BANGLADESH ON A NEW JOURNEY

BANGLADESH ON A NEW JOURNEY

Moving beyond the Regional Identity

Edited by
Sreeradha Datta

BLOOMSBURY
NEW DELHI • LONDON • OXFORD • NEW YORK • SYDNEY

BLOOMSBURY INDIA
Bloomsbury Publishing India Pvt. Ltd
Second Floor, LSC Building No. 4, DDA Complex, Pocket C – 6 & 7,
Vasant Kunj, New Delhi, 110070

BLOOMSBURY, BLOOMSBURY ACADEMIC INDIA and the Diana logo are
trademarks of Bloomsbury Publishing Plc

First published in India 2024
This export edition published 2024

Copyright © Sreeradha Datta and contributors, 2024

Sreeradha Datta has asserted her right under the Indian copyright act to be
identified as the Editor of this work

Bloomsbury Academic India
An imprint of Bloomsbury Publishing Plc

All rights reserved. No part of this publication may be reproduced or transmitted in
any form or by any means, electronic or mechanical, including photocopying,
recording or any information storage or retrieval system, without the prior
permission in writing from the publishers

This book is solely the responsibility of the author and the publisher has had no
role in the creation of the content and does not have responsibility for anything
defamatory or libellous or objectionable

Bloomsbury Publishing Plc does not have any control over, or responsibility for,
any third-party websites referred to or in this book. All internet addresses given in
this book were correct at the time of going to press. The author and publisher regret
any inconvenience caused if addresses have changed or sites have ceased to exist,
but can accept no responsibility for any such changes

ISBN: HB: 978-93-56404-21-2 eBook: 978-93-56404-23-6
2 4 6 8 10 9 7 5 3 1

Typeset by Manipal Technologies Limited
Printed and bound in India by Replika Press Pvt. Ltd.

Bloomsbury Publishing Plc makes every effort to ensure that the papers used in the
manufacture of our books are natural, recyclable products made from wood grown
in well-managed forests. Our manufacturing processes conform to the
environmental regulations of the country of origin.

To find out more about our authors and books visit www.bloomsbury.com and sign
up for our newsletters

CONTENTS

Acknowledgements   vii
Foreword
    C. Raja Mohan   ix
Prologue: Bangladesh in the World: Progress, Pitfalls and Prospects
    Michael Kugelman   xi

Introduction: Bangladesh on a New Journey:
Moving beyond Regional Identity
    Sreeradha Datta   1

Part I   Introduction   19

1. The Making of the Bangladesh Doctrine: Strategic Autonomy and Development Deterrence
   Rashed Al Mahmud Titumir   21
2. Nation Building, Religion and Foreign Policy in Bangladesh
   Brigitta Schuchert   49
3. Construction and Reconstruction of Identity of the Bangladeshi Diaspora in the UK and the US
   Ali Riaz   75
4. Bangladesh's Domestic and International Efforts to Address Climate Change
   Ashley Johnson   91

Part II   Introduction   111

5. Bangladesh and the Outside World: A Story of Exploring Convergences, Connectivity and Continuity
   M. Humayun Kabir   113
6. Smaller States in a Multipolar Asia: The Case of Bangladesh
   Johannes Plagemann   137
7. From the Bay of Bengal to the Indo-Pacific: Extra-Regional Powers Vying for Bangladesh's Attention
   Sreeradha Datta   148
8. The Evolving Dynamics in Bangladesh and Southeast Asian Relations: A Long Road of Constraints and Opportunities
   Don McLain Gill   169

Part III Introduction 185

9 Bangladesh and India: An Evolving Relationship
  Deb Mukharji 187

10 China–Bangladesh Relations: Review and Prospects
  Li Jianjun 203

11 Bangladesh–Pakistan Relations: Old and New Dimensions
  Amna Ejaz Rafi 220

12 Bangladesh–US Bilateral Relations
  Nilanthi Samaranayake 237

13 Bangladesh: Australia's Blind Spot
  Andrew Hunter 250

Epilogue: The Road Ahead for Bangladesh—Prospects to Emerge as the 'Next Frontier' of Asia
  Ramita Iyer 265

About the Editor and Contributors 281
Index 287

ACKNOWLEDGEMENTS

Ubuntu—a word I recently came across—loosely means I am because we are—aptly describes my journey as an academic and researcher. My work is indeed a reflection of all those from whom I imbibed knowingly or intuitively over the years. Family, friends, well-wishers and now my students continue to influence my thoughts and writings.

I, not unlike many of my South Asian generation, have been deeply affected by the partition of the subcontinent and later, the birth of Bangladesh. The two milestone events also wound their way in my research endeavours. A harrowing experience for many, including my family, I attempted to understand the region and its people through their eyes. My Ma, Krishna Datta, however, stands tall in the bevy of an exceptional family, given her ability to see the larger picture.

It could be my roots, or maybe other factors, but I have, time and again, returned to examine Bangladesh. This compelling preoccupation made me seek newer aspects to cover, ensuring in this volume a rather exceptional experience. This volume would not have been possible without the support of a fantastic group of scholars from across the globe and I am especially thankful to Professor C. Raja Mohan. It was a privilege to begin a second book under the aegis of the Institute for South Asian Studies (ISAS), National University of Singapore, while he was the director. The journey started with Professor Raja's idea to do a book on *Bangladesh at 50: Development and Challenges* during a challenging professional and personal time, and it has come to a completion with this volume.

Professor C. Raja Mohan also introduced me to Dr S. Narayan, a bureaucrat who finds joy in academia, and who, besides being my co-author previously, has now become my most reliable critic and mentor. I would like to mention the support of Professor Iqbal Singh Sevea, Director ISAS and particularly of my dear friend Mr Hernaikh Singh, Deputy Director, ISAS.

No work of mine, especially on Bangladesh, would have been possible without Matiur Rahman, editor *Prathom Alo*, Amb Deb Mukharji, Professor Rahman Sobhan and countless other friends from Bangladesh, including Professors Amena Mohsin, Mustafizur Rahman and Debapriya Bhattacharya and Major Arefin who continue to share their insights so liberally.

A year ago, shifting to full-time teaching at the OP Jindal Global University has been exceptionally joyful. I am very grateful to Professor

Sreeram Chaulia and the School of International Affairs team for making this possible. I was indeed glad to have my younger colleagues Dr Soham Das and Dr Sriparna Pathak to trouble endlessly, as well as Dr Gunjan Singh and Dr Avinash Godbole, both of whom made my transition to Jindal University seamless. I certainly miss many of my younger colleagues from the Vivekananda International Foundation, and the foundation director, Dr Arvind Gupta, and General Ravi Sawhney, whose morning calls add sparkle to my day.

The pleasure of being able to see the sky and sea merge frequently has been possible due to my husband Arup's move to Goa—our home that I enjoy visiting greatly. This past year has been one of travel and family time, which was only made possible by my daughter, Dishari, and her inimitable ways. While I once again cope with the empty-nest syndrome, I am truly grateful for all the wonderful opportunities that have come our way.

I want to acknowledge the immense support of Chandra Sekhar and his team at Bloomsbury.

I dedicate this book to Shri Pranab Mukherjee (former President of India). I first met him when he visited the Institute of Defence Studies and Analyses (IDSA) in his capacity as its president. While flipping through my first book on Bangladesh, *Bangladesh: A Fragile Democracy* (an outcome of my IDSA project), he had advised me to focus on specific aspects and subsequently, over the years, I continued learning much through many of our interactions while he held various official positions. If there is any Indian Bangladesh greatly admires, it is Pranab-da; his contribution to strengthening the India–Bangladesh bilateral ties remain unparalleled.

I am hoping there are no glitches, but I am responsible, if at all.

A big thank you to all.

FOREWORD

This edited volume by Sreeradha Datta examines Bangladesh's growing regional salience and global value amidst the return of great power rivalry. Bangladesh's location at the crossroads of the eastern subcontinent, the Himalayan mastiff, China and Myanmar might not have been considered strategic during the Cold War, but it now draws compelling geopolitical attention. Bangladesh's centrality in the Bay of Bengal, which is adjacent to the South China Sea, makes Dhaka an important regional actor in the new Indo-Pacific geography.

The new strategic significance of Bangladesh is reinforced by its impressive economic performance in recent decades. Bangladesh has replaced Pakistan as the second-largest economy in South Asia. And unlike Pakistan, Bangladesh has enjoyed political stability and is willing to embark on sub-regional economic integration within South Asia and between the eastern subcontinent and Southeast Asia. These positive features are bound to accelerate Dhaka's economic growth and political influence.

While plenty of literature exists on the sources and drivers of Dhaka's economic success and the complex domestic politics, there is little significant work on the foreign policy of Bangladesh. Datta and her colleagues fill this major gap in the regional and global appreciation of Dhaka's geopolitics and the evolution of its foreign policy.

This volume also neatly complements Datta's co-edited volume, *Bangladesh at 50*, which focuses on the political and developmental trajectory of Bangladesh during its first 50 years as an independent nation. I had the privilege of supporting that valuable and well-received project as the director of the Institute of South Asian Studies, National University of Singapore. I am delighted to see Datta extend that important work to cover the international relations of Bangladesh.

Bangladesh is now moving beyond its traditional regional identity to seek its rightful place in the world. That, in turn, is bound to make a big difference to Asian geopolitics and the discourse on global issues. This book unpacks this significant moment in Dhaka's regional and international trajectory.

C. Raja Mohan
Visiting Research Professor,
Institute of South Asian Studies,
National University of Singapore

Prologue

BANGLADESH IN THE WORLD: PROGRESS, PITFALLS AND PROSPECTS

Michael Kugelman

On 12 September 2022, Bangladesh Prime Minister Shaikh Hasina inaugurated the 46th Indo-Pacific Armies Management Seminar (IPAMS) in Dhaka. The annual event, described as the largest conference of land forces from the Indo-Pacific, featured—in the words of a US army readout—'an elaborate show highlighting Bangladesh's customs and culture', and an 'inspirational message' from Hasina (Shimooka 2022). Co-hosted by the Bangladesh and American armies, it featured top army leaders from 23 countries.

By serving as the physical host for the conference in 2022, Bangladesh was showcasing its global convening power. However, this wasn't the first time Dhaka hosted the event. It did so in 2014, and back in 1993 as well. Its strength as a global convener—for geopolitical events but also other major forums, such as international arts festivals—has long been nothing new.[1]

Indeed, headlines over the last few years have highlighted Bangladesh's increasing global influence, but the country has been a key actor worldwide for decades. In fact, it has been a major player since shortly after its independence. That said, it is only over the last few years that Bangladesh has truly come into its own on the global stage. And yet, a series of challenges threaten to hold Bangladesh back from charting even greater heights abroad. How and if it addresses these obstacles will go a long way towards determining its trajectory as a global player.

A Long Legacy of Global Influence

Evidence of Bangladesh's entrenched global footprint is easy to find. Indeed, what the casual observer may regard as relatively new manifestations of global clout is actually quite long-standing. For example, Bangladesh has been among the top-three global exporters of garments over the last few years—but ready-made garments (RMG) first became Bangladesh's top export back in 1988. Scholarship shows that the biggest expansion in the industry was from 1995 to 2010. Net garment exports became Bangladesh's 'most significant' foreign exchange earner in 1998 (Sarkar 2018). The story of the country's much-ballyhooed, globe-girdling garment industry goes way back.

Similarly, Bangladesh is one of the biggest contributors to United Nations (UN) global peacekeeping forces today—but that's been the case for a long time, more than three decades, in fact. It provided more troops for UN peacekeeping missions than any other country in 2015, 2014 and 2011 (Rashid 2022).

More broadly, the country has been an active diplomatic player since its earliest days, thanks in great part to the unrelenting international engagements of Sheikh Mujibur Rahman, Bangladesh's independence hero and first president and prime minister. Consider that, on its first anniversary of independence, Bangladesh had already secured formal recognition from 54 countries. Bangladesh joined the Non-Aligned Movement in 1973, just two years after independence, and Rahman would soon endear himself to a range of global leaders, from Cuba's Fidel Castro to the heads of Arab Gulf states (Rahman 2021).

Under Rahman, Bangladesh played a notable role in the 1973 Yom Kippur War: It sent medical workers from its military to help Syrian troops near the Golan Heights, and tea to Egyptian soldiers in Sinai (Zamir 2021). These acts helped earn Bangladesh wider acceptance within the Islamic world. It gained membership in the Organisation of Islamic Cooperation (OIC) in 1974. Some observers may look at Bangladesh's much more recent diplomatic successes—such as the lead role it played with a small group of other countries to start the process of establishing a new UN convention on crimes against humanity in late 2022—as an indication of something new, but in reality, there are quite a few precedents of active diplomacy going back many decades (Gramer and Rathi 2022).

To be sure, the tone and direction of Bangladesh's foreign relations would change after Rahman's assassination in 1975 and the imposition of military rule. But the point here is to underscore that Bangladesh didn't take long to start leaving its imprint on different parts of the world.

For whatever reason, the story of Bangladesh's long-standing global prominence has not been properly understood around the world, especially in the West—even though its size and location make it impossible to overlook.[2] This may be because of an insufficient strategic focus on Bangladesh in Western capitals, a lack of soft power and a diaspora that tends to be relatively small in many Western countries. Not surprisingly, global media coverage of Bangladesh is often reductive, emphasising stories about flash floods and factory fires and not nearly enough in between.

Here, a brief digression is in order. It's worth recalling how Bangladesh first came into the public consciousness, on a mass scale, in the West. In the summer of 1971, just months after independence, two superstar musicians—sitarist Ravi Shankar and ex-Beatle George Harrison—hosted a celebrity concert in New York City to raise funds for Bangladeshis hit by conflict and floods. Separately, Harrison released the song 'Bangla Desh'. The concert became a massive and popular success, and it is still regarded today as one of the best charity concerts ever produced. Harrison's song, a top hit in Europe and the US, was a poignant plea for relief aid. It included lyrics such as 'Bangladesh, Bangladesh/Where so many people are dying fast/And it sure looks like a mess/I've never seen such distress'. The concert and the song, focusing on Bangladesh's dire humanitarian needs, arguably became the first major frame of reference for many in the West about the newly independent nation.

Due to the huge popularity and reach of both the charity concert and Harrison's song, the tragic circumstances that accompanied Bangladesh's independence—war and natural disaster—would become a powerful initial shaper of Western public perceptions of the country. The question arises: Did this perception linger in the years that followed, thereby contributing to an inability or unwillingness of many observers to recognise Bangladesh as the country into which it quickly began to evolve—an increasingly confident, influential, and self-sufficient nation, with the will and capacity to exert agency overseas? It is certainly a point to ponder.

Bangladesh Comes into Its Own on the World Stage

The last few years have truly marked a new phase for Bangladesh's presence in the world. Its economic growth story, and the global economic influence that comes with it, have resulted in a series of recent major achievements. In 2020, a year when many countries suffered major pandemic-induced setbacks to growth, Bangladesh's economy grew by 3.5 per cent. Around that same time, Bangladesh also enjoyed a nearly 25 percentage point drop in its poverty rate since 1991, and—according to the UN—it is expected to exit from least-developed-country status by 2026.[3] In 2022, Bangladesh completed or was close to completing a series of large infrastructure projects—a new metro service in Dhaka, a massive new bridge and an underwater tunnel—illustrating its status as one of the fastest-developing economies in the region (a region where infrastructure is one of the biggest needs) and the world on the whole. Growth projections now estimate Bangladesh—buoyed by its garment industry, robust foreign investment and overall macroeconomic stability—could become the world's 24th largest economy by 2036 (Centre for Economics and Business Research 2021).

In December 1971, a senior US State Department official, Ural Alexis Johnson, predicted in a policy meeting in Washington that Bangladesh would soon become an 'international basket case'. National Security Adviser Henry Kissinger (who, contrary to popular belief, was not the first to use the derogatory term) replied, 'But not necessarily our basket case' (Nasir 2010). More than 50 years later, Bangladesh is an international success story, not a basket case. And no American official today would ever think of distancing themselves from that success story: America is the single largest market for Bangladeshi goods, and also the largest source of foreign direct investment (FDI) in Bangladesh.

Indeed, Dhaka's growing relations with Washington also signify just how far Bangladesh has come. In a milestone moment for Bangladesh's foreign policy, Afreen Akhter, a deputy assistant secretary in the state department's Bureau of South and Central Asian Affairs, stated in a speech in Washington on Victory Day in December 2022 that Bangladesh is a 'truly important strategic partner' (*Prothom Alo* 2022). For the world's superpower to describe its relations with Dhaka in those terms—a designation it gives to relatively few partners—is to acknowledge the importance that Washington accords to Dhaka's global role.

Geopolitical developments had, in fact, already been trending in this direction. For several years, US government strategy documents have described Bangladesh as a key part of Washington's Indo-Pacific policy, the core US Asia policy. In early 2023, Donald Lu, the top South Asia official at the state department, visited Dhaka and pledged continued cooperation across a wide array of spaces (his visit came just days after Eileen Laubacher, the top South Asia official at the National Security Council, made her own trip to Dhaka). This all represents a remarkable turnaround from the period soon after independence (and the period leading to independence), when Kissinger and other senior US officials didn't hesitate to refer to Bangladesh in the most bitter and denigrating terms.[4]

Over the last few years, more broadly, Bangladesh has emerged on the global stage as a net economic, humanitarian and security provider. In 2021, it announced an offer of $200 million in credit to Sri Lanka—another milestone moment for a country long perceived as a recipient, not a supplier, of aid. The country has also earned global attention for the delicate task of hosting hundreds of thousands of Rohingya refugees, most of whom fled violence in neighbouring Myanmar in 2017. Meanwhile, Bangladesh has continued to be a top provider of troops to UN peacekeeping missions.

Potential Challenges to Bangladesh's Place in the World

These net provider activities, however, have not been easy to sustain. Dhaka may have showcased its capacity to be an economic aid provider in 2021 but during the next year, global shocks triggered by Covid-19 and the Russian invasion of Ukraine hit Bangladesh's economy hard, resulting in the same rising inflation, food and fuel shortages, and plunging foreign reserves that afflicted countries around South Asia, and the world more broadly (Cookson 2022). Dhaka's hosting of Rohingya refugees has run into problems over the last few years amid reports of poor conditions, and even deadly attacks, in the large camps housing them in Cox's Bazar; a controversial decision to relocate some Rohingya to an isolated island; and news of thousands of desperate Rohingya who fled Bangladesh by boat and subsisted—and in some cases perished—in terrible conditions at sea while looking for new countries to take them in (Chowdhury and Barua 2022). Apart from these, Bangladesh's UN peacekeeping activities have been marred by past allegations of sexual assault against some of its troops while they were participating in those missions abroad (though many more peacekeeping troops from South Africa and the Democratic Republic of Congo have been accused than have those from Bangladesh) (*Prothom Alo* 2016; Khan 2018).

Sustaining—and increasing—Bangladesh's prominent position overseas will face a series of challenges more broadly in the coming years. Its ability to successfully respond to these challenges will influence, to a considerable degree, just how far it can go on the global stage.

Great Power Rivalry

In September 1974, soon after Bangladesh gained membership in the UN, Sheikh Mujibur Rahman made a speech before the UN General Assembly that famously proclaimed, 'Friendship to all, malice toward none.' It would become the guiding principle undergirding Bangladesh's non-aligned and independent foreign policy, and it has endured to the present day. (However, it should be noted that Rahman's quote borrowed heavily from another gifted orator: President Abraham Lincoln, in his second inauguration address delivered more than 100 years earlier, used the phrase, 'With malice toward none, with charity for all.')

This view on foreign policy was ingrained in Rahman's mind even before independence. While in prison in the late 1960s, he wrote a scathing criticism of Pakistan for not having followed an independent foreign policy:

> The newly created state of Pakistan should have followed a neutral and independent foreign policy. We should not have made enemies of any country. It was our duty to become friends with all countries of the world. It should have been a sin for us to even think of joining any military bloc.[5] (Rahman 2012)

Bangladesh's non-aligned position has enabled it to cultivate relations with a wide range of countries and embedded it in the global diplomatic architecture for decades. In recent years, this has meant balancing relations with Washington, New Delhi, Beijing and Moscow, even amid sharpening competition and intensifying rivalry between some of those states. But with this competition and rivalry reaching fever pitches—thanks to a deadly India–China border spat in 2020 and Russia's invasion of Ukraine in 2022, among other key trigger points—Dhaka's balancing act has become more difficult to carry out.

Dhaka, in line with non-alignment, seeks a proactive foreign policy—one in which it dictates the terms of its engagement with the world and chooses what types of partnerships to pursue. This is the policy that has helped it secure, and sustain, a strong foothold in international diplomatic relations. This strategy has also helped it closer to home, with its neighbour Myanmar, an instructive recent example. While Washington and some other Western capitals have approached relations with Naypyidaw through democracy and other values-based lenses, Dhaka—much like New Delhi—has refused to let moral considerations dictate its policy towards Myanmar, and especially towards that country's brutal junta. Instead, it has taken a strict realist approach, seeking to carefully maintain a workable relationship with Naypyidaw given the delicacies of Bangladesh–Myanmar ties: Dhaka is keen to ensure that the junta's conflicts with insurgents not spill into Bangladesh, and it also hopes to carry out difficult negotiations with the junta about repatriating Rohingya refugees. Given those goals, Bangladesh's interests would not be well served by taking a confrontational position that calls the junta out for its brutalities and lack of democracy.

And yet, today, Bangladesh is increasingly at risk of getting dragged into great power rivalries and strategic tug-of-wars of which it has no desire to be a part. China's deepening footprint in Bangladesh, mainly through the vehicle of the Belt and Road Initiative (BRI), has fuelled intensified

Indian engagement with Dhaka to push back against Beijing. Washington has sought to scale up engagement with Dhaka as well, in part because of a desire to counteract China's growing influence in Bangladesh (it's also notable that in recent years, and especially after the establishment of China's first overseas military base, in Djibouti, Beijing has deepened its naval presence in Bangladesh's broader maritime neighbourhood, and especially in the western parts of the Indian Ocean region).

Additionally, after the Russian invasion of Ukraine, Washington stepped up high-level outreach to Dhaka. Victoria Nuland, the number two official at the state department, visited Dhaka in March 2022, just a few weeks after the invasion. While official Washington messaging emphasised that the Indo-Pacific policy would be the main focus of her trip, Nuland—known as one of Washington's most prominent Russia hawks—most likely spent some of her time trying to get Bangladesh to take a harder line against the invasion. However, Bangladesh and Moscow have enjoyed cordial relations since 1971, with Russian investment flowing into Bangladesh to the present day (Bangladesh, like India and Pakistan, abstained from voting on several UN General Assembly resolutions condemning Russia's invasion).

To this point, Dhaka has successfully managed this intense state of play, which amounts to the geopolitical equivalent of the walls closing in. Bangladesh's relations with all four countries remain strong, and, in the case of Washington, are growing. But Dhaka is constantly being tested. In March 2021, Gowher Rizvi, an international affairs aide to Hasina, chose his words carefully in explaining how Dhaka approaches its relations with Beijing, New Delhi and Washington. He said that Bangladesh partners with China on BRI, and that Beijing plays a key role in development projects in Bangladesh, but that 'we are very willing to be a part of the Indo-Pacific relationship,' and—strikingly—India 'is our most important partner and you cannot conceive of anything different' (Krishnankutty 2021).

Was this suggesting an alignment with India, and possibly the US, over China? That's likely not what Rizvi meant but it appears to be what Beijing may have thought. Several weeks after Rizvi's comment, China's ambassador to Bangladesh, Li Jiming, admonished Dhaka not to join the Quad—the increasingly influential security grouping that includes Washington and New Delhi as members and aims to counterbalance China's power—and even warned that China–Bangladesh relations would be 'substantially damaged' if Dhaka were to join the group (Papri 2021). In reality, Dhaka did not—and does not—have any desire to join the Quad. Li's message was likely meant to pressure Dhaka not to get any closer to New Delhi and Washington.

Dhaka's conundrum vis-à-vis the US–Russia rivalry came into sharp relief during an actual foreign policy crisis in January 2023. A Russian ship bearing parts for a Moscow-funded nuclear power plant was due to dock in a port in Bangladesh, but the US embassy warned Dhaka that the ship was sanctioned by Washington because it had links to the Russian military. Dhaka opted for a middle-ground approach. It denied permission to the ship to dock, and instead it arranged for it to go to an Indian port, where the goods were to be transferred to another ship that was not sanctioned by Washington (in an interesting twist, however, India ended up not allowing the Russian ship to offload its goods) (Kugelman 2023). Moscow was displeased about having its ship turned away from Bangladesh. Also, enlisting the assistance of India—a close friend of Moscow and Washington—helped defuse the crisis and, by extension, enabled Dhaka to successfully manage the US–Russia rivalry. But it was also a reminder of Dhaka's continued friendship with New Delhi, which China does not like. Beijing probably wasn't thrilled about Dhaka's decision to bring India into the crisis.

Bangladesh's task as a balancer is tougher now than it was earlier in its existence, during the Cold War, because the world was more bipolar back then and dominated by US–Soviet rivalry. Today, Dhaka must manage three major great power rivalries. Some may point to India's own experience as an example of how non-aligned states can manage multifaceted great-power competition. But Bangladesh arguably has a tougher job than India. New Delhi faces the challenge of navigating US–Russia rivalry, but India, an avowed strategic competitor of Beijing's, gains some benefits from US–China competition. Indeed, that latter rivalry has helped India increase its global clout through its growing strategic partnership with Washington and involvement in the Indo-Pacific institutional architecture, from the Quad to the Indo-Pacific Economic Framework for Prosperity (IPEF). Dhaka, however, with its 'friendship to all, malice to none' mantra, must keep its relations with all four countries on an even keel, even as they each aim to draw Bangladesh more into their respective orbit.

Economic Concerns

Dhaka and its supporters may shrug off the country's economic troubles in 2022 as a temporary consequence of Covid-induced supply chain bottlenecks and soaring world commodity costs triggered by the war in Ukraine—global shocks that interrupted Bangladesh's growth story but will eventually recede, allowing the country's economy to return to the *status quo ante*.

However, even before the global economic shocks of 2022, concerns were starting to mount about the sustainability of Bangladesh's remarkable growth. Back in 2021, economist Shahid Yusuf published a detailed critique of Bangladesh's economy that identified a long list of red flags: Consistently low rates of total factor productivity, which is a measure of the efficiency of production—a key determinant of long-term income growth; heavy dependence on a sole export (garments), which has resulted in reductions of shares of exports in GDP; sluggish investment in new industries, in part because concerns about firms' reliability, quality and compliance have kept FDI rates down and limited the presence of top foreign multinationals in Bangladesh; high tariff barriers, leading to rent-seeking behaviour from inward-looking domestic companies; unreliable electricity supply because of neglected transmission and distribution infrastructure; and corruption (Yusuf 2021).

Another concern is climate change. Bangladesh, a low-lying, low-riparian nation, is one of the countries' most vulnerable to climate change—in a very climate-change vulnerable region. One can't overstate the potentially catastrophic long-term economic impacts of global warming, from massive agricultural losses to the destruction of businesses. Bangladesh, to its credit, has been ahead of the curve in South Asia, and it has implemented a series of mitigation and adaptation measures in recent years—including the incorporation of climate-disaster scenarios into military training exercises. An emerging global norm around the need for the world to help climate-vulnerable states build resilience—as reflected in an agreement at the 2022 UN climate summit to establish a new loss and damage fund—is also encouraging. But the irreversible reality of global warming, coupled with Bangladesh's large-scale vulnerability, means that the country won't be able to escape climate change and its potentially devastating economic effects.

This isn't to suggest Bangladesh's economy is doomed. But if these issues aren't sufficiently addressed, the country's growth outlook could become significantly less rosy—and then its growth story, a top driver of its prominent role in the world, could suffer a major blow. If garments continue to dominate Bangladesh's export mix but struggle to keep up with competitors, and especially if Bangladesh is left on the outside looking in as other growing economies diversify their export mixes (as the likes of South Korea and India, and most recently Vietnam have already done), then Bangladesh could find itself locked out of key markets. A consistently subpar business environment could make the country a less popular destination for foreign financiers. And if the economy begins to experience more and more stress in the coming years, Dhaka could struggle to be the net financial aid provider that it became—at least briefly—in 2021.

Domestic Politics

The last decade has brought major and well-founded concerns about democratic backsliding in Bangladesh. From elections described by international observers as rigged to harsh crackdowns on the opposition, the ruling party has faced frequent criticism from international media, foreign affairs analysts, and Western governments. Dhaka may push back against such concerns, regarding them as exaggerated or unnecessary meddling in its internal affairs. But many if not most of these concerns come from actors in the West, a top-priority region for Bangladesh's economic, diplomatic and broader strategic interests. If the democratic backsliding trend intensifies in the coming months and years—regardless of whether the ruling party once again wins re-election in the next national polls—the country could face some challenges in relations with many of its Western partners.

Bangladesh's internal situation has already dealt setbacks to its international relations. Washington's decision in late 2021 to slap sanctions on the Rapid Action Battalion (RAB), a top Bangladesh security agency, because of concerns about human rights violations, delivered a blow to a relationship that has otherwise experienced considerable progress in recent years. Even after that move to sanction the RAB, much of Washington's public messaging about Bangladesh has continued to identify human rights as a top priority for the relationship—suggesting that it is not about to let Dhaka off the hook anytime soon. Indeed, given that the Biden administration emphasises values, rights and democracy promotion in its foreign policy, the human rights focus it attaches to US–Bangladesh relations is likely to remain sharp as long as Biden occupies the White House. On a related note, perceptions in Washington of Dhaka's slow progress to institute reforms that provide stronger safeguards for worker rights have ensured that America's Generalized System of Preferences (GSP) trade privileges to Bangladesh, revoked since 2013, have not been reactivated.

Additionally, Bangladesh's democratic backsliding will not help improve the country's image abroad. To be sure, the country has long earned praise as a moderate Muslim-majority country, and it has regularly been categorised as such by the UN. However, over the last few years, many observers—including Western officials—fear it has become a politically intolerant, one-party state with authoritarian tendencies. It does not take much to find news stories and analyses on Bangladesh these days that don't paint a pleasant picture: Security forces using live ammunition on protestors, government acquisitions of surveillance technologies from Israel, the use of digital security laws to arrest and jail government critics, and so on.[6] Also, the US sanctions on the RAB risk undercutting global perceptions of Bangladesh's security forces, which have already suffered given the sexual abuse allegations against some Bangladeshis serving abroad as UN peacekeepers.

Bangladesh's Future Path

To be sure, these types of challenges haven not stopped other countries from maintaining and deepening their role on the global stage. Many regional and global powers and other globally influential states today are either democracies faulted for rights violations (India, Israel, Brazil) or not democracies at all (China, Russia, Saudi Arabia). Periodic economic slowdowns have not limited China's rise. Great-power rivalry hasn't constrained non-aligned India. But many of these countries compensate with other key qualities, benefits or forms of leverage that Bangladesh lacks, or has in shorter supply, which enable these other countries to withstand these challenges more effectively than can Bangladesh. These other characteristics include large militaries, diversified export economies, the ability to quickly deploy large amounts of capital worldwide, soft power, long-established global reputations as strategically important countries; the possession of critical assets and resources (such as oil), and permanent memberships in the most powerful global bodies (such as the UN Security Council).

Since independence, Bangladesh has blazed its own non-aligned trail to become an economically and diplomatically significant player. For that reason, it does not need advice from others—and especially not from this South Asia analyst sitting far away in Washington—about its best path forward. Still, there should not be anything controversial about this very simple point: Bangladesh's role on the world stage will be further enhanced by addressing the factors that could potentially constrain it. After several consecutive elections in Bangladesh marred by rigging allegations, many Western governments will carefully observe the country's next national elections to see how free and fair they are. Navigating relations with those governments will be less difficult for Dhaka if international election observers characterize those polls as free and fair.

Additionally, taking steps to better foolproof the economy would ensure the continuation of Bangladesh's growth story—and it would save Dhaka from potential trouble with FDI, and with economic and trade diplomacy down the road. Simply resting on the laurels of its past economic successes isn't a winning strategy. Correctives could entail a stronger focus on creating sustainable, value-added, globally competitive new exports beyond garments, and better addressing quality and reliability concerns within major domestic firms. Such efforts, to be sure, would require both public and private sector buy-in.

Dhaka will need help from the world, too. And that assistance can best be rendered on the geopolitics front. Great-power competition is not going anywhere anytime soon. That is not just because of the sheer intensity of contemporary great-power competition but also because multipolarity is creating the space for multiple competitive actors and theatres, and because multilateralism and broader global cooperation are not robust enough to scale back these different areas of competition and contention. Bangladesh is keen to avoid getting dragged into all this. It would benefit from the major powers agreeing to view their relationships with Bangladesh through the lens of Bangladesh—and not through the lens of US–China, US–Russia or India–China rivalry.[7] It is a tall order, for sure. But in the end, if these countries truly seek better relations with Dhaka, then it would serve their interests to orient their relations with Dhaka in a way that helps advance Dhaka's interests as well.

Over more than five decades, Bangladesh has authored one of the most impressive—albeit unsung—success stories in economic growth and diplomatic engagement to become the nation it is today. But it still has much work to do, and especially in a world far more geopolitically complex than what it experienced during its first few decades as an independent nation.

Notes

1   Bangladesh has been hosting a Dhaka Literature Festival since 2011.
2   Awareness of Bangladesh's strategic location has been enhanced by the work of Robert Kaplan, an influential foreign affairs analyst who has written about the great importance of the Indian Ocean region. See Robert D. Kaplan, *Monsoon: The Indian Ocean and the Future of American Power* (New York: Random House, 2011).
3   A UN General Assembly resolution passed in 2021 laid out a five-year timeframe for Bangladesh to graduate from least-developed-country status. See https://documents-dds-ny.un.org/doc/UNDOC/GEN/N21/355/26/PDF/N2135526.pdf?OpenElement.
4   For an excellent account of the Nixon administration's views of Bangladesh during the country's earliest days, see Gary J. Bass, *The Blood Telegram: Nixon, Kissinger, and a Forgotten Genocide* (New York: Alfred A. Knopf, 2013).

5   These thoughts and many of his other prison musings would later be published in a posthumous autobiography, Sheikh Mujibur Rahman, *The Unfinished Memoirs* (Dhaka: University Press Limited, 2012).
6   For more information, see Shaikh Azizur Rahman, 'Bangladesh Arrests Thousands of Political Activists Ahead of Opposition Protest', *Voice of America*, 7 December 2022. https://www.voanews.com/a/bangladesh-arrests-thousands-of-political-activists-ahead-of-opposition-protest/6867314.html; Al Jazeera Investigative Unit, 'Bangladesh Bought Mass Spying Equipment from Israeli Company', *Al Jazeera*, 2 February 2021. https://www.aljazeera.com/news/2021/2/2/bangladesh-bought-surveillance-equipment-from-israeli-company; and Ali Riaz, 'How Bangladesh's Digital Security Act Is Creating a Culture of Fear', Carnegie Endowment for International Point, 9 December 2021. https://carnegieendowment.org/2021/12/09/how-bangladesh-s-digital-security-act-is-creating-culture-of-fear-pub-85951.
7   To better understand what this model of relationship with Dhaka might look like for Washington, see Anu Anwar and Michael Kugelman, 'America Should Bet on Bangladesh', *Foreign Policy*, 1 December 2021. https://foreignpolicy.com/2021/12/01/us-bangladesh-relations-dhaka-india-china-bri/.

References

'Bangladeshis among UN Peacekeepers Accused of Sexual Abuse,' *Prothom Alo*, January 30, 2016. https://en.prothomalo.com/international/Peacekeepers-accused-of-sexual-abuse.

'Bangladesh a Truly Important Strategic Partner: US'. *Prothom Alo*, December 17, 2022. https://en.prothomalo.com/international/americas/fbuj17bjy1.

Chowdhury, Kamran Reza and Sunil Barua. '2 More Rohingya Killed by Armed Groups in Bangladesh Camp," *Benar News*, October 27, 2022. https://www.benarnews.org/english/news/bengali/bangladesh-rohingya-killed-at-camps-10272022153121.html.

Cookson, F. 'What Happened to Bangladesh's Economy?' *Dhaka Tribune*, October 25, 2022. https://www.dhakatribune.com/business/2022/10/25/what-happened-to-bangladeshs-economy.

Gramer, R. and A. Rathi. 'How an Unusual Coalition Outfoxed China and Russia at the UN'. *Foreign Policy*. December 23, 2022. https://foreignpolicy.com/2022/12/23/united-nations-china-russia-treaty-crimes-against-humanity-international-law/.

Khan, Maliha. 'Sexual Abuse at the Hands of UN Peacekeepers,' *The Daily Star*, May 25, 2018. https://www.thedailystar.net/star-weekend/sexual-harassment/sexual-abuse-the-hands-un-peacekeepers-1581139.

Krishnankutty, Pia. 'We're Part of China's BRI but India Our "Most Important Partner": Bangladesh Foreign Advisor,' *The Print*, March 24, 2021. https://

theprint.in/diplomacy/were-part-of-chinas-bri-but-india-our-most-important-partner-bangladesh-foreign-advisor/627369/.

Kugelman, Michael. 'Bangladesh becomes a US-Russia Battleground,' *Foreign Policy*, January 5, 2023. https://foreignpolicy.com/2023/01/05/bangladesh-us-russia-battleground-embassy-dhaka-nonalignment/.

Nasir, A.M.B. 'The Myth of International Basket Case'. bdnews24, October 6, 2010. https://bdnews24.com/opinion/comment/the-myth-of-%E2%80%9Cinternational-basket-case%E2%80%9D.

Papri, Jesmin. 'Bangladesh: Chinese Envoy's Warning against Joining Quad "Very Unfortunate,"' *Benar News*, May 11, 2021. https://www.benarnews.org/english/news/bengali/bd-ch-quad-folo-05112021153119.html.

Rahman, A. 'Friendship to All, Malice to None'. *Daily Sun*, May 25, 2021. https://www.daily-sun.com/post/554375/%E2%80%98Friendship-to-all-malice-to-none%E2%80%99.

Rahman, S.M. *The Unfinished Memoirs*. Translated by Fakrul Alam. Dhaka: University Press Limited, 2012.

Rashid, M. 'Bangladeshis Hailed for UN Peacekeeping'. *New Age*. May 29, 2022. https://www.newagebd.net/article/171810/bangladeshis-hailed-for-un-peacekeeping.

Sarkar, M.M.I. 'Garments Exports in Bangladesh: The Unexpected Success Story', *Social Scientist* 46 (September–October 2018): 61–70.

Shimooka, R. '46th Indo-Pacific Armies Management Seminar'. U.S. Army, September 12, 2022. https://www.army.mil/article/260093/46th_indo_pacific_armies_management_seminar.

'World Economic League Table 2022, 13th edition'. Centre for Economics and Business Research, 2021. https://static.poder360.com.br/2021/12/cebr-ranking-economia-mundial-26dez-2021.pdf.

Yusuf, Shahid. 'Bangladesh: Growth Miracle or Mirage?', *Center for Global Development*, June 16, 2021. https://www.cgdev.org/blog/bangladesh-growth-miracle-or-mirage.

Zamir, M. 'Bangabandhu Sheikh Mujibur Rahman and the Islamic World'. *The Business Standard*, March 17, 2021. https://www.tbsnews.net/bangladesh/bangabandhu-sheikh-mujibur-rahman-and-islamic-world-217903.

Introduction

BANGLADESH ON A NEW JOURNEY: MOVING BEYOND REGIONAL IDENTITY

Sreeradha Datta

Bangladesh's Growth Story Stymied by Challenges

As Bangladesh steps into its 52nd year, it is now being identified as one of the 10 fastest-growing economies globally. The year-long celebrations marking the half-century of this South Asian nation bespoke pride and joy as it also coincided with Bangladesh's dual graduation from low-income country to lower-middle-income country, and from the group of least developed country to developing country status by 2026. The sustained progress in various economic and social indicators echo a fascinating growth story of a nation that overcame several challenges at its birth—including West Pakistan's genocidal campaign, extreme poverty, and political instability—to achieve several milestones that have, in recent times, captured the imagination of the global community.

The past five decades began on a high note of Independence in December 1971 from its erstwhile Pakistani identity to form Bangladesh, a separate state. The journey since, however, has been rather tumultuous. Bangladesh's history has been scattered with low and dark moments, making its economic turnaround a compelling argument for the Bangladeshi miracle. The country's growth figures over the last few years have strongly addressed many of the doubts that were initially raised by Western nations.

Growth Story

Bangladesh's journey as an independent nation began on a very difficult note, with long periods of political instability, but what is remarkable is its sustained growth rate and economic development despite the turbulent political journey it has undertaken. Indeed, it can even showcase some positive indicators that a number of its other South Asian neighbours may not be able to match. Bangladesh's growth has been possible due to its investment in human development and market-friendly policies, enabling an environment for entrepreneurship to emerge. Beginning with deep pockets of poverty to achieving a sustainable growth rate of over 6 per cent and beyond for over three decades is what makes the Bangladesh growth story fascinating.

The country, as has been well documented, was almost written off, especially by Western powers during its early years. From then to now, Bangladesh has traversed a long fruitful journey from being a 'basket case' to becoming a 'developing giant on the world stage' (*Dhaka Tribune* 2019). With its growth and developmental achievements, Bangladesh has successfully positioned itself as a critical neighbour in the region and an attractive partner for extra-regional players too. Significantly, the country has been able to provide and build a substantial middle-income population, attract substantial foreign direct investment (FDI) and foreign remittance and host the Bay of Bengal Initiative for Multi-Sectoral Economic Cooperation (BIMSTEC) secretariat and mark its presence in other regional and global communities. Much of Bangladesh's achievements have been due to its ability to introduce internal measures leading to the growth of agricultural output and huge export driven by ready-made garments, among other markers of growth. Additionally, a large number of migrant labourers outside the country bring in considerable remittances and investment in the construction sector. These factors have been identified as important drivers of growth.

Another indicator of the country's development has been its remarkable infrastructure, and one of the crowning achievements has been the inauguration of the 16.1-kilometre-long Padma Bridge in June 2022. Built to connect the capital city Dhaka to its south and southwest districts, the bridge has become a source of national pride. A self-funded project of nearly US$4 billion, this bridge has also been a recipient of global accolades and a successful demonstration of Bangladesh's commitment to development.

Its growth is easily witnessed in the increase in the per capita income from US$273 in 1975 to US$1,888 in 2020, recording a 6 per cent growth rate despite being affected by the Covid-19 pandemic. However, on account of the Ukraine crisis, the ensuing global energy shortage and low economic growth along with some other domestic factors, Bangladesh has, in recent times, raked up a high import bill with a significant dip in its foreign exchange reserve, thus requiring a US$4.5 billion support from the International Monetary Fund (IMF). Although there has been a recent dent in its economic 'miracle', one cannot take away from Bangladesh's success in chalking a destiny of its own and looking after its people and their aspirations (Subramanian

2021). The country lifted its people from deep-rooted poverty to providing better social, medical and cost-effective quality of life for its burgeoning middle-income population and developing impressive infrastructure. Bangladesh's consistent economic growth despite the political instability is often referred to as Bangladesh Paradox or the Bangladesh Miracle. It behoves us to recall, in this context, that Pakistan also experienced a similar journey. It was one of the *fastest-growing economies* in South Asia for most of the 1960s and 1970s. However, it started borrowing heavily in the 1980s—when it started borrowing money not just for development but consumption as well; it relied heavily on the IMF and western countries, particularly the US, and evidently never stopped. The downslide continues and while the comparisons may seem inappropriate presently, the irony in the situation is difficult to ignore.

One of Bangladesh's distinctive characteristics and strengths also lies in a deeply aware and vigilant civil society—a population that has always remained politically aware and indeed has shaped the destiny of the nation. East Pakistan was patient in the wake of the early years of discrimination and deprivation a situation that continued till it emerged as an independent nation in 1971, but when consistently denied their rights, especially in the parliamentary elections of 1970 where, despite the Awami League's (AL's) massive majority, the then Pakistani president, General Yahya Khan—using every possible subterfuge in collaboration with Foreign Minister Zulfikar Ali Bhutto—ensured that it did not form the government (Datta 2022).

The Desire for a Cultural Identity

Mujibur Rahman, president of East Pakistan Awami League, stood firm on the demand for autonomy and the right to form a government. The Bangladeshis' desire for freedom and liberty, both politically as well as culturally, grew out of their years of repression and exploitation at the hands of the Pakistani authoritarian leaders. Inevitably, the liberation struggle was strewn with many difficulties, leading to the loss of thousands of lives and an overwhelming cross-border refugee movement in the face of brutality and torture (Dasgupta 2016). No Bengali family in Pakistan remained immune to the vagaries of that period. The violence unleashed by the Pakistani military has left wounds that have continued to fester. Many Bangladeshis are yet to overcome the torture they experienced or witnessed at the hand of the Pakistani forces. The recent declaration of the (April 2023) International Association of Genocide Scholars, about the genocide and other crimes against humanity that

Pakistan committed during the 1971 Liberation War of Bangladesh, is a small step towards healing many festering wounds, while opening up an opportunity for greater international acceptance of the unfortunate history (*LatestLY* 2023).

The release and return of Mujibur Rahman to Dhaka[1] after the signing of the 'Instrument of Surrender' between India and Pakistan to assume his role as the first prime minister of Bangladesh was not only a validation of the struggle and hardship that the Bengalis of Pakistan suffered but also a watershed event in South Asia with wide ramifications for the region and outside. Mujib, popularly known as 'Bangabandhu', was arrested when he led a non-cooperation movement against the Pakistani military leaders and taken to Karachi where he remained till January 1972. The Mujibur led AL government and was tasked with the job of nation-building under very challenging political, social and economic conditions. In his attempt to deliver and live up to the people's expectations, he resorted to a few unpopular political experiments including forming a one-party state, the Bangladesh Krishak Sramik Awami League, banning activities of any other political parties, and disagreeing with some of his core political team members.

The Bangladeshi domestic polity, however, underwent a drastic change with his assassination in 1975. The early socialists and democratic initiatives faltered in the face of coups and counter-coups and Bangladesh soon gave way to an authoritarian system. The army, in the face of ongoing political splits and disarray, held strong and was able to emerge as the political answer to the nation during this early volatile period. Each military leader that assumed power (Ziaur Rahman, 1975–1981 followed by M. Ershad, 1980–1990) sought legitimacy by appealing to religious leaders and forming political parties, the Bangladesh Nationalist Party (BNP) and Jatiya Party respectively. This thus introduced the religious element into politics, something that Mujib apparently tried to keep away from. The military and religious factors have since then cast a shadow over the political discourse of Bangladesh (Datta 2004).

It was only in 1991 with the return of the electoral multiparty democracy that the Bangladesh armed forces withdrew from its primary function. But the military continues to play its part in the politics of the nation; during a brief interregnum between 2006 and 2008, they once again, through the facade of a caretaker government, assumed political control. However, reading the mood of the people, they retreated, and Bangladesh ushered in another era of parliamentary politics. The security forces have also, from time to time, been invited to intervene during domestic law-and-order crises. Indeed, despite Bangladesh's parliamentary democracy, the armed forces as mentioned earlier, wield influence domestically while being appreciated internationally as they are the largest contributor to the UN Peacekeeping force they continue to serve. The birth of two mainstream political parties namely, the BNP and the Jatiya Party from the army barracks, have left an indelible imprint in domestic politics that AL is unable to shake off and, in fact, is being forced to embrace.

Political Islam

All mainstream political parties have used Islam for both legitimacy as well as greater domestic outreach. The prevailing divisive political atmosphere offers greater manoeuvrability to the radical Islamist forces to seek greater patronage. Over the years, the AL and the BNP have repositioned themselves. While the BNP has not hesitated to form a coalition with Islamic political parties, namely the Jamaat-e-Islami (JI). While even in the best of times the JI has not managed more than a few seats in the Jatiya Sangsad (national parliament) elections, they have essentially played the role of a queen-maker in Bangladesh. The Awami League, popularly known for its secular credentials, enjoyed Jamaat support from outside when it formed a government in 1996. Subsequently, AL has been seen compromising with the hardliner organisation, Hefazat-e-Islam as well. Since 2013, the government has allowed Hefazat greater social space and has justified these actions as a way to counter the other strident Islamist groups. In sharp contrast to the earlier position of prioritising its cultural identity over its religious one, Bangladesh has witnessed the identity of being Islamic gaining increasing acceptance, legitimacy and popularity. At the same time, through its two main women leaders, the country has found a voice and cause to ensure greater women's participation in all spheres of society and the state. Not only does Bangladesh boast of a considerable woman workforce, especially in its ready-made garment sector that contributes to its commercial strength and export earnings, but the reservation of women seats in the parliament has also encouraged grassroots and urban women to engage in the decision-making process.

Fragile Democracy

While the transition towards democratic tendencies in the post-Ershad period, in 1991, was slow and painful, changes were brought in through ballots and not bullets. Arguably, Bangladesh has successfully held elections since 1991, but its ability to uphold democratic norms has not been very laudable. Periodically elected governments have, over the years, feebly tried to uphold them. However, while the past three terms of the AL rule have not broken any fresh ground, it seems to have further shrunken the democratic space. The present Sheikh Hasina-led AL coalition government has been in power since 2009 and has virtually ruled without any opposition for nearly a decade. The deep political schism that always existed in Bangladesh has only deepened over the course of the past decade. Indeed, the next few months to the next parliamentary elections, scheduled for January 2024, look uncertain. The last two elections (2014 and 2019) were largely one-sided and the parliament functioned without a legitimate opposition. While the AL leaders continue to chime the developmental narrative that has been unveiled by Sheikh Hasina, and shower self-accolades over the trebling of its per capita income in the last decade, the moot question is whether this will be enough to satisfy the people in the face of some rather blatant executive overreach and institutional manipulation. There is very little separation of power in reality. The resignation of Chief Justice Surendra Kumar Sinha—when he refused to uphold a law that sought to give parliament the power to sack judges in July 2017—is a case in point (Bergman 2018). Similarly, there have been several instances where observations or rulings by the judiciary have been brazenly ignored by the executive (Huda 2021).

The separation of powers exists only on paper; the government is not hesitating to stampede over any contrarian ideas and suggestions that have the slightest scope to threaten its tight grip over political and financial power. The impudence of the government in the face of strong accusations of a rampant violation of human rights and breach of the rule of law surfaces blatantly. Evidently, the Bangladeshi government is increasingly resorting to restricting the contours of a democratic state structure, having moved the nation into what is now being popularly referred to as 'hybrid democracy' (Riaz 2019). For all purposes, the country has only been an electoral democracy and in the past decade, there has been a distinct erosion of that too. The ruthlessness through which any voice that does not echo the government is being brought to the books and the intolerance shown towards any other political view and the constant harassment of targeted liberal thinkers and journalists have only pointed shrinking of any liberal space. The introduction of the Digital Security Act by the present government reflects its deep sense of insecurity manifested through its hardline positions (Riaz 2021).

The one distinct feature of Bangladesh, however, has been its strong civil society. They have in the past intervened successfully to turn around difficult situations and there is an underlying belief that these constituent stakeholders will not allow the present circumstances to reach unmanageable levels. Although the government has through various measures stymied many organisational efforts, the indomitable spirit of the citizenry is to be saluted. In the face of dire conditions, their intrinsic strength has always been reliable.

Interestingly, while the BNP has begun its electoral run and rallies are being organised in some areas, the lack of BNP leadership is its biggest failing for the upcoming election in 2024. Begum Khaleda Zia, the leader of BNP, as well as Tarique Zia, the heir apparent, have been incarcerated on many grounds of corruption. While Khaleda remains confined in Dhaka with failing health, Tarique's return from London— where he is currently—is impossible because of the legal charges he faces. Despite the challenges, the party has not broken down and some seasoned BNP political leaders have been holding the fort for nearly a decade and a half, ever since AL government took over in 2009. Arguably, their political absence from the main arena of action has dented them operationally, physically as well as psychologically. Both AL and BNP have long received nearly similar percentages of electoral support, but BNP, living in the margins for a while, might face some limitations (Datta 2023). The BNP, as in the past two elections, continues to seek an interim government to oversee elections as they are not sanguine about the fairness of the electoral outcome under the present government and its administration. The same demand by the AL in the past had led to the introduction of a caretaker government but it now refuses to follow the earlier institution on grounds of the political maturity of the present government. Very briefly, the bringing in of the caretaker government was a unique introduction to a polity which was deeply polarised with very little trust amongst the political parties, which were divided into ideological lines. The elected government, once its term is over, will leave office along with the dissolution of the parliament, and the caretaker government is headed by a chief advisor (usually the last retired chief justice) and jointly elected 10 technocrats, for a maximum period of three months. As per the constitutional provisions, the caretaker government will 'assist the Chief Election Commissioner in holding impartial, free and fair elections' (Datta 2009). The possibility of the ruling party coming to some arrangement with few other political parties to contest the election to save face may be an option on the electoral table. Given the last electoral experience of vote-rigging and ballot manoeuvres, much of the recent development seems heading towards a rather opaque situation. An Indian newspaper has quite aptly termed the situation as Dhakakracy (Datta 2023). While some others have used hybrid regime to explain the unfolding political landscape in Dhaka, it's a pity that parties, when in power, wilfully manipulate the situation for myopic gains (Hassan 2021).

While the AL has been successful in shepherding a confident nation as it steps into its 50-plus years, spread with various significant economic milestones, Bangladesh remains unsuccessful in getting out of the rabbit hole of corruption. Unfortunately, the present government too has not been able to escape the taint of some notoriety, including corrupt and fraudulent practices, including several scams and misappropriation of funds by private banks, which have come to light periodically. Although the government and its leaders have either denied or offered absurd justifications, the patience of the masses can never be taken for granted. Rural Bangladesh remains mired in poor conditions at the cost of urban unequal growth. The point of concern is that this time around, the public may not accept the fait accompli thrust on them by its leadership. Bangladeshis, periodically in 1991, 1996 and 2008, have shown they are capable of putting across their opinion and choices frankly and unreservedly. Another electoral manipulation could be the black swan moment that Bangladesh does not need. Lessons from previous mistakes should be a stark reminder to avoid any similar moves. However, it is a point worth noting that despite its political reality and shrinking plurality, Bangladesh has made great strides in its foreign policy outreach.

Bangladesh's Growing Outreach

Given its economic worries from its initial days, Bangladesh has pursued its external relations with a focus on access to markets, concessions, and bilateral and multilateral aid. Its foreign policy has been driven by self-interest and centred on gaining an advantage from its relationships to enhance its economic development. Bangladesh has established stable bilateral with all major powers from Asia, America, Europe and the Muslim world. While India and China are likely to continue their engagement with Bangladesh, its broader outreach has been acquired through leveraging its unique geography (situated at the head of the Bay of Bengal, within the larger the Indo-Pacific region that is witnessing growing interests of major powers), staying away from political alliances, and showcasing its growth story with its plans to move into a knowledge-intensive society, beyond apparel manufacturing.

The recent announcement of the Indo-Pacific Outlook (April 2023) by the government reflects its strategic clarity about the geopolitical developments in its extended neighbourhood (*Dhaka Tribune* 2023). Some of the major powers engaged in the Indo-Pacific were urging Bangladesh to join the coalition, thus the latter clarifying its position just before PM Hasina's visit to Japan was interesting. It's not very often that Dhaka is seen articulating a policy in such specific terms. The 15-point explainer covers its security concerns while ensuring that this foreign policy formulation will also contribute to its economic growth and development. It does signal a newfound confidence about all the regional partnerships that Dhaka has forged with many of the capitals, not only within the neighbourhood but a more extended Indo-Pacific community and globally as well.

The growing bilateral and regional partnership that Bangladesh enjoys presently is a sharp contrast to its initial years. When except for India, Russia and a few other countries, most of the bigger powers did not lend support to the Liberation War for Bangladesh. During the early days of the war, many nations, including the US, backed West Pakistan and tried to undermine India's intervention and military action against the aggression by West Pakistan (Bass 2013). India, Bhutan, Russia, the German Democratic Republic, Bulgaria, Mongolia, Poland, Burma (now Myanmar) and Nepal were the first countries to recognise Bangladesh. The Pakistani government tried threats to break off relations with some countries which had recognised Bangladesh. In Europe, the UK was among the first countries to recognise Bangladesh as an independent and sovereign nation in early February 1972. And by the end of the month, in total 47 countries had accorded recognition to Bangladesh. The journey of this South Asian state from being shunned and marginalised in its struggle for independence to now enjoying the interests of the neighbourhood to the extra-regional powers has been fascinating.

A number of factors have lent salience to Bangladesh's growing bilateral partnership and stable ties all across the globe. Over the years, its leaders have fallen back on Mujib's foreign policy dictum of 'we want friendship to all and malice towards none', to explain many of Bangladesh's foreign policy overtures. Aspiring to influence and steer, Bangladesh has been at the forefront of regional organisations in the South Asian region, having initiated the South Asian Association for Regional Cooperation (SAARC) and is now a partner in the Bay of Bengal Initiative for Multi-Sectoral Technical and Economic Cooperation. It is seeking to be the hub to connect the South Asian region to Southeast Asia, through a 'sectoral dialogue' partnership in Association of Southeast Asian Nations (ASEAN). In the present context, with the Bay of Bengal assuming greater salience and the Indian Ocean as part of the Indo Pacific with its growing strategic salience has become a focal point for major powers' jostling, Bangladesh's ability to turn around and effectively use its geographical position to its advantage has been rather fascinating.

Back in 1974, the country had already established ties with the Muslim world when it gained membership in the Organisation of

Islamic Cooperation (OIC). Ever since then, it has steadily stepped up bilateral and multilateral relations. In 1983, the Dhaka International Islamic Bank Limited was established as the first interest-free bank in Southeast Asia. This part of the world has also been a substantial contributor to Bangladesh's growth through the remittance generated, constituting 7 per cent of its GDP. Remittances from more than 10 million citizens abroad from over 160 countries have become a key source of foreign exchange (Islam 2023). Saudi Arabia has been the largest source of remittances, followed by UAE, Qatar, Oman, Bahrain, Kuwait, Libya, Iraq, Singapore, Malaysia, the US, the UK and others.

As it moves from one milestone to another, Bangladesh is emerging as a middle-income country and exiting from the category of less-developed nations. It is also now contemplating seeking concessions, to enjoy all the LDC-specific international support measures— particularly duty-free and quota-free market access to the country's exports—for an extra three-year period, as the removal of taxes will have an immediate effect on the price of its goods and subsequent export orders.

The Bangladesh Aid Group was established under the aegis of the World Bank in 1974 with 26 participating governments and institutions. Aid to Bangladesh has remained at a high level since the consortium came into existence. That apart, the Asian Development Bank, the Japan International Cooperation Assistance and the Islamic Development Bank have provided Bangladesh with developmental assistance and 2019 witnessed over US$6 billion in aid inflow. Although foreign direct investment has not been large in Bangladesh, despite the pandemic, the number of international financial projects tripled to 14, reaching US$4.7 billion in 2021. However, Bangladesh continues to be vigilant. The crash of the Sri Lankan economy has also raised many concerns and it is expected that they would be treading cautiously in the coming years.

Despite the economic growth, the challenges of the Covid-19 pandemic and its consequences will impact the future trajectory. The worries ahead are many. Apart from the social and public health crises, the dwindling economy will inevitably impact the majority of the population and Bangladesh will have to skilfully manage the budgetary cuts on many fronts. Its domestic governance will need to be supported by its relations with the external world which has long supported Bangladesh over the past 50 years.

This book, therefore, examines some of the aspects of Bangladesh's foreign policy, that shares convergence with some states over civilisational values and ideas of socialism, democracy and similar ideologies, while working with governments that follow divergent political systems too. The ongoing discourse of big versus small nations and how Bangladesh has negotiated through that passage of moving from one side of being a small nation to the other side has been discussed too. Bangladesh is no more boxed in its geography; on the contrary, the shift of geopolitical focus has enabled Dhaka to engage with extra-regional powers with greater manoeuvrability. This volume also looks at the increasing regional resonance of Bangladesh, not only with India but also with others, including Nepal and Bhutan. Bangladesh is grappling with growing concerns about climate change and Islamisation which not only have domestic implications but have also been examined through the foreign policy prism. Some vital bilateral ties have been included in this volume also.

This volume begins with a prologue by Michael Kugelman that identifies Bangladesh's progress, pitfalls and prospects. He believes that the story of Bangladesh's global prominence has not been properly understood around the world, more so in the West. In fact, their Liberation War struggle had sparked an interest amongst many and Western music icons such as George Harriosn, Eric Clapton, got involved in raising awareness about the crises that were unfolding in this corner of the globe. Bangladesh took a few years to firmly plant its footprint on the global stage. Right from the time of Mujib, Bangladesh had pursued to establish a global presence through bilateral and multilateral fora. And yet, a series of challenges threaten to hold Bangladesh back from charting even greater heights abroad. According to Kugelman, how and if it at all Bangladesh addresses these obstacles will go a long way in determining its trajectory as a global player.

In the first chapter of the first section of the book, Rashed Titumir sketches out a Bangladeshi policy doctrine through the lens of an alternative framework beyond the conventional concepts of liberalism and realism. Given the context of Bangladesh's geographical location, its size and strength—and its weaknesses—the author has chosen four different scenarios that would help construct the country's security and defence strategy framework. He argues for a Bangladeshi white paper outlining its policy strategy, which would enable leveraging the strength of its population dividend and locational advantage, and maximising its economic potential.

Brigitta Schuchert writes about Bangladesh's need for international legitimacy and economic support to define its national image on the international stage. She examines this national identity, a contested space with deep fissures between visions of Bangladesh as a Muslim-majority secular nation, or Bangladesh as an Islamic nation first, while explaining how Islam has played a distinct role in establishing Bangladesh's diplomacy with leading Muslim-majority countries. The understanding of Bangladesh's national identity by its ruling party has played an instrumental role in the foreign policy partnerships the country has prioritised and how Bangladesh messaged its interests externally. Schuchert explains how its positioning as a secular nation and as a Muslim-majority country has supported pragmatic interests and shaped the country's diplomatic outreach.

Ali Riaz discusses the 'diasporic identity' of Bangladeshis living abroad. The shifts that the Bangladeshi community, especially in North America, has undergone in their identification with 'home' and 'host' countries have contributed to the construction and reconstruction of various identities and have followed a particular trajectory. He explains how the migrant community found ways to preserve their culture living far away from home, leading to a hyphenated identity of the community. He argues that they subsequently embraced a globalised identity based on religion and that the transformation from an ethnicity-based identity to a religion-based identity has been mediated through the diasporic identity.

Ashley Johnson looks at the challenges of climate change through the lens of domestic strategies, policies and plans enacted or proposed for mitigation of and adaptation to global warming. It assesses the select past and current partnerships that have been instrumental in Bangladesh's progress to implement these efforts and how it is using its knowledge and resources to aid other vulnerable states in South Asia and the broader Indo-Pacific region.

The second section begins with Humayun Kabir's analysis of Bangladesh's engagement with the outside world over the last five decades. He elaborates on domestic economic and political compulsions that have essentially driven the foreign policy decisions from the very beginning of its journey as a nation, and which have continued across the regimes. Even as Bangladesh has taken long development strides, its foreign policy decisions have supported its establishment as an independent, active and contributing member of the international community. Kabir also adds a note of caution: In the face of fast-changing technology advancements taking place, Dhaka will need to introduce urgent adjustments to successfully navigate the emerging multipolar and multi-partner world.

Johannes Plagemann argues that the tense multipolarity prevalent in Asia today accrues a greater bargaining power in bilateral relations to secondary and tertiary states, such as Bangladesh. Plagemann points out that at the same time, multipolarity severely restricts weak states' collective power through coalitions in multilateral settings. Bangladesh's foreign policy posture today is emblematic of the wider changes in the international system. Over time it has been able to reduce its dependency on traditional donors while seeking friendly relations with all major powers active in the region. It has improved its traditionally strained relations with neighbouring India and deepened relations with China through infrastructure investments and military procurement. He traces, amongst others, Bangladesh's development from aid dependency to—however tepid—donor country, which epitomises the resurgence of the Global South more widely.

Sreeradha Datta brings out how a variety of factors have enabled Bangladesh to leverage its geographical location to play a distinct role in its growing outreach and how the contemporary political environment looming over the neighbourhood geography has lent Bangladesh greater relevance in global affairs. With the ongoing refocus on the Indo-Pacific, the extra-regional powers see a potential strategic advantage in engaging with Bangladesh, especially when the strategic asset of the region is seeing powers big and small engaging with each other. Undoubtedly, the contemporary strategic developments in the region and outside have coincided with Bangladesh's growth to ensure its pivotal role in the region. At the same time, Bangladesh has been able to take advantage of a competitive power jostling in the region and outside to establish itself as a reliable partner.

Don McLain Gill focuses on Bangladesh's relations with Southeast Asia. He argues that the strengthening of Bangladesh–Southeast Asian relations seems to be a logical and inevitable progression, as both regions are increasingly becoming interconnected economies brought by a globalising international political–economic landscape. While ASEAN seeks to bolster engagements with a wide array of emerging states—of which Bangladesh is also an important partner—Dhaka has equally endeavoured to reinvigorate its partnership with states in the region at bilateral, multilateral, and institutional levels. McLain discusses the growing partnership in the background of the geopolitical tension caused by the violence unleashed on the Rohingya population, leading to forcible exodus across the borders. The 9,00,000 Rohingya refugees have been hosted by Bangladesh under very difficult circumstances and while the two governments have had some discussions about repatriation, the political instability within Myanmar has added further complexity to the issue. According to McLain, Bangladesh must also continue to maintain its foreign policy momentum with its southeastern neighbours, which can enable conducive conditions to address not only the critical issue of Rohingyas. (Myanmar does not engage with other countries much and there is a perception that ASEAN members are in a better position to impress upon Myanmar to alter its policies towards the Rohingya population.)

In the next chapter, Li Jianjun discusses how the formation, maintenance and development of the traditional friendship between China and Bangladesh benefits from China's active practice of the five principles of peaceful coexistence in its foreign exchanges, from the two countries' respect and support for each other's development, and domestic and foreign policies. The strategic cooperative partnership between China and Bangladesh gradually grew through the diplomatic engagement of the two countries. He suggests that the cornerstone of Bangladesh's China policy is to maintain the same friendly relations with China, India, the US and other countries; at the same time, with the help of China, it wants to reduce its economic dependence on India and the US, to obtain economic benefits from the competition between China, India and the US in the long run. The China factor sometimes has become an important tool for Bangladesh to balance India and the US. As long as Bangladesh's future China policy remains friendly and neutral, the long-term prospects of their relations will continue to develop steadily.

Deb Mukharji, while analysing the present 'golden chapter' in Indo-Bangladeshi relations, has cautioned that both sides need to understand the complexities of this bilateral relationship if pitfalls are to be avoided. Certainly, recent years have shown a steady upward trend in economic relations and some understanding of mutual core concerns, even if some issues may remain unaddressed. While the future parameters of Bangladeshi society and polity would continue to evolve, a positive trend that Mukharji brings to light is that even if its impact on relations with India can only be indirect, despite many years of contrary state indoctrination, the youth of Bangladesh, far removed from 1971, still value the sacrifices and cherish the values that underpinned the war of liberation.

Amna Ejaz Rafi traces the historical journey of Bangladesh's Liberation War and suggests that the situation may have unfolded differently if the leading political parties of Pakistan would have taken a cooperative approach during the crisis period. She questions the Bangladeshi quest for a 'formal' and an 'unconditional apology' for the genocide of '3 million Bengalis and rapes of 2,00,000 Bengali women', from Pakistan. The author also discusses the drastic changes in circumstances that occurred with Mujib's assassination and the changing political scenario. While diplomatic links resumed between Bangladesh and Pakistan, their issue of apology has come in the way of a more cooperative relationship. The chapter explores how Bangladesh and Pakistan can mend fences regardless of the bitterness of the past and what impediments obstruct the establishment of meaningful friendly relations between the two countries. It also explores purposeful areas of cooperation and how the two countries can positively transform their uneven ties by promoting economic, political, educational and cultural relations in the years to come. Rafi suggests that Bangladesh and Pakistan can be partners in the regional integration that is unfolding.

Nilanthi Samaranayake traces the Bangladesh–US ties from the genesis of the new nation. Given the context of the Cold War and the close ties that Washington shared with Islamabad, the break-up of Pakistan was seen unfavourably. And that memory is not lost on the Bangladeshis as yet. Despite the tepid beginnings, presently Bangladesh and the US have established strong ties spanning economic and political ties. The US is a large market for Bangladesh's ready-made garment industry, which has contributed substantially to Bangladesh's emergence as a powerhouse. The Agency for International Development (USAID) has also hosted large programmes in Bangladesh. Moreover, the US is the largest source of FDI. Although Dhaka has held out on signing the two foundational defence agreements that the US has proposed, the growing security and military relations have lent another aspect to the increasingly strong bilateral ties, including addressing the non-traditional security threats that Bangladesh has to deal with regularly. Despite the growing bilateral ties, there is a deep schism between the two nations on a few core issues, namely democratic governance and law and order. The US has imposed sanctions on Bangladesh's Rapid Action Battalion and seven current and former officials for human rights abuses further adding to the underlying tension. With elections around the corner, these issues continue to inhibit bilateral ties.

Andrew Hunter focuses on the lack of Australian attention on Bangladesh which is anomalous with its current geo-economic objectives and inconsistent with the approach taken by its regional partners. He asks why Australia, although concerned about China's increasingly assertive international engagement, pays little attention to a country with a population of over 160 million, located in an area of geo-strategic significance. He, however, does find room for optimism and points out how Bangladesh's striking economic growth trajectory has recently captured Canberra's attention. It is a welcome sign that Australia now recognises the economic opportunity that Bangladesh offers. Hunter believes that the irresistible economic and strategic forces are such that it is only a matter of time before Australia sharpens its focus on Bangladesh.

Ramita Iyer ties up this volume on a positive albeit cautionary note. She observes Dhaka is uniquely placed to reap significant economic and strategic gains, but will need skilful diplomacy to navigate an increasingly complex international landscape.

Note

1 The tripartite talks among President Yahya Khan, Foreign Minister Zulfikar Bhutto and Awami Leader Mujibur Rahman over the victory of Awami League in the 1970 parliamentary elections and the rightful recognition of Mujibur as the Prime Minister ultimately broke down, and troops stationed in East Pakistan began a large-scale suppression of the people of East Pakistan at midnight on 25 March 1971. Mujibur Rahman was arrested and taken to Karachi where he remained till the independence of Bangladesh.

References

'Bangladesh Formally Announces Its Indo-Pacific Outlook', *Dhaka Tribune*, 24 April 2023. https://www.dhakatribune.com/bangladesh/2023/04/24/bangladesh-formally-announces-its-indo-pacific-outlook.

Bass, G.J. *The Blood Telegram: Nixon, Kissinger, and a Forgotten Genocide*. First Edition. New York: Alfred A. Knopf, 2013.

Bergman, D. 'Bangladesh: Ex-Chief Justice Alleges He Was "Forced" to Resign', *Al Jazeera*, 2018. https://www.aljazeera.com/news/2018/9/28/bangladesh-ex-chief-justice-alleges-he-was-forced-to-resign.

Dasgupta, A. 'Exile and Freedom: Bangladesh Liberation War Refugees, 1971'. In *Displacement and Exile: The State-Refugee Relations in India*, edited by Abhijit Dasgupta. New Delhi: Oxford University Press, 2016. https://doi.org/10.1093/acprof:oso/9780199461172.003.0004.

Datta, S. *Bangladesh, a Fragile Democracy*. New Delhi: Shipra Publications, 2004.

———. *Caretaking Democracy: Political Process in Bangladesh, 2006–08*. New Delhi: Institute for Defence Studies and Analyses, 2009.

———. 'India–Bangladesh Bonhomie at 50: 1971 and the Present'. 25 March 2022. New Delhi: VIF, 2022. https://www.vifindia.org/book/2022/march/25/India-Bangladesh-Bonhomie-at-50-1971-and-the-Present.

———. 'India–Bangladesh: Carving a New Destiny for South Asia'. *NatStrat*, July 2023. https://natstrat.org/articledetail/publications/india-bangladesh-carving-a-new-destiny-for-south-asia-28.html.

'Forum Demands Immediate International Recognition of Bangladesh Genocide Committed in 1971'. *LatestLY*, 26 April 2023. https://www.latestly.com/agency-news/world-news-uk-forum-demands-immediate-international-recognition-of-bangladesh-genocide-committed-in-1971-5085515.html.

Hassan, Shorab. 'From Democracy to a Hybrid Regime'. 2 January 2021. https://en.prothomalo.com/opinion/op-ed/from-democracy-to-a-hybrid-regime.

Huda, M.N. 'Separation of Powers Key to Functioning Democracy'. *The Daily Star*, 2021 https://www.thedailystar.net/opinion/straight-line/news/separation-powers-key-functioning-democracy-2046057.

Islam, S. 2023. 'Bangladesh Sees Economic Ray of Light as Exports, Remittances Rise'. *Nikkei Asia*, 2023. https://asia.nikkei.com/Economy/Bangladesh-sees-economic-ray-of-light-as-exports-remittances-rise.

Riaz, Ali. *Voting in a Hybrid Regime, Explaining the 2018 Bangladeshi Election*. Singapore: Springer, 2019.

———. 'How Bangladesh's Digital Security Act Is Creating a Culture of Fear', Carnegie Endowment for International Point, 9 December 2021. https://carnegieendowment.org/2021/12/09/how-bangladesh-s-digital-securityact-is-creating-culture-of-fear-pub-85951.

Subramaniam, A. 'The Paradoxes of the Bangladesh Miracle'. *Project Syndicate*, 6 November 2021. https://www.project-syndicate.org/commentary/bangladesh-economic-miracle-outperforming-india-and-pakistan-by-arvind-subramanian-2021-06.

'UK High Commissioner: Bangladesh a Developing Giant on World Stage', *Dhaka Tribune*. 4 April 2019. https://archive.dhakatribune.com/bangladesh/event/2019/04/04/uk-high-commissioner-bangladesh-a-developing-gianton-world-stage.

Part I

INTRODUCTION

The challenging circumstances during the birth of Bangladesh and the concomitant domestic compulsion shaped Bangladesh's foreign policy especially during the initial years. The template established by Mujibur Rahman continues to provide the premise for Bangladesh's external relations with other nations. Mujib's formulation of 'friendship to all, malice towards none' enabled Bangladesh to befriend all other nations spread across the globe. It is a practice that continues to this day. Worldwide recognition for the newly emerged Bangladesh was the primary focus for its leaders and Mujib reached out to all major powers, notwithstanding their political position during the Liberation War of Bangladesh. Indeed, awareness of the political developments in this corner of South Asia was limited for most of the extra-regional states and at the same time Pakistan's engagement with major powers ensured that many of them preferred to ignore the ensuing struggle between East Pakistan and West Pakistan. Thus, recognition for Dhaka was impinged on the Cold War power matrix. Much of Mujibur's initial years were spent trying to convey the circumstances of Bangladesh's birth to other nations and each state recognition that came Dhaka's way was indeed another acknowledgement of its struggle.

Before the actual war broke out, then Indian prime minister Indira Gandhi travelled abroad to Europe and North America to draw the attention of the international community towards the plight of people in East Pakistan, but it was journalist Anthony Mascarenhas's article in the *Sunday Times* (June 1971) that spread the word far and wide. India sent delegations to 70 countries, of which 13 were at the ministerial level, which also led to the flow of humanitarian help and support pouring in from some quarters. Nonetheless, the US and China's tilt towards Pakistan continued, and the United Nations (UN) was unable to address the issue effectively, as Cold War politics continued to influence state behaviour. To overcome much of this initial hesitation, Mujib laid out a broad foreign policy formulation to help tide over its economic limitations. Apart from India, Russia, Bhutan, East Germany, Myanmar, Poland and a few others followed in recognising Bangladesh. Canada, after some initial reservations, gave in and provided Bangladesh with much-needed aid (apart from India and Russia) and assisted Bangladesh to slowly lift itself from its very poor economic conditions.

Bangladesh has also faced severe climate change issues including rising sea levels that have not only drawn the attention of the international community to this part of the world but have also given Bangladesh a voice to articulate its positions on many critical issues. Prime Minister Sheikh Hasina while initiating new programmes to address the challenges of climate change has also launched a Mujib Climate Prosperity Plan Decade 2030 in 2021.

While Dhaka's Indian Ocean Outlook as explained by Bangladesh Foreign Minister A.K. Abdul Momen (April 2023) was timed well with Prime Minister Sheikh Hasina's visit abroad, it is not very often that the government has etched out its foreign policy contours so clearly. Understandably, Article 25 of the Bangladesh Constitution outlines the broad principles of its foreign policy. These include promotion of international peace, security and solidarity, and most other non-controversial but accepted norms for respecting national sovereignty and equality, as well as following the principle of non-interference in the internal affairs of other countries, while lending its support to oppressed peoples struggling against imperialism, colonialism or racialism.

Thus, the need for constructing a doctrine which will outline the policy in the face of the emerging geostrategic contours is an important aspect that has not received adequate attention in Bangladesh. As explained in the chapter on the Bangladeshi diaspora, the role of the diaspora, which is one of the largest and is spread over a broad expanse of the globe, has contributed to a certain imagery of Bangladesh and Bangladeshis. While the chapter here focuses largely on the American and European diaspora, their growing presence and impact is noticeable. The changing domestic narrative where religion is finding greater appeal amongst a certain sector of people has also influenced the perspective of other nations of Bangladesh.

1

THE MAKING OF THE BANGLADESH DOCTRINE: STRATEGIC AUTONOMY AND DEVELOPMENT DETERRENCE

Rashed Al Mahmud Titumir

Introduction

Bangladesh has completed over 50 years as an independent state. Following the golden jubilee of independence, it is timely to reflect on the achievements and position of the country in the international arena. Particularly, to ponder on some key questions: What kind of roadmap is needed for the future Bangladesh, taking into account the aspirations of common people on the basis of equality, human dignity and social justice, the three main pillars of the Liberation War? How should it coordinate its national security policy with its development policy? What will be the strategies and procedures of this integrated policy and the institutions and organisations associated with it? These aspects need to be systematically reviewed to formulate the core guiding principles as regards the country's journey towards becoming a prosperous, developed nation.

The word 'doctrine' has a variety of connotations, most of which are having to do with core values. However, in geopolitical discourse, the phrase can be understood as the authoritative principles that offer the framework within which a nation's security, economic, foreign and defence policies might be developed. A doctrine differs from a national security strategy in that the latter specifies the tactics to be used in order to carry out the aims described in the former. A national security doctrine can also be seen as a country's 'grand strategy'. A nation's defence and security policies are guided by a national security doctrine or grand strategy. In addition, it helps a country recognise and build the components of complete national power. Doctrines primarily serve as a declaration of a nation's fundamental interests. These pragmatic and grounded remarks might be aspirational, ideological or declaratory (Iyer-Mitra 2014). The creation of a national doctrine aids in the identification and ranking of the geopolitical interests of the nation.

It includes all the measures taken by the government to advance and safeguard its interests in national security through economic, social, political, diplomatic and military channels.

Up until the 1990s, national security was only concerned with maintaining security at the state level and was referred to as territorial integrity. As a result, the concept of national security overlooked the security of the individual. However, there are shifts in thinking following the collapse of the bipolar world system, and alternative strategies are being discussed. It is maintained that the security of the state may not guarantee the security of the people. Equal in importance is the security of the individual in terms of one's well-being, dignity and growth. Particularly in developing and underdeveloped countries, the security concerns may differ considerably. For example, the 'southern half of the earth' is believed to be unstable due to poverty rather than a lack of military equipment. The enormous challenges that these nations are dealing with are essentially political, economic and social in nature, and therefore, it legitimately raises concerns of the stability of these countries (Mohammad 2009). An established doctrine discourages adventurist behaviour and gives the populace confidence that the necessary safeguards are in place to protect them. Further, a lack of a national security/defence vision is also the root cause of the insufficient national security of a number of nations.

Many countries in the world have specific doctrines which are mainly reflected in the security policy of the state. It is in this light that foreign and defence policies are formulated. Likewise, it is also necessary to have a doctrine in the case of Bangladesh to guide its future advancement. Following such a doctrine will enable the executive branch to manage and fulfil its mandated missions and vision. Various articles of the Constitution of Bangladesh contain guidelines for its foreign policy, especially instructions articulated in Article 25 on the 'promotion of international peace, security and solidarity', which provides a foundation for outlining the core tenets of the doctrine (Government of Bangladesh 2019).

For a nation with nuclear-armed neighbours, a comprehensive doctrine allows the various government agencies and branches of the armed services to develop their individual tactical and operational doctrines. In its absence, national strategy will continue to remain subject to ad-hoc decisions.

In the public domain, no official or unofficial policy document exists that describes Bangladesh's defence strategy, military doctrine or warfighting tactics. It is assumed that in the country's 50-plus years of existence, it is yet to develop a national security strategy. Bangladesh is now working towards 'Forces Goal 2030' with the intention of modernising its armed forces (Anwar 2022). An in-depth understanding of the paradigm of national security strategy, focusing on the economic, political and social security factors, is paramount for Bangladesh (Chowdhury 2017).

The state of Bangladesh, with long enough experience in international engagements with actors in the region and beyond during the past half a century, is now passing a critical momentum to carry out such an exercise. Against this backdrop, an attempt has been made to briefly analyse the various regional and international contexts as well as to find out the nature of the Bangladesh Doctrine. This is an attempt to steer discussions, and by no means, is comprehensive.

Context: The Known-Unknown Quandary

Many commentators termed the Covid-19 pandemic as a great disruption with shocking consequences to the economy, society and in domestic and international politics (Sakwa 2020; World Bank 2020). Such a situation, borrowing the words of former Austrian finance minister Joseph Schumpeter, can be seen as creative destruction; it is possible to break the old mould in such a crisis and move towards a creative new approach to build a better society and address the limitations of conventional liberalist or realist conceptions of the world, which has been marred with an incessant drive for profit or power (Aghion et al. 2021; Segers and Gaile-Sarkane 2020; Schumpeter 2003).

Currently, there are some known and some unknown issues that characterise the global scene. For example, if the Quadrilateral Security Dialogue (Quad) is considered, consisting of Australia, India, Japan and the US, the objective or organisational structure is not clearly discernible, given that the members' perspectives on the future regional order and their strategic interests, including their relationship with China, often diverge, indicating a lack of 'coherent strategic intent' among the countries involved (Satake 2020; O'Neil and West 2020; Rai 2018). In contrast, when the North Atlantic Treaty Organization (NATO) and Warsaw Pact were formed after the Second World War, most of the actors involved had a clear notion about their goals, objectives, and strategies, which made it easier to make decisions by other actors (Palmer 2014; Mastny 2001).

The current known-unknown quandary, however, can also create perplexing situations. As is evident, the USA may not opt for persistent policy choices. For example, at one point, China was given a seat on the United Nations Security Council (UNSC), because the USA was in a Cold War with the then Soviet Union. Henry Kissinger, then a very influential diplomat in the Nixon administration, forged an alliance with China. Admittedly, the USA played a major role in the rise of today's China. However, it is often argued that the latter's rise did not align with the former's expectations, the US revised its approach towards China (Harding 2015; Xiang 2001).

In the case of the US's Asia-Pacific Partnership, the known-unknown quandary has become more apparent. Initially, the approach was 'pivot to Asia'. This was followed by the Asia-Pacific Strategy, and now it is replaced with the Indo-Pacific Strategy as a framework for regional order with strategic implications for containing China's rise (Heiduk and Wacker 2020; Medcalf 2018; Saeed 2017). Although this partnership is already in its third stage, there is not profound clarity about institutional structure, scope and areas of work the Asia-Pacific (He and Feng 2020; Tellis 2020; Choong 2019). There is also quadrilateral security dialogue, commonly known as QUAD, involving Australia, India, Japan and USA, witnessing ups and downs. For example, in 2008 Australia withdrew, reflecting its ambivalence over the tension between the USA and China while Australia resumed in 2010 with enhanced military cooperation between the Australia and the USA. This suggests that the USA must retain its economic momentum and cultivate a kind of strategically competitive hostile relationship with China, which means it would not declare clearly where its initiative or strategy will lead between them. Similarly, there is ambiguity surrounding the implications of the idea among India's neighbouring countries.

With regard to China, which is experiencing rapid economic growth, though slowed down in recent years while also making great strides in knowledge, science and technology, the country is too addressing the problem of growing inequality (Jain-Chandra et al. 2018). Although China is emerging as a powerful nation, it is yet to reconcile at least three different kinds of contradictions. First, China believes that its economy will one day be the largest in the world, while officially still being a developing country because its economy is still in the early stage of structural transformation (Roach 2017). Second, to become a superpower like the USA, which promotes democracy and human rights as ideals, a nation needs to develop soft power on which account China is still lacking (Xinbo 2001). At present, China is emphasising economic development, but that alone cannot create strategic allies, without normative or ideological legitimacy in the relationship. Third, China's central leadership, while acknowledging its strategic success, has yet to demonstrate bureaucratic efficiency in various areas, including its soft power as the world's second-largest economy (Keck 2013). These contradictions pose mounting challenges for China with implications for its neighbouring region and beyond.

In the aftermath of the Covid-19 pandemic, every country is preoccupied with managing its own affairs. Although some commentators classify the coronavirus as a black swan, according to Nassim Taleb, the global pandemic is a 'white swan'—a catastrophe that is bound to happen eventually (Lustenberger 2020).[1] Due to the structure of the modern world and its interconnectedness, pandemics are unavoidable, so countries need to be prepared for any such unforeseen events (Norman et al. 2020).

The ability of nations to deal with any black swan event may be improved by taking measures like strengthening institutions, markets, diplomatic ties, and regional/global agreements since the time and type of severity of similar extreme events are hard to predict (Vegh et al. 2018). As such, the present situation can be utilised as a backdrop for building a forward-moving Bangladesh. In this regard, the core dictum of the country's foreign policy must be contained—'Friendship to all, malice to none'—while formulating the state's policies and advancing its national interests (Momen 2021). In other words, Bangladesh needs to play a pacifist and defensive role. In this way, it can rise in the international arena and that is why Dhaka needs a specific doctrine to direct its journey forward.

Four Scenarios

Bangladesh is the eighth most populous country in the world although it ranks 94th in terms of its geographic size. Most of the land area of Bangladesh is bordered by India and some parts by Myanmar, with China in the close vicinity. It occupies a strategically significant position, and particularly, has huge advantages over the Bay of Bengal. Bangladesh lies at the centre of South Asia and Southeast Asia, and is a source of connecting China's southern landlocked region. The bay is a reservoir of huge natural resources. Furthermore, the US, China and India have held separate major military exercises here, involving many countries, including Bangladesh, Malaysia, Singapore, Thailand, Singapore, Japan and Australia.

The aspirations of the people of Bangladesh are immense as there are broad similarities among the people, considering ethnicity, language, culture and religion. In this context, an illustrative attempt has been made to chalk out the Bangladesh Doctrine in light of four scenarios to steer further discussions.

In this respect, the relationship has been categorised as (*i*) balanced relation with great powers; (*ii*) a relationship with a specific superpower and its allies; (*iii*) a joint relationship with the neighbours and (*iv*) an independent and mutually inclusive policy (Table 1.1).

A payoff matrix illustrates the move of the players (Figure 1.1). The first element of the payoff represents the payoff of Bangladesh, the second represents the payoff of superpower A and its allies, the third element of the payoff cell embodies the payoff of great power C and its allies. The strategies of superpower and great power are the imposition of restriction in unfavourable cases and none in favourable cases. The first element of the payoff represents the payoff of Bangladesh (*B*). It is thus assumed that $B_2 \geq B_1$. In this case, Bangladesh may prefer a payoff

Table 1.1: Four Alternative Scenarios—Necessary and Sufficient Conditions

	First scenario: Joint initiatives with neighbours	Second scenario: Alliance with superpower/ great power	Third scenario: Relationships with balance	Fourth scenario: Independent, mutually inclusive policy
Necessary conditions	Comparative geographic advantage => strategic interest maximisation	Coalition with superpower => relative regional autonomy	Balancing mutual engagement => maximisation of benefits	Assertive strategy to realise demographic dividend, resource exploration and development deterrence => optimal use of factors of production
Sufficient conditions	Pursuing power/ability of a nation => optimal use of factors of production	Consensus political settlement => efficient use of factors of production	Weak political settlement => no efficient use of resources	Consensus in political settlement and normative legitimacy for pursuing strategic autonomy
Outcomes	Excessive dependence and limited autonomy	Rise with power(s) or trap and backlash	Risks, unpredictability leading to vicious circle	Optimisation, consensus, stability and growth

Source: Prepared by the author.

Figure 1.1: Alternative Scenarios and Payoffs

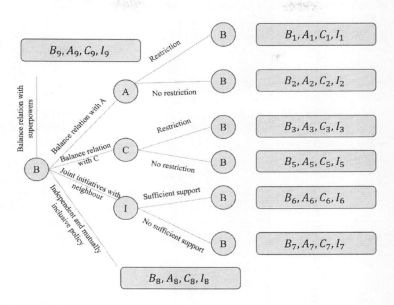

Source: Prepared by the author.

of B_2. Similarly, a pattern may arise in the case of great power C. It is also assumed that B_6, $B_7 \geq B_1$, B_2, B_3, B_4, B_5. It is also assumed that $B_9 \geq B_8 + i$, $i = 1, 2, \ldots$. The ultimate result of this game will depend on the probability of the imposition of restrictions by one superpower/great power if Bangladesh joins another power bloc. An independent, mutual relationship may be a suitable strategy for Bangladesh for growth and development.

In the first scenario, the necessary condition ascertains that a relatively weak actor assumes derivation of maximum benefits if it can strike a balance through the preservation of mutual engagements for divergent objectives within and outside the region. While the sufficient condition purports that in a situation of a weak political settlement, the state largely tries to keep the balance amongst the powers that eventually causes a sliding down to a further weakened state with an attendant vicious cycle. This means that a relatively weak country can reap maximum benefits if it maintains a balanced relationship with other countries in the region and beyond as a necessary condition. Usually, in a situation of weak political settlement, the state essentially tries to strike a balance between the various superpowers. This attempt further weakens the state and plunges it into a vicious circle.

In the second scenario, the necessary condition entails that an actor prefers a coalition with a superpower beyond its geography for securing relative autonomy in the region. The sufficient condition, however, asserts that an efficient utilisation of factors of production depends on the consensual political settlement across the board for both nations. In other words, a state may ally with a superpower/great power outside the territory as a necessary condition for ensuring regional relative autonomy. But the effective use of the factors of production depends on the political settlement where political consent, a peaceful political situation and balanced power are necessary conditions to keep the wheel of the economy moving. Consequently, the outcome may be either rise with the superpower/great power or fall into a trap and cause a backlash, depending on how well necessary and sufficient conditions are met.

In the third scenario, the necessary condition implies that in a state of regional tension, the actor with comparative geographic advantage maximises strategic interest while the sufficient condition demonstrates that the power of a nation depends on its ability to optimise the factors of production—land, labour, capital and technology. In other words, states in a geographically advantageous position are able to pursue the highest strategic interests as a necessary condition in the event of regional tensions. But in this situation, the pursuing power of a nation as a sufficient condition depends on the effective utilisation of its factors of production. When the productivity of the means of production is high, capital is easily formed and dependence is reduced. If a state embarks on joint initiatives with its neighbours based on comparative geographic advantage but falls short of utilising productive potentials, the outcome that follows is excessive dependence, limited autonomy, and arrested development. Such excessive dependence on a neighbour may prove to be unsustainable.

In the fourth scenario, the necessary condition demonstrates that an optimisation strategy for an actor is to assert itself through the exploitation of its resources, including its geo-strategic position, while the sufficient condition assumes that a transformation from a weak state, dominated by the interplay of regional and global powers, is to build consensus in political settlement in order to optimise the utilisation of factors of production. For a country to move forward, it must ensure the maximum and productive use of its resources as well as its geo-strategic location. The necessary condition for a successful transition of a weak state between the domination of regional and international powers is the need for a consensual political settlement. It will produce the ideological legitimacy of the state and create a system of a government that is accountable to the people, which will ensure the efficient use of the means of production leading to optimal use of resources, stability and growth.

In order for Bangladesh to move forward in light of its own specific doctrine, it is necessary to fulfil certain necessary and sufficient conditions. One of the prerequisites is the efficient use of factors of production and increase in productivity to harness its potential and achieve the 2041 goal of becoming a developed country (Titumir 2021; Titumir and Rahman 2017). In this case, it is important to accelerate the formation of capital, including human resources. If there are increase in skills and productivity of the labourers, their wages will also rise. So, there is no alternative to increasing investment and research in education, health, universal social security and technology. At present, Bangladesh has the highest number of population in the age group of 15 to 65, which is defined as economically active population. If properly utilised, this large working-age population will be a huge resource for increasing production and productivity, and thus, can attain high economic development by means of this demographic dividend (Navaneetham and Dharmalingam 2012). Therefore, realising the demographic dividend will have to be Bangladesh's basic economic strategy (Titumir and Rahman 2018).

Following the first demographic dividend as the central goal in the realm of economic strategy, a peaceful, prosperous Bay of Bengal is the second core of the proposed Bangladesh Doctrine and both necessitate deterrence for sustenance of durable development. Deterrence is a diplomatic strategy of influencing one party's choices by altering its expectations of another party's actions (Schelling 1960).[2] Although it was more relevant during the Cold War period, a deterrence theory's portrayal of how political opponents might be inhibited by threats of force is still relevant today (Quackenbush 2011). The concept of development deterrence as it is proposed here is not similar to the conventional 'militaristic' one. Rather, the main difference is in the purpose of the strategy, that is to safeguard development activities and ensure stability and security of property rights in a situation where possible threats from an adversarial power are present and, thus, might inhibit investment and production, including exploration and utilisation of productive and/or natural resources. In both cases, deterrence is most effective when there are established and clear-cut boundaries which are connected to core national interests, communicated by messages that are clear and credible and supported by known capabilities about what will happen if those boundaries are crossed (Freedman 2020).

Drawing insights from the case of spatial competition, utilising game theory, which has been used to study of strategic or interactive decision-making, a new framework of deterrence for development can be considered (Priyarsono 1992). In the context of taking up development initiatives or investment activities by a party in a region with a potential threat of appropriation by an adversary, development deterrence would lead to a higher level of social welfare and better outcomes, as a result of an increase in the marginal social benefit than what would happen in the absence of deterrence for development [as shown in Figure 1.2(a), potential welfare gains due to deterrence, and the deadweight loss without deterrence, as demonstrated in Figure 1.2(b)].

There are many examples. For an instance, although a small, vulnerable country, Singapore has been able to create deterrence for development by rapidly expanding military power after its independence in 1965, which evidently contributed to its peaceful development (Cheong 2017; Kwan 2016; Lee 2000). Therefore, in light of the experiences of other similar countries, Bangladesh also needs to move towards achieving effective, modern, mechanised multi-platform based military capabilities to address different dimensionalities of land, air, sea and cyber-space. The basic structure of foreign policy needs to centre on a peaceful Bay of Bengal while the defence policy gravitates around deterrence for development, that is, to consolidate the country's position as a reliable or credible power. This would require transformation and capability development of the armed forces including strengthening of land, aerial and naval power to be able to credibly address any security challenges that might hamper the realisation of the country's development potential and resource exploration in the Bay of Bengal. Additionally, development deterrence would play a crucial role in ensuring strategic autonomy,[3] which, in turn, would reduce external dependence, safeguard national interests and expand economic opportunities (Anghel et al. 2020).

In the contemporary globalised world, policymaking is increasingly conditioned by regional and international considerations that go well beyond national boundaries. If policies of external engagement are not driven by domestic compulsions, a consequent strategy may not bring beneficial outcomes. For example, Alfredson and Cungu (2008, 17)

Figure 1.2: Deterrence for Development—A New Framework

(a)

(b)

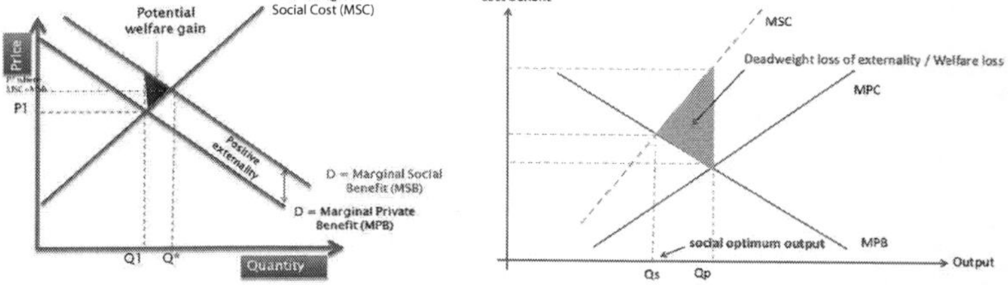

Source: Prepared by the author.

provide a summary and critique of the dominant approaches and theories of negotiation that supports the argument on why domestic compulsion leads to a beneficial strategy while a structural approach that mainly focuses on power or position often leads to a 'lost opportunity for mutually beneficial agreement'. In a classic paper on the increased popularity of using game theory in international politics, Snidal (1985) stresses that the rationality, realism and zero-sum game-driven research are plagued with problems. He argues that 'the ultimate promise of game theory lies in expanding the realm of rational-actor models beyond the restrictive confines of the traditional Realist perspective to a more complex world where concern is less exclusively with problems of conflict and as much with problems of cooperation.'

The novel approach proposed here underpins that 'social property relationships—political settlement,[4] distribution of power and resources—generate compulsions in a particular historical and institutional setting that determines the design and direction of policies and actions taken by a state' (Titumir and Rahman 2019a; 2019b). This is premised on the basis that countries' engagements with the outside world emanate from how material foundations are settled inside the country, and thus political settlement based upon domestic compulsions determines the external policies of a state. So, the political settlement is the sufficient condition which drives necessary conditions, and the effective political settlement stems from the people's approval through normative legitimacy.[5]

It is emphasised that the agreements of strategic cooperation must be based on normative legitimacy. The relationship between nations, based upon normative legitimacy, promotes effective collaboration and results in mutually inclusive development. The legitimacy of the people or approval of citizens is at the heart of any meaningful development strategy. When there is a political consensus and social recognition over the distribution of power and resources as well as the productive class is interested in entrepreneurial activities backed by a supporting set of institutions and policies, these create conditions for a mutually inclusive pathway to progress. Such a political settlement only focuses on mutual development needs and priorities rather than being at the recipient end of divergent geopolitical interests (Titumir and Rahman 2019a; 2019b).

First Scenario: Relationships with Balance

If a weak country maintains a balanced relationship with other powerful nations by reconciling divergent interests for mutual engagement as a necessary condition, whether a relatively weak country can reap strategic gains to the fullest extent. That is briefly what the first scenario postulates. If this were to be followed, Bangladesh can strike a balanced relationship with major powerful nations in the region and beyond. As a small state, Bangladesh's strategy may focus on deepening its connections with them on the political and economic levels so that they remain important to it and its success aligns with their interests. While this is the most deliberated strategy suggested for a relatively weak country, it may turn out to be the most dangerous in the long run.

The first concern is about the durability of such an arrangement, especially regarding how long it can be balanced, since balance is susceptible to changes in the stability of power in regional and global spaces. Hence, a shift in priorities of powers may leave the weak country in a poorer state. The geo-strategic compulsions determine a country's adversaries and allies. The balancing act in the changed circumstance leave a small country's interests at stake. Depending on the circumstances, it may even go to the level of animosity when strategic compulsions are reversed, turning allies into adversaries or fierce competitors. Consider the example of Sino-USA relations during the hostility of the USA with the former Soviet Union. At times, the US was at odds with the then Soviet Union and Henry Kissinger, an influential diplomat in the Nixon administration, formed an alliance with China during the height of the Cold War. However, with the rise of China, a 'downward spiral' in Sino-American relation is observed, as illustrated by the recent episodes of the trade war between the two countries (Layne 2020; Sachs 2019). The experiences in the case of China and similar historical evidence in the case of other South Asian countries suggest that weak political settlement and dependence on powerful states may lead to further weakening of the state, even trapping it into a vicious cycle.

Another fragility points out to the possibility of fallout due to the great power game characterised by frequent friction and unpredictability. For example, the USA is the single largest market for Bangladesh's main export item, ready-made garments, representing almost 85 percent of the country's total export. The USA is the destination of one-fifth of the garments exported from Bangladesh. On the other hand, Bangladesh depends on China for its imports of raw materials and capital equipment crucial for utilisation of the productive activities in the country (Samaranayake 2019). China has remained Bangladesh's biggest trading partner since 2009. Due to such a tilted pattern of trade dependence on two contending great powers today, any disequilibrium in the balancing strategy runs the risk of falling out, rendering the country unable to advance its strategic and economic interests.

Finally, for effective balancing in such a scenario, a small state needs to have its own power or strategic leverage that makes it relevant to the great powers and their allies in the neighbourhood. Since neighbours can pose a strategic hurdle when it comes to balancing, even in the scenario when a state deems the neighbouring state to be directly geopolitically essential in its strategic map. The dilemmas faced by Bangladesh with regard to its relations with India and China can be considered as an example (Hossain and Islam 2020; Datta 2008). Although some observers argue that Bangladesh has performed well in managing competing rival powers in the region by securing connectivity investments (Plagemann 2021), the contested nature of domestic politics in Bangladesh and lack of consensus over its core national interests suggest only bleak prospects for pursuing an independent and mutually beneficial strategy in the long run (Kumar 2014). This is because even if a state tries to achieve a balance between the major powers, under a weak political settlement, this attempt may make the state weaker. It could be dragged deeper into a vicious cycle that may result from the difficulty in balancing numerous conflicting interests and resolving disagreements over how their shared goals should be attained.

Therefore, a small country making a balance with powerful countries may consequentially be fatalistic in the long run due to the perception of opportunism (or balancing), because of the degree to which the parties believe one another to be acting opportunistically may have an adverse impact on the functioning of a balanced strategic alliance (Parkhe 1993). The first option thus is not sustainable for Bangladesh in the long run.

Second Scenario: Alliance with Superpowers

The second scenario argues that a state may form an alliance with a superpower as a requirement for ensuring relative regional autonomy. However, the efficient utilisation of productive resources depends on the political settlement of the two countries involved. To keep the economic wheel turning, there is a need for an inclusive political settlement, wherein the relations between the state and society or 'the social contract' is robust and legitimate, which guarantees a stable political environment and a balance of the relative holding of power of different groups and organisations contesting the distribution of resources. So, it needs to find out when an alliance with a major power, namely, an alliance with the US or China for instance, is desirable for Bangladesh and whether it would advance the core objectives of the country to secure relative autonomy in the region.

As a background, it is necessary to elaborate on the context of Sino-USA ties in relation to Bangladesh forming an alliance with a major power. China and the USA have a bilateral relationship that combines both competition and cooperation. There is desire that the world's two largest economies must cooperate for the global stability, trade and development (Sheng and Geng 2017). The stability of the current world order ultimately depends on the capacity of the competing global powers to agree on compromises about their economic goals and military commitments. However, it is often highlighted that there could be a deadly 'trap' because of mistrust or misconceptions about the rival's acts and intentions, as China's ascent is challenging US global dominance (Allison 2017). Bangladesh, thus, needs to be wary of its approach towards aligning with either one of these two contending parties.

Historically, many cases show that forming a successful alliance with a superpower has a lot of advantages. As seen in the cases of Japan, Taiwan, South Korea, Malaysia and even Thailand, the USA and other Western countries have greatly contributed to their rise by forming and maintaining a strong alliance (Dollar and Stromseth 2021). The challenge is that in the current situation, the agenda of the great powers is not clearly known, making it problematic for countries like Bangladesh to choose a side while opting to confidently pursue its goals for inclusive economic development.

One of the key advantages that a successful alliance with a great power may guarantee access to foreign markets and investments. Regarding trade benefits, Bangladesh's relation with the USA, a superpower, and a great power like China is faced with a unique pattern. In terms of trade, Bangladesh imports more from China than it exports, resulting in a huge trade deficit. On the other hand, the country exports more to the USA than it imports, leading to a huge trade surplus in favour of Bangladesh (Table 1.2). In 2021, China was Bangladesh's top source of imports with nearly $16.9 billion leading to a trade deficit of $16.23 billion. In the same year, the USA was Bangladesh's top export destination paying about $6 billion with $3.47 billion dollars of trade surplus. A comparative analysis on Bangladesh's trade relationship with China and the USA and other western nations suggest that due to the existing pattern of Bangladesh's interdependence on China and the West, a bias towards a particular side may have potential adverse consequences for the country.

With regard to its geo-strategic position, Bangladesh is at the crossroads between US's Indo-Pacific Strategy and China's Belt and Road Initiative (BRI), giving the country strategic leverage while at the same time leading to a much more challenging decision-making process. In the Indo-Pacific region, the USA is working to push a new strategic investment and connectivity programme that is considered by many as an effort to challenge China's expanding influence by fortifying

Table 1.2: Bangladesh's Trade Relations with China and USA, 2010–2021 ($ million)

Year	Bangladesh–China			Bangladesh–USA		
	Export	Import	Balance	Export	Import	Balance
2010	190.98	4,681.43	-4,490.45	3,247.48	534.10	2,713.38
2011	299.64	6,575.18	-6,275.54	3,824.24	787.69	3,036.55
2012	314.40	6,092.13	-5,777.73	3,702.39	573.09	3,129.3
2013	401.93	6,972.53	-6,570.6	3,948.05	650.59	3,297.46
2014	691.67	7,846.10	-7,154.43	4,052.55	876.52	3,176.03
2015	675.08	8,848.85	-8,173.77	4,164.91	940.16	3,224.75
2016	716.12	10,028.79	-9,312.67	3,962.32	861.29	3,101.03
2017	693.39	10,433.75	-9,740.36	3,839.76	1,435.28	2,404.48
2018	540.30	13,144.05	-12,603.75	4,178.82	1,727.47	2,451.35
2019	595.89	13,265.78	-12,669.89	4,607.35	1,946.83	2,660.52
2020	445.77	10,862.60	-10,416.83	4,051.88	2,071.12	1,980.76
2021	624.23	16,913.11	-16,288.88	5,981.71	2,513.71	3,468

Source: Direction of Trade Statistics (IMF 2022).

relationships with India, Japan and Australia (Palit and Sano 2018). In fact, it is a continuation of the USA's long-standing strategy toward Asia and the Pacific, with a stronger focus on the Indian Ocean region. The US strategy appears to offer few alternatives to combat China, given the scope of the latter's economic involvement in Indo-Pacific nations and its status as the top trading partner of practically all Asian economies, including India, Japan and Australia (Manning 2018). It seems conceivable that none of the countries could afford to lose each other's main trading partners, with economic compulsions triumphing over conflicting strategic goals.

Since the efficient use of the factors of production depends on political settlement, where political consent and a peaceful political environment are necessary conditions, forging an alliance with a major power against another could have the unintended consequence of falling into a trap and producing a negative backlash for Bangladesh.

Third Scenario: Joint Initiatives with Neighbours

The third scenario posits that when there is regional tension, countries that are in a geographically advantageous position can pursue their highest strategic objectives by entering into joint initiative with neighbours. However, in this scenario, a nation's ability to pursue its goals as a necessary condition depends on the efficient use of its productive resources. If the productivity of the factors of production is high, capital may be easily generated and invested in accelerating economic development, ultimately reducing foreign reliance. Otherwise, excessive dependence on neighbours may emerge, which would eventually prove unsustainable in the long run. If the neighbouring country is in a known-unknown quandary, this initiative might not work because the prevailing political consensus and general people's approval in the country might not be in favour of such an exclusive partnership. Also, the success of such initiatives would largely depend on whether the neighbouring states has the power to advance the development aspirations of the people of both countries.

Following this outline, Bangladesh could work jointly with its neighbouring country, namely India. India is a regional power in Asia, with its sphere of influence being South Asia (Mohan 2022). Having a huge population of over a billion people, this nation continues to struggle with persistent underdevelopment, poor infrastructure, severe investment deficit and a larger demand for connectivity both within the nation and across the region (Nataraj 2014). Although India's ambition is growing, its economy is fraught with several setbacks that show that the country has a poor ability to achieve optimal use of factors of production, thus limiting the ability of the nation to achieve inclusive economic development either inside the border or in its neighbourhoods (Rodrik 2015; Rodrik and Subramanian 2004).

Notwithstanding occasional regional disputes in South Asia, Bangladesh's comparative geographic advantage to form a successful partnership with India may suggest that the country can maximise its strategic interests by taking this path. Before assessing how and to what extent Bangladesh's alliance with India as a core strategy can serve its objectives, there are several internal bottlenecks in India that needs to be considered. First, India has a severe capital shortage issue. This is supported by data on current account deficits which stretched to its highest level in almost a decade as the country's domestic savings and foreign investments decreased while trade deficit increased (Behera and Yadav 2019). The deficit on the current account was $23 billion, or 2.7 per cent of the GDP in the last quarter of 2021 and it is expected to rise further (Figure 1.3). Notably, India's border security and maintenance costs are particularly high due to its extensive borders (15,106.7 km of land border and 7,516.6 km of coastline including island territories), as well as its ongoing disputes with neighbours, limiting its investment capacity in more productive areas of the economy (SATP 2008).

Figure 1.3: Widening Current Account Deficits in India, 2012–2021 ($ billion)

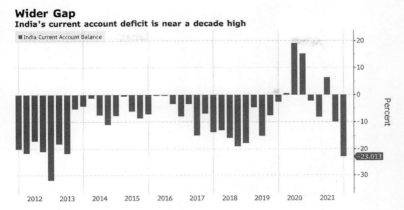

Source: Reproduced from Roy (2022).

Second, India has exceptionally high levels of poverty and inequality. India, for instance, is the country with the greatest concentration of poor people; it was home to one-fourth of 736 million of the world's severely poor in 2015 (World Bank 2018). One in five Indians lives in poverty with the greatest rates of poverty among the lower tribes or castes to the tune of five out of six multidimensionally poor people in India (UNDP 2021). Additionally, there is a significant amount of inequality based on socioeconomic factors, religious and regional divides. For instance, 62 per cent of India's impoverished live in seven low-income states, which also house 45 per cent of the country's population (World Bank 2016).

Third, India has the second-largest labour force in the world after China with more than 500 million working-age people, but the quality of India's human capital remains poor despite some improvement in skill development in recent years (Asian Development Bank 2015). In terms of providing skills necessary for young people to find employment, India trails behind many of its counterparts. According to India Skills Report (2021), only fewer than half (45.9 per cent) of Indian youth were employable in 2021 (Figure 1.4), indicating a severe skill shortage plaguing the economy (Jha et al. 2021). Overall, high unemployment and a lack of skilled workers are two factors that define the labour market (Mehrotra and Parida 2019).

Another reason why taking joint initiatives exclusively with India is marred with uncertainties is that Bangladesh has high trade deficits with India while South Asia is the least integrated region in the world in terms

Figure 1.4: Trends in the Rate of Employability of Indian Youth, 2015–2021

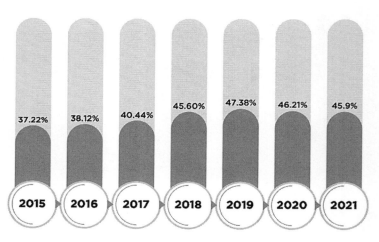

Source: India Skills Report (2021).

of trade and economic exchanges despite having much homogeneity in history, culture, language, preferences and having taken initiatives like the formation of the South Asian Association for Regional Cooperation (SAARC). For example, the percentage of trade within South Asia in the region's overall trade is roughly 5 per cent (Raihan 2014). While there could be sizeable economic and welfare gains for countries in South Asia if there was greater regional integration, the reality is that intra-regional trade currently only represents one-third of its potential, with an estimated $23 billion shortfall per year (World Bank 2020). Moreover, there seems to be limited scope for regional integration due to a range of factors, including a higher cost of trade within the region (costs for shipping containers within South Asia are 50 per cent higher than those within OECD countries) and equal purchasing capacity of consumers among the countries (World Bank 2020).

Considering the above scenario, India's ability to steer development needs for another country seems arrested since its ability depends on its optimal use of the factors of production. Thus, it can be argued that India has restrained capacity to help enhance Bangladesh's growth trajectory. When comparative geographic advantage does not lead to strategic interest maximisation and nations fail to attain optimal use of productive resources by taking bilateral initiatives, the outcome is excessive dependence and limited autonomy without mutual development. So, taking joint initiatives with India as the core strategy does not seem to be a viable option for Bangladesh.

Finally, the issue of regional tension involving India and China has clear repercussions for Bangladesh. China is also India's top trading partner, and the two nations have a long history of mutually beneficial trade and cultural interactions. The bilateral relationship between the nations continues to be strained by strategic mistrust and sporadic escalation of tensions resulting from border disputes, as well as the memories of two brief wars waged by the two nuclear-armed neighbours in the last 60 years, resulting in various military conflicts—the Sino-Indian War of 1962, the border clashes in Nathu La and Cho La in 1967, and several standoffs including in Sumdorong Chu in 1987, the Doklam Plateau in 2018 and Galwan Valley in 2020 (Deepak 2020; Ray 2019). India's position on China's role is guided by the realist conviction of competitive and conflictual comprehension as Delhi is worried that Beijing's presence in the area could diminish its dominance while furthering latter's commercial, economic and geopolitical interests in nations that fall under its sphere of influence (Pradhan 2019). The political elite in India perceives China's rise as a threat, and its position in this regard is likely due to geopolitical considerations involving the 'Indo-US alignment of interests in the Indian Ocean region' (Rahman 2015). Bangladesh's interaction with India is greatly conditioned by these developments, which brings the case of the final scenario that argues for an independent and mutually inclusive policy.

Fourth Scenario: Independent, Mutually Inclusive Policy

The fourth scenario posits that for a country to move forward, it must ensure the maximum and productive use of its resources as well as its geo-strategic position by taking an independent, mutually inclusive policy. The necessary condition for a successful transition of a weak state between the domination of regional and international superpowers is the need for a consensual political settlement. It will produce the ideological legitimacy of the state and create a system of accountable government to the people, which will ensure the efficient use of the means of production.

In a dynamic situation, the Bangladesh Doctrine needs to be propositional without resorting to a reaction-based strategy. So, what are the elements in case of Bangladesh? The first element is realisation of the demographic dividend, ensuring full utilisation of the labour force, enhancing skills and productivity and preparing an entrepreneurial class that is ready to reap such benefits. Secondly, the most critical element for an independent, mutually inclusive policy is leveraging the full advantage of the Bay of Bengal (BoB), situated in the southern portion of Bangladesh. The Bay connects some of the most crucial trade routes between the Indian Ocean and the Pacific Oceans. The geopolitical and economic importance make the area a focal point of the strategic rivalry in the Indo-Pacific as well as a 'cockpit for economic growth' for South and Southeast Asian nations. After the resolution of maritime boundary disputes with Myanmar and India in 2012 and 2014, respectively, the Bay acquired significant connotation for Bangladesh. A total of 1,18,813 square kilometres (or 81 per cent of the country's land area) of territorial sea, 200 nautical miles (nm) of an exclusive economic zone (EEZ) and a sizeable piece of the extended continental shelf in the Bay of Bengal is demarcated for Bangladesh. The BoB provides the country with momentous opportunities to explore resources like gas, oil, minerals and fisheries and harness the blue economy for the growth of the nation.

Bangladesh's approach towards the BoB must be focused on an optimisation strategy to assert itself through the exploitation and utilisation of its resources, including its geo-strategic position. For instance, Bangladesh has been creating several economic zones, and many nations are showing their interest in this. However, not much progress has been made towards the idea of an offshore economic zone, which could be a crucial goal. The proposition should be embodied in the concept of a peaceful BoB with greater cross-border trade and increased connectivity for capitalising on the potential of a blue economy (Titumir and Rahman 2019b).

Development deterrence is needed for property rights stability for the exploration of resources in the BoB. As the region is marked by a variety of geopolitical conflicts and rivalries, this necessitates conscious efforts in harnessing cooperation and confidence building. The development deterrence ensures ensure secured property rights. Secondly, if multiple parties invest in the BoB, it would be an imperative in everyone's best interest to assure peace and stability in the BoB. The first step in translating the idea of a peaceful, prosperous BoB into action is for Bangladesh to embark on an inclusive offshore investment regime. When many countries invest, every country is a stakeholder in ensuring that the BoB does not move towards a conflict zone.

The strengthening of ties with Myanmar is another element in such an endeavour. There are several ongoing tensions involving the two countries. The Rohingya crisis, drug trafficking, separatist uprisings in the hill tract regions and concerns associated with border security are among the most pressing issues. Due to severe violence and persecution in the Rakhine State, about 7,27,000 Rohingya refugees have fled to Bangladesh since August 2017. 9,21,000 Rohingyas were living in several camps in Cox's Bazar, Bangladesh, as of 4 September 2018 (ISCG 2018). Despite engagements with international organisations, Bangladesh has made little headway in handling the problem or stopping the flow of refugees. The government of Myanmar does not appear to be genuinely interested in solving the issue, and repatriation efforts are delayed. Given all these challenges, getting to a working strategic relation with Myanmar needs to be a strategic priority for Bangladesh.

Myanmar is Bangladesh's land corridor to Southeast Asia with vast potential for economic cooperation in the ASEAN region. It would be necessary to resolve current issues between the nations in order to realise the connectivity potential. In fact, Bangladesh's tense relations with Myanmar seem to be 'a fork in the path' to optimal cooperation with China's land corridor connecting the region. However, India is wary of China's expanding economic and political ties with its neighbours. Since China and India are competing with one another for influence, resources and markets outside of their immediate area, there is no guarantee of resolution unless Bangladesh strategically manoeuvres the situation in its favour.

Therefore, Bangladesh needs an independent, mutually inclusive strategy for accommodating the relevant countries. For such a transformation, the country requires to build consensus in its political settlement for optimising the potential, including utilisation of factors of production. Therefore, the optimisation strategy needs to be centred on investing in human capital for realising the demographic dividend, securing a peaceful BoB by ensuring inclusive participation of all interested parties and maintaining stability through deterrence for development, underwritten by a political settlement through peoples' legitimacy.

Conclusion

Bangladesh must fulfil a number of necessary and sufficient conditions in order to advance in accordance with its own doctrine. The effective use of factors of production and an improvement in productivity are essential. Accelerating the formation of capital, including human capital, is crucial. Therefore, boosting spending and research in technology, universal social security, health care and education is the only viable option to realise the demographic dividend. If used properly, this large pool of people who are in the working age group could be the main asset for the nation's sustained, durable economic growth.

The inclusive, peaceful BoB as the cornerstone of Bangladesh's foreign policy will foster an inclusive, peaceful rise of collaborative synergetic co-development, and can act as an example of live and let live stability. The deterrence for development is a prerequisite for establishing such a peace in the Bay of Bengal. The success of the trinity is contingent upon an inclusive political settlement.

Notes

1. In 'The Black Swan: The Impact of the Highly Improbable', Nassim Taleb (2008) posited the analogy of the white swan and the black swan to refer to phenomena that are highly improbable but when they occur, they come with enormous consequences. In *Crisis Economics*, Nouriel Roubini (2010) defined financial crises as 'white swans', which are more like hurricanes: they are the predictable result of built-up economic and financial vulnerabilities and policy mistakes.
2. According to the US Department of Defense, deterrence can be defined as 'the prevention of action by the existence of a credible threat of unacceptable counteraction and/or belief that the cost of action outweighs the perceived benefits' (cited in Taylor 2021).
3. The concept of 'strategic autonomy' can be defined as the ability to make decisions and then act on those decisions independently as well as decide when, where, and whether to engage with allies (Anghel et al. 2020). It does not refer to self-sufficiency but rather to means and resources for minimising external dependence in strategic areas where such dependence can jeopardize autonomy while still working with allies in a multilateral context (Libek 2019).
4. The concept of 'political settlement' is defined as the forms of distribution of power within a given society (Khan 2010). Whether the prevailing political settlement or distribution of power within it promotes and fosters particular institutions and policies that would lead to the creation of a group interested in the transformation of the productive capacities of the economy will determine how much gain the country can realise from opportunities made available by a country's engagement with other countries (Titumir and Rahman 2019a).
5. Legitimacy refers to popular consensus or political support for political community, political regimes and for their actions or decisions, and the stability of a political system depends on normative legitimacy arising from the convergence between political culture and political structures (Westle 2007). Moreover, legitimacy is considered to be a key component of a country's development and its entrepreneurial success (Díez et al. 2015).

References

Aghion, P., C. Antonin, and S. Bunel. *The Power of Creative Destruction: Economic Upheaval and the Wealth of Nations.* Cambridge, MA and London, England: Harvard University Press, 2021.

Ahmad, Wasim, Ali M. Kutan, and Smarth Gupta. 'Black Swan Events and COVID-19 Outbreak: Sector Level Evidence from the US, UK, and European Stock Markets,' *International Review of Economics & Finance* 75 (2021): 546–557.

Alfredson, T. and A. Cungu. *Negotiation Theory and Practice: A Review of the Literature.* FAO Policy Learning Programme, Food and Agriculture Organization of the United Nations, 2008.

Allison, G. 'The Thucydides Trap: When One Great Power Threatens to Displace Another, War is Almost Always the Result—But It Doesn't Have to Be'. *The Foreign Policy*, 9 June 2017. http://foreignpolicy.com/2017/06/09/the-thucydides-trap/.

Anghel, S.E., B. Immenkamp, E. Lazarou, J.L. Saulnier, and A.B. Wilson. *On the Path to 'Strategic Autonomy': The EU in an Evolving Geopolitical Environment.* Strasbourg: European Parliamentary Research Service, September 2020.

Anwar, A. 'Bangladesh's National Security Conundrum'. *Dhaka Tribune*, 20 September 2022. https://www.dhakatribune.com/longform/2022/09/20/bangladeshs-fragile-national-security.

Asian Development Bank. *Human Capital Development in the People's Republic of China and India: Achievements, Prospects, and Policy Challenges.* Manila: Asian Development Bank, 2015.

Behera, H.K. and I.S. Yadav. 'Explaining India's Current Account Deficit: A Time Series Perspective'. *Journal of Asian Business and Economic Studies* 26, no 1 (2019): 117–138.

Chakma, B. 'The BRI and Sino-Indian Geo-Economic Competition in Bangladesh: Coping Strategy of a Small State'. *Strategic Analysis* 43, no 3 (2019): 227–239.

Cheong, D. 'As a Small Country, Singapore Has to Be Friends With Everyone, But at Times It Needs to Advance Its Own Interests'. *The Straits Times*, 18 July 2017. https://www.straitstimes.com/singapore/as-a-small-country-singapore-has-to-be-friends-with-everyone-but-at-times-it-needs-to.

Choong, W. 'The Return of the Indo-Pacific Strategy: An Assessment'. *Australian Journal of International Affairs* 73, no 5 (2019): 415–430.

Chowdhury, C.A. 'Need for National Security Strategy: Relevant Concept and Paradigm and Context of Bangladesh'. *NDC Journal* (2017): 69–87.

Datta, S. 'Bangladesh's Relations with China and India: A Comparative Study'. *Strategic Analysis* 32, no 5 (2008): 755–772.

Deepak, B.R. 'Cooperation and Conflict in India–China Relations: A Crisis of Confidence Building'. In *India and China: Beyond the Binary of Friendship and Enmity*, edited by B.R. Deepak, 59–76. Springer: Singapore. 2020.

Díez, E., C. Prado-Román, F. Díez-Martín, and A. Blanco-González. 'The Role of Normative Legitimacy in the Development of Efficiency-Driven

Countries'. In *Entrepreneurship, Regional Development and Culture*, edited by M. Peris-Ortiz and J. Merigó-Lindahl, Berlin: Springer, 2015.

Dollar, D. and J. Stromseth. 'The US Must Urgently Rethink Its Economic Policies in Asia'. *Brookings*, 17 February 2021. https://www.brookings.edu/blog/order-from-chaos/2021/02/17/us-must-urgently-rethink-its-economic-policies-in-asia/.

Freedman, L. 'Introduction—The Evolution of Deterrence Strategy and Research'. In *NL ARMS Netherlands Annual Review of Military Studies 2020: Deterrence in the 21st Century—Insights from Theory and Practice*, edited by F. Osinga and T. Sweijs, 1–10. The Hague: TMC Asser Press, 2021.

Fu, R.T., D.J. Gill, E. Hundman, A.P. Liff, and G.J. Ikenberry. 'Looking for Asia's Security Dilemma'. *International Security* 40, no 2 (2015): 181–204.

Government of the People's Republic of Bangladesh. 'The Constitution of the People's Republic of Bangladesh'. Dhaka: Legislative and Parliamentary Affairs Division, Ministry of Law, Justice and Parliamentary Affairs, The Government of the People's Republic of Bangladesh. 2019.

Grieco, K.A. 'Reality Check #11: America's Indo-Pacific Strategy Requires Tough Choices'. The Atlantic Council. 2022. https://www.atlanticcouncil.org/content-series/reality-check/reality-check-11-americas-indo-pacific-strategy-requires-tough-choices/International Monetary Fund. 'Direction of Trade Statistics (DOTS)'. Washington D.C.: International Monetary Fund, 2022.

ISCG. 'Situation Report Rohingya Refugee Crisis'. Cox's Bazar. Inter-Sector Coordination Group (ISCG). 27 September 2018. https://reliefweb.int/sites/reliefweb.int/files/resources/iscg_situation_report_27_sept_2018.pdf.

Iyer-Mitra, A. 'National Security: The Need for a Doctrine'. Observer Research Foundation. 10 February 2014. https://www.orfonline.org/research/national-security-the-need-for-a-doctrine/.

Harding, H. 'Has US China Policy Failed?' *The Washington Quarterly* 38, no 3 (2015): 95–122.

He, K. and H. Feng. 'The Institutionalization of the Indo-Pacific: Problems and Prospects'. *International Affairs* 96, no 1 (2020): 149–168.

Heiduk, F. and G. Wacker. 'From Asia-Pacific to Indo-Pacific: Significance, Implementation and Challenges'. SWP Research Paper, September 2020.

Hossain, D. and M.S. Islam. 'Understanding Bangladesh's Relations with India and China: Dilemmas and Responses'. *Journal of the Indian Ocean Region* 17, no 1 (2021): 42–59.

Jain-Chandra, M.S., N. Khor, R. Mano, J. Schauer, M.P. Wingender, and J. Zhuang. 'Inequality in China—Trends, Drivers and Policy Remedies'. *IMF Working Paper WP/18/27*, International Monetary Fund, 2018.

Jha, S., E. Panda, and A. Sing. 'India Skills Report 2021: Key Insights Into the Post-Covid Landscape of Talent Demand and Supply in India'. 2021. https://indiaeducationforum.org/pdf/ISR-2021.pdf.

Keck, Z. 'Destined to Fail: China's Soft Power Push'. *The Diplomat*, 7 January 2013. https://thediplomat.com/2013/01/destined-to-fail-chinas-soft-power-offensive/.

Khan, M. 'Political Settlements and the Governance of Growth-Enhancing Institutions'. Working Paper, SOAS, University of London, 2010. http://eprints.soas.ac.uk/9968/1/Political_Settlements_internet.pdf.

Kumar, A. 'Domestic Politics of Bangladesh and India–Bangladesh Relations'. *Strategic Analysis* 38, no 5 (2014): 652–667.

Kwan, B.T. 'Singapore's Development and Use of Military Power: Diplomacy, Deterrence, Compellence and Counter-Coercion'. 20 February 2011. https://issuu.com/tohboonkwan/docs/issuu_saf_compellence/3.

Layne, C. 'Preventing the China–US Cold War From Turning Hot'. *The Chinese Journal of International Politics* 13, no 3 (2020): 343–385.

Lee, K.Y. *From Third World to First: The Singapore Story, 1965–2000.* Singapore: Times Media, 2000.

Libek, E. 'European Strategic Autonomy: A Cacophony of Political Visions'. International Centre for Defence and Security (ICDS). 2019. https://icds.ee/en/european-strategic-autonomy-a-cacophony-of-political-visions/.

Lustenberger, M. 'The Corona Pandemic: A White Swan, Not a Black Swan'. *Portfolio Strategies, LGT*. 2020. https://www.lgt.com/en/magnet/investment-strategies/the-corona-pandemic-a-white-swan-not-a-black-swan/#button2.

Manning, R. 'US Indo-Pacific Strategy: Myths and Reality'. *Global Affairs*, 21 September 2018. https://eng.globalaffairs.ru/valday/US-Indo-Pacific-Strategy-Myths-and-Reality-19763#_ftn1.

Mastny, V. *Learning From the Enemy: NATO as a Model for the Warsaw Pact.* Zurich: Forschungsstelle für Sicherheitspolitik und Konfliktanalyse, ETH Zürich, 2001.

Medcalf, R. 'Reimagining Asia: From Asia-Pacific to Indo-Pacific'. In *International Relations and Asia's Southern Tier*, edited by G. Rozman and J.C. Liow, 9–28. Singapore: Springer, 2018.

Mehrotra, S. and J.K. Parida. 'India's Employment Crisis: Rising Education Levels and Falling Non-Agricultural Job Growth'. Working Paper, Centre for Sustainable Employment, Azim Premji University, 2019.

Mohammad, G. 'Introduction'. In *National Security Bangladesh*, 1–8. Dhaka: The University Press Limited. 2009.

Mohan, C.R. 'India and South Asia: The Elusive Sphere of Influence'. *ISAS Insights: Detailed Perspectives on Developments in South Asia*. Singapore: Institute of South Asian Studies, National University of Singapore, 2022. https://www.isas.nus.edu.sg/papers/india-and-south-asia-the-elusive-sphere-of-influence/.

Momen, A.K.A. 'Bangladesh's Foreign Policy Compulsions, Constraints and Choices'. *The Daily Star*, 23 August 2021. https://www.thedailystar.net/views/in-focus/news/bangladeshs-foreign-policy-compulsions-constraints-and-choices-2158201.

Nataraj, G. 'Infrastructure Challenges in India: The Role of Public-Private Partnerships'. ORF Occasional Paper No. 49, Observer Research Foundation, India, 2014.

Navaneetham, K. and A. Dharmalingam. 'A Review of Age Structural Transition and Demographic Dividend in South Asia: Opportunities and Challenges." *Journal of Population Ageing* 5, no 4, (2012): 281–298.

Nicholas, N. 'The Black Swan: The Impact of the Highly Improbable'. *Journal of the Management Training Institute* 36, no 3, (2008): 56.

Norman, J., Y. Bar-Yam, and N.N. Taleb. 2020. 'Systemic Risk of Pandemic Via Novel Pathogens–Coronavirus: A Note'. New England Complex Systems Institute 26, 2020. https://jwnorman.com/wp-content/uploads/2020/03/Systemic_Risk_of_Pandemic_via_Novel_Path.pdf.

O'Neil, A. and L. West. 'The Quadrilateral Security Dialogue and Indo-Pacific Minilateralism: Resurrection Without Renewal?' In *Minilateralism in the Indo-Pacific: The Quadrilateral Security Dialogue, Lancang-Mekong Cooperation Mechanism, and ASEAN*, edited by B. Singh and S. Teo, 27–41, London and New York: Routledge, 2020.

Palit, A. and S. Sano. 'The United States' Free and Open Indo-Pacific Strategy: Challenges for India and Japan'. *ISAS Insights*, No 524, Institute of South Asian Studies, National University of Singapore, 4 December 2018.

Palmer, D.A.R. 'The NATO-Warsaw Pact Competition in the 1970s and 1980s: A Revolution in Military Affairs in the Making or the End of a Strategic Age?'. *Cold War History* 14, no 4 (2014): 533–573.

Parkhe, A. 1993. 'Strategic Alliance Structuring: A Game Theoretic and Transaction Cost Examination of Interfirm Cooperation'. *Academy of Management Journal* 36, no 4 (1993): 794–829.

Plagemann, J. 'Small States and Competing Connectivity Strategies: What Explains Bangladesh's Success in Relations With Asia's Major Powers?'. *The Pacific Review* 35, no 4 (2021): 1–29.

Pradhan, R. 'China's Silk Road Strategy and India's Apprehension'. *IUP Journal of International Relations* 13, no 4 (2019): 69–78.

Priyarsono, D.S. 'Welfare Implications of Entry Deterrence in a Spatial Market'. *The Annals of Regional Science* 26, no 4 (1992): 319–330.

Quackenbush, S.L. 'Deterrence Theory: Where Do We Stand?' *Review of International Studies* 37, no 2 (2011): 741–762.

Rahman, M.M. 'South Asia's View on China's One Road One Belt Initiative'. Fudan IIS Working Paper Series, University of Fudan. 2015.

Rai, A. 'Quadrilateral Security Dialogue 2 (Quad 2.0)—A Credible Strategic Construct or Mere "Foam in the Ocean"?'. *Maritime Affairs: Journal of the National Maritime Foundation of India* 14, no 2 (2018): 138–148.

Raihan, S. 'South Asia's Greater Integration in Asia: A Non-Indian Perspective'. *The Daily Star*, 4 August 2014. https://www.thedailystar.net/perspective/south-asias-greater-integration-asia-1443142.

Ray, J.K. 'India–China Relations Reconsidered: A Realist Perspective on India's Border Dispute with Its Neighbour'. *Revista UNISCI/UNISCI Journal No. 49*, 2019.

Roach, S.S. 'China's Contradictions'. Project Syndicate, 2017. https://www.project-syndicate.org/commentary/xi-jinping-political-report-19th-congress-by-stephen-s--roach-2017-10.

Rodrik, D. and A. Subramanian. 'From "Hindu Growth" to Productivity Surge: The Mystery of the Indian Growth Transition'. NBER Working Paper No. 10376, National Bureau of Economic Research, March 2004.

Rodrik, D. 'Premature Deindustrialization'. NBER Working Paper 20935, National Bureau of Economic Research, February 2015. http://www.nber.org/papers/w20935.pdf.

Roubini, Nouriel and Stephen Mihm. *Crisis Economics: A Crash Course in the Future of Finance*. New York: Penguin Press, 2010.

Roy, A. 'India's Current Account Deficit Widens to Near Decade High'. *Bloomberg*, 21 March 2022. https://www.bloomberg.com/news/articles/2022-03-31/india-s-current-account-deficit-widens-to-near-decade-high.

Sachs, J.D. 'Will America Create a Cold War With China'. *China Economic Journal* 12, no 2 (2019): 100–108.

Saeed, M. 'From the Asia-Pacific to the Indo-Pacific: Expanding Sino-US Strategic Competition'. *China Quarterly of International Strategic Studies* 3, no 4 (2017): 499–512.

Sakwa, R. 'Multilateralism and Nationalism in an Era of Disruption: The Great Pandemic and International Politics'. *Journal of International Analytics* 11, no 3 (2020): 129–150.

Samaranayake, N. 'China's Engagement with Smaller South Asian Countries'. Special Report No. 446, Washington, D.C.: United States Institute of Peace, 2019.

Satake, T. 'The Future of the Quadrilateral Security Dialogue: Possibilities and Challenges'. In *Minilateralism in the Indo-Pacific: The Quadrilateral Security Dialogue, Lancang-Mekong Cooperation Mechanism, and ASEAN*, edited by B. Singh and S. Teo, 42–56, London and New York: Routledge, 2020.

SATP. 'Chapter 3: Border Management'. Annual Report 2007–2008, South Asian Terrorism Portal, 2008. http://www.satp.org/satporgtp/countries/india/document/papers/mha07-08/chapter3-07.pdf.

Schelling, T.C. *The Strategy of Conflict*. Cambridge, MA: Harvard University Press, 1960.

Schumpeter, J. *Capitalism, Socialism and Democracy*. London and New York: Routledge, 2003.

Segers, J.P. and E. Gaile-Sarkane. 'From Creative Destruction to Creative Disruption: Lessons for Selected and Strategic Industries'. In: 24th World Multi-Conference on Systemics, Cybernetics and Informatics (WMSCI 2020): Proceedings. Vol. 3, pp. 103–107. Orlando, United States of America: International Institute of Informatics and Systemics (IIIS).

Sheng, A. and X. Geng. 'This is Why a Positive Relationship Between China and the US Matters for the Average Worker'. World Economic Forum, 28 April 2017. https://www.weforum.org/agenda/2017/04/this-is-why-a-positive-relationship-between-china-and-the-us-matters-for-the-average-worker.

Snidal, D. 'The Game Theory of International Politics'. World Politics, 38, no 1 (1985): 25–57.

Taylor, A. 'Conventional Deterrence and the US Navy: Why the Future Needs to Happen Now', Center for International Maritime Security, 2021. https://cimsec.org/conventional-deterrence-and-the-us-navy-why-the-future-needs-to-happen-now-pt-i/.

Tellis, A.J. 'Waylaid by Contradictions: Evaluating Trump's Indo-Pacific Strategy'. *The Washington Quarterly* 43, no 4, (2020): 123–154.

Titumir, R.A.M. 'Economic Growth in Bangladesh'. In *Numbers and Narratives in Bangladesh's Economic Development*, 1–32. Singapore: Palgrave Macmillan. 2021.

Titumir, R.A.M. and M.Z. Rahman. 'Changes in Population Age Structure and Economic Development: The Case of Bangladesh'. *Florya Chronicles of Political Economy* 3, no 1 (2017): 1–54.

———. 'Strategic Implications of China's Belt and Road Initiative (BRI): The Case of Bangladesh'. *China and the World* 2, no 03 (2019a).

———. 'Economic Implications of China's Belt and Road Initiative (BRI): The Case of Bangladesh'. *China and the World* 2, no 04 (2019b).

United Nations Development Programme. '2021 Global Multidimensional Poverty Index (MPI): Unmasking disparities by ethnicity, caste and gender. New York: UNDP, 2021.

Vegh, C.A., G. Vuletin, and D. Riera-Crichton. *From Known Unknowns to Black Swans: How to Manage Risk in Latin America and the Caribbean*. Washington, D.C.: World Bank Publications, 2018.

Westle, B. 'Political Beliefs and Attitudes: Legitimacy in Public Opinion Research'. In *Legitimacy in An Age of Global Politics*, 93. London: Palgrave Macmillan, 2007.

World Bank. 'Infographic: India's Poverty Profile'. Washington, D.C.: World Bank, 2016. http://www.worldbank.org/en/news/infographic/2016/05/27/india-s-poverty-profile.

———. 'Poverty and Shared Prosperity 2018: Piecing Together the Poverty Puzzle'. Washington, DC: World Bank, 2018.

———. 'Global Economic Prospects'. Washington, D.C.: The World Bank Group, 2020.

———. 'World Bank's Approach to South Asia Regional Integration, Cooperation and Engagement, 2020–2023'. World Bank, 2020. https://documents1.worldbank.org/curated/en/377981601447389283/pdf/Brief.pdf.

Xiang, L. 'Washington's Misguided China Policy'. *Survival* 43, no 3 (2001): 7–24.

Xinbo, W. 'Four Contradictions Constraining China's Foreign Policy Behavior'. *Journal of Contemporary China* 10, no 27 (2001): 293–301.

2

NATION BUILDING, RELIGION AND FOREIGN POLICY IN BANGLADESH

Brigitta Schuchert

In December 1971, Bangladesh emerged as an independent nation—behind the new country was a brutal civil war that had drawn in global and regional powers and plunged the nation deeply into debt. On the road ahead was a path towards nation building, recognition and gaining much-needed aid. Led by the charismatic Sheikh Mujibur Rahman (hereafter Mujib), Bangladesh's founding leader had to build national identity in the aftermath of the trauma of civil war violence that had seen the othering of ethnic, religious, and political communities. In creating a sense of nationhood, Mujib primarily emphasised a national identity around the language of a shared liberation struggle and this— along with Bangladesh's identity as a Muslim-majority country—have echoed through to this day.

At its independence, Bangladesh (previously East Pakistan) became the world's 35th Muslim majority country with the fourth-largest Muslim population.[1] While Muslims were a substantial majority of the population in Bangladesh (approximately 90 per cent in 1971), the early national moment had built on a sense of identity distinctly different from what had once been the separate wing of the country (West Pakistan). Beyond the drivers that helped consolidate a sense of nationalism separate from the 'two-nation theory', the eventual independence was also driven by deep economic grievances against the industrial and political centre of the country in the West, as well as regional and global trends of the post-colonial Cold War period (Raghavan 2013).

Bangladesh's statehood also emerged after much of the world had come to the support of West Pakistan either tacitly, rhetorically or, in the case of some countries including Saudi Arabia and Jordan, in military aid—with support of the Nixon administration in the US despite a formal aid cut-off (Gandhi 2014; Raghavan 2013). Bangladesh's foreign policy began with a push to define its national image on an international stage seeking legitimacy and the aid that may have come with it. In the years since independence, however, this national identity has also been a contested space with fissures between visions of Bangladesh as a Muslim-majority secular nation or Bangladesh as an Islamic nation first. While Islam and religious ties have consistently been intertwined with the country's pragmatic interests, the understanding of Bangladesh's national identity by its ruling leaders has also played a role in how the country has messaged its interests externally.

As argued by Peter Mandaville and Shadi Hamid, 'In nearly every Muslim-majority country that aspires to regional or global influence, Islam is an important and sometimes the only ideological currency that "mixes" effectively with more narrowly defined realpolitik' (2018). In purely realpolitik terms, Bangladesh may have less concern with global influence than leading countries in the Muslim world, such as Saudi Arabia, Iran and Turkey. Islam, nonetheless, offers a degree of 'ideological currency', both in its relations with other Muslim-majority countries and, at times, as a means of garnering domestic legitimacy or as leverage for opposition parties to pressure the ruling government. Far from being the only ideological currency, however, Bangladesh's history, rooted in a civil war and secular ideals in its founding, has also served as a guiding principle for its response to independence struggles and relationships with postcolonial nations. The country's constitutional roots in secularism can be a powerful currency as well—both in domestic political struggles and foreign policy. Both these identities—as a secular nation and as a Muslim-majority country—have supported pragmatic interests and shaped the country's diplomatic outreach.

This chapter examines Islam's role in Bangladesh's foreign policy by focusing on Dhaka's relations with the Muslim world since its independence. Assessing how and when religion shapes foreign policy is a difficult exercise, as it is never the sole guiding factor or an isolated variable (Mandaville 2014). This chapter is by no means an exhaustive look at Bangladesh's relations with the entirety of the Muslim world or meant to suggest that Bangladesh's policies towards the Muslim world are in any way monolithic. Instead, it aims to assess pivotal moments in Bangladesh's diplomacy with leading Muslim-majority countries and examine how this has shaped the identity Bangladesh has worked to project abroad.

The chapter first examines how religion and secularism were used in rhetoric during Bangladesh's independence movement and subsequent approach towards international recognition and nation building under the successive administrations of Mujib and the later military rule of General Ziaur Rahman and General M. Ershad. It then moves into a discussion of the role Islam has played in the parliamentary period, which has been driven by competition between the Awami League (AL)—led by Mujib's daughter Sheikh Hasina, which has built party support in part through calls to the secularism of the original Constitution—and the centre-right Bangladesh Nationalist Party (BNP), led by General Ziaur Rahman's widow Khaleda Zia. While Sheikh Hasina has consolidated Awami League power in the country over the past decade and pushed much of the opposition to the outskirts of Bangladeshi politics, religion has continued to be an important tool for building authority and conversely, used by opposition groups to undermine the government's legitimacy.

Securing Legitimacy: Religion and Secularism in Nation Building

The role of secularism and Islam has repeatedly come to the forefront in contests between Bangladesh's main political parties and in the fluctuating periods of military and civilian rule (Siddiqi 2010). Driven by grievances, including unbalanced political representation in West Pakistan, fears of erosion of Bengali language and culture and resource and economic disparities between Pakistan's eastern and western wings, Bangladesh's independence was deeply rooted in Bengali national identity. Its independence has also been represented as a rejection of the fundamentally religious national identity at the heart of Pakistan's foundation. As many scholars have emphasised, however, it is important not to oversimplify nation building in Bangladesh as a binary contest between a religious and secular visions of nationhood.

While post-partition policies led from the political centre in West Pakistan's Punjab province deepened a sense of division between Pakistan's eastern and western wings, Bengali nationalism was not simply a reactionary response to grievances from the majority Bengali-speaking East Pakistan towards the federal centre in the West. As detailed by Neilesh Bose, pre-partition Bengali Muslim League leaders, along with prominent writers and intellectuals, actively negotiated and conceptualised an idea of Pakistan that would blend and maintain space for Bengali culture and ideas of 'nation' (Bose 2014). Negotiating where Bengal and Bengali identity fit within the nation of Pakistan had also been shaped by translation and religious scholarship by 19th-century Bengali Muslim reformers for a Bengali audience, which, as Sufia M. Uddin has noted, 'attempted to create a unified subcontinental Muslim culture and community but inadvertently also reinforced a uniquely Bengali vision of Muslim community' (Uddin 2006).

Sana Aiyer has further stressed that partition narratives focusing primarily on West Pakistan and Punjab have created a false dichotomy between religious communalism on the one hand and secular nationalism on the other. In the lead up to partition, politicians in Bengal had 'produced a peculiar form of identity politics that appealed to not only religious sentiment in their consolidation of community and solidarity but also regional loyalty that cut across the religious divide' (Aiyar 2008). This was seen, for instance, in the politics of Fazlul Huq, the prime minister of undivided Bengal before partition and leader of the agrarian rights-focused Krishak Praja Party. Holder of multiple seats of political importance during his time in politics, Huq presented the Lahore Resolution calling for an independent state for Muslims at the All-Indian Muslim League meeting in 1940, but simultaneously had strong rifts with Jinnah and the Muslim League over the regional interests of Bengali Muslims (Aiyar 2008).

Much of the groundwork for what was eventually an independent Bangladesh was laid not by religious separatism, however, but by economic grievances, unbalanced political representation and national/regional identity politics that had long been negotiated in different political spheres. The push for greater independence, as spearheaded by Mujib, was predominately framed around class struggle and demands for greater economic and political autonomy (Raghavan 2013). When Bangladesh emerged as a People's Republic, after witnessing widespread ethnic and religious violence and a war that brought in India and outside powers, the vision espoused in the 1972 Constitution was one of upholding 'the ideals of nationalism, socialism, democracy and secularism' (Constitution Project 2021). Notably, the ideas of secularism differed from the historically Western-rooted concept of secularism as the strong separation between religion, the affairs of the state and public life (Heir 2003). As Mujib asserted, 'secularism does not mean the absences of religion ... our only objection is that nobody will be allowed to use religion as a political weapon' (quoted in Uddin 2015). As such, secularism was set in opposition to religious exclusion rather than the absence of religion in public spaces (Bhuiyan 2021).

The role of religion/secularism in Bangladesh's national identity has been repeatedly debated the over 50-odd years since independence. In 1979, the term 'secular' was removed from the Constitution during the military rule under Ziaur Rahman following Mujib's assassination in 1975. Zia also lifted the ban on religious parties, including Jamaat-e-Islami, which had been banned in 1972 due to its opposition to the separation of Pakistan's two wings during the civil war and support of the Pakistan army (Bhattacharjee 2020). In 1988, under the subsequent military rule of General Ershad, a constitutional amendment was added declaring Islam the official religion of the country.[2] Although Islam remains the national religion, the Constitution also enshrines religious tolerance, and the commitment to secularism of the 1972 Constitution was reinstated to an amended constitution under the Awami League in 2011 (Uddin 2015).

These tensions have also shaped Bangladesh's political landscape and domestic politics. Its two main political parties, the BNP and the AL, brought this question into their respective party identities and negotiated coalition building with religious political parties (Ahmed 2021). Religion, and appealing to majoritarian sentiments, has also been a powerful tool in opposition politics—particularly as the main secular party (the AL) has been marred by its own charges of backsliding towards authoritarianism, corruption and intolerance of dissent (Sikdar and Shohag 2016).

Beyond the question of the role of Islam in Bangladesh's domestic politics, the country's identity as a Muslim-majority nation has, at times, also been a component of its foreign policy. In the first few years after independence, gaining recognition and legitimacy—as well as securing financial aid and investment after the war—were the core foreign policy priorities of Mujib's government. Gaining international recognition, however, was shaped far more by Cold War-era politics than religious nationalism. Stressing 'friendship towards all, malice towards none'—the guiding line of Bangladesh's foreign policy to this day—its early foreign policy largely followed the framework of the Non-Aligned Movement (NAM). The Soviet Union was the first major power to recognise Bangladesh, and the Warsaw Pact countries were among the first to establish diplomatic relations with newly independent Bangladesh. Despite Nixon and Kissinger's independent relationship with Pakistan's military leader Yahya Khan as the US worked to reopen ties with China during the 1971 war, the US soon followed with recognition in 1972 (Ahmed and Liton 2016).

A more pressing challenge in Bangladesh's immediate independence was the rift between the newly independent country and—with its population now cut in half—Pakistan. Bangladesh's diplomatic outreach to the Muslim world and beyond was met with resistance from Pakistan, which boycotted the 1972 Afro-Asian Solidarity Summit in Cairo due to the presence of a delegation from Bangladesh, and left the Commonwealth of Nations after its recognition of Bangladesh in 1972, not rejoining until 1989 (*The New York Times* 1972; BBC 2014). During the 1971 war, Muslim countries across the Middle East had voiced their support for a united Pakistan. The Nixon administration in the US had turned a blind eye or supported partners in the Middle East—including Iran, Jordan and Turkey—in routing military equipment to Pakistan despite a congressional freeze on arms exports (Karim 2019; Gandhi 2002).

In the immediate years after independence, Mujib's foreign policy towards the Muslim world focused on securing legitimacy for Bangladesh and countering the narrative that Bangladesh's independence movement and commitment to secularism in its Constitution had been a reaction against an Islamic state in South Asia—a narrative that was being put forth by Pakistan as well as Jamaat leaders (Hasan 2019). Beyond the Arab world, Muslim-majority countries that had supported Pakistan in the war were also slow to recognise Bangladesh. Turkey, like Bangladesh, was a Muslim-majority nation with secularism protected in its Constitution. However, it did not recognise Bangladesh until 1974, when Pakistan did (Colakoğlu 2019). Muslim-majority states of Southeast Asia, in contrast, were early to recognise Bangladesh, with Indonesia and Malaysia jointly extending their recognition in February of 1972 (*Straits Times* 1972). Iraq became the first Arab country to recognise Bangladesh in 1972 (Sajen 2022).

Mujib's diplomatic outreach to Muslim-majority countries, however, focused beyond religious ties to solidarity among non-aligned nations of the developing world. This stance was highlighted in Bangladesh's foreign minister's attendance at the 1972 Afro-Asian Solidarity Summit and Mujib's attendance at the NAM summit in Algiers the following year (Rashid 2009). Algeria was also early in its recognition of Bangladesh, but this recognition may have been more to do with a shared narrative of liberation wars rather than religious solidarity (Feroze 2021). While pushing for Bangladesh's presence in multilateral fora, the Mujib government also made specific diplomatic overtures to Muslim-majority countries in the Middle East, including sending tea to Egypt and Syria, foreign minister trips to multiple Muslim- majority countries and hosting foreign ministers from across the Muslim world (Rahman 2020). A key turning point was Mujib's attendance at the Summit of the Organisation of the Islamic Conference (today the Organisation of Islamic Cooperation) held in Lahore in 1974, which was followed by several Arab Gulf states, including Bahrain and the United Arab Emirates extending support (Zarif 2020).

The importance of gaining the support of the Muslim world was perhaps most strongly indicated in Bangladesh's early stance towards Israel, which recognised Bangladesh soon after its independence on 7 February 1972 (Chowdhury 2020). Bangladesh, in contrast, has yet to recognise the state of Israel and has voiced support to Palestine and the Palestinian Liberation Organization (PLO) since the 1970s. A year after Israel's recognition of Bangladesh, Bangladesh expressed strong opposition to Israel in the 1973 Arab-Israeli war and—despite its young economy—sent relief supplies and a medical team to Palestinians during the conflict (Mohsin 2021). Support for Palestine aligned with not only religious solidarity but also the image Mujib projected of Bangladesh as a supporter of oppressed populations and liberation struggles internationally.

The connections between support of Palestine and Bangladesh's presentation of itself as a support of oppressed groups globally was made perhaps most clearly in Mujib's 1974 speech to the UN. In his speech, he aligned Bangladesh's independence with liberation struggles in South America, Asia and Africa, while also stressing, 'Our Arab brethren are still fighting for the complete liberation of all illegally occupied territories, and the legitimate national rights of the people of Palestine have yet to be restored' (Mohsin 2021). While noting shared religious ties with the Arab world, as was seen in Mujib's foreign policy more broadly, his speech also placed Bangladesh's stance within the broader context of liberation struggles and solidarity with oppressed groups internationally.

Mujib's diplomacy from 1971 to his death in 1975 was, in many aspects, a balancing act between the distinct characteristics of Bangladesh's independence struggle, conceptions of secularism and identity as a Muslim-majority country. Beyond the need to establish strong bilateral ties for economic, political and military support, Mujib sought to gain Bangladesh's legitimacy through its admittance into international institutions. Muslim-majority countries—most notably Indonesia and Egypt, who were among NAM's founders along with India, the former Yugoslavia, and Ghana—were key voices in carving a 'third route' for non-aligned countries in the Cold War era. However, beyond NAM countries, Mujib also sought acceptance into groups emphasising shared religious ties, such as the Saudi Arabia-led Organisation of Islamic Cooperation (OIC). Muslim-majority countries with postcolonial legacies—many that had only become independent from colonial rule less than two decades prior—played a key role in bringing Bangladesh into the fold of religious-based multilateralism—such as Algeria's president sending a private aircraft to transport Mujib to the Lahore summit in 1974 (Weinraub 1974). Getting the support of countries in the Gulf, however, involved a more concerted diplomatic effort, with Saudi Arabia holding reservations over Bangladesh establishing itself as a secular nation and not recognising the country until after Mujib's death in 1975 (Hasan 1976).

The tensions over the role of religion in Bangladesh's identity and domestic politics came visibly to the forefront under the military rule of Major General Ziaur Rahman (1977–1981) and the subsequent leadership of Major General Hussain Muhammad Ershad (1982–1990). In the 15 years of military rule, both Zia and Ershad ushered in a greater role of religion in politics, offering a form of legitimacy that the authoritarian military-led government lacked. Soon after coming to power, Zia lifted the ban on religious political parties, allowing the Islamist political party Jamaat-e-Islami, which had been banned from politics for its support of West Pakistan and crimes committed during the war, to participate in national politics. Zia's government additionally established a Religious Affairs Ministry and brought figures with strong ties to religious parties and organisations into the cabinet (Riaz 2008). Ershad would later add Islam as the state religion to the Constitution in 1989. The push for a stronger Islamic identity after Zia's coup was not only a matter of domestic politics but also Bangladesh's foreign policy. Zia removed the secularism enshrined in Article 12 of Bangladesh's Constitution and further instituted an amendment calling for Bangladesh to 'consolidate, preserve and strengthen fraternal relations among Muslim countries based on Islamic solidarity' (Wohab 2020).

As Zia and Ershad redefined Bangladesh's identity domestically, they also opened the doors for relationships with the Muslim world that were both ideological and pragmatic. As president, Zia worked to further develop Bangladesh's relations with multiple Muslim-majority countries with foreign trips to Saudi Arabia, Iran, Egypt, Pakistan, as well as Kuwait and Iraq. Funds from across the Muslim world supported development projects in Bangladesh—including an over $500 million railway project supported by Saudi Arabia (Hasan 1983). Saudi Arabian and Kuwaiti investors were also pivotal to start of the Islami Bank Bangladesh, which began in 1983 with the aim of supporting Sharia-compliant banking and as 'the First Islamic bank in South East Asia', with approximately 70 per cent of its initial funding from the Middle East (*The Economist* 2017; Bahree 2016; Islami Bank Bangladesh Limited n.d.)

The ties with the Muslim world deepened under the Ershad administration, which continued the regular high-level visits to countries across the Muslim world as well as hosting high-level dignitaries—including PLO leader Yasser Arafat (Mujib notably had also built ties with Arafat). Ershad's outreach supported Bangladesh economically through bilateral trade agreements and loans with countries including Turkey, Kuwait, Indonesia, a substantial increase in aid from OPEC countries, and funding for infrastructure projects (Hasan 2020). The stark contrast with the hesitancy of a number of Gulf countries to support the newly independent Bangladesh under Mujib with the period under Ershad was seen clearly with the full backing of many Muslim countries for Bangladesh's security council seat at the UN in 1978 (Hasan 2020).

Lacking the democratic credentials to claim popular support, Zia and Ershad nevertheless strove to gain legitimacy internationally and through domestic appeal. This involved gaining support from the AL's former opposition, including the religious right, as well as continuing to build support and recognition internationally (Murshid 2001). Zia's constitutional changes and efforts to link Bangladeshi nationalism with Islam alleviated objections from Saudi Arabia and others in the Muslim world about Mujib's brand of secularism. The 20 years following Bangladesh's independence also laid the groundwork for narrative competition over the roots of Bangladesh's identity, reckoning with the civil war and role of Islam in politics, which would play out over periods of parliamentary rule by the Zia-founded BNP—later led by his widow Khaleda Zia—and the AL under Mujib's daughter, Sheikh Hasina.

Foreign Policy and Domestic Politics: The Awami League and Bangladesh Nationalist Party

When Bangladesh entered a parliamentary system in the 1990s, ties with the Muslim world had deepened with benefits for Bangladesh's globally established recognition and gradually improving international leadership role and economic development. However, domestically, Bangladesh faced the challenge of moving away from over a decade of military rule, weakened electoral systems and two political parties with competing narratives of national identity. While Zia's BNP, which more closely linked Bangladesh's national identity with Islam, and the AL under Sheikh Hasina, which focused more on secularism, emphasised different narratives of Bangladesh's founding and national identity, there was little incentive to make drastic foreign policy changes or move away from the economic benefits and diplomatic ties that came with improved relations with the Muslim world. Further, the AL had lost the initial nationalist galvanisation from the early independence years and had to factor the re-emergence of more hard-line religious parties into its political manoeuvring (Riaz 2008). While foreign policy decisions appeared to be driven by a more pragmatic political understanding, contentious issues in the Middle East or Muslim world more broadly also generated a base of support that opposition parties could easily mobilise around.

This dynamic was illustrated early in Bangladesh's move towards multiparty elections as the general election in 1991 coincided with turmoil breaking out across the Middle East following Saddam Hussein's invasion of Kuwait. Zia and Hasina shared a policy stance supporting coalition forces against Iraq (Chowdhury 2020). Despite the anti-American sentiment among many in Bangladesh during the Gulf War, the leading religious party Jamaat-e-Islami also voiced its opposition to Iraq's Kuwait invasion

(Hossain 1997). In the Ershad administration and the interim election government after he was unseated, Bangladesh met this rhetorical support by sending approximately 5,000 troops to offer support to the Saudi-US coalition—a significant commitment, given Bangladesh's small and still emerging military (Sun 1991). Ershad also supported a coalition among Asian Muslim countries demanding Iraq's withdrawal from Kuwait, and offered advice to the H.W. Bush administration based on the former's previous close ties with Saddam Hussein (Bush Presidential Library 1990).

While support for the coalition seemed less controversial, sending troops proved to be a source of domestic discontent, sparking protests and stone throwing at the US, Saudi Arabian and Egyptian embassies as well as broad condemnation from opposition parties (Hossain 1997). Prior to the war, Bangladesh and Iraq had warm relations—Iraq was the first Arab country to recognise Bangladesh—and Ershad and Saddam Hussein reportedly had a strong personal relationship (Bush Presidential Library 1990). Bangladesh's response, while not popular with domestic audiences, underscored the pragmatic approach of its relations with the Middle East. Bangladesh had a sizeable overseas workers' population living in Kuwait along with interests in strengthening relations with Saudi Arabia and its ally, the US—both with the capacity to offer substantial loans for Bangladesh's economic development. The country's decision to send troops to Gulf in 1991 marked a clear stance in a conflict briefly dividing the Middle East.

Bangladesh was more united in its response in denunciation of 9/11 terror attacks (Zia and Hasina both offered Bangladesh's ports and air space for US operations in Afghanistan while election campaigning), as well as later condemnation of later US wars in Iraq (Litner 2004). Khaleda Zia led Bangladesh through the onset of the US 'Global War on Terror' (GWOT). The BNP-led government—then governing in coalition with Jamaat and another Islamist political party, the Islami Oikya Jote (IOJ)—may have been cautious in appearing to offer overt support to the US-led war, and IOJ and Jamaat leaders had voiced support for the Taliban and Osama bin Laden prior to 9/11 (Riaz 2008). In the early years of the GWOT, Zia maintained that there was no Islamic fundamentalism in Bangladesh, despite a spate of bombings including political assassination attempts of then opposition leader Hasina, which was met by opposition from the AL (Vaughn 2006). In 2003, Bangladesh joined much of the Muslim world—and many other countries as well—in condemning the US invasion of Iraq (*Hindustan Times* 2003).

While Hasina's criticisms in this period were less focused on Zia's foreign policy during the GWOT, the AL's reproach drew on the motifs of US counterterror priorities at the time. Following attacks targeting AL rallies—including a bombing that killed AL Finance Minister

A.M.S. Kibria, and four others and a grenade attack at an AL rally that Sheikh Hasina narrowly escaped—the AL accused the BNP of 'letting loose communal extremist forces' and shallow efforts to address militancy (Vaughn 2006). In the case of the BNP, the need to maintain a fragile coalition likely acted as a constraint on the party's initial response, while for the AL, using the rhetoric of the time for the GWOT allowed the party to draw contrast and critiques of the BNP government.

Zia and Hasina's messaging around the GWOT in the early 2000s also reflected an ongoing balancing act between maintaining domestic support and projecting either the AL or the BNP vision of Bangladesh's national identity. While Zia stressed Bangladesh's role as a moderate Muslim country that opposed terrorism but did not face the same challenges of extremism domestically, Hasina and the AL pointed to the growing terrorism threat domestically that they argued was exacerbated by the BNP coalition-led government (Zee News 2005). In the lead up to the 2008 elections, after a two-year period of military rule under a caretaker government, the AL campaigned on its secular credentials and promised to uproot terrorism and corruption. However, in practice, this contributed to the arrests of a number of critics and political opponents (US Department of State, Bureau of Democracy, Human Rights and Labor 2009).

Under the AL, the governing party since 2009, Bangladesh aimed to project an international image as a secular democracy and quickly fulfilled promises of adding the secularism clause back into Bangladesh's Constitution (Habib 2011). The AL also maintained the constitutional commitment towards 'fraternal relation' with the Muslim world through economic and multilateral cooperation, and agreed to maintain Islam as the state religion (Bangladesh Awami League 2013). In multilateral fora, Bangladesh stressed a foreign policy agenda related to its identity as a developing country as well as a Muslim-majority nation. For instance, Bangladesh is a member 'Developing Eight' (D-8) grouping, which focuses on cooperation between 'major developing Muslim majority countries', along with Turkey, Malaysia, Indonesia, Iran, Egypt, Nigeria and Pakistan (D-8 Organisation for Economic Cooperation n.d.). The groupings have helped support Bangladesh's economic development gains by facilitating trade among members (Standing Committee for Economic and Commercial Cooperation of the Organisation of Islamic Cooperation n.d.). Bangladesh has also, in recent years, used both the D-8 and the OIC to draw attention to other foreign policy concerns, primarily the Rohingya refugee crisis and its push for Myanmar to repatriate the displaced Rohingya population (OIC 2019). Although this has led to little diplomatic success in changing Myanmar's behaviour, it has drawn financial support for Rohingya relief efforts from countries including Saudi Arabia and statements issued largely supporting Bangladesh's calls for repatriation (Al-Haj 2017).

Maintaining warm relations with the Muslim-majority countries and invoking Islam as a shared aspect of identity remained an aspect of Bangladesh's foreign policy under the AL government, which has often pragmatically balanced responses to domestic and international pressures. As others have argued, Sheikh Hasina's AL has also been constrained by the rise of religious right-wing parties and secularism's weaknesses as a clear political rallying point. For instance, as argued by Tahmina Rahman, rather than creating a clear 'Bangladesh-oriented' concept of secularism, 'many leftist politicians have opted for the strategy the AL has been using since the mid-1990s, showcasing the piety of their leaders to offset anti-religious allegations' (Rahman 2022).

While it has been rare that the AL has publicly voiced a stance that would invite strong censure from hard-line religious parties in Bangladesh, it has chosen to remain quiet on sensitive issues. For instance, while experiencing mass protests calling for a boycott of France after French President Emanual Macron referred to Islam as being 'in crisis', the Hasina government did not issue any public comment, unlike other Muslim-majority countries and the OIC which condemned Macron's statements and Islamophobia worldwide (Mahmud 2020). In other instances, however, the Hasina government has acted in its own clear domestic interests, despite international rebuke. For instance, the AL government has moved forward with its promise of a war crimes tribunal for atrocities committed during the 1971 war, which was met with strong objections from a number of international human rights groups for not following international standards and led to Turkey withdrawing its ambassador from the country in 2016 (Reuters 2016; Human Rights Commission United States Congress 2016). In this instance, domestic politics eclipsed external objections, with the tribunals enjoying broad support as well as targeting AL's opposition in Jamaat and the BNP (Riaz 2008; Ramani 2016). In a less visible case in 2017, reports also tied government pressure to resignations and replacement of the chairman and vice chairman of Islami Bank Bangladesh—which has, over the years, drawn attention for the high-level management affiliations with Jamaat-e-Islami—despite the move frustrating major stakeholders from Saudi Arabia and elsewhere (*The Economist* 2017).

However, Bangladesh has also chosen to be vocal on issues that have received some level of consensus among many Muslim-majority countries, most notably the support of an independent Palestinian state and strong condemnation of the state of Israel. This has, at times, led to vocal stances against US policy in the Middle East, such as the move by the Trump administration to move the US embassy from Tel Aviv to Jerusalem—a policy stance that was broadly unpopular with the international community in both the Muslim world as well as among America's traditional allies in Europe (bdnews24 2017). While Bangladesh's leadership may be hesitant to change its long-standing policy on issues that garner a high amount of sensitivity, such as relations with Israel and Palestine, the Hasina administration has also appeared willing to wait out protests on other foreign policy issues such as Bangladesh's relationships with France—a key trading partner for the country's ready-made garment industry.

While quiet on Saudi Arabia, the UAE and later Bahrain's move towards normalisation of ties with Israel under the Abraham Accords, Bangladesh has reiterated its non-recognition policy. Despite removing a clause on Bangladeshi passports that stated the passports' validity everywhere except Israel—a move that some thought may have been testing the waters of a shifting public stance towards Israel—Bangladesh was quick to backtrack and affirmed all travel to Israel was still banned (Sumon 2021). While rooted in early and continued solidarity with Palestine, Bangladesh's stance is likely also shaped by strong public sensitivities surrounding the matter as well as weighing the public fallout that would likely follow any indications of a policy shift. As recently as January 2023, Bangladesh state media reported Sheikh Hasina reaffirming Bangladesh's support of Palestine in a meeting with seven OIC envoys and her call for Muslim *Ummah* to collectively do the same. Hasina further emphasised the continuity between her stance and the stance of Bangladesh's founding leader—messaging support for Palestine and Bangladesh's leadership role within multilateral institutions internationally while domestically reiterating the position on Palestine as a core aspect of AL history (Bangladesh Sangbad Sangstha 2023).

Even so, the removal of the clause in passports in became quick fodder for the opposition. The clause was removed without any public announcement and came only days after Jamaat-led rallies against Israel following May 2021 aerial strikes in Gaza. The BNP was quick to respond, calling the move to remove the clause from the passports 'amoral' and stating that the party would send medical supplies to Palestinians impacted by the conflict (Nafiu 2021). Beyond being a policy that represents shared stances across many countries in the Muslim world, Israel also has the potential to stir up strong domestic reactions, which have been mobilised by political actors across Bangladesh. In 2016, Sheikh Hasina alleged that the BNP and Jamaat alliance had worked with Israel to try and remove her from the government (*The Daily Star* 2016). Stances on Israel have proven to be an effective way to stir up support and criticism of the opposition while burnishing each party's commitment to Muslim rights abroad. While each party has often approached polarising religious issues differently based on whether they sit at the centre or periphery, both the AL and BNP have ultimately, as Mubashar Hasan and Geoffrey Macdonald have argued, 'wielded Islam for political advantage ... [and promoted] Muslim solidarity in foreign policy' (Hasan and Macdonald 2022).

Economic Growth: Building Party Legitimacy

Touting Bangladesh's economic growth has also been a key factor for leaders—most recently the AL—to build political legitimacy. Ties with the Middle East and Gulf countries have been a core component of Bangladesh's economy. Transforming from what was once infamously called a 'basket case' to one of the world's fastest-growing economies, economic development has been a key feature of Bangladesh's domestic and foreign policy. Economically devastated by the 1971 war, gaining recognition, opening trade ties and securing economic aid were core components of Bangladesh's early foreign policy. Under Zia, improved relations with Saudi Arabia were also, in part, an effort to secure an improved rate on oil imports (which Zia was unable to establish), as well as export labour to Gulf states, which has provided substantial remittances to Bangladesh to this day (Murshid 2001). During the Ershad administration, Saudi Arabia, Pakistan, Kuwait and Libya also increased financial assistance to Bangladesh's education sector, contributing to the number of madrassas in Bangladesh doubling from 1981 to 1991 (Murshid 2001). Saudi Arabia and Kuwait, in particular, continue to fund madrassas, mosques and cultural centres across Bangladesh (BD News 2017).

Since its independence and origins in a government-controlled economy under Mujib, Bangladesh has also undertaken multiple market reform efforts to draw in increased foreign direct and private investment, as well as liberalise trade (Brookings Institute 2018). Despite multiple economic setbacks—driven by internal issues including corruption, unemployment and inflation—and economic burdens from multiple natural disasters, including droughts and devastating cyclones, Bangladesh's economy has been frequently highlighted as a success story, even in the midst of the pandemic (World Bank 2021; Devarajan 2022). This repeated economic success narrative, however, has hit a recent roadblock as inflation, regular power outages and rising costs of food and fuel led to widespread protests in the fall of 2022 (Mahmud 2022). In 2022, Bangladesh joined Sri Lanka and Pakistan in seeking aid from the IMF and became the first country of the three to secure a deal in early 2023 (Reuters 2023).

Facing these ongoing shocks—as well as the internal weaknesses in its economy that experts have warned have gone unresolved and predate the pandemic and Russia's war in Ukraine—Bangladesh will likely need to continue to lean into the economic development gains of its international ties (Riaz 2022a). For Gulf states, these ties are most apparent in Bangladesh's remittances sector, which made up 8 per cent of its GDP in 2018 and was the second-highest source of Bangladesh's foreign exchange earnings (Mujeri and Mujeri 2020). With Bangladesh's independence aligning with the oil boom in the Gulf states, Saudi Arabia and the UAE have been among the top sources of remittances from the country's overseas work population (Titumir 2021). Malaysia, meanwhile, leads Bangladesh's remittances from East Asia (Titumir 2021).

However, with remittances linked to sustaining Bangladesh's economic growth and meeting development goals, countries contributing significantly to remittance inflows may also have a higher level of influence and leverage. The power of countries like Saudi Arabia and the UAE to shape economies across South Asia came through clearly in the Covid-19 pandemic as concerns grew of a remittance contraction following restrictions on the number of migrants across South Asia (Molavi 2020). The substantial population of migrants across South Asia and the dependency many economies have on remittances sent home by workers has also offered Gulf states troubling amounts of leverage. For Bangladesh, this came to the forefront as Saudi Arabia began deporting Rohingya refugees who had migrated to Saudi Arabia from Myanmar years earlier—many of whom had never lived in Bangladesh—and pushed for over 54,000 Rohingya to be issued Bangladeshi passports (Ullah 2020).

As Bangladesh's foreign policy is predominantly driven by economic development goals, it has prioritised maintaining positive economic and trading relations with various countries of the Muslim world despite regional rifts such as tensions between Iran and Saudi Arabia, or Saudi Arabia and Qatar. On the diplomatic front, Bangladesh's involvement in disputes has generally been kept to statements of rhetorical support that echo statements from Muslim-majority states. For instance, Bangladesh joined in with other Gulf states as well as several North African countries in condemning Houthi missile attacks and voicing support for the Saudi-backed Hadi government in Yemen (*The Daily Star* 2015). As a country with a small military, the Bangladesh armed forces have focused on peacekeeping missions with the UN—although it has jointly worked on mine-sweeping and civilian construction in Saudi Arabia while stopping short of sending troops to engage militarily in Yemen. Bangladesh has stressed that its troops have had no military involvement in Yemen despite some defence cooperation with Saudi Arabia (Bhuiyan 2019).

Bangladesh's rhetorical support of Saudi Arabia in the Yemen war is not surprising—economic ties and remittances from Saudi Arabia dwarf those from Yemen, and Bangladesh has been pursuing not only economic but also stronger defence relations with Saudi Arabia (Zaman 2018). However, in conflicts when Bangladesh has sizeable stakes in positive relations with both countries, Dhaka has often chosen not to take a clear position. For instance, the country stayed silent in the Qatar–Gulf crisis of 2017, which included states where Bangladesh has a significant overseas worker population and has historically positive relations (Mushtaq 2017). Similarly, while many smaller South Asian states were quick to condemn the assassination of Iranian nuclear scientist Mohsen Farkhrizadeh, Bangladesh made no official statement, while Pakistan, with similarly strong ties with Saudi Arabia, took almost a week to officially condemn that attack (Tolany 2020).

While Bangladesh has generally positive ties with most Arab Gulf states (each of the Gulf Cooperation Council states along with Jordan received mangoes in a recent gift from Bangladesh to friends in the region), the country's bilateral ties with Saudi Arabia appear to supersede many of its other ties with countries in the Muslim world—with Hasina making multiple official visits during her time in office, as well as inviting Crown Prince Mohammad Salman to visit to Bangladesh on the sidelines of the G20 summit in Delhi (*The Daily Star* 2021; *Saudi Gazette* 2018; *Prothom Alo* 2023).

The Domestic Politics Balancing Act

National identity and religion in Bangladesh have played an important role in not only how the two leading political parties have messaged domestically but also how Bangladesh has projected itself to external partners. Debates over the role of religion and secularism in Bangladesh's identity have often centred on Bangladesh's domestic policies, including the role of religious political parties and how national identity is projected within the Constitution and historical memory. However, less attention has generally been given to the role of religious identity in Bangladesh's foreign policy and the projection of its image and national interests abroad. From securing legitimacy soon after independence to contemporary defence and economic agreements, Bangladesh's relationships with the Muslim world have been a central and pragmatic driver of the country's foreign policy. While much of Bangladesh's foreign policy has been driven by pragmatism and economic interests, evoking a shared identity and sense of solidarity amongst Muslim-majority countries has also helped Bangladesh foster ties bilaterally and in multilateral forums.

While Bangladesh has made notable economic strides over the past decades, the growth is beginning to show signs of strain. The country faces a weakened currency and declining foreign exchange reserves along with rising inflation and repeated power outages warning of an impending energy crisis (Riaz 2022). This may raise questions of how much economic gain can be used to offer political legitimacy with more citizens frustrated by the state of the economy (International Republican Institute 2023). The BNP, for instance, has used the growing economic crisis to mobilise rallies across the country (*The Daily Star* 2022). While Bangladesh has secured funding through the IMF, economic strain along with electoral apathy will likely challenge the sources of legitimacy the AL has built while becoming the dominant party in Bangladesh and increasingly pushing opposition to the margins (Hasan 2023).

How the country chooses to respond to polarising issues across the Muslim world also has the potential to mobilise opposition parties and shape domestic opinion. As Bangladesh heads into elections, anticipated in early 2024, it will be important to watch whether leadership in Bangladesh is constrained by demands from its opposition parties and needs to secure political legitimacy at home and abroad—even as the AL has increasingly entrenched itself as a singular party in Bangladeshi politics (Riaz 2022b). Even as the Hasina government has rhetorically championed the country's secularist credentials abroad and its commitments to religious freedom, gender equality and democracy—often accompanied by boasting the strides Bangladesh has made economically—it has also at times worked domestically to fracture Islamist opposition by conceding to religious nationalist demands (Beschloss and Hasina 2019; Hasan and Macdonald 2022).

Projecting legitimacy has, in many ways, been at the heart of the role of religion and secularism in each era of Bangladesh politics. Whether it was emphasising the secularism within Bangladesh's founding policies or relying on the support of religious leadership, each administration in Bangladesh has had to establish itself as the authentic portrayal of the country's national identity while navigating domestic politics. As argued by Ali Riaz, while Islamist political parties do not have the power to win elections outright, they can play the role of 'kingmaker' in Bangladeshi politics, and catering to demands of religious actors, or parties can solidify support and manage overt opposition (Riaz 2018). Efforts to cater to religious parties can often be seen more dramatically in domestic politics than in foreign policy. This includes, for instance, the AL government amending the Information Communications Technology Act in 2013—later replaced by the 2018 Digital Security Act—which has led to the arrest of bloggers and journalists, and even Sufi singers, who have reportedly engaged in 'acts of defamation' (Hardig and Sajjad 2020; Nag 2020). The AL government has also quietly removed or relocated statues protested by hard-line Islamist groups such as Hefazat-e-Islami, including the removal of a female statue personifying justice outside the country's supreme court building in 2017 (Nag 2020).

The AL's policies have oscillated between crackdowns on oppositions—through reported arrests and intimidation—and trying to secure critical vote banks and prevent a stronger coalition of opposition parties (Human Rights Watch 2022; Mahmud 2018). The international impact of extremism domestically may be most immediately visible in Bangladesh's relationships in its neighbourhood. In 2021 alone, there were several instances of anti-Hindu communal violence, including attacks on temples following Prime Minister Modi's visit in March and attacks on Hindu homes, businesses and temples during Durga Puja in October that year (Paul 2021; Hassan 2021). As Hindu nationalist politics have also contributed to repeated instances of anti-Muslim violence and communalism in India, both countries could see a strain on the political relationship due to religious majoritarianism, communalism or violence at home.

Still, even while facing a domestic balancing act at home, the Awami League government has often worked to continue to project an image of multi-religious and secular ideals internationally. Hasina's response to the 2021 Durga Puja attacks was swift, in a speech after she drew on the national narrative from the 1971 war, emphasising that Hindus and Muslims fought alongside one another for Bangladesh's independence—coming out with the statement, 'Each unto his or her religion, festivals are for all' (Mandal 2021). The statement echoes the ways the language of secularism can continue to play a valuable messaging role in Sheikh Hasina's political image to domestic and international audiences.

Following the US withdrawal from Afghanistan in 2021, Hasina raised concerns over the impact the rise of the Taliban in Afghanistan or religious extremism in the region may have on stability in the country. With the Taliban takeover aligning with the 17th anniversary of the grenade attacks at her rally in 2004, in a state news interview on the anniversary, Hasina emphasised the support for the Taliban under previous BNP rule—asserting that opposition members had received training in Afghanistan to launch attacks against the AL—while stressing her government's commitment to 'the founding principles of creation of Bangladesh' (Chaudhury 2021). As has been done with messaging in the past, these comments seek to align the ruling party's vision with widespread international sentiment while simultaneously projecting the AL's image as preserver of constitutional values at home. In a rare condemnation of another state, in April 2023 Hasina accused the United States of seeking regime change in Bangladesh noting the US 'has the power to topple the government in any country and the Muslim countries, in particular, are having a tough time' (*Dhaka Tribune* 2023). The comment, which followed rising criticisms from the US on democratic backsliding in Bangladesh ahead of 2024 elections, placed Bangladesh in alignment with Muslim countries internationally—as well as with the broader narrative critical of US double-standards in the Global South—while simultaneously discounting claims of democratic backsliding to domestic audiences.

It is worth asking what the most important drivers of popular legitimacy will be for Bangladesh as the country heads into upcoming parliamentary elections. In the more than 50 years since Bangladesh's independence, multiple frameworks of nationalism have played a part in shaping how the country portrays itself to its citizens and to audiences abroad. With eyes on Bangladesh in an election year, national and international narrative building is likely to be front and centre for the Awami League and opposition parties seeking to portray themselves as the true protector and representative of the Bangladeshi state.

Notes

1 Other Muslim-majority countries as of December 1971 included: Afghanistan, Albania, Algeria, Bahrain, Burkina Faso, Chad, Egypt, Gambia, Guinea, Indonesia, Iran, Iraq, Jordan, Kuwait, Lebanon, Libya, Malaysia, Mali, Mauritania, Morocco, Niger, Nigeria, Oman, Pakistan, Saudi Arabia, Senegal, Sierra Leone, Somalia, Sudan, Syria, Tunisia, Turkey, the UAE and Yemen. Census data acquired from: Houssain Kettani, 'Muslim Population in Africa: 1950–2020,' *International Journal of Environmental Science and Development* 1, no 2 (June 2010); Kettani, 'Muslim Population in Asia: 1950–2020,' *International Journal of Environmental Science and Development* 1, no 2 (June 2010); Kettani, 'Muslim Population in Europe: 1950–2020,' *International Journal of Environmental Science and Development* 1, no 2, (June 2010) and ARDA, The Association of Religious Data Archives, https://www.thearda.com/.

2 See Article 2A, 'Bangladesh's Constitution.'

References

'2008 Country Reports on Human Rights: Bangladesh'. US Department of State, Bureau of Democracy, Human Rights and Labor, February 25, 2009. https://2009-2017.state.gov/j/drl/rls/hrrpt/2008/sca/119132.htm.

'Address by Sheikh Mujibur Rahman, Prime Minister of Bangladesh'. United Nations General Assembly, 29th Session, New York, September 25, 1974. https://bdun.org/wp-content/uploads/2020/03/Bangabandhu_speech_on_September_25_1974_at_the_UNGA_in_English.pdf.

Ahmed, K.A. 'As Bangladesh Turns 50, Its Ongoing Battle for Secularism Deserves Great Attention – and Praise'. *Scroll.in*, April 11, 2021. https://scroll.in/article/991937/as-bangladesh-turns-50-its-ongoing-battle-for-secularism-deserves-greater-attention-and-praise.

Ahmed, I. and S. Liton. 'Nixon Was Advised to Recognise Bangladesh'. *The Daily Star*, March 24, 2016. https://www.thedailystar.net/frontpage/nixon-was-advised-recognise-bangladesh-1198774.

Aiyar, S. 'Fazlul Huq, Region and Religion in Bengal: The Forgotten Alternative of 1940 –43'. *Modern Asian Studies* 42, no. 6, (November 2008): 1214–1215.

Al-Haj, T. 'UN Official Praises Saudi Role in Rohingya Relief Efforts'. *Alarabiya News*, October 27, 2017. https://english.alarabiya.net/features/2017/10/27/As-Rohingya-crisis-prolongs-gap-between-needs-and-response-deepens.

Bahree, M. 'Islamic Bank: Bangladesh's Most Watched Bankers'. *Forbes*, July 5, 2016. https://www.forbes.com/sites/meghabahree/2016/07/05/islami-bank-bangladeshs-most-watched-bankers/?sh=40718215611d.

Bangladesh Awami League. 'Election Manifesto of Bangladesh Awami League, 9th Parliamentary Election, 2008'. News Article. October 1, 2013. https://www.albd.org/articles/news/31125/Election-Manifesto-of-Bangladesh-Awami-League,-9th-Parliamentary-Election,-2008.

'Bangladesh's Constitution of 1972, Reinstated in 1986, with Amendments Through 2014'. Constitute Project, 2021. https://www.constituteproject.org/constitution/Bangladesh_2014.pdf?lang=en.

'Bangladesh: Crackdown on Political Opposition'. Human Rights Watch, October 10, 2022. https://www.hrw.org/news/2022/10/10/bangladesh-crackdown-political-opposition.

'Bangladesh PM Urges Muslim Nations to Stand Firm by Palestinians'. *New Age Bangladesh*, January 31, 2023. https://www.newagebd.net/article/193180/bangladesh-pm-urges-muslim-nations-to-stand-firm-by-palestinians.

'Bangladesh Secures $4.7 Bln from IMF as Other South Asian Countries See Delay'. Reuters, January 31, 2023. https://www.reuters.com/world/asia-pacific/imf-board-approves-47-bln-support-program-bangladesh-2023-01-30/.

'Bangladesh Won't Accept US Recognition of Jerusalem as Israeli Capital: Hasina'. bdnews24, December 17, 2017. https://bdnews24.com/bangladesh/2017/12/07/bangladesh-wont-accept-us-recognition-of-jerusalem-as-israeli-capital-hasina.

Basu, K. 'Why is Bangladesh Booming?' Brookings Institute, May 1, 2018. https://www.brookings.edu/opinions/why-is-bangladesh-booming/.

Bergman, D. 'As Bangladesh Court Reaffirms Islam as State Religion, Secularism Hangs on to a Contradiction'. *Scroll.in*, April 2, 2016. https://scroll.in/article/805988/as-bangladesh-court-reaffirms-islam-as-state-religion-secularism-hangs-on-to-a-contradiction.

Beschloss, A.M. and S. Hasina. 'A Conversation with Prime Minister Sheikh Hasina of Bangladesh'. Council on Foreign Relations, September 25, 2019. https://www.cfr.org/event/conversation-prime-minister-sheikh-hasina-bangladesh

Bhattacharjee, J. 'A New Party by Jamaat-e-Islami Reformists in Bangladesh'. Observer Research Foundation, May 11, 2020. https://www.orfonline.org/expert-speak/a-new-party-by-jamaat-e-islami-reformists-in-bangladesh-65961/.

Bhuiyan, H.K. 'Bangladeshi Troops Won't Engage Militarily in Saudi Arabia'. *Dhaka Tribune*. February 14, 2019. https://www.dhakatribune.com/bangladesh/military-affairs/2019/02/14/bangladeshi-troops-won-t-engage-militarily-in-saudi-arabia.

Bhuiyan, M.J.H. 'The Contested Concept of Secularism in Bangladesh'. *The American Journal of Comparative Law* 69, no. 3, (September 2021): 399–448. https://doi.org/10.1093/ajcl/avab014.

'BNP, Jamaat Joined Hands with Israel To Oust Govt: PM'. *The Daily Star*, May 18, 2016. https://www.thedailystar.net/politics/bnp-jamaat-join-hands-israel-oust-govt-pm-1225783.

Bose, N. 'Purba Pakistan Zindabad: Bengali Visions of Pakistan, 1940–1947'. *Modern Asian Studies* 48, no. 1, (January 2014): 1–36.

'Brief History of D-8'. D-8 Organisation for Economic Cooperation. https://developing8.org/about-d-8/brief-history-of-d-8/.

Chaudhury, D.R. 'Bangladesh PM Sheikh Hasina Warns Radicals in Wake of Taliban Takeover'. *The Economic Times*, August 24, 2021. https://economictimes.indiatimes.com/news/international/world-news/hasina-warns-radicals-in-wake-of-taliban-takeover/articleshow/85572877.cms.

Chowdhury, U. 'Why Bangladesh Should, Belatedly, Recognize Israel'. *Hareetz*, May 12, 2020. https://www.haaretz.com/israel-news/.premium-why-bangladesh-should-belatedly-recognize-israel-1.8834838.

———. 'Bangladesh and the First Gulf War'. *Dhaka Tribune*, October 24, 2020. https://www.dhakatribune.com/opinion/op-ed/2020/10/24/op-ed-bangladesh-and-the-first-gulf-war.

'Co-Chairs Urge Stay of Execution in Bangladesh Case for Lack of Due Process'. Human Rights Commission United States Congress, May 6, 2016. https://humanrightscommission.house.gov/news/press-releases/co-chairs-urge-stay-execution-bangladesh-case-failing-due-process-standards.

Colakoğlu, S. 'Turkey-Bangladesh Relations: A Growing Partnership between Two Friendly Nations'. Middle East Institute, June 25, 2019. https://www.mei.edu/publications/turkey-bangladesh-relations-growing-partnership-between-two-friendly-nations.

Devarajan, S. 'Success Despite the Odds: South Sudan and Bangladesh'. Brookings Institute, January 14, 2022. https://www.brookings.edu/blog/

future-development/2022/01/14/success-despite-the-odds-south-sudan-and-bangladesh/.

'Dhaka Backs Saudi Efforts in Yemen'. *The Daily Star*, March 21, 2015. https://www.thedailystar.net/backpage/dhaka-backs-saudi-efforts-yemen-74714.

'Economic Crisis Is Not War Driven'. *The Daily Star*, December 4, 2022. https://www.thedailystar.net/news/bangladesh/news/economic-crisis-not-war-driven-3186636.

Feroze, S. 'Exclusive Interview of Algerian Ambassador to Bangladesh'. *The Daily Observer*, March 22, 2021. https://www.observerbd.com/news.php?id=304712.

'Final Communique of the 14th Islamic Summit Conference'. May 31, 2019, https://www.oic-oci.org/docdown/?docID=4496&refID=1251.

Gandhi, S. 'The Tilt: The U.S. and the South Asian Crisis of 1971: National Security Archive Electronic Briefing Book No. 79'. The National Security Archive, 2002. https://nsarchive2.gwu.edu/NSAEBB/NSAEBB79/.

Habib, H. 'Bangladesh: Restoring Secular Constitution'. *The Hindu*, June 25, 2011. https://www.thehindu.com/opinion/lead/bangladesh-restoring-secular-constitution/article2132333.ece.

Härdig, A.C. and T. Sajjad. 'Between the Secular and the Sacred: The Changing Role of Political Islam in Bangladesh'. Woodrow Wilson International Center, Washington DC, 2020.

Hasan, M. *Islam and Politics in Bangladesh: The Followers of Ummah*. Singapore: Springer, 2020.

———. 'Can Bangladesh's Election Commission Act To Boost Its Credibility?' *The Diplomat*, March 10, 2023. https://thediplomat.com/2023/03/can-bangladeshs-election-commission-act-to-boost-its-credibility/.

Hasan, M. and G. Macdonald. 'The Persistent Challenge of Extremism in Bangladesh'. United States Institute of Peace, June 23, 2022. https://www.usip.org/publications/2022/06/persistent-challenge-extremism-bangladesh.

Hasan, S. 'Foreign Policy of Bangladesh'. *Pakistan Horizon* 36, no. 4, (1983): 65–80.

Hassan, A.M. 'Communal Cauldron Bubbles over in Bangladesh'. *The Diplomat*, October 19, 2021. https://thediplomat.com/2021/10/communal-cauldron-bubbles-over-in-bangladesh/.

Heir, F.B. 'Religion an American Foreign Policy: Prophetics, Perilous, Inevitable'. Pew Research Center, February 5, 2003. https://www.pewforum.org/2003/02/05/religion-and-american-foreign-policy-prophetic-perilous-inevitable/.

Hossain, I. 'Bangladesh and the Gulf War: Response of a Small State'. *Pakistan Horizon* 50, no. 2 (1997): 39-55.

'IBBL at a Glance'. Islami Bank Bangladesh Limited. https://www.islamibankbd.com/abtIBBL/abtIBBLAtaGlance.php (accessed March 26, 2023).

'India Unhappy with US Tole in Upcoming Bangladesh Polls', *Dhaka Tribune*, December 12, 2023. https://www.dhakatribune.com/bangladesh/foreign-affairs/322843/report-india-unhappy-with-us-role-in-upcoming.

'Iraq War Takes Toll on Bangladesh'. *The Hindustan Times*, March 28, 2003. https://www.hindustantimes.com/world/iraq-war-takes-toll-on-bangladesh/story-INUbiIRKF6teaFvkUVpXML.html.

'Islamic Banking Grows in Bangladesh, No Thanks to the Authorities'. *The Economist*, August 24, 2017. https://www.economist.com/finance-and-economics/2017/08/24/islamic-banking-grows-in-bangladesh-no-thanks-to-the-authorities.

Jones, O.B. *Bangladesh in Eye of the Storm*, 146–186. New Haven: Yale University Press, 2003.

Karim, R. 'The Role of the Arab World in the Liberation War of Bangladesh'. *International Journal of Innovative Science and Research Technology* 4, no. 10 (October 2019). https://papers.ssrn.com/sol3/papers.cfm?abstract_id=3487598.

'Khaleda Denies Existence of Islamic Fundamentalists in Bangladesh'. Zee News, March 16, 2005. https://zeenews.india.com/news/south-asia/khaleda-denies-existence-of-islamic-fundamentalists-in-bangladesh-207084.html.

Litner, B. 'Religious Extremism and Nationalism in Bangladesh'. In *Religious Radicalism and Security in South Asia*, edited by Satu P. Limaye, Robert G. Wirsing, and Mohan Malik, 413–436. Honolulu: Asia-Pacific Center for Security Studies, 2004.

Mahmud, F. 'Bangladesh's Ruling "Secular" Awami League Strengthens Ties with Islamist Parties'. *Asia Time*, December 7, 2018. https://asiatimes.com/2018/12/bangladeshs-ruling-secular-awami-league-strengthens-ties-with-islamist-parties/.

———. 'Why is Bangladesh Protesting France'. *Al Jazeera*, November 5, 2020. https://www.aljazeera.com/news/2020/11/5/what-prompted-the-prolonged-anti-france-protest-in-bangladesh.

———. 'Bangladesh Anger of Fuel Prices Echoes Sri Lanka, Pakistan'. *Nikkei Asia*, August 17, 2022. https://asia.nikkei.com/Politics/Bangladesh-anger-over-fuel-prices-echoes-Sri-Lanka-Pakistan.

Mandal, D. 'Govt, Media, Opposition – Bangladesh Can Teach India How to Handle Hate Crimes'. *The Print*, October 22, 2021. https://theprint.in/opinion/govt-media-opposition-bangladesh-can-teach-india-how-to-handle-hate-crimes/754719/.

Mandaville, P. *Islam and Politics*. New York: Routledge, 2014.

Mandaville, P. and S. Hamid, 'Islam as Statecraft: How Governments Use Religion in Foreign Policy'. Brookings Institute, November 2018. https://www.brookings.edu/research/islam-as-statecraft-how-governments-use-religion-in-foreign-policy/.

Maniruzzam, T. 'The Fall of the Mujib Regime and Its Aftermath'. *Asian Survey* 16, no. 2 (February 1976): 119–129.

'Memorandum of Conversation: Meeting with President Hussain Muhammad Ershad of Bangladesh'. Bush Presidential Library, The White House. October 1, 1990. https://bush41library.tamu.edu/files/memcons-telcons/1990-10-01--Ershad.pdf.

Mohsin, S. 'Why Remove "Except Israel" from Passports?' *The Daily Star*, May 31, 2021. https://www.thedailystar.net/opinion/news/why-remove-except-israel-passports-2101785.

Molavi, A. 'Economic Contraction across the Gulf Chokes the Flow of Remittances to South Asia'. The Arab Gulf States Institute in Washington, May 26, 2020. https://agsiw.org/economic-contraction-across-the-gulf-chokes-the-flow-of-remittances-to-south-asia/.

Mujeri, M.K. and N. Mujeri. *Bangladesh at Fifty Moving Beyond Development Traps*, Palgrave MacMillan, 2020.

Murshid, T.M. 'State, Nation, Identity: The Quest for Legitimacy in Bangladesh'. In *The Post-Colonial States of South Asia: Democracy, Development and Identity*, edited by Amita Shashstri and Jayaratnam Wilson, 158–199. London: Palgrave MacMillan, 2001.

Mushtaq, S.B. 'Qatar-Gulf Crisis: Impact on Bangladesh'. *The Diplomat*, June 27, 2017. https://thediplomat.com/2017/06/qatar-gulf-crisis-impact-on-bangladesh/.

Nafiu, R.M. 'BNP: Removal of "Except Israel" from Passports Exposed Govt's Amoral Position'. *Dhaka Tribune*, May 24, 2021. https://www.dhakatribune.com/bangladesh/2021/05/24/bnp-removal-of-except-israel-from-passports-exposed-govt-s-amoral-position.

Nag, M. 'Bangladesh's Dangerous Islamist Appeasement – and What It Portends'. *The Diplomat*, December 22, 2020. https://thediplomat.com/2020/12/bangladeshs-dangerous-islamist-appeasement-and-what-it-portends/.

'National Survey of Bangladesh, March-April 2023', Center for Insights and Survey Research, A Project of the International Republican Institute, August 8, 2023. https://www.iri.org/news/survey-research-for-bangladesh-2023-dissatisfaction-with-countrys-direction/.

'Pakistanis Boycott Conference in Cairo'. *The New York Times* Archives, January 11, 1972. https://www.nytimes.com/1972/01/11/archives/pakistanis-boycott-conference-in-cairo.html.

Palma, P. 'Bangladesh Sends Mangoes to Asian Friends'. *The Daily Star*, July 5, 2021. https://www.thedailystar.net/news/bangladesh/news/bangladesh-sends-mangoes-asian-friends-2123471.

Paul, R. 'Bangladesh Violence Spreads after Modi's Visit, Attack on Hindu Temples, Train'. Reuters, March 28, 2021.

'PM Hasina invites Saudi Crown Prince Salman to Visit Bangladesh,' *Prothom Alo*, September 10, 2023. https://en.prothomalo.com/bangladesh/pknazaypo2.

'Profile: Common Wealth of Nations—Timeline'. BBC, September 26, 2014. https://www.bbc.com/news/world-africa-16908628.

'Observatory of Economic Complexity'. OEC Bangladesh. https://oec.world/en/profile/country/bgd (accessed June 27, 2021).

Raghavan, S. *1971 A Global History of the Creation of Bangladesh*. Cambridge: Harvard University Press, 2013.

Rahman, A.K.M.A. 'Bangabandhu Built Bangladesh's Relations with the Muslim World'. In *A Special NDC Journal on the Birth Centenary of the Father of the Nation Bangabandhu Sheikh Mujibur Rahman*, 26–34. Dhaka: National Defence College, 2020.

Rahman, T. 'From Revolutionaries to Visionless Parties: Leftist Politics in Bangladesh'. Carnegie Endowment for International Peace, September 6, 2022. https://carnegieendowment.org/2022/09/06/from-revolutionaries-to-visionless-parties-leftist-politics-in-bangladesh-pub-87806.

Ramani, S. 'Here's How the Bangladesh Government Is Making Religious Violence More Likely'. *The Washington Post*, July 21, 2016. https://www.washingtonpost.com/news/monkey-cage/wp/2016/07/21/heres-how-the-bangladesh-government-is-making-religious-violence-more-likely/.

Rashid, H.U. 'Non-Aligned Conference and Bangladesh'. *The Daily Star*, July 13, 2009. https://www.thedailystar.net/news-detail-96760.

Riaz, A. 'Bangladesh: A Tale of Two Systems'. In *Faithful Education: Madrassahs in South Asia*. New Brunswick: Rutgers University Press, 2008.

———. 'Why Bangladesh's Mainstream Parties Rely on Islamists'. *Deutsche Welle*, December 19, 2018. https://www.dw.com/en/why-bangladeshs-mainstream-parties-rely-on-islamists/a-46801270.

———. 'Bangladesh's Economic Crisis: How Did We Get Here'. The Atlantic Council, August 5, 2022a. https://www.atlanticcouncil.org/blogs/southasiasource/bangladeshs-economic-crisis-how-did-we-get-here/.

———. 'Bangladesh's Quiet Slide into Autocracy'. *Foreign Affairs*, April 29, 2022b. https://www.foreignaffairs.com/articles/bangladesh/2022-04-29/bangladeshs-quiet-slide-autocracy.

Sajen, S. 'Bangladesh Prime Minister's Visit to Saudi Arabia: Quest for Enhanced Friendship'. *Saudi Gazette*, December 9, 2018. https://saudigazette.com.sa/article/549829.

———. 'First Arab Recognition for Bangladesh'. *The Daily Star*, July 8, 2022. https://www.thedailystar.net/backpage/news/first-arab-recognition-bangladesh-1926709.

Shawon, A.A. 'June 7, 1966: Six Points Were Bengalis' Charter of Freedom'. *Dhaka Tribune*, June 6, 2020. https://www.dhakatribune.com/bangladesh/2020/06/06/june-7-1966-six-points-were-bengalis-charter-of-freedom.

Siddiqi, D.M. 'Political Culture in Contemporary Bangladesh: Histories Ruptures and Contradictions'. In *Political Islam and Governance and Bangladesh*, 7–26. New York: Routledge, 2010.

Sikdar, M.M. and M.M.H. Shohag. 'Democracy and Authoritarianism: Understanding Three Decades of Bangladesh Politics'. *Research on Humanities and Social Science* 6, no. 24 (2016): 7– 20.

Sumon, S. 'Bangladesh Denies Normalization with Tel Aviv Despite Removing Caveat from Passports'. Arab News, May 24, 2021. https://www.arabnews.com/node/1863571/world.

Sun, L.H. 'Bangladesh Defends Response to Disaster'. *The Washington Post*, May 8, 1991. https://www.washingtonpost.com/archive/politics/1991/05/08/bangladesh-defends-response-to-disaster/f308e501-8708-4b2e-b3a6-33fb90639252/.

'The Government Initiates a Coup at Bangladesh's Biggest Bank'. *The Economist*, April 6, 2017. https://www.economist.com/asia/2017/04/06/the-government-initiates-a-coup-at-bangladeshs-biggest-bank.

'The World Bank in Bangladesh'. World Bank, March 23, 2021. https://www.worldbank.org/en/country/bangladesh/overview.

'Trade Preferential System among the Member States of the OIC'. Organisation of Islamic Cooperation. http://www.comcec.org/en/tps-oic/.

'Turkey Strongly Condemns Execution of Jamaat-e-Islami Leader'. *The Daily Sabah*, May 12, 2016. https://www.dailysabah.com/asia/2016/05/12/turkey-strongly-condemns-execution-of-jamaat-e-islami-leader.

'Turkey Withdraws Bangladesh Ambassador after Execution of Islamist: Erdogan'. Reuters, May 12, 2016. https://www.reuters.com/article/us-turkey-bangladesh/turkey-withdraws-bangladesh-ambassador-after-execution-of-islamist-erdogan-idUSKCN0Y311M.

Titumir, R.A.M. *Numbers and Narratives in Bangladesh's Economic Development*. Palgrave MacMillan (ebook), 2021.

Tolany, A. 'Here's What the Murder of Mohsen Fakhrizadeh Could Mean for Iran and Pakistan'. *South Asian Voices*, December 9, 2020. https://southasianvoices.org/heres-what-the-murder-of-mohsen-fakhrizadeh-could-mean-for-iran-and-pakistan/.

Uddin, A. 'Politics of Secularism and the State of Religious Pluralism in Bangladesh'. *Journal of South Asian and Middle Eastern Studies*, (Spring 2015): 42–54.

Uddin, S.M. *Constructing Bangladesh: Religion, Ethnicity, and Language in an Islamic Nation*, 140. Chapel Hill: The University of North Caroline Press, 2006.

Ullah, A. 'Rohingya Fear Deportation after Saudi Arabia Calls on Bangladesh to Give Minority Passports'. *Middle East Eye*, October 14, 2020. https://www.middleeasteye.net/news/saudi-arabia-rohingya-bangladesh-deportation-passports.

Vaughn, B. 'Bangladesh: Background and U.S. Relations'. Congressional Research Services, September 7, 2006. https://www.everycrsreport.com/files/20060907_RL33646_9d9a57ec2d092b5c841fa8a9e4b8c9170d92fa34.pdf.

———. 'Islamist Extremism in Bangladesh'. Congressional Research Services, January 31, 2017. https://fas.org/sgp/crs/row/RS22591.pdf.

Weinraub, B. 'Pakistan Admits That Bangladesh Exists as a Nation'. *The New York Times*, February 23, 1974. https://www.nytimes.com/1974/02/23/archives/pakistan-admits-that-bangladesh-exists-as-nation-prime-minister.html.

Wohab, A. '"Secularism" or "No-Secularism": A Complex Case of Bangladesh'. *Cogent Social Sciences* 1, (November 2021). DOI: 10.1080/23311886.2021.1928979.

'"Yes" To Mujib'. *The Straits Times*, February 26, 1972. Newspapers SG Archive, Reel Number NL06967, accessed June 5, 2021. https://eresources.nlb.gov.sg/newspapers/Digitised/Article/straitstimes19720226-1.2.67.1.

Zaman, S.S. 'Dhaka Wants Stronger Defence Ties with Riyadh'. *Dhaka Tribune*, May 18, 2018. https://www.dhakatribune.com/bangladesh/foreign-affairs/2018/05/18/dhaka-wants-stronger-defence-ties-with-riyadh.

Zarif, M.M. 'Recognition, as Equals'. *The Daily Star*, March 17, 2020. https://www.thedailystar.net/opinion/news/recognition-equals-1881703.

3

CONSTRUCTION AND RECONSTRUCTION OF IDENTITY OF THE BANGLADESHI DIASPORA IN THE UK AND THE US

Ali Riaz

The voluntary migration of people from the land now known as Bangladesh has a long history, but it accelerated in the 1980s, in the second decade of the country's independence, as both short-term labour migrants and long-term immigrants moved to various countries in relatively large numbers and continued to do so through subsequent decades. The independence of Bangladesh in 1971 and the growing number of migrants beginning in the 1980s shaped the size and nature of the Bangladeshi immigrant community in various countries, especially in Western countries such as the UK and the US. The Bangladeshi migrant community has become part of the host community but like other immigrant communities, it continues to maintain a distinct identity. The identity, however, has not remained constant but changed over time. This chapter attempts to map the formation and transformation of the self-identification of Bangladeshis in the host countries, particularly in the UK and the US.

I argue that the Bangladeshi community has undergone perceptual shifts in their identification with the 'home' and the 'host' countries. These perceptual shifts have contributed to the construction and reconstruction of various identities. It is neither unusual nor unexpected that an immigrant community would undergo a transformation regarding their identity; it is not unique to Bangladeshis living abroad, as other communities have displayed such a tendency. Continuous and perpetual negotiations between the migrant's current spatial location and relationship with the host country shapes these identities. As such, various identities are constructed and reconstructed over time. The processes of construction and reconstruction are a conscious decision and results of a social process of how others (which includes not only the host community but also other migrants) view them.

In the case of the Bangladeshi diaspora, the transformation, especially as the marker of identity, has followed a particular trajectory.

In the early stage of their migration, the group identity was based on their culture, that is, common language, heritage, rituals, practices and solidarity groupings. As is the case with any migrant community, culture served as the context of and gave rise to a particular identity. But the expansion of community and generational variation brings changes to culture and paves the way for identities to diverge from cultural contexts, which gives rise to the idea of identity in the first place (Riaz 2014). This change creates a 'diasporic identity', a phenomenon easily discernible in any immigrant community. The diasporic identity, in turn, gives rise to a hyphenated identity of the community—and this was palpable among the Bangladeshi diaspora with the rise of Bangladeshi-American/British-Bangladeshi identities. But subsequently, a sizable segment of the community not only transcended the 'traditional' cultural identity, but their marker of identity transcended their host country's 'geography-bound' national identity as well. They embraced a globalised identity based on religion. The transformation from an ethnicity-based identity to a religion-based identity has been mediated through the diasporic identity.

This chapter shows the pathway of identity reconstruction of the Bangladeshi diaspora, the milestones of this process and the factors which played significant roles in this process over the past five decades. It uses the UK and US as case studies, with the UK having largest number of Bangladeshi migrants, and the US seeing considerable growth in Bangladeshis since the 1990s. However, it should be noted that these are not the only two countries where they have migrated.

The Diasporic Identity

Comprehending the diasporic identity requires a clarification of what is meant by 'diaspora'. The concept has gained salience in recent decades, as globalisation has become the defining feature of our time, creating a web of movement and various forms of migration. Besides, various disciplines have utilised it to explain the mindset and roles in society of those located away from their ancestral homeland. In its most rudimentary understanding, the term refers to a community located outside its home; there is an implicit assertion that the community members have been displaced. Some have argued that 'the notion of diaspora rests on three co-ordinates: homeland, displacement and settlement. In other words, a diaspora is constituted when communities of settlers articulate themselves in terms of displacement from a homeland' (Sayyid 2000). I argue that migration, while necessary, does not inevitably create a diaspora community and contribute to a diasporic identity. Instead, for a diaspora to emerge, specific processes of mobilisation must take place. De-territorialisation remains the indispensable condition for the construction of diaspora in the common understanding of the concept; both physical space and the psychological state of the community are vital elements in understanding the diasporic identity.

In dominant discussions on diaspora, settlement or the eventual return to the 'homeland' feature prominently. But this element has increasingly become problematic too; because for many migrant communities, the return to the homeland in a physical sense is neither a practical option nor even a dream. This is partly due to the expansion of the families but also partly due to the realisation that the homeland has changed. A key factor in this regard has to do with one aspect of globalisation: communication. Thanks to new communication technologies such as the internet and satellite television, the homeland is now easily accessible, virtual as it may be, to those who live far away.

The primacy of space and reified notions of belonging and the 'roots' of migrants in places of origin have been underscored in existing discussions on diasporic identity. The relationship between these two (homeland and diaspora) are projected and understood as inseparable and simplistic. Andre Levy has criticised this uncomplicated pairing, calling it the 'solar system model' (Levy 2005). In his formulation, the 'home' remains a symbolic centre rather than a place to return to. I contend that in understanding the identity formation and changes of the Bangladeshi community outside Bangladesh in the past decades, a simplistic unidirectional relationship with the 'homeland' should be avoided. Instead, we need to adopt Stuart Hall's framework: 'Diaspora does not refer to those scattered tribes whose identity can only be secured in relation to some sacred homeland to which they must return at all costs' (Hall 1997).

The Bangladeshi diaspora, whether in the UK or the US, continuously negotiates its current location (space) and their relationship with the host society and their 'homeland'. As the community no longer subscribes to the 'myth of return'/an ideology of return, the homeland has now taken a new meaning akin to what Andre Levy and Alex Weingrod described as 'center':

> [Centers] are places where immigrants and their descendants formerly lived, or a purported place of identification … and towards which they develop positive memories and a personal attachment… What mainly differentiates between [Homelands and Centers] is the moral requirement to Return: Centers are places where one might visit and enjoy, but they are not conceived of as the Ancient Home where one should Return and where one truly belongs. (Levy 2005, 69)

Such a process allows them to, in the words of Hall, constantly produce and reproduce themselves anew through transformation and differences. This has been the case of the Bangladeshi diaspora.

We should also acknowledge identity formation as a dynamic process and that 'the fully, unified, completed, secure, and coherent identity is a fantasy' (Hall 1992). In agreement with Amartya Sen, I am also of the opinion that, in our daily lives, we live with multiple identities. Sen argues that having these multiple identities simultaneously, some based on religion, some based on ethnicity, does not assign any one particular identity to an individual. Sen insists that multiplicity of identities does not create any contradiction. He noted that 'Given our inescapably plural identities, we have to decide on the relative importance of our different associations and affiliations in any particular context' (Sen 2006).

Based on this framework, I will demonstrate that in the past decades, the Bangladeshi diaspora community has undergone the process of a perceptual shift from an ethnicity-based identity to a religiously informed identity.

Community Formation and Group Identity

Migration is a lonely process where an individual or, at best, a family moves to a new land with hopes and dreams, whether it is economic opportunity or to build a different life. They face a challenge of settlement, particularly if the host country has a smaller community of migrants from the same country. But over time, migrants build a community. Community building and attaining a group identity have a symbiotic relationship, where one influences the other. It has been equally true for Bangladeshis migrating to the UK and the US.

Although the contact between Britain and South Asians, particularly the people from what is Bangladesh, began in the 17th century, sporadic settlements started in the 18th century. In the following century, the settled Bengali population grew but not in great numbers. By the early 1920s, many Bangladeshis who arrived in London as *lascars* (seamen) decided to stay. The number of immigrants was small in the early phases but grew steadily in the post-colonial period and surged in the 1980s.

Community formation began in the 1970s. 'During the 1970s, the first generation of Bangladeshi Muslims was joined by a second generation, and wives and dependents arrived in the 1980s to complete community formation' (Eade 2006). This engendered a perceptual shift among male migrants that the place they lived was no longer an alien land but a home, a temporary one and not *the* home, yet a home, nevertheless. Although in their minds, the image of home remained, the place where they lived before and one that they longed for, and where they would 'eventually' return, the migrants soon began to recognise that until that moment arrived, they were 'here'. This perceptual shift on the part of the male members of the community brought about an underlying alteration in their relationships with their fellow migrants and society. This was the first step in the process of creating a distinct group identity. Community formation entailed the emergence of three interrelated supportive social networks: networks of a neighbourhood, marriage networks and religious and cultural networks (Brown 2006; Gardner and Shuker 1994). These interconnected networks, especially since most migrants came from a particular region of Bangladesh (i.e. Sylhet), enabled them to reproduce socio-religious ethos, practices and identity.

Throughout the 1970s and 1980s, a slow process of chain migration (marriage and kinship), the arrival of new migrants (for education, employment and business) and the expansion of catering businesses (creating job opportunities) paved the way for the formation and consolidation of the Bangladeshi diaspora community in Britain. The community became more diverse and increased in size as people from other parts of Bangladesh arrived and families grew. The expansion of the community created various kinds of organisations and the dynamics changed.

It is equally notable that before 1970, there was a presence of a different group of people from then East Pakistan, primarily students at various universities in Britain. They were studying a wide range of disciplines, although students of law were quite significant. Some of them were engaged with the larger community while many were not. The number of these students was small. A bridge between these two groups was established in 1971 when the independence war started in Bangladesh and support for the movement brought a majority of the community together.

The beginning of the Bangladeshi diaspora community formation in the US has been somewhat similar to Britain in the sense that one of the main strands of migration began with the seamen who jumped the ships (Bald 2015). Unlike Britain, however, this was largely a 20th-century phenomenon and took place in the shadow of the Immigration Act of 1917 and its predecessor, the Chinese Exclusion Act of 1882; these laws prohibited immigration from South and Southeast Asia and the Pacific, thus making these new immigrants completely invisible within the community. However, like those in Britain, some of these seamen in the US married local women; in the case of Britain, they were English or Irish (Adams 1988, 48), in the case of the US, they were predominantly African American or Puerto Rican women, owing to strict segregation (Bald 2015).

The community formation, however, can be traced back to the mid-1960s. Shafiqur Rahman points to two stages of Bangladeshi diaspora community formation in the US: post-1965 and post-1990. Rahman writes, 'The small number of students from East Pakistan (now Bangladesh), who arrived after 1965, are generally considered the founders of the Bangladeshi diaspora, which later expanded greatly by new arrivals under various US immigration programs (Opportunity Visa and Diversity Visa) in the 1990s' (Rahman 2011). The first generation of immigrants, that is, those who arrived in the 1960s, lived in various parts of the country and were least connected to each other. Those in New York and the vicinity (for example, New Jersey) formed smaller organisations but others were far less connected to the ethnic/national groups. Rahman identified these immigrants as mostly students who stayed after completion of their degrees. But the composition of the Bangladeshi community changed afterwards, especially in the 1980s. Almost 90% of the members of the community were professionals and were engaged in various jobs. Rahman noted that the composition changed dramatically after 1992, when various lottery visas were introduced and 'low skilled and less educated people began to arrive'. (Rahman 2011, 31)

As these new Bangladeshi immigrants 'settled in large cities where other Bangladeshis were already concentrated', the geographical proximity unleashed new community dynamics (Rahman 2011, 32). There is no denying that geographical concentration helped new immigrants cope with adverse situations and helped to tap into the social capital. But it also contributed to spatial segregation. In the case of Britain, it is well documented that spatial segregation leads to a situation where white and minority ethnic communities live 'parallel lives' that do not intersect at any point; Bangladeshis are the most conspicuous example of this. They live in areas described as the most deprived in the UK. This not only has immediate health and opportunity issues but also significantly impacts life chances and upward mobility. It has been concluded that 'in relation to the occupational returns to education, living in ethnically-segregated residential areas tends to have a negative impact upon the employment prospects and occupational returns to education among Bangladeshis in the UK' (Khattab et al. 2010). In the US, although there have not been such studies regarding Bangladeshis, studies have shown similar impacts on the African American community.

What is pertinent for our discussion on identity is that such segregation impacted the social fabric of the Bangladeshis, their worldview and their political activism. Most importantly, the spatial aspect seriously affects the self-perception of Bangladeshis and outsiders' views of the community. It is true that these features do not impact all members of the community equally; impacts vary by age, gender, and profession.

Bangladesh's independence war in 1971 significantly contributed to bringing the community together in the UK and the US. This is not to say that all of those who migrated from then East Pakistan lent support to the cause of Bangladesh, but a large segment came together and transcended class and other social differences. The somewhat homogeneity of the community, regarding their social strata, made it far easier; in Britain, the community was larger and their actions became more visible than that of the Bengali diaspora in the US. Geography played a part too. As the community in Britain was concentrated in London, it was easier for them to congregate, while the fragmented nature of the Bengali community in the US made it difficult. Nevertheless, a group identity based on their ethnicity became the defining feature.

From Identity to Identities: Perceptual Shifts and Activism

In the 1970s, especially until the mid-1970s, the Bangladeshis in Britain were organised along ethnic lines and welfare societies were created by members of the Bangladeshi community. These organisations, particularly the Pakistan Welfare Organization, were established in the 1950s and continued to serve under the changed reality after the emergence of Bangladesh under the new name, Bangladesh Welfare Organization. The goals of the organisations included providing welfare support, keeping the community together and working with local governments to expand social services. Considering that most Bangladeshi migrants came from the Sylhet district, some of these organisations blended their identity of their home country's region and their need for support in the host country. These organisations did not highlight any other identity and were not viewed by the members as the vehicle for establishing their group identity. Therefore, in essence, these organisations were secular in nature. Their presence was limited within their own community and remained invisible to the host country's community at large. The community was 'cohesive yet confined' (Barton 1986).

But the situation took a turn in the mid-1970s as racism in Britain rose with the tacit support of the Conservative Party, particularly its policies about immigration. Throughout the mid-1970s, members of the Asian community, including the Bengali population, faced not only spatial segregation but also racial discrimination and rampant racist attacks and harassment from various strata of society. The emerging National Front, a white supremacist organisation, orchestrated attacks on members of the Asian community almost daily. These attacks, particularly the brutal murders of Ishaq Ali and Altab Ali in 1978, engendered three significant changes within the Bengali community, which had implications for group identity. Firstly, there was a realisation among the Bangladeshi-origin youth that the existing community organisations, such as the Bangladesh Welfare Organization, were neither prepared nor willing to transcend the age-old identity and take a more prominent role in protecting the community. Thus, a fracture emerged between the old members of the community and the younger generation. The latter went on to establish new organisations such as the Bangladesh Youth League (BYL), the Bangladesh Youth Movement (BYM), the Bangladesh Youth Association (BYA), Bangladesh Youth Front (BYF), Bangladesh Youth Approach (BYA) and Progressive Youth Organization (PYO), to name but a few. Subsequently, the Federation of Bangladeshi Youth Organisations (FBYO) was established.

Secondly, the community, particularly the younger population, joined the larger anti-racist movement spearheaded by the Asian Youth Movement (AYM) and similar anti-racist organisations. Although the Bengali population was aware that they were being targeted, they consciously decided to merge within a larger community of resistance—which included Black and other Asian communities. This was a clear departure from an insular community-based identity and the adoption of a different group identity.

Thirdly, it imparted a sense of British identity. According to Caroline Adams, it was a part of the coming of age of the Bangladeshis (Adams 1988). As narrated by Suroth Ahmed (Faruk), a community activist, it was a time of change in the mindset of the Bangladeshi immigrants: 'The killing of Altab Ali gave the voice to the Bengali people that we are here to stay and to live…. Many people had a mindset, that we are here to earn and go back to Bangladesh, but the mindset was changed after Altab Ali's killing. We decided to establish ourselves in Britain' (Trialbyjeory 2013).

This was the second perceptual shift of community identity. Despite this shift, the foundation of identity was rooted in ethnic identity as the community organisations continued to organise events that were part of Bengali culture, irrespective of religion. It should also be noted that not all members of the community adopted the new kinds of identity; the generational difference was easily discernible—the older generation was more comfortable in their insular community while the younger ones were embracing a newer identity. Besides, there were other ways of redefining community identity, religion being one. Among the youth, a pan-Islamic organisation, the Federation of Students' Islamic Societies (FOSIS, established in 1962), had some influence, and so did the Islamic Youth Movement (IYM). Among the older generation, it was the ethos of their home country, which included traditions of Sufis, saints and shrines, that had appeal. These were distinctly different from other Muslim communities.

As such, in the late 1970s and early 1980s, the Bengali diaspora community in Britain was adopting various identities with contestations among these identities palpable. Moreover, these were not passive identities but also a source of activism. The anti-racism movement, which brought together various minority communities, dissipated in the late-1980s. This left the younger generation bereft of a multi-community platform and very little organised form to express their discontent and despair.

During the same period, Bangladeshis in the US were treading a different path. On the one hand, the Bangladeshi associations were gaining ground while on the other hand, the members of the community were pursuing the American Dream, personal endeavours to achieve professional and personal successes. The Bangladeshi organisations were more focused on cultural activities than using these as a vehicle to be a part of the larger community. Smaller size, lack of spatial proximity of the community members and the composition of the community played distinctly different pathways between those in the UK and the US. The relative invisibility, compared to the Bangladeshis in England, was also because of the absence of any historical contact between the US and Bangladesh. British colonial rule had provided the British-Bangladeshis greater visibility. In Britain, 'Asian' largely meant people of South Asian descent. In contrast, in the US, 'Asian' was used to largely refer to the East Asian communities, particularly the Chinese, for historical reasons. Institutional racism, which was ingrained in the US system, had hindered social and professional mobility. South Asians, including Bangladeshis were not part of the civil rights movements. The members of the Bangladeshi community were hardly present in the southern states of the US to become engaged in the movement. Therefore, although the Bangladeshi community grew after 1971, there was no effort to make their ethnic identity the principal marker of their identity or use it as a source of activism. The situation began to evolve in the 1990s, especially after the composition of the community began to change after new Bangladeshi immigrants started to come to the US under various diversity visas.

Foregrounding Muslim Identity and Contestations

The 1990s saw a remarkable shift in the identity politics of the Bangladeshis in Britain. It was around this time that the Muslim identity gained salience among a section of British-Bangladeshis, especially the younger generation. Studies about the British-Bangladeshi community conducted in the subsequent decade not only bear out this trend but also show a rapid acceleration of such identification.[1] 'More and more young Bengalis now identify themselves first and foremost as Muslims rather than as Bengali or Bangladeshi' (Gardner and Shuker 1994). John Eade's study in 1994, based on interviews with 20 Bengali-speaking youth who were either born in Bangladesh or Britain with Bengali ancestry, showed them wrestling with multiple identities but also revealed the growing inclination towards a Muslim identity (Eade 1994). A female respondent stated in that study that 'if you had to go on a one to ten scale of who you are, what you are, it [goes] Muslim, Bengali and then British and then whatever the things that make me up. If you take the top two away that wouldn't be me. If you take the British bit away, I think that would still be me.' Prioritising Islam over other markers of identity was a key response of several respondents. For example, one respondent said, 'if I was to describe myself, I would say I am British Bengali Muslim, if you like, but my religion is more important to me than my culture at the end of the day.' Another respondent explained that s/he views her primary identity as a Muslim and then his/her national identity as British. However, the respondent did mention that one of his/her identity is based on the Bengali ethnicity.

While each of these youth, in some form or other, acknowledges the existence of several aspects of his/her identity involving ancestry, location and faith, each underscored his/her religious identity as the core element.

I received similar responses in my interactions with youngsters in the summer of 2007 during fieldwork focusing on identity politics of the British-Bangladeshi community. Many youth attending various colleges and universities insisted that Islam is an integral part of their lives. However, some admitted that they are not devout Muslims and do not practice Islam. 'I may not be practising, but how can I deny that I am a Muslim? Islam is my culture,' commented a young male participant in an informal group discussion. Often, they described Bengali as a language they do not speak, although that is their parents' preferred language of communication.

The multiplicity of identities was featured in our discussion, as it was reflected in a comment by a participant who migrated in childhood: 'I don't think I can say I am a Bengali ... [definitely] I am not Bangladeshi, I can describe myself as British, but then my parents are from Bangladesh, perhaps I am Bengali by birth ... but I surely am a Muslim.' Another participant, born and raised in Britain, commented, 'you see, you can be a Bengali and a Muslim; you can be a Bangladeshi and a Muslim; you can be a British and a Muslim; you can be here or there—but you can be Muslim anywhere. That is why you should be Muslim first. That is only things that stays with you all the time.' Justin Gest, in a 2010 study, found similar sentiments among a group of Bangladeshi youth in East End. '"Without Islam, I have no identity," Ebrahim, a student as Queen Mary University, says. "My practice is weak, yeah. I have little time in life for Islam. But it's still my base. When I have nothing else, it'll always be there."' Gest quotes another youth who insists, 'I am a Muslim. Not a Barelwi, Tablighi Jamaat, Salafi, Hanafi or whatever. I'm a Muslim. I'm not British or Bengali. I'm Muslim' (Gest 2010). The statement demonstrates that the respondent deliberately chooses Islam over other potential identities. Ismail, a high school student, says to Gest, 'I don't feel an identity crisis, because I feel like I have a relationship with God and so I don't have any problem saying that I am a Muslim' (Gest 2010).

While the Muslim identity was gaining salience among one section of the members of the community, another section highlighted their ethnic roots, particularly the secular nature of it. The community leaders closely associated with the ethnic Bengali culture intensified their efforts to highlight their Bengali identity by inscribing secular nationalist symbols on public spaces such as Shahid Minar[2] and *shapla* (water lily),[3] by organising Baishakhi Mela,[4] through observance of the Shahid Dibosh,[5] and by demanding that Brick Lane be named Banglatown, to name but a few. Until the mid-1990s, efforts to highlight the secular ethnic symbols were largely uncontested but by the end of the decade, these were criticised as un-Islamic activities, as wasteful spending, as efforts to divert the younger generation from their Islamic duties, as a decadent culture of mixing between male and female and an influence of Hindu traditions.

A wide range of factors was behind the salience of the religious identities which I have described elsewhere (Riaz 2013); these include the relationship between political parties in Bangladesh and the growing influence of Islamist parties and the expedient politics of the perpetrated secular parties, the appeal of Islamist youth groups in the UK—for example, the Young Muslim Organisation (YMO) and the Hizb-ut Tahrir (HT)—the failure of the secular leadership and the irrelevance of the existing welfare organisations. These were matched by the government's welfare policies which encouraged religious identification of community groups, the UK's foreign policy towards Muslim-majority countries, the actions of the government after the publication of Salman Rushdie's *Satanic Verses* in 1988, engagement in the Gulf War in 1991 and 2003.

The appeal of Muslim identity to a segment of community members of the Bangladeshi diaspora in the US grew later, but it was connected to the transformation of the composition of the community and the cultural shift. In the 1990s, as the Bangladeshi community grew, so did its insularity. Kibria described this as 'family-centred transnationalism' (Kibria 2011). That is 'marked by the relative detachment from a local community' while remaining connected to the members of the family in Bangladesh. The availability of media, both locally printed Bengali newspapers and Bangladeshi television channels, has allowed them to connect to the 'home' and replicate the culture (Rahman 2011).

Within this new immigrant community, various contesting ethos cohabited. Some practiced the traditional ethnicity-based secular culture, some remained ambivalent towards religious identity while others embraced it. Various cultural organisations, language and music schools, and a national organisation represented the 'secular' strand. Most of them were Hometown Associations (largely based on the administrative districts in Bangladesh). This was akin to the trend in the UK. Kibria notes that the Bangladeshi diaspora in the US channelled their energies towards building organisations based on interests, such as alumni associations (Kibria 2011). The generational difference also became palpable, as was the case in the UK. Rahman noted that there was an ambivalence among the first-generation Bangladeshi parents regarding adopting religious identity. Yet, they tend to encourage the children to practice Islamic ethos and practice. Their primary rationale was that these practices would help them to remain free from the popular culture, which they considered "bad".

> At the same time, first-generation Bangladeshis show discomfort when their children embrace a revivalist Islam in the transnational context not only because that Islam can slide to an exclusionary and even an extremist version of Islam but also can take their children from the Bangladeshi Islam that they practice. (Rahman 2011)

Religious organisations and newly built mosques represented the third strand. These three strands continue to remain in the social milieu of the Bangladeshi diaspora in the US.

The Role of the Society and the State

Group identity is not entirely a voluntary process, i.e., a group does not decide exclusively on its own volition how it (and its members) wants to be identified. Identities are constructed in two ways—how 'we' want to be seen and how others perceive us. These two meanings are influenced by the social ecosystem within and outside the community, and they involve actors—individuals and the state.

In the case of identity construction and transformation of the Bangladeshi diaspora, society and state have contributed immensely both in the UK and the US. As I have alluded to previously, the immigration policy of the UK in the 1960s shaped the perception of the Bangladeshi, and the welfare policy of the British state in the 1990s underscored religious identification. The most telling indicator of the government's preference for religious groups as opposed to ethnic community organisations was the comment of UK Home Secretary Michael Howard in 1994. He told a Muslim delegation that they should return when they established a unified Muslim organisation to speak with one voice (McLoughlin 2006). Subsequently, those bodies based on faith received more funding than their welfare and social counterparts, leading to their ability to provide more services and expand their reach.

In contrast, the government policy after the 9/11 attacks in the US and during the so-called Global War on Terror (GWOT) made the Muslim community suspect and put under surveillance. The media created a frenzied reaction, portraying immigrants as the 'enemy within'. Diaspora Bangladeshis were facing discrimination and harassment, and increasingly adopted a global identity to be a part of a larger community. The backlash of the GWOT and consequent changes in security policies, notwithstanding UK foreign policy, also contributed to the perceptual shift that emboldened the Islamist groups, broadened their appeal, and helped a segment of the Bangladeshi diaspora to identify themselves as Muslim rather than Bengalis. Their reaction was also a marker of their claim of British citizenship, i.e., they opposed these policies as citizens.

The most significant impact post-9/11 on the immigrant community was evident in the US. Political leaders, government agencies and the media, in large measure, spoke in a manner that not only enhanced Islamophobia but also xenophobia. The relatively invisible Bangladeshi community became visible in media and social discourse as a 'Muslim community' rather than an ethnic group. The new prominence came at a cost; they too became subject to public and media scrutiny and suspicion. Both Kibria and Rahman have extensively discussed how the state-encouraged and society-adopted discourses have put Bangladeshis in a precarious condition. These engendered two responses among the Bangladeshi diaspora. The first was the rejection of the binary of 'either-Muslim-or-American'. The rejection was because Bangladeshis didn't see a contradiction between these two identities. In post-9/11, media and public discourses in the US created narratives wherein Islam and US citizenship were constructed as mutually exclusive categories. Bangladeshis consciously avoided being categorized as Muslim. As one may recall, a perception was propagated that being Muslim implied that they are lesser American, therefore their civil liberties can be curtailed.

The second response was to some extent embrace the religious identity, more than ever before. Because such identity offers them a stable identity and recognition within the multicultural United States. Despite these two ostensibly conflicting responses, one thing became evident 'They want[ed] their Muslim identity recognized but they do not want their religious identity to eclipse their other identities' (Rahman 2011, 19).

Thus, a religion-informed identity found a strong basis among the Bangladeshis diaspora in the US.

Conclusion

The foregoing discussion on the diaspora identity of the Bangladeshis in the UK and the US shows that group identity has undergone significant transformation in the past decades. Group identity is not a homogenous characteristic; various elements, for example age, gender, social status and geography, influence how s/he view themselves, and how they are viewed by others. Material constraints influence their choices as well. In the case of a community, the identity can be doubly imagined/constructed—by those who claim to represent them, through the creation of associations with specific goals, to establish their claim on the available resources, and by the state 'which must reify ethnic segments as perpetual communities in order to control conflict or allocate resources in an "equitable" manner' (Werbner 1991).

Therefore, this discussion is a broad stroke of the processes and characteristics of the community. Besides, in the case of diasporic identity, the transformation does not imply that one is to be replaced with another with complete disavowal/denial/rejection of the previous one; it is not a complete erasure of one and then the inscription of another. Instead, the process of transformation produces fluidity and layered identities. In one sense, the changes mean that individuals move away from 'an ideal construct' to 'a pragmatic acculturation'. Members of a diasporic community, in the words of Stuart Hall, 'must learn to inhabit two identities, to speak two cultural languages, to translate and negotiate between them' (1992). We can go further by saying that they must inhabit multiple identities and speak multiple cultural languages. Bangladeshi diaspora, in this sense, is inhabiting the world of multiplicities.

Notes

1   Examples of such studies include Eade, J., 'Nationalism and the Quest for Authenticity: The Bangladeshis in Tower Hamlets', *New Community*

16, no 4 (1990): 53–68; Eade, J. and D. Garbin, 'Changing Narratives of Violence, Struggle and Resistance: Bangladeshis and the Competition for Resources in the Global City', *Oxford Development Studies* 30, no 2 (2002): 137–149; Glynn, S., 'Bengali Muslims: The New East End Radicals?' *Ethnic and Racial Studies* 25, no 6 (2002): 969–988; Hussain, D., 'Globalization, God and Galloway: The Islamisization of Bangladeshi Communities in London', *Journal of Creative Communications* 2, nos 1&2 (2007): 189–217; Eade, J. and D. Garbin, 'Bangladeshi Diaspora: Community Dynamics, Transnational Politics and Islamic Activities (with a Focus on Tower Hamlets, Oldham and Birmingham)', Report for the Foreign and Commonwealth Office, London, 2003; Gardner, K. and A. Shuker, 'I'm Bengali, I'm Asian, and I'm Living Here', in *Desh Pardesh: The South Asian Presence in Britain*, edited by R. Ballard, 142–164, London: Hurst & Co. 1994.

2   Shahid Minar is a monument to commemorate the martyrs of the Language Movement of 1952. The first permanent replica of the Shahid Minar outside Bangladesh was established in Oldham of England by the local Bengali community in 1996, and then at the East End of London, in a park named after Altab Ali, in 1999.

3   The national icon of Bangladesh. A square with a sculpture of the water lily was established in Oldham in 2000.

4   A public fair to celebrate the Bengali New Year. Although small-scale efforts to organise fairs to celebrate Bengali culture started in the early 1990s, the Baishakhi Mela in its current form began in 1997. It is held on the second weekend of May each year. The programmes include music, dance, and drama performances.

5   Shahid Dibosh—Martyr's Day is observed on 21 February in Bangladesh to commemorate the death of the students killed by police gunfire in 1952 while demanding recognition of Bengali as a state language in Pakistan. The movement is considered the fountainhead of the Bengali nationalist movement and the day is commemorated as a day of remembrance and renewal of commitment to Bengali nationalism

References

Adams C. (ed.). *Across Seven Seas and Thirteen Rivers: Life Stories of Pioneer Sylhetti Settlers in Britain*. London: Tower Hamlets Arts Project, 1988.

Bald, V. *Bengali Harlem and the Lost Histories of South Asian America*. Boston: Harvard University Press, 2015.

Barton, S.W. *The Bengali Muslims of Bradford*. Leeds: Community Relations Project, University of Leeds, 1986.

'Bengali Reflections on the Seventies: We thought the racism was a natural phenomenon.' Trialbyjeory, June 1, 2013. https://trialbyjeory.com/2013/06/01/bengali-reflections-on-the-seventies-we-thought-the-racism-was-a-natural-phenomenon/.

Brown, J. *Global South Asian: Introducing the Modern Diaspora*, 43. Cambridge: Cambridge University Press, 2006.

Eade, J. 'Identity, Nation and Religion: Educated Young Bangladeshi Muslims in London's "East End"'. *International Sociology* 9, no. 3, (1994): 377–394.

———. 'The Brick Lane Test'. *Axess*, no. 2, (February 2006). http://www.axess.se/nglish/2006/02/theme_eade.php.

Gardner, K. and A. Shuker. 'I'm Bengali, I'm Asian, and I'm Living Here'. In *Desh Pardesh: The South Asian Presence in Britain*, edited by R. Ballard, 150, London: Hurst & Co., 1994.

Gest, J. 'Reluctant Pluralists: European Muslims and Essentialist Identity Structures'. Paper presented at Political Studies Association Conference, 2010. http://www.psa.ac.uk/journals/pdf/5/2010/306_1270.pdf (accessed on 15 July 2010).

Hall, S. 'Old and New Identities, Old and New Ethnicities'. In *Culture, Globalisation and the World-System: Contemporary Conditions for the Representation of Identity*, edited by A. King, 31–68. Minneapolis: University of Minnesota Press, 1977.

———. 'The Question of Cultural Identity'. In *Modernity and Its Future*, edited by S. Hall, D. Held, and A. McGrew, 277. Cambridge: Polity Press, 1992.

Khattab, N., R. Johnston, I. Irkeci, and T. Modood. 'The Impact of Spatial Segregation on the Employment Outcomes amongst Bangladeshi Men and Women in England and Wales'. *Sociological Research Online* 15, no. 1, (2010): 3. http://www.socresonline.org.uk/15/1/3.html (accessed on May 15, 2012).

Kibria, N. *Muslims in Motion: Islam and National Identity in the Bangladeshi Diaspora*, 45. New Brunswick, NJ: Rutgers University Press, 2011.

Levy, A. 'A Community That Is Both a Center and a Diaspora: Jews in Late Twentieth Century Morocco'. In *Homelands and Diasporas: Holy Lands and Other Places*, edited by A. Levy and A. Weingrod, 69, Stanford: Stanford University Press, 2005.

McLoughlin, S. 'The State, New Muslim Leaderships, and Islam as a Resource for Public Engagement in Britain'. In *European Muslims and the Secular State*, edited by McLoughlin and J. Cesari, 60, Aldershot: Ashgate Publishing, 2006.

Rahman, S. *The Bangladeshi Diaspora in the United States After 9/11: From Obscurity to High Visibility*, 30. El Paso, Texas: LFB Scholarly, 2011.

Ramamurthy, A. 'The Politics of Britain's Asian Youth Movements'. *Race & Class* 48, no. 2, (2006): 38–60.

Riaz, A. *Islam and Identity Politics among British-Bangladeshis: A Leap of Faith*. Manchester: Manchester University Press, 2013.

———. 'Being Bengali Abroad: Identity Politics among the Bengali Community in Britain'. In *Being Bengali: At Home and in the World*, edited by M.N. Chakraborty, 159–180. London: Routledge, 2014.

Sayyid, S. 'Beyond Westphalia: Nations and Diaspora—the Case of the Muslim *Umma*'. In *Un/Settled Multiculturalisms: Diasporas, Entanglements, Transruptions*, edited by B. Hesse, 37–38. London/New York: Zed Books, 2000.

Sen, A. *Identity and Violence: The Illusion of Destiny*, xii–xiii. London: Penguin, 2006.

Werbner, P. 'Black and Ethnic Leaderships in Britain: A Theoretical Overview'. In *Black and Ethnic Leadership: The Cultural Dimensions of Political Actions*, edited by Werbner and M. Anwar, 21. London: Routledge, 1991.

4

BANGLADESH'S DOMESTIC AND INTERNATIONAL EFFORTS TO ADDRESS CLIMATE CHANGE

Ashley Johnson

Introduction

A confluence of geographical factors makes Bangladesh one of the country's most vulnerable to natural disasters and the impacts of a changing climate. As observed in Germanwatch's recent Climate Risk Index, Bangladesh ranks seventh among the top 10 countries most impacted by extreme weather events between 2000 and 2019, totalling 185 events within that period (Eckstein 2021). Over the past two decades, cyclones alone have caused between $3 and $5 billion in damages (Ozaki 2016).

With 580 kilometres of coastline bordering the Bay of Bengal and more than 150 perennial rivers—the Water Development Board lists a total of 405 rivers, including seasonal flows (Bangladesh Water Development Board 2021)—cyclones and flooding present regular and severe threats. Melting Himalayan glaciers have altered flood patterns and the availability of water resources, with an estimated 22 per cent decrease in cubic meters available per capita in Bangladesh by 2030 (Munirazzaman 2015, 8). Managing the 54 transboundary rivers with India presents additional considerations for data sharing and early warning systems, complicated by the limited number of agreements on river management (Munirazzaman 2015, 10); the Joint Rivers Commission remains an important bilateral agreement for data sharing but is viewed to be largely ineffective (Samaranayake 2018). The Sundarbans have for long been a critical resource for managing coastal flooding and lessening the inland reach of cyclones, particularly as half of the country is only 7 metres above sea level (Ozaki 2016). However, regularly occurring storms, coastal erosion and pollution from agricultural and industrial run-off are contributing to the destruction of the mangrove forests, reducing this natural barrier (Karim 2020).

Adding to these challenges are demographic factors that compound the devastating impacts of natural disasters. Bangladesh is one of the most densely populated countries in the world, with more than 1,000 people per square kilometre. The Intergovernmental Panel on Climate

Change estimated that 27 million people are vulnerable to the fallout of rising sea level by 2050, as there are significant numbers of communities that depend on industries tied to coastal ecosystems to sustain their livelihoods (Olsson et al. 2014). Another 5 per cent of the population lives on the riverine sandbanks, or *chars*, which are regularly eliminated during heavy rain and flooding, forcing relocation (Bangladesh Climate Change Resilience Fund 2014). As coastal and riverine communities repeatedly lose their primary sources of income and have to rebuild, many citizens, predominantly men, are relocating to urban areas for better economic prospects, it is estimated that nearly 4,00,000 move to Dhaka each year alone (World Bank Office 2007). Women and children are often then left behind, and in many cases have minimal skills, resources or support, making them more vulnerable to climate disasters, disease and poverty.

As a result, climate adaptation has long been a critical policy priority for both urban and rural policymakers and has established a deep foundation of local expertise on resiliency and recovery efforts that serve as best practices and lessons learned for others seeking to manage the impact of natural disasters. Yet the costs of preparation, response and rebuilding are high. Bangladesh still ranks among the least-developed countries (although with a recent recommendation for graduation by the Committee for Development Policy of the UN), which limits the scale of domestic financing that can be earmarked for disaster management and climate resiliency (UN Department of Economic and Social Affairs 2021). To address the issues at stake outlined above, partnerships with development organisations and other invested countries are necessary to finance strategies for climate resiliency.

This chapter considers these challenges through the lens of domestic strategies, policies and plans enacted or proposed for mitigation of and adaptation to climate change. It then assesses select past and current partnerships that have been instrumental in Bangladesh's progress to implement these efforts and how the country is using its own knowledge and resources to aid other vulnerable states in South Asia and the broader Indo-Pacific region. Finally, it outlines a few recommendations to continue strengthening existing areas of cooperation and build out new opportunities.

Domestic Strategies to Address Climate Change

Action on climate change falls into two primary categories: mitigation and adaptation. Mitigation is proactive, working to reduce and prevent the negative impacts caused by the increasing levels of greenhouse gases and climate change. Adaptation is more responsive, altering patterns of behaviour to accommodate changes in natural habitats or resource availability. Many policies for mitigation and adaptation overlap—planting trees can be a carbon sink to reduce greenhouse gas (GHG) emissions and a natural barrier to floods by reducing run-off, as a simple example.

However, in the discussions held at the Conference of Parties, the decision-making body of the UN's Framework Convention on Climate Change (UNFCCC), and other international fora, much of the responsibilities for mitigation are aimed at more developed countries. These economies were able to develop with few restrictions on how they powered their growth, and as a result, relied heavily on more accessible or cost-effective fossil fuels with dire environmental consequences. It is important to consider the need for developed countries to do their 'fair share' and to aid developing countries in obtaining and deploying clean energy technologies to ensure that they can both meet the basic needs of their citizens but also sidestep the errs of past development trajectories (Adhikari 2021). It is through this lens that Bangladesh's domestic efforts must be considered.

Mitigation

Despite being among the most vulnerable to the impacts of climate change, Bangladesh contributes less than 0.35 per cent of global GHG emissions (Ministry of Environment, Forest and Climate Change 2020, 1). However, national policymakers have still outlined strategies to aid global efforts to limit GHGs. The updated Nationally Determined Contribution (NDC) submitted in December 2020 re-emphasises Bangladesh's unconditional commitment to reduce GHGs by 5 per cent of business-as-usual (BAU) levels in across the three main energy subsectors—power, fuel and electricity use in industrial processes, and transport—by 2030, or 12 metric tons of oil equivalent of carbon dioxide (Ministry of Environment, Forest and Climate Change 2020, 7). It also committed to expand this target economy wide, to also include sectors such as agriculture and cement production. Although this is comparatively minor when viewed alongside the commitments of larger economies, it can be considered proportionally appropriate given Bangladesh's overall contributions and status as a growing economy.

With international support, the targeted emissions reduction triples, and both the unconditional and conditional commitments may increase if certain standards are still met for domestic prosperity and well-being.[1] In addition to this overarching goal, the NDC outlines further targets within specific sectors, including a 9 per cent reduction in BAU emissions in the transportation sector and a 21 per cent reduction in energy consumption per unit of GDP in all sectors by 2030 (Ministry of Environment, Forest and Climate Change 2020, 8).

Energy and Power Mix

Critical to reducing GHG emissions is assessing Bangladesh's national energy mix. Natural gas makes up approximately 55 per cent of total energy supply (International Energy Agency 2021), a rate which increases to more than two-thirds when looking only at the power sector (Energy Futures Initiative 2021, 53). This is largely due to the available domestic supply of natural gas, of which production was estimated to be 2,754 million cubic feet per day in 2017 by the Ministry of Power, Energy and Mineral Resources (Lu et al. 2017). It is also estimated that there could be 34 trillion cubic feet of untapped gas supply.

Coal plays a significant role in the energy and power mix as well, although to a lesser extent than some other countries in South Asia. There have been plans to significantly increase the use of coal in Bangladesh's energy mix, with capacity of coal-fired power plants increasing more than four times to 1.1 gigawatts between 2017 and 2019, which have raised concerns among climate-focused organisations (Enerdata 2021). The June 2021 announcement by the government that it would eliminate plans for 10 coal-fired power plants, including a 1,320-megawatt plant on Moheshkhali Island, was seen as an important step with consideration to achieving the NDC. However, questions remain if the move was sufficient (*Business Standard* 2021).

Despite dependence on fossil fuels, there are important efforts to expand the role of renewable energy. Nearly one-third of the primary energy supply comes from renewable sources; however, it is almost entirely made up of biomass (International Renewable Energy Agency 2021). Biomass presents numerous concerns for indoor air pollution, which is estimated to result in 49,000 premature deaths each year in Bangladesh and has resulted in large programmes to improve cooking stoves. Hydropower has increased in the past several years but ensuring continuous water flow amid increased flooding and droughts will inhibit the ability to use hydropower as a reliable, baseload source of electricity. Policy plans to increase solar power penetration have also been a primary focus; the government aims to generate 2,000 megawatts of electricity through utility scale and solar home systems (SHS) by 2030 (Ministry of Environment, Forest and Climate Change 2020, 8), a goal on which some progress has been made; there are nearly six million SHSs in Bangladesh, providing power to about 11 per cent of the population (Ministry of Environment, Forest and Climate Change 2020, 7). Development organisations and the private sector are also active in this space; Grameen Shakti developed microcredit lending and other microfinance plans to help install 1.8 million SHSs (Elahi 2021).

Adaptation

Guiding the majority of Bangladesh's efforts on adaptation is the Bangladesh Climate Change Strategy and Action Plan (BCCSAP) 2009, which covers six key areas pertaining to both mitigation and adaptation to climate change (Ministry of Environment, Forest and Climate Change 2009). The BCCSAP was catalysed by the National Adaptation Plan (NAP), which has been in development for over 15 years, beginning with the National Adaptation Programme of Action in 2005 as part of an effort with the United Nations Development Programme (2021). Seemingly central to this effort is alignment with the Green Climate Fund (GCF), a key supporter in financing adaptation plans, and the Climate Fiscal Framework. Other programmes of note, some of which will be discussed further in the following sections, including the Forest Investment Plan, the Bangladesh Climate Change Trust Fund and the Bangladesh Delta Plan 2100 (a non-exhaustive list of these numerous organisations and policies may be found in Table 4.1) (Ministry of Environment, Forest and Climate Change 2020, 11). Evaluations of these initiatives point to four key, interrelated areas for adaptation of with a few examples from each highlighted below.

Gender and Economic Empowerment

Women in Bangladesh, like in many places around the world, have typically had fewer opportunities for economic independence, and are often required to stay at home or work in less favourable conditions. Although progress has been made to increase the number of women in political positions (mostly notably Prime Minister Sheikh Hasina, who will soon conclude her fourth term) which is often viewed as a key step to ensuring policies achieve the intended targets, upward trends of representation have not remained consistent. The most common industries in which women find work are in agriculture, community services and manufacturing, and with the impact of disasters and climate change on food security and community resilience, it is of particular importance to consider the impact this has on women (Khanam 2014).

At the national level, the Ministry of Environment, Forest and Climate Change put forth the Climate Change and Gender Action Plan for Bangladesh (ccGAP) nearly a decade ago. This initiative aims to ensure gender equality in the plans and responses to climate change, specifically food security and health; disaster management; infrastructure; and low carbon development (Ministry of Environment and Forest Bangladesh 2013). At a more local level, initiatives like the Community Climate Change Project (as part of a World Bank project under the Bangladesh Climate Change Resilience Fund) supported a crab cultivation programme, which aimed to help train women in running small-scale fisheries as a way to generate income and a food source and ties into efforts on food security (World Bank Group 2017).

Table 4.1: Select Policies and Organisations Shaping Bangladesh's Climate Efforts[2]

Domestic	
Organisations/Ministries	**Related Policies**
Ministry of Environment, Forest and Climate Change	Bangladesh Climate Change Strategy and Action Plan 2009
	National Adaptation Plan and National Adaptation Programme of Action
	Bangladesh Climate Change Trust Fund
	Climate Change and Gender Action Plan for Bangladesh
	Nationally Determined Contribution; also see the 'Roadmap and Action Plan for Implementing Bangladesh NDC: Transport, Power and Industry Sectors'
Ministry of Planning	Bangladesh Delta Plan 2100
Ministry of Finance, Economic Relations Division	National Policy for Development Cooperation; Climate Fiscal Framework
Ministry of Agriculture	Bangladesh Rice Research Institute
Prime Minister's Office	Access to Information (a2i)
Ministry of Energy and Natural Resources	Gas Sector Master Plan Bangladesh 2017
Ministry of Foreign Affairs	Foreign Service Academy; and general foreign policy and diplomacy
International	
Forum/Organisation	**Related Efforts/Policies**
Climate Vulnerable Forum	Midnight Survival Deadline for the Climate; NDCs
Green Climate Fund	Supports technology transfers and access, among other development efforts
Climate Leaders' Summit	NDCs; advocating for developing country support
United Nations Development Programme	National Adaptation Plan, National Adaptation Programme of Action
United Nations Office for South-South Cooperation	Support for a2i and the South-South Matchmaker

Source: Compiled by the author.

Food Security
One of the greatest threats to food security in Bangladesh is the tainting of freshwater sources by increased salinity from rising sea levels. Agriculture is an income generator for more than 87 per cent of households in rural areas, and increased agricultural yields have benefits for poverty levels and malnutrition, among other benefits (World Bank 2016). Rice in particular has been negatively impacted by increasing salinity, with a yield reduction of 80 kilograms on average over the past decade (Johnson 2017). If this trend is not reversed, reduction in crop yields increases the percentage of the population living in poverty by 15 per cent, a statistic that directly detracts from one of the government's top three goals as outlined in the NDC (Hijioka et al. 2014). This is also impacting fisheries, as both salinity and increased temperatures have made fish more susceptible to viruses and has destroyed their habitats (International Centre for Climate Change and Development 2019). Food and freshwater insecurity are not isolated to the coastal, rural areas of Bangladesh; increasing urbanisation will continue to exert strain on available resources in urban centres as well.

One example of a strategy to identify solutions to food security and develop saline-resistant crops is the Bangladesh Rice Research Institute (BRRI), which was established as an autonomous branch under the Ministry of Agriculture in 1973 (Bangladesh Rice Research Institute 2016). BRRI has had many successes, releasing 80 rice varieties that can yield two to three more times than regular rice (Bangladesh Rice Research Institute 2016, 4). Although the impact of these breakthroughs has been beneficial, there are concerns about the limits of scientific progress and that the rate of sea level rise and salinity intrusion may outpace future breakthroughs. The most resilient strains of rice can withstand salinity levels of 8 deci Siemens per meter (d/Sm) and scientists at BRRI believe they can achieve up to 12 d/Sm, a level which has already been exceeded in some areas (Roy 2014).

Community Resilience
Efforts to strengthen community resilience are manifested through both physical infrastructure and human capacity development. Local communities have long been finding ways on their own to cope with climate change and variability, and many of these methods are being adopted at a larger scale in both urban and rural communities. Although often of minimal benefit when faced with winds from a cyclone, for those who are unable to leave areas alongside riverbanks or the coast, raising the foundation of homes by building on stilts has aided in avoiding flooding (although the height may continue to increase as floods become more intense and sea levels rise); expanding the size of

homes as they can be built out over water; and increasing ventilation which has an additional benefit of lowering temperatures (Jabeen 2010).

Another major focus for infrastructure investment from both the national government and development organisations are cyclone shelters (Hasan 2022). Thousands of shelters have been built to provide a secure place for communities to evacuate during cyclones and flooding, and to improve the usefulness of these structures, they were often designed to serve as community centres and schools in non-emergency times. However, utilisation proved to be a challenge, as many were concerned about losing their possessions or livestock if they evacuated their homes, with the replacement costs for these items too high. In response, experts from BRAC University and the United Nations Development Programme have worked to generate funding to fortify homes that better resemble shelters (Miyaji et al. 2020). The Ministry of Environment, Forest and Climate Change has also encouraged the use of floating beds to better utilise increased water cover and saline-resistant crops (Johnson 2017). The floating beds (mats woven from banana tree leaves covered with soil) can also be used in urban areas and have positive implications for food security. Approximately 6,000 such beds have been funded by the Bangladesh Climate Change Trust thus far.

Often less at the forefront of conversations on climate change and disaster management is healthcare and the capacity training needed to ensure communities with fewer resources are able to receive medical care. This is one area among many in which BRAC, a notable NGO in Bangladesh, has focused. Specifically focusing on women, BRAC awarded special grants to train women on how to educate others on the prevention of spreading disease in the aftermath of a disaster and to also aid with the psychological trauma that accompanies such events; these community volunteers were referred to as Shasthya Shebikas (Reichenbach and Shimul 2011). Another effort by Grameen Shakti leveraged efforts from the establishment of rural solar PV to support off-grid health clinics which ensured refrigeration for lifesaving medicines and lighting so that clinics could stay open longer.

Environmental Protection
The benefits of forests as a carbon sink, barrier for flooding and erosion and source of economic livelihood are widely studied and were the drivers of the 2017 Forest Investment Plan (FIP), which aimed to increase geographical coverage of forests to 20 per cent by 2020 (Government of the People's Republic of Bangladesh 2017). This goal has not been met however, with a little more than 14 per cent of land covered by forests, according to most recent data provided by the

World Bank (n.d.). As stakeholders would seek to achieve the targets for afforestation, they often found competing goals in other development plans that counteracted ongoing work in forestry management.

One example of this is the Bangladesh Delta Plan 2100 (BDP 2100) (Ministry of Planning, Bangladesh 2018). Designed to enhance environmental security in one of the most densely populated portions of the country with a critical blue economy that contributes to national growth, the BDP 2100 also incorporates broader strategic planning on issues such as those mentioned above. Although it emphasises the need to approach climate resiliency and water security in the delta region with a holistic approach, there remain concerns that there isn't enough integration among other plans that seek to protect other ecosystems.

Bangladesh and the World: International Collaboration and Leadership

The depth of local expertise in Bangladesh has been the foundation of improvements in climate change adaptation efforts. As a result, the government has been prioritising a whole-of-government approach to climate action by ensuring key ministries have climate divisions and offering courses on climate change for public servants joining the foreign service (Huq 2021). Given the impact of climate change on security, human welfare and economic development, local adaptation efforts must both inform domestic national strategies and international efforts and is an increasingly important diplomatic tool.

By matching on-the-ground knowledge with financing from multilateral organisations and international partners, there are numerous examples that can be used and learned from in global efforts to adapt to climate change and strengthen economic development. Essential to international success in climate change mitigation and adaptation is ensuring that others are hearing and learning from these lessons. As a result, Bangladesh's active engagement in regional and international organisations and diplomatic partnerships are critical.

International Organisations

Bangladesh is an active participant in numerous international organisations and fora on climate change adaptation and mitigation. It has emerged as an important voice in highlighting what is already happening domestically and what other countries may expect to experience in the future. Most recently, Bangladesh has been receiving attention for its work with the Climate Vulnerable Forum, a cohort of the 48 most climate-vulnerable countries. In the middle of its second leadership term of the forum, Bangladesh launched the Midnight Survival Deadline for the Climate initiative, which pushed countries to submit enhanced NDCs before midnight on 31 December 2020 in advance of the 26th Conference of Parties (COP26) held in Glasgow in November 2021 (Climate Vulnerable Forum n.d.).

Another key area of Bangladesh's ongoing advocacy in international climate efforts is on South–South Cooperation, or economic and technical cooperation among countries in the Global South. Advancing South–South cooperation has been acknowledged as one of the key priorities of the Permanent Mission of the People's Republic of Bangladesh to the UN in larger international discussions and also prominently featured in several initiatives within Bangladesh (People's Republic of Bangladesh to the United Nations n.d.). One example of this is in the National Policy for Development Cooperation, the official framework published by the Economic Relations Division on how to efficiently and effectively deploy foreign assistance (Economic Relations Division n.d.). Like foreign direct investment received in Bangladesh, mobilisation of resources for South–South cooperative efforts must also be earmarked with considerations to transparency and achievable impact (Economic Relations Division n.d., 11). Another initiative is Access to Information (a2i) which seeks to build on the whole-of-government approach for climate action to create a whole-of-society effort to streamline access to data and information and improve livelihoods. Key areas of a2i's innovations include skills training for youth, digital finance apps, increased accessibility for marginalised groups, a Sustainable Development Goal (SDG) tracker, and a hub for South–South cooperation, among others (Access of Information n.d.). The South–South Matchmaker is one innovation that arose as part of the South–South Network for Public Service Innovation, which identified public service challenges in developing nations and matched them with countries that successfully overcame or identified steps to address similar issues in order to 'export' solutions (United Nations Office for South–South Cooperation n.d.). In one of the featured examples, Bangladesh leveraged another a2i innovation—the SDG tracker—to help Peru 'set localized sustainable goals, targets and indicators', through the 'identification of data sources and gaps' (United Nations Office for South–South Cooperation n.d.). Other examples in the matchmaking case studies include creating a holistic digital service platform for public services and expanding access to internet in rural areas, as well as vocational training programmes, among others.

An additional factor in Bangladesh's leadership and ability to share best practices is the support received from international development banks and funds, such as the Green Climate Fund (GCF). The GCF provides funding through numerous mechanisms—grants, concessional debt, equity instruments—for projects led by the recipient countries, acknowledging that local stakeholders have identified the most effective way to achieve certain targets but often need financial support to bring those plans to fruition. In Bangladesh, the GCF has provided support upwards of $350 million for projects on improved cooking stoves, climate resiliency for women and other vulnerable populations, and sustainable forestry, among others (Green Climate Fund n.d.).

South Asia

As Ambassador Tariq A. Karim has noted, power dynamics among South Asian states are complicated, given the relatively recent independence and sovereignty of some countries and the complex legacy of colonialism and partition (Karim 2020). This leads to a general sense of mistrust, particularly of India, as its size and economic status often gives it more leverage when negotiating in regional fora on issues pertaining to matters of national and non-traditional security issues alike. However, Bangladesh's overall positive relationship with India and its own successful ongoing economic rise positions Bangladesh well for increased leadership in regional institutions and collaborative efforts.

Indeed, Bangladesh has already played a critical role in numerous regional fora that are concerned with the wide-ranging impacts of climate change on security, economic development and social well-being. For example, it was the country that largely initiated the formation of the South Asian Association for Regional Cooperation (SAARC) with former president Ziaur Rahman's submitted proposal to other South Asian leaders and diplomatic efforts to assuage concerns of loss of sovereignty and alignment of nations against others (Iqbal 2006). Although it is widely noted that SAARC is underfunded to accomplish the action plans it sets, there are valuable resources for regional cooperation on climate change, disaster management and environmental protection—transboundary issues that can be acted on with fewer concerns for national security.

Beyond its international and regional efforts to highlight the need for collective action on climate change, Bangladesh has continued its efforts in sharing locally led adaptation best practices on a bilateral basis within South Asia as well. To strengthen cooperation with the Maldives, another nation rapidly facing the dire consequences of climate change, Bangladesh signed six memorandums of understanding (MoUs) with the former in February and March 2021. The MoUs cover a range of issues including fisheries, cultural exchange, human resources and training for climate action (The President's Office of the Republic of Maldives 2021). While it is too early to assess the progress of implementation, these high-level government meetings underscore the direction of foreign policymaking in the region and what will continue to be top-line items in their respective agendas in other regional and global dialogues.

Another area of bilateral focus that requires immediate action is the issue of climate migration between Bangladesh and India. Like Bangladesh, India's coastal states are inundated with flooding and battered by cyclones, and both countries have seen extremely high numbers of displaced persons as a result of climate and natural disasters, such as the three million people that had to evacuate during cyclone Amphan in May 2020 (Center for Disaster Philanthropy 2020). While the issue of climate migration is frequently discussed among political leaders, there remain no official policies for climate refugees and it continues to be an area of tension (Pasricha 2021). This is a challenge for which international partners must also better prepare; as natural disasters continue to intensify in impact and frequency, climate migration will expand beyond regional borders. More developed countries have already shown their lack of preparedness (and in some cases unwillingness) to accept climate refugees, and we are only facing the early stages of this problem.

United States

The US private sector, notably the energy and textile/manufacturing industries, has long been aware of the economic potential of Bangladesh and there is a growing realisation among US policymakers of the importance of this partnership. In the past few years, expanded efforts by the departments of commerce and state, among others, have increased trade delegations and initiatives that focus on Bangladesh, including the most recent United States Agency for International Development (USAID) and Bangladesh Advancing Development Growth through Energy (BADGE) initiative (US Embassy Dhaka 2021; *The Daily Star* 2021). Given the increased focus on cleaner energy transitions and action on climate change under the Biden administration, BADGE has the potential to aid in Bangladesh's mitigation efforts. The country's strategic location in the Bay of Bengal and ties to both India and China make it an important actor as the US and others balance their regional strategies for diplomatic and economic development. Its climate leadership has also been noted by the US and was one of the key issues discussed in the call between Foreign Minister A.K. Abdul Momen and Secretary of State Antony Blinken in February 2021 (US Department of State 2021).

From an aid perspective, numerous agencies and NGOs have been working with the government of Bangladesh and local organisations to help provide needed financial and technical support. While there is a wide spectrum of issues these partnerships cover, strengthening women's rights and independence through micro-grants and other programmes to help provide economic opportunities for women to be self-sustainable are frequently priority areas. For example, USAID funds activities such as the Bangladesh Aquaculture and Nutrition and Livestock for Improved Nutrition (US Agency for International Development 2021). These aim to educate women and provide resources so that they can raise livestock and dry fish with the simultaneous goal of improving nutrition and food security.

Additional areas for future consideration lie in several of the initiatives outlined in the post-event press release from the White House on the Leaders' Summit on Climate that took place in April 2021. Prime Minister Hasina was one of 40 leaders invited to join the summit and, in her remarks, she emphasised the need for technology transfers that focus on green economic growth and carbon-neutral innovations (*Dhaka Tribune* 2021). 'Promoting innovation to bring clean technologies to scale', was one of the many areas in which the Biden administration hopes to strengthen as a result of a reinvigorated US climate policy (White House 2021). Given Bangladesh's own work on developing innovative platforms to expand access to job training, food security and electricity, increased efforts by the US and others to improve funding and deployment of innovative technologies is a potential area for collaboration.

Conclusion

Bangladesh is in a unique position, in that it has identified the problems, outlined a number of solutions, but is constrained by its ability to fully implement many of these plans, the large scale of financing needed and the actions of third parties. In the coming years, there are a few action items for consideration to both expand Bangladesh's own leadership abroad and strengthen domestic environments for resiliency and adaptation.

Domestically, there are three areas in which accelerated action could have wide-ranging benefits. First, energy mixes must continue to de-carbonise. Eliminating poverty and ensuring reliable energy access should not be sacrificed in this process, but increasing trade for natural gas to bypass coal-fired power additions and utilising existing development partnerships for technology transfers or scaling up existing renewable and zero-carbon efforts can aid in this transition. Additionally, continuing to incorporate and relying on local-led adaptation will remain critical. The International Institute for Environment and Development, in partnership with International Centre for Climate Change and Development, BRAC and others, have laid out eight principles in which strategies can better incorporate and depend on grassroots knowledge and contributions (Soanes et al. 2021). Lastly is the need to de-conflict overlapping mandates. A whole-of-government approach to addressing climate change is necessary but to most effectively implement programmes that utilise the depth of knowledge from local and national experiences, clearly articulated roles and policies will be imperative.

Internationally, Bangladesh can continue to utilise its growing economic presence in the Indo-Pacific to enact change by incorporating climate into trade agreements and cooperative efforts moving forward. This rising economic status is also important in helping voice the concerns of small nations that are the most vulnerable to climate change.

For foreign actors observing and assisting Bangladesh, there are several takeaways that should be factored into their own strategies. One is to begin laying the groundwork to prepare immigration services to welcome and absorb the coming influx of climate migrants. At COP26, developing countries pushed for the establishment of the Glasgow Loss and Damage Finance Facility to mobilise financing that would aid vulnerable communities experiencing environmental deterioration and could help reduce the urgency of migration; the final outcome from negotiations did not provide any new funding and outlined a 2024 start date for the effort (Huq 2022). Some progress was made at COP27 with the establishment of a loss-and-damage fund seen as one of the highlights of the meeting. The details of how this fund will be structured are intended to be finalised at the upcoming COP28 in November 2023 (this was the status at the time of this publication going to press), which will continue to ensure that the issue of climate vulnerability and migration will be at the forefront of this international dialogue.

The second is to take into consideration the funding challenge the country is facing. By graduating from a least-developed country ranking, Bangladesh will lose some of its international support, despite still experiencing rising costs from damage caused by natural disasters and lacking the depth of resources to recover as quickly as developed countries might. Although it is important to acknowledge the progress Bangladesh has made, technology transfers and other support mechanisms will remain critical. Finally, take into consideration the locally led adaptation strategies outlined by countries like Bangladesh and the efforts they are making to support other similar economies.

This will maximise the effectiveness of aid provided and help accelerate progress in adaptation efforts.

Notes

1 Factors on which additional strengthening of Bangladesh's NDC for GHG mitigation are dependent: maintaining an 8 per cent rate of economic growth; eradication of poverty by 2020; and secure food and nutrition supplies for all. See 'Nationally Determined Contributions.' 13, Ministry of Environment, Forest and Climate Change.
2 Please note this is a non-exhaustive list and largely summarises the organisations, ministries and policies discussed in this chapter. The BCCSAP states that there are more than 35 ministries/agencies in Bangladesh alone contributing to climate change adaptation and mitigation strategies. More information on domestic efforts can be found on page 20 in the BCCSAP 2009. This list also does not include local government agencies working in this space, which is another sector worth exploring in more depths.

References

'About'. Climate Vulnerable Forum. https://thecvf.org/about/ (accessed 28 June, 2021).

Adhikari, M. 'An Economically Sustainable Approach to the Energy Transition in Developing Countries'. The National Bureau of Asian Research, USA, April 9, 2021. https://nbr.org/publication/an-economically-sustainable-approach-to-the-energy-transition-in-developing-countries/.

'Agriculture Growth Reduces Poverty in Bangladesh'. World Bank, last modified May 17, 2016. http://www.worldbank.org/en/news/feature/2016/05/17/bangladeshs-agriculture-a-poverty-reducer-in-need-of-modernization.

'Bangladesh Climate Change and Gender Action Plan'. Ministry of Environment, Forest and Climate Change, xvi–122, November 2013. http://nda.erd.gov.bd/files/1/Publications/CC%20Policy%20Documents/CCGAP%202009.pdf.

'Bangladesh Climate Change Strategy and Action Plan 2009'. Ministry of Environment, Forest and Climate Change, xvii–78, September 2009. https://www.iucn.org/downloads/bangladesh_climate_change_strategy_and_action_plan_2009.pdf.

'Bangladesh—Community Climate Change Project'. World Bank Group, i–43, August 22, 2017. https://documents1.worldbank.org/curated/en/277981504638164950/pdf/ICR00004072-08222017.pdf.

'Bangladesh Delta Plan 2100: Bangladesh in the 21st Century'. Ministry of Planning, 4–37, September 4, 2018. http://plancomm.portal.gov.bd/sites/default/files/files/plancomm.portal.gov.bd/files/dc5b06a1_3a45_4ec7_951e_a9feac1ef783/BDP%202100%20Abridged%20Version%20English.pdf.

'Bangladesh Development Series Paper No. 17'. World Bank Office, Dhaka, ix–138, June 2007. https://documents1.worldbank.org/curated/en/938981468013830990/pdf/404240BD0Dhaka10ALSO03582401PUBLIC1.pdf.

'Bangladesh Govt Scraps Plans for 10 Coal Plants, Pursues Green Option'. *Business Standard*. June 29, 2021. https://www.business-standard.com/article/international/bangladesh-govt-scraps-plans-for-10-coal-plants-pursues-green-options-121062900016_1.html.

'Bangladesh to Help Maldives Combat Climate Change: PM'. *The Daily Star*, February 10, 2021. https://www.thedailystar.net/environment/climate-change/news/bangladesh-help-maldives-combat-climate-change-pm-2042453.

'Bangladesh, National Adaptation Plan'. United Nations Development Programme. https://www.bd.undp.org/content/bangladesh/en/home/projects/national-adaptation-plan--nap-.html (accessed on June 26, 2021).

'Bangladesh: National Policy on Development Cooperation'. 1–15. Economic Relations Division. https://erd.portal.gov.bd/sites/default/files/files/erd.portal.gov.bd/page/8de61198_58fb_47fe_8462_a39372d6b621/FINAL%20DRAFT%20NPDC%20(1).pdf.

'BRRI at a Glance'. Bangladesh Rice Research Institute, 1–6, 2016. http://brri.portal.gov.bd/sites/default/files/files/brri.portal.gov.bd/page/c8743e0a_87bf_46d6_9a16_bf6cd00db1c8/BRRI_At%20a_Glance_10-8-16.pdf.

'Climate-Smart Development: Empowers Bangladesh Communities'. *Newsletter*, no 4 (June 2014):1–4, Bangladesh Climate Change Resilience Fund.

'Consolidated 2020 energy and emissions statistics with 2021 estimates, including Covid-19 impact and structural changes,' in *Global Energy Trend 2021*, June 29, 2021. https://www.enerdata.net/publications/reports-presentations/2021-energy-climate-trends.html.

'Cyclone Amphan'. Center for Disaster Philanthropy, 2020. https://disasterphilanthropy.org/disaster/cyclone-amphan/.

Eckstein, D., V. Kunzel, and L. Schafer. 'Global Climate Risk Index 2021: Who Suffers Most from Extreme Weather Events? Weather-Related Loss Events in 2019 and 2000–2019'. *Germanwatch*, (January 2021): 1–48. https://germanwatch.org/sites/default/files/Global%20Climate%20Risk%20Index%202021_2.pdf.

Elahi, N. 'How Grameen Shakti is Providing a Sustainable Renewable Energy Solution in Rural Bangladesh'. *Climate Tribune*, (2021): 24–26. http://www.icccad.net/wp-content/uploads/2021/08/CT_July_2021.pdf.

'Ensuring Livelihood Security for Climate Vulnerable Communities in Coastal Bangladesh'. International Centre for Climate Change and Development, 1–4, 2019. http://www.icccad.net/wp-content/uploads/2019/09/Ensuring-Livelihood-Security-for-Climate-Vulnerable-Communities-in-Coastal-Bangladesh_ICCCAD_Helvetas_Policy-Brief_Final-Version.pdf.

'Fact Sheet: President Biden's Leaders' Summit on Climate'. White House, April 23, 2021. https://www.whitehouse.gov/briefing-room/statements-releases/2021/04/23/fact-sheet-president-bidens-leaders-summit-on-climate/.

'Forest Area (% of Land Area) – Bangladesh'. World Bank. https://data.worldbank.org/indicator/AG.LND.FRST.ZS?locations=BD (accessed on 30 June, 2021).

'Forest Investment Plan 2017'. Government of the People's Republic of Bangladesh, 1–119, 2017. https://bforest.portal.gov.bd/sites/default/files/files/bforest.portal.gov.bd/notices/e24e37f4_3101_4cde_921c_bf898a2b716d/FIP_Report_Draft_09.10.17.pdf.

'Gender Equality and Women's Empowerment'. US Agency for International Development, last modified June 1, 2021. https://www.usaid.gov/bangladesh/gender-equality-and-womens-empowerment.

Hasan, M.M. 'Building Resilience in Coastal Communities: Perspectives From the Bay of Bengal'. The National Bureau of Asian Research, 2022. https://www.nbr.org/publication/building-resilience-in-coastal-communities-perspectives-from-the-bay-of-bengal/.

Hijioka, Y., E. Lin, J.J. Pereira, R.T. Corlett, et al. 'Asia'. In *Climate Change 2014: Impacts, Adaptation, and Vulnerability. Part B: Regional Aspects. Contribution of Working Group II to the Fifth Assessment Report of the Intergovernmental Panel on Climate Change*, 1327–1370. Cambridge: Cambridge University Press. 2014. http://www.ipcc.ch/pdf/assessment-report/ar5/wg2/WGIIAR5-Chap24_FINAL.pdf.

Huq, S. 'Bangladesh's Climate Diplomacy Needs to Take a Whole-of-Society Approach'. *The Daily Star,* May 5, 2021. https://www.thedailystar.net/opinion/politics-climate-change/news/bangladeshs-climate-diplomacy-needs-take-whole-society-approach-2088229.

———. 'Why COP26 Failed to Address Loss and Damage from Climate Change'. Organisation for Economic Co-operation and Development, 2022. https://oecd-development-matters.org/2022/01/25/why-cop26-failed-to-addressloss-and-damage-from-climate-change/.

Iqbal, M.J. 'SAARC: Origin, Growth, Potential and Achievements'. *Pakistan Journal of History and Culture* 27, no. 2 (2006): 130–140. http://www.nihcr.edu.pk/Latest_English_Journal/SAARC_Jamshed_Iqbal.pdf

Jabeen, H., C. Johnson, and A. Allen. 'Built-In Resilience: Learning from Grassroots Coping Strategies for Climate Variability'. *Environment and Urbanization* 22, no. 2, (2010): 415–431. https://journals.sagepub.com/doi/pdf/10.1177/0956247810379937.

Johnson, A. 'Bangladesh's Climate Change Challenge'. The National Bureau of Asian Research, 2017. https://nbr.org/publication/bangladeshs-climate-change-challenge/.

Karim, T.A. 'Bangladesh's Role in Forging a Bay of Bengal Community'. The National Bureau of Asian Research, February 18, 2020. https://nbr.org/publication/bangladeshs-role-in-forging-a-bay-of-bengal-community/.

Khanam, S.A. 'Woman Security is Social Security: Bangladesh Perspective'. *Peace and Security Review* 6, no. 13, (2014): 42–53.

'Key Agreements Signed between the Maldives and Bangladesh'. The President's Office of the Republic of Maldives, March 18, 2021. https://presidency.gov.mv/Press/Article/24336.

'Leaders' Summit on Climate: PM Hasina for Immediate Action Plan'. *Dhaka Tribune,* April 22, 2021. https://www.dhakatribune.com/world/2021/04/22/pm-hasina-places-4-suggestions-to-deal-with-climate-challenge.

Lu, G., P. Jorgensen, B. Svensson, A. Lemp, et al. 'Gas Sector Master Plan: Bangladesh 2017'. Ministry of Power, Energy and Mineral Resources Government of the People's Republic of Bangladesh Ministry of Power, 2017. https://policy.asiapacificenergy.org/node/3509.

Miyaji, M., K. Okazaki, and C. Ochiai. 'A Study on the Use of Cyclone Shelters in Bangladesh'. *Japan Architectural Review* 3, no. 4, (2020): 590–600. https://onlinelibrary.wiley.com/doi/pdf/10.1002/2475-8876.12177.

Munirazzaman, A.N.M. 'Water and Disaster Management in South Asia: Threats to Peace and Security'. *South Asia Journal* 12 (Winter 2015): 1–15.

'Nationally Determined Contributions 2020 (Interim)'. Ministry of Environment, Forest and Climate Change, 1–18, December 31, 2020. https://www4.unfccc.int/sites/ndcstaging/PublishedDocuments/Bangladesh%20First/Updated_NDC_of_Bangladesh.pdf.

Olsson, L., M. Opondo, P. Tschakert, A. Agrawal, et al. 'Livelihoods and Poverty'. In *Climate Change 2014: Impacts, Adaptation, and Vulnerability. Part A: Global and Sectoral Aspects. Contribution of Working Group II to the Fifth Assessment Report of the Intergovernmental Panel on Climate Change*, 793–832. Cambridge and New York: Cambridge University Press. 2014. https://www.ipcc.ch/site/assets/uploads/2018/02/WGIIAR5-Chap13_FINAL.pdf.

Ozaki, M. 'Disaster Risk Financing in Bangladesh'. ADB South Asia Working Paper Series, no. 46, (September 2016): 1–26. https://www.adb.org/sites/default/files/publication/198561/sawp-046.pdf.

Pasricha, A. 'In South Asia, Rising Ocean Pushes Out Those Living at the Shore'. *Voice of America*, September 5, 2021. https://www.voanews.com/south-central-asia/south-asia-rising-ocean-pushes-out-those-living-shore.

'Rivers Information'. Bangladesh Water Development Board. Last modified July 2, 2021. https://www.bwdb.gov.bd/en/rivers-information.

Reichenbach, L. and S.N. Shimul. 'Sustaining Health: The Role of BRAC's Community Health Volunteers in Bangladesh, Afghanistan and Uganda'. *Economic Studies* 28 (September 2011): 224–333. http://research.brac.net/monographs/Monograph_49.pdf.

Roy, P. 'Coastal Bangladesh Turns Too Salty for Salt-Tolerant Rice'. *The Third Pole*, December 8, 2014. https://www.thethirdpole.net/en/climate/coastal-bangladesh-turns-too-salty-for-salt-tolerant-rice/.

Samaranayake, N. 'Bangladesh: The Strongest Advocate of Basin-Wide Management'. In *Raging Waters: China, India, Bangladesh and Brahmaputra River Politics,* 71–99. 2018. Quantico, Virginia: Marine Corps University Press.

'Secretary Blinken's Call with Bangladeshi Foreign Minister Momen'. US Department of State, February 23, 2021. https://www.state.gov/secretary-blinkens-call-with-bangladeshi-foreign-minister-momen/.

Soanes, M., A. Bahadur, C. Shakya, B. Smith, et al. "Principles for Locally Led Adaptation: A Call to Action." International Institute for Environment and Development, 1–41, January 2021. https://pubs.iied.org/sites/default/files/pdfs/2021-01/10211IIED.pdf.

'South–South Cooperation'. Permanent Mission of the People's Republic of Bangladesh to the United Nations. https://bdun.org/bangladesh-priorities-at-the-un/south-south-cooperation/ (accessed 15 August, 2021).

'The South–South Matchmaker: South–South 1-Network for Public Service Innovation 2017– 2018 Best Practices'. United Nations Office for South–South Cooperation, 6–67, 2018. https://a2i.gov.bd/publication/south-south-matchmaker/.

'The Future of Natural Gas in a Deeply Decarbonized World: Expert Workshop Summary Report'. Energy Futures Initiative, 1–114, 2021. https://static1.squarespace.com/static/58ec123cb3db2bd94e057628/t/60c6d79fb49a1c21bd45921c/1623644077072/GlobalGasStudy_v08.pdf.

'The Least Developed Country Category: 2021 Country Snapshots'. United Nations Department of Economic and Social Affairs, 1–99, May 5, 2021. https://www.un.org/development/desa/dpad/wp-content/uploads/sites/45/Snapshots2021.pdf

'USAID Launches a New Clean Energy Project: Bangladesh Advancing Development and Growth Through Energy (BADGE)'. US Embassy, Dhaka. https://bd.usembassy.gov/usaid-launches-a-new-clean-engergy-project-bangladesh-advancing-development-and-growth-through-energy-badge/ (accessed on 22 June, 2021).

'Welcome to a2i'. https://a2i.gov.bd/ (accessed September 1, 2021).

Part II

INTRODUCTION

Given that Bangladesh became an independent nation during the Cold War, it had to navigate through strong alliances and different strategic orientations to build bilateral and regional partnerships during the 1970s. Except for India, then Soviet Union and a handful of others, the bigger powers did not lend support to Bangladesh's Liberation War. Major powers, including the US and the UK's strategic interests aligned them with West Pakistan. However, over time, Bangladesh was not only able to overcome much of the latent hostility it faced in the initial years to emerge as a suitable bilateral partner for nations in different regions, it was also able to leverage its geographical location and the growing geo-strategic interests emerging in the region around Bangladesh. For long, the country was perceived as a small state flanked by two large Asian neighbours, walking a tightrope in its relationship with both the larger nations. But, with a strong youth demographic, growing spending power and sustained economic growth, this South Asian state has undergone transformational progress. This distinct change has been noticed in many quarters of the region and outside, leading to a different worldview about Bangladesh.

That apart, with global attention riveted on the Indian Ocean and the Bay of Bengal, Bangladesh's strategic location is making it an attractive partner. The convergence of strategic interests in maintaining the rule of law and keeping the sea lanes of communications free has drawn in many regional and extra-regional powers to the Indo-Pacific. Many of these powers are directing their sight on Bangladesh and several factors are making it appear as an attractive partner. In this broadening of Bangladesh's strategic interests, Dhaka is seeing itself as an entity which is larger than the South Asian identity entity with a larger scope in Indo-Pacific geopolitics. Traditionally, Bangladesh has always advocated for regionalism and the new developments in the surrounding geography have given it the opportunity to explore that scope through multifold regional partnerships. It has also expressed a desire to piggyback India and Japan to engage more closely with Southeast Asian economies, as India is building extensive cross border transport facilities with its Southeast Asian neighbours and Bangladesh joining these economic corridors will enable deeper economic linkages with these strong ASEAN economies.

Apart from the traditional partners in Asia, namely India and China, Bangladesh is engaging closely with Japan and Korea, which has led some to suggest that Bangladesh is also pursuing a 'Look East' policy. The Rohingya refugee crises has come in the way of a more substantial engagement with Myanmar but Bangladesh's interest in the Southeast Asian economies is evident. Many of them, including Singapore, are showing considerable trade and economic interests in Bangladesh, which is gradually being viewed as a reliable partner. In 2021, Singapore became Bangladesh's third-largest importing partner. Dhaka's foreign policy maturity is reflected in its equal friendship with not only India and China but also in its ability to reach out effectively to other powers, both big and small. The growing strategic salience of Bangladesh will find more resonance in the days ahead unless there are untoward domestic developments.

This is not to suggest that Dhaka's recognition as an important player is not strewn with difficulties. While much of the contemporary attention it enjoys is impinged on its growth and progress, the lack of fiscal discipline that has led to the present credit-debt ratio difficulty that it is facing points to challenges that lie ahead. Irresponsible financial decisions may reflect badly when the world is entering another high inflationary phase. Many factors have converged for Bangladesh to be seen as an important strategic partner but that view may falter if not halt if Bangladesh is unable to manage its future economic and political matters.

5

BANGLADESH AND THE OUTSIDE WORLD: A STORY OF EXPLORING CONVERGENCES, CONNECTIVITY AND CONTINUITY

M. Humayun Kabir

Backdrop

Bangladesh defies economic and political gravity. Since its 1971 War of Independence with Pakistan, the country has been known for its tragedies: wrenching poverty, natural disasters and now one of the world's biggest refugee crises, after the influx of 7,50,000 Rohingya Muslims fleeing persecution in neighbouring Myanmar. With remarkably little international attention, Bangladesh has also become one of the world's economic success stories.

This is how Gwen Robinson (2018), editor-at-large of *Nikkei Asian Review*, described Bangladesh. Although her remarks may seem a little exaggerated at first read, there is perhaps some truth to it. During the glorious Liberation War in 1971, Bangladesh was written off, first, geopolitically[1] and second, economically[2] by many in the international community. However, Dhaka rose up like a phoenix from the ashes not only to prove all the negative predictions wrong, but it also emerged as a dynamic actor in the geopolitical transformation in South Asian and in the Indian Ocean region in its own right. The question is how and why Bangladesh has been able to practically defy these preconceived expectations. One perhaps needs to deconstruct the texture, trend and tenacity of Bangladesh to understand such a 'paradox' or 'miracle',[3] which is what this chapter aims to do.

The Shape and Trajectory of Bangladesh Involvement Abroad

The entry of Bangladesh into the international community as a new state was neither easy nor pleasant. In most of the contemporary discourse, the creation of Bangladesh was seen through a geopolitical lens, while the real story centred on the indomitable and odds-defying spirit of the people of Bangladesh for complete independence. It would therefore not be an exaggeration to say that the foreign policy of Bangladesh was born on the battlefield. The Proclamation of Independence of 10 April 1971 captured the essence of the commitment of the Provisional Government of Bangladesh to global norms and practices as the guiding principles of an ongoing Bangladesh movement for independence. It affirmed, 'We further resolve that we undertake to observe and give effect to all duties and obligations that devolve upon us as a member of the family of nations and to abide by the Charter of the United Nations.'[4] It further expressed its commitment to 'ensure for the people of Bangladesh equality, human dignity and social justice' and the justification for putting this proclamation out.[5]

As the massive flow of refugees from Bangladesh to India continued since the launching of a military campaign by the Pakistani regime on 25 March 1971, a two-front war effort was initiated by the newly formed provisional government. One was the intensification of armed resistance against the military campaign by Pakistan in Bangladesh, and the other was the intensification of the diplomatic campaign to secure the support of the international community for the cause of Bangladesh. While the broadly perceived 'civil war' and the humanitarian crisis unleashed by the exodus of refugees were the predominant narratives in the global network, the Provisional Government of Bangladesh tried hard to create an alternative set of narratives.

Nonetheless, the geopolitical fault line continued to frame the armed struggle of the people of Bangladesh against Pakistan. In the end, however, owing to active diplomatic and military support by India, Bangladesh could defeat the Pakistani military machine under a joint command on 16 December 1971, and consequently, achieve its much-cherished freedom from occupation. Regardless, the narrative on Bangladesh continued to be defined more by geopolitical calculations than by the success of the aspirations of the people of Bangladesh (Butt 2017). This may explain why even after Bangladesh gained independence, many countries around the world were hesitant to recognise it as an independent state, although many tacitly acknowledged its existence.[6]

Search for Identity and Exploring Opportunities

In an independent Bangladesh, the issue of creating a new model of inclusive identity away from the two-nation theory on which Pakistan was set up in 1947 had become a priority. One of the first tasks before

Bangabandhu Sheikh Mujibur Rahman, even before he took charge of the new government on 12 January 1972, was to demonstrate the separate identity of Bangladesh and conceptualise a framework for the foreign policy of a free and independent country. Accordingly, he declared, 'friendship to all and malice to none' as the principle and essence of Bangladesh's engagement with the outside world. In order to concretise his foreign policy principle, he quickly moved on to express his gratitude to then Indian prime minister Indira Gandhi for her sustained personal campaign for his release and for firmly standing by the cause of Bangladesh. Accordingly, he made a stopover in New Delhi during his return journey from his detention in Pakistan via London. He had also invited her to visit Bangladesh, which she accepted. Simultaneously, he also requested for the withdrawal of Indian troops from Bangladesh and PM Gandhi kept her word—the troops were withdrawn before she made a visit to Bangladesh in March 1972. During her visit, a 25-year-long Treaty of Friendship and Cooperation was signed almost along the lines of the Indo-Soviet Treaty signed in August 1971 (Ministry of External Affairs 1972). Clearly, this treaty was a formal effort to consolidate the existing bond between Bangladesh and India. In a way, it also highlighted the desire of the Bangladesh government to demonstrate its identity as an independent nation and an equal partner in the domain of diplomacy.[7]

Despite criticism from many domestic political and civil society actors in Bangladesh on the Mujib government being too close to India, both leaders worked closely with each other and demonstrated a constructive attitude towards strengthening the bilateral relations and reducing the tensions in the region. Close bilateral relations also facilitated the signing of a landmark agreement in 1974 to clear the way for the demarcation of the land boundary between Bangladesh and India, although its implementation took more than four decades of delay (Bhattacharjee 2018). A Bilateral Trade and Transit Agreement was also signed in 1972 to formalise the economic relationship between these two close neighbours.

As the initial euphoria of the post-liberation phase gradually waned and hard realities started to set in,[8] the government was forced to think of adding new elements to its foreign policy priorities to meet the rising expectations of the people and the international community. Accordingly, the Bangladesh government continued to make its tentative outreach to build a relationship with China despite its refusal to recognise the country (Jahan 1974).[9] The message emanating from the appointment of Khawaja Mohammad Kaiser as ambassador of Bangladesh to Burma (present-day Myanmar) was clear; he was sent with an obvious goal of building a bridge with the Chinese authorities,[10] where he had served as Pakistani ambassador during the entire period in 1971. In a similar vein, Bangladesh felt the need to make an outreach to Muslim countries, apparently for three reasons. The first was to establish its credentials as an independent state with a Muslim-majority population; it was indeed required to neutralise the toxic narrative circulating in the external world. The narrative essentially tried to portray the War of Liberation of Bangladesh as a conspiracy of India to break Pakistan, which was an Islamic nation. This served two purposes: (*i*) it could delegitimise the creation of Bangladesh by showing it as a part of systematic conspiracy hatched and executed against an independent State, Pakistan, and (*ii*) at the same time it could obscure the strong determination of the people of Bangladesh to resist military occupation and pursue their legitimate aspiration to get independence from Pakistan. The second objective was to mount pressure on Pakistan to recognize Bangladesh as an independent nation while the third one was to get access to oil resources in the Middle East and Gulf regions.[11] Therefore, it appears that the outreach to both China and the Arab countries was more dictated by the domestic compulsions in Bangladesh in the form of the strong urge of the people and the need of economy to diversify its outreach to other countries with a view to demonstrating its autonomy of decision-making as an independent country. What was seen in the subsequent years was indeed an acceleration of pace on the foundations laid out during the first few years of its existence.

Along the same line, several other independent yet complex diplomatic moves increased the diplomatic leverages of Bangladesh. In addition to Sheikh Mujibur Rahman's attendance at the Commonwealth Head of Government Conference in Ottawa in 1973, his decision to attend the Non-Aligned Summit in Algiers in 1973 sealed the recognition and support of Arab countries in favour of Bangladesh. According to Professor Rounaq Jahan, Bangladesh had subtly played up its 'Muslim' image to gain Arab recognition. It also took an extra initiative to impress the Arab countries by sending a medical team to the Arab side during the Arab-Israeli war of 1973 (Jahan 1974). The other initiative was the decision by Sheikh Mujibur Rahman to join the Organisation of Islamic Cooperation (OIC) meeting in Lahore in February of 1974 after securing the recognition of Pakistan. Indeed, since then, successive Bangladesh governments have deepened the engagement with the OIC and it has served Bangladesh well (Rahman 2021). The return visit of then Pakistani Prime Minister Zulfikar Ali Bhutto to Bangladesh in June 1974 and the withdrawal of the objection by China thereafter facilitated the securing of membership of Bangladesh at the UN. These diplomatic moves were clearly designed to enlarge the space for Bangladesh in the international community and to establish itself as a non-aligned country.

Bangladesh became a member of the UN, an act that was formalised at the 36th session of the UN General Assembly in September 1974. It was perhaps one of the finest hours of Bangladeshi diplomacy at the global level and almost completed the diplomatic effort by Bangladesh to establish itself as a full, active and responsible member of the international community. In parallel, Sheikh Mujibur Rahman's visit to Washington in September 1974 also sent a 'strong message to the world that Bangladesh had moved away from the perceived Indo-Soviet alliance' (Rashid 2005). The follow-up visit of then US Secretary of State Henry Kissinger to Dhaka in October 1974 was yet another force multiplier for Bangladeshi diplomacy, notwithstanding the fact that it had created tensions, both at the domestic and regional level, with long-term consequences.

Self-Preservation: The Reconstruction Phase

Although the Bangladesh government was pursuing a value-driven foreign policy, its domestic pressures compelled it to also explore interest-based opportunities outside. The urgency to respond to the needs of repatriation and resettlement of Bangladeshi refugees from India, reconstruction and restoration of shattered infrastructures, and the reduction of widespread poverty, including food support to the poor, who numbered around 71.3 per cent of the total population, practically dictated the policy priorities of the government (Hossain 2014). Bereft of any domestic capacity to fall back on, it sought support from the UN agencies, World Bank, ADB and other development partners for assistance. Records show that in the initial years, Bangladesh was desperate to secure development assistance from international partners, particularly from bilateral donors. Indeed, bilateral aid provided the bulk of the support to Bangladesh with a focus on food aid, assistance of humanitarian nature and support for the budget as well as the Annual Development Programme (ADP). During the 1970s, almost 100 per cent support for the budget came from the Official Development Assistance (ODA), while 58 per cent of support came for the Annual Development Programmes or the ADP (Raihan 2010; Hasan 2011). Again, a bulk of the external support came in the form of grants, which was 90.5 per cent in 1971–1972; this has reduced to 6 per cent in 2017–2018. Grants mostly covered the areas of food and commodity support (Economic Relations Division, Ministry of Finance 2019).

Among the countries, US, Japan, Germany, Canada and the UK were among the top bilateral donors (Economic Relations Division, Ministry of Finance 2019), while India and the then-Soviet bloc also extended humanitarian and economic support in the post-Independence period. This massive financial support received from the Western countries since 1972 laid the foundation for Bangladesh's economic sustenance and recovery as well as subsequent developments, including in the social sector.[12] Indeed, heavy reliance on foreign aid had, to a large extent, influenced the very nature of engagement of Bangladesh with the international community, including some influence on the domestic governance arrangements (Chattopadhyay 2018).[13] It may be mentioned that although Bangladesh started its journey with a predominantly state controlled economy, it soon had to adjust its policies by way of opening up the economy to the private sector and incentivise investment in the social sector. Encouragement from the World Bank and other western nations, including those in the Paris Club, played a significant role in this process of transformation. Indeed, except for a brief period of tension between the donor community at the Paris Club and the Bangladesh government on the economic philosophy under the one-party structure, which was introduced in January 1975 with a 'socialist' orientation,[14] the influence of the liberal economic philosophy of the donor community grew. Over time, the preferences of the development partners converged with the new economic priorities pursued by the subsequent governments in Bangladesh.

The brutal assassination of Sheikh Mujibur Rahman in August 1975 and the following turmoil in Bangladesh had, to some extent, rattled domestic politics with a corresponding impact on its relationship with the outside world, including its vital relationship with India (Maniruzzaman 1976). However, despite some hiccups in the wake of the change-over in 1975 (Maniruzzaman 1976), Bangladesh and India quickly retrieved the momentum on their bilateral relationship, leading up to the signing of a five-year Ganges Water Sharing Agreement in 1977. The visit by President Ziaur Rahman to India and the return visit by Prime Minister Morarji Desai to Dhaka helped keep the relationship on track. Subsequently, however, the return of Indira Gandhi to power in 1980 added some discomfort, as she had reportedly held a strong view about the government in Bangladesh at that time (Franda 1981).

Securing recognition as an independent nation from other members of the international community, particularly from the extended neighbourhood, and the Muslim countries, the UN and other international bodies created an expanded diplomatic space for Bangladesh. Its strong endorsement by the UN member states as a non-permanent member of the UN Security Council during 1978–1980[15] and securing the post of executive secretary at the UN Economic and Social Commission for Asia and the Pacific (UN ESCAP) in 1981 were viewed as a ringing endorsement of Bangladesh as a responsible member of the international community.

By 1975, Bangladesh became a member of the UN's List of Least-Developed Countries (LDC),[16] allowing it to receive non-reciprocal market access to developed countries. In the following years, Dhaka also succeeded in drawing positive attention of the donor community at the Paris Club. By the late 1970s, as Bangladesh's economy gradually started to implement policy reforms, it also received strong support from Western governments and the World Bank to take new initiatives on the economic front that were focused on pushing the struggling economy to a new productive level (Islam 2003).[17] While President Zia's slogan of 'Bangladeshi nationalism' was mainly intended to mobilise support in favour of his domestic political agenda, it also unleashed the economic energy of the people[18] and sent an unmistakable message to the international community that his administration was ready to undertake bold initiatives to forge new relationships. Indeed, strong international support played a critical role in helping Bangladesh recalibrate its relationship with neighbours and other partners in the international community. It is noteworthy that during the difficult first decade, Bangladesh diplomacy was characterised by modesty, objectivity, agility and professionalism on which the subsequent initiatives were built in the successive decades.

Seeking Legitimacy through Expanded External Engagements

The second decade opened with traumatic developments at home with some ripple effects felt in Bangladesh's foreign policy as well. After Zia's tragic death in May 1981, a military coup was staged in March 1982 by General H.M. Ershad, the army chief, who took advantage of the prevailing political volatility (Auerbach 1982). What was striking was that during his tenure, Bangladesh made significant diplomatic moves with notable successes. Among the initiatives, he reached out to India to mend the frayed relationship during the time of BNP led government. As a result, a number of high-level visits took place and a number of agreements were signed with India—the Ganges Water Sharing agreement in 1982 and a Memorandum of Understanding (MoU) on the exchange of enclaves, including the perpetual leasing of the Tin Bigha corridor to Bangladesh, in October 1982. The relationship with Muslim countries deepened due to his open religious affiliation, along with that of China, although the relationship with the Soviet Union dipped.

Three other foreign policy achievements also stood out, creating a long-term strategic space for Bangladesh as a peace-loving and proactive nation. First, SAARC was launched from Dhaka in December 1985, which was perhaps yet another feather in the cap of Bangladeshi diplomacy (*The Commonwealth Journal of International Affairs* 1987). It established Bangladesh as a peace entrepreneur in South Asia, and it received wide appreciation for its noble initiative. Indeed, after the elapse of several decades since the launching of SAARC, people in many South Asian countries still strongly associate the image of Bangladesh with that of SAARC. Second, Foreign Minister Humayun Rasheed Chowdhury was elected as the president of the 41th UN General Assembly session in 1986 with overwhelming support. His election drew global attention and offered a rare opportunity to stay at the centre of global spotlight. Third, Bangladesh could put its foot at the door of UN peace-keeping operations in 1988 through its participation at the UN Mission to monitor the armistice between Iran and Iraq in that year and since then Bangladesh has become a 'consistently contributing' member of the UN peacekeeping operations. Currently, Bangladesh enjoys the number one position in terms of troop contribution to the peacekeeping missions.[19] In parallel, Bangladesh was also elected as the chair of the G-77 and China group in 1982 and under the leadership of Ambassador Farooq Sobhan, the group played a significant role in influencing the important deliberations and outcomes at the UN. It also gave Bangladesh a global profile.

Besides, two other diplomatic moves initiated during the 1980s had far-reaching positive consequences for Bangladesh. One of them was the opening of the manpower market in Saudi Arabia[20] in 1982, with the dispatch of workers to the Jeddah municipality, and in the Malaysian labour market in the mid-1980s.[21] Likewise, some domestic policy initiatives undertaken during this period had huge multiplier effects on the reputation of Bangladesh as a nation. The generous policy support extended to the burgeoning Readymade Garments (RMG) sector in the form of the bond facility played a transformative role in the field of export potential of Bangladesh (O'Shea 2015). Indeed, over the years, the export of huge volumes of RMG to the global market changed the image of Bangladesh as a trading nation and established it as an economic powerhouse. At the same time, the courageous Drug Control Policy introduced in 1982 also had a huge positive impact on the promotion of the domestic pharmaceutical sector, which, incidentally, is one of the major export items of Bangladesh to over 60 countries (Reich 1994; Gay 2017). In a similar vein, the government's active support for the establishment of the Grameen Bank[22] under the Bangladesh Bank rule in 1983 made a huge impact nationally in terms of reducing poverty through empowering rural women as well as lifting the reputation of Bangladesh as a socially creative nation globally. Indeed, Grameen Bank, Bangladesh Rural Advancement Committee (BRAC) (Whisson et al. 2021) and other NGOs played a key role in transforming the country's socio-economic landscape and aided in the creation of a new model in development (Khandker 1998; Azam and Alam 2012).

It appears that General H.M. Ershad wanted to earn domestic legitimacy through his diplomatic achievements abroad. Although his entire tenure was bumpy from a political point of view, diplomatic successes achieved during this period remain outstanding, and indeed, several current achievements in diplomacy may trace their beginnings to those days.

An Opening World and Engaged Bangladesh

The 1990s opened up a new vista of opportunities for Bangladesh in the outside world, building on earlier stepping stones. The accelerated process of globalisation created a new space for the country with regard to the movement of products, profits and persons across the larger global market. Transforming the very character of the relationship with the European Union (EU) and the US through the increased volume of ready-made garments (RMG) exports to these markets gave Bangladesh a new identity beyond its aid dependence. The establishment of World Trade Organization (WTO) in 1995 helped to further institutionalize such a transformation on a global scale, creating a wide scope for Bangladesh to explore further opportunities. Likewise, it also opened up markets for the movement of the labour force to the US, Canada, Australia and EU countries under various schemes. Thus, a new Bangladeshi diaspora community started to take shape in many countries around the world. Acquisition of WTO membership by China in 2001 was perhaps the largest accelerator in terms of expanding the consumer markets in the West (Tran 2020; Wang 2008). Bangladesh became the beneficiary of such a transforming process as a member of WTO with a positive impact on its exports, economy and employment (Kibria 2020). Since then, the three largest economies—US, China and Germany—were at the leadership of the process at WTO, and opportunities at the global level continued to bloom, which benefitted Bangladesh (Kibria 2020).

On the domestic front, the BNP, under the leadership of Begum Khaleda Zia, reaped the benefit of its determined opposition to President Ershad and won the 1991 general elections. Despite the high level of euphoria, due to domestic political turmoil, not many foreign policy initiatives could be undertaken during the first half of the 1990s.[23] Nonetheless, some of the creative financial reforms, such as the introduction of the value-added tax (VAT) helped transform the revenue collection capacity of the government in a significant way. Another forced innovation was the inclusion of a provision in the Constitution in 1996 for the formation of a non-party caretaker government to oversee the future general elections in Bangladesh.[24] According to constitutional experts, 'Bangladeshi non-party caretaker government is one of the more interesting constitutional innovations of recent times' (*The Lawyers and Jurists* 2017). This provision has since been abolished by the Supreme Court and hence removed from the Constitution in 2011. In the meantime, many countries around the world have replicated this model quite successfully.

One of the hallmarks of an ambitious foreign policy of the new AL government under Sheikh Hasina in the late 1990s was to take initiatives to resolve the long-standing issues with India, with a particular focus on the sharing of the waters of the Ganges River and ending the armed insurgency in the Chittagong Hill Tracts. Accordingly, in December 1996, Bangladesh and India signed a 30-year-long Ganges Water Sharing Agreement (Chowdhury 2018; Hanasz 2014) and a Peace Accord in Chittagong Hill Tracts (CHT) (Miti 2020) was signed in 1997 with tacit support from India.

The AL government also pursued a robust policy at the global level, and consequently, Bangladesh became a non-permanent member of the UN Security Council during the period 2000–2001. Two initiatives undertaken by Bangladesh during its tenure at the council remain landmark achievements: (*i*) the adoption of a resolution at the council on the Role of Women in Peace and Security, which was to be commemorated on the International Women's Day[25] every year and (*ii*) holding consultations with the troop contributing countries (TCCs) in the UN peacekeeping operations to protect their interests.[26] Both these resolutions not only earned goodwill for Bangladesh but also put it at the forefront of serving the collective interests of the member states at the UN.

With the change of government in 2001, the new BNP-led government under Begum Khaleda Zia tried to explore a new window of opportunity on the eastern front in the form of articulating a Look East Policy with a focus on strengthening relations with ASEAN, including Myanmar, as well as China and Japan. As the domestic political environment became tense and conflict- ridden, the government tried to deflect some of the pressure by undertaking some initiatives on the external front, such as seeking membership of the ASEAN Regional Forum, which was granted in 2006.[27] However, gaining tangible benefits from such an opening is yet to materialise.

A Polarised World and Proactive Bangladesh

Soon after it assumed power in 2009, the Awami League government under Prime Minister Sheikh Hasina set a three-point foreign policy priority with a focus on regional connectivity. They included pursuing an India-positive foreign policy to promote connectivity and widen collaboration (Chakma 2012; Momen 2021);[28] a policy of active and open regionalism in South Asia and beyond;[29] and developing a close relationship with Western countries. India's support to Bangladesh in taking a strong stand against extremism also helped in easily galvanizing support from the Western countries.

Based on these strategies, Bangladesh built an India-positive foreign policy framework and garnished it with a regional approach. Accordingly, it decided to unilaterally allow India to use the Chittagong and Mongla ports (Ministry of External Affairs 2010). Gradually it spawned into the nucleus of a larger sub-regional approach. In 2015, Bangladesh, Bhutan, India and Nepal agreed to form a sub-regional framework for cooperation called the Bangladesh, Bhutan, India and Nepal (BBIN) Initiative, which is yet to become operational (Warren and Nag 2016).

Two other landmark developments marked the progress in bilateral relations between Bangladesh and India. One was the demarcation of a 4,000-kilometre-long land boundary along the Bangladesh–India borders, which was sealed in 2015 during the first visit of Prime Minister Modi to Bangladeshi in June 2015 (Ministry of External Affairs 2010). The other one was the demarcation of the maritime boundary between the two countries, the verdict of which was delivered by the Hague Court of Arbitration in 2014 (Constance 2014; UNB 2020; Mirdha 2021).

Some movement took place on the economic front as well. India has granted 98 per cent duty waiver benefits under the South Asian Free Trade Area (SAFTA) and bilateral frameworks since 2011.[30] While India has extended bilateral loans worth $7.36 billion to Bangladesh since 2010, Indian investment in Bangladesh has remained relatively modest (Mahmood 2021).[31] Nonetheless, India will continue to play a significant role in the economic matrix of Bangladesh, with all its attendant opportunities and challenges. Mindful of the changing economic realities, Bangladesh is now trying to meet the emerging challenges by intensifying its initiatives to attract foreign investment. It is also exploring economic opportunities through the signing of preferential trade agreements (PTAs) and free trade agreements (FTAs) with several countries ahead of its graduation to the level of a low-income developing country by 2026 (UNB 2020; Mirdha 2021). Accordingly, the government has focused on economic diplomacy as the number one priority for its engagement outside (Bhattacharya 2019).

On the maritime side, Bangladesh is eager to exploit the resources from the 'blue economy' and work with regional partners in this pursuit. In this context, the country has highlighted the scope for expanding economic cooperation among the members of the Indian Ocean Rim Association (IORA) (UNB 2021). Further, under its current chairmanship of IORA, it may intensify its efforts to draw attention to and engage with the IORA partners to explore peace and economic cooperation in this domain in a meaningful manner. A few other recent developments, however, have demanded a qualitatively different approach to the Bay and Bengal and Indian Ocean domain, particularly after President Xi Jinping announced China's Belt and Road Initiative (BRI) (Chatzky and McBride 2020) in 2013 and then US president Donald Trump initiated the country's Indo-Pacific Strategy in 2017 (Ford 2020), which has been refined by President Biden in 2021. Both initiatives aim at advancing their strategic and economic interests in the Indo-Pacific region and notably, Bangladesh has extended its support to both these ideas with an accent on their economic priorities (Tribune Desk 2019).

The emerging message from the extended region is clear: the countries in this neighbourhood, including China and Japan, have their eyes fixed on exploring the economic potential of the region while simultaneously pursuing military strategic objectives; they do not see them as mutually exclusive (Heydarian 2021). In light of Dhaka's upcoming graduation, there is a growing realisation in Bangladesh that it should also actively explore all opportunities to engage with emerging economic groupings such as the Regional Comprehensive Economic Partnership (RCEP) (Khan 2021) and pursue its economic interests, including capitalising on the opportunities created by the digital economy and benefitting from its interactions with China, India and the US (Pedrosa and Findlay 2020; Madan 2021). Likewise, Covid-19 and its devastating impacts have perhaps sensitised regional countries to unforeseen risks and the diminishing returns from the geopolitical tensions in the face of the ferocity of non-traditional threats, such as health, food, energy, cybersecurity, environment and climate, among others (Gong 2021).

Challenges

On its part, Bangladesh is aware of the unfolding strategic importance of the region and the countries along the Indian Ocean periphery. In recent years, several issues of huge strategic importance, both at the regional level as well as the global level, have tested the strength and agility of Bangladesh diplomacy. Five of them deserve special mention—the Rohingya issue, the Covid-19 pandemic, the war in Ukraine, the digital economy and governance issues.

Rohingya Repatriation

Initially unfolded as a humanitarian crisis in 2017, the Rohingya issue has now turned into a regional security threat with the potential for far-reaching negative consequences for the regional (Tribune Desk 2019). It has also created a new space for competition among regional and global actors. Regardless, despite the fact that the international community has stood firmly for the early, 'voluntary, safe and sustainable return of the Rohingyas,' not a single Rohingya has been able to return to their homeland as 'Myanmar failed to create conditions conducive' to facilitate their return (TBS Report 2021). Unfortunately, the strengthening of radical nationalism within Myanmar and the recent intensification of armed conflicts in Myanmar, particularly in the Rakhine State on the one hand and the growing geopolitical divide among the relevant powers on the other, have continued to complicate the resolution of this human tragedy (UN 2018). Indeed, despite Chinese effort in recent months to convince Myanmar to start at least a pilot repatriation is yet to bear fruit in the face of deep-seated mistrust among the Rohingya population in Bangladesh about the commitment from the Myanmar regime to address their concerns and the questionable ground realities in the Rakhine State.[32] The reluctance of some of the UN agencies and some Western powers to back the pilot repatriation has created another drag in the potential repatriation process.[33] The lack of pressure on Myanmar by India and Russia, on the other hand, to create a congenial environment for the return of the Rohingyas continues to be a source of frustration. In addition, in the wake of the military takeover in Myanmar in February 2021, Russia has become a major source of arms supply to the regime with a view to advance its strategic interests in the region. This has not only helped perpetuate the military rule in the country, it has also further complicated the process of Rohingya repatriation. Needless to say, unless resolved soon and on a sustainable basis, and through an active initiative of India, China, ASEAN, EU, US and the UN, the Rohingya issue will continue to remain a major foreign policy challenge for Bangladesh and pose a strategic challenge for the extended region (Hossain 2021).

Covid-19

As if the burden of the Rohingya influx from Myanmar in 2017 was not enough, the outbreak of Covid-19 in early 2020 came as yet another geopolitical shock to Bangladesh. Although Dhaka could recover from the Covid-19 crisis with a relatively modest loss, its domestic policy as well as diplomacy were severely tested during this crisis. At the domestic level, Bangladesh responded to the unfolding pandemic through a number of innovative policy initiatives, including the imposition of a calibrated lockdown, offering financial stimulus to various actors and sectors.[34] It also conducted aggressive diplomacy to procure Covid-19 vaccines from practically all sources (Bhuiyan 2021; Tajmim 2022). Several initiatives were noteworthy. At the bilateral level, Bangladesh reached out to all vaccine-producing countries—India, China, Russia, US and COVAX facilities—to procure vaccines on an urgent basis. The Bangladesh foreign minister was at the forefront in approaching all countries and agencies producing and supplying Covid-19 vaccines (Tajmim 2022). In such a pursuit, Bangladesh had to often navigate through the maze of geopolitical tensions between India and China, as well as between the US and China, as each one of them had pursued their own Covid-19 diplomacy to advance their strategic objectives. Regionally, Bangladesh also responded to the Indian initiative to mobilize financial resources under the SAARC platform (Star Online 2020). It also sought support from friendly countries to assist Bangladesh in manufacturing Covid-19 vaccines locally, even though the outcome was not very encouraging. At the multilateral level, Bangladesh joined India and South Africa in requesting for the waiver of intellectual property rights at the WTO to facilitate local production of Covid-19 vaccines in developing countries (bdnews24 2021). At the UN level, Bangladesh's call for declaring these vaccines as a global public good was well appreciated.[35] Bangladesh also successfully drew the attention of the international community towards the plight of migrant workers and refugees, and the adverse impact of the Covid-19 pandemic on climate vulnerable countries.[36]

War in Ukraine

The military conflict in Ukraine came as yet another test for the diplomatic strength and agility of Bangladesh. Indeed, the Ukraine war has challenged Bangladesh on many fronts. It faced a tough choice between standing by its long-held principles of respecting the sovereignty and territorial integrity of all nations as well as resolving conflicts through peaceful means, as enshrined in the UN Charter, and protecting its material interests through maintaining its economic growth momentum. As the pressure mounted due to supply chain disruption leading to higher import bills, declining export earnings and remittances, rising risk of falling foreign exchange reserves, among other things, the heat of the Ukraine war was acutely felt in Bangladesh, threatening its domestic political and social stability. This issue assumed a particular salience following the collapse of the Sri Lankan government in July 2022 (Rabbee 2022). These drivers indeed helped shape the response of Bangladesh along a two-pronged strategy. First, it paid extra attention to protect its economic interests in an uncertain global environment. In her statement at the UN General Assembly, Hasina was categorical in calling for the end of the Ukraine–Russia conflict to alleviate the economic sufferings of the people around the world. She also underscored the unintended negative consequences sanctions and counter-sanctions had wrought on various countries, including and beyond the targeted countries. She further added that such actions had hugely affected the vulnerable sections of society, such as women and children in many countries (Bangladesh Sangbad Sangstha 2022). In parallel, Bangladesh was also extra conscious not to jeopardize its commercial interest, given the Russian support in building and completing the landmark $12.65 billion nuclear power plant (BBC 2011; Biswas 2022).

Second, at the diplomatic level, Bangladesh decided to pursue a rather cautious policy line and maintained its non-aligned stand on the war in Ukraine. The abstention of Bangladesh during the voting on the resolution at the UN General Assembly on 2 March 2022, condemning Russia for violation of the territorial integrity of Ukraine (Tribune Desk 2022), reflected such an understanding, although Bangladesh voted in favour of a resolution rejecting the annexation of eastern Ukrainian territory in October 2022 (Toosi and Heath 2022). Yet, two opposite trends posed some strategic dilemmas for Bangladesh. First, the US decision to impose sanctions against some leaders of the Rapid Action Battalion (RAB), a paramilitary outfit, in December 2021 for alleged violation of human rights in Bangladesh did not please the leadership, and may have had some role in framing its perspective on the Ukraine issue (*The Daily Star* 2021). Additionally, the growing Russian proximity to the military regime in Myanmar and their continued indifference shown towards the repatriation of Rohingya refugees added a new layer of complexity for Bangladesh. However, against the growing pressure from the US and other Western countries to ensure a free, fair and inclusive and internationally recognised parliamentary election in 2024, the Bangladesh government seems to have positively viewed the Russian position as a kind of counter weight against the US policies. The recent visit of Russian Foreign Minister Sergey Lavrov to Bangladesh and his remarks could be seen from that perspective.[37]

Geopolitics and Digital Economy

Bangladesh's strong economic relationship with China, India, Japan, the US and the EU as well as the large concentration of its expatriate workers in Middle Eastern and Southeast Asian countries, its developmental needs and the emergence of the digital economy in the ASEAN region, are framing the future diplomatic landscape for Bangladesh. With the onset of de-globalizing trends and the growing preference for a shorter value chain for products and services, a new context has appeared before Bangladesh to adjust its diplomatic focus. The urgency for the exploration of opportunities from the blue economy and the need to take a fresh look at the emerging economic groupings in the form of Regional Comprehensive Economic Partnership (RCEP) led by the ASEAN and the Comprehensive and Progressive Agreement for Trans-Pacific Partnership (CPTPP), led by Japan among others, have multiplied the pressure.[38] In parallel, the economic interest and involvement of the US, UK and EU in the Indo-Pacific domain will be an additional attraction. Notwithstanding attendant challenges, it may open up an additional window of opportunity for Bangladesh.

Governance Issues and Growing Radicalisation

The recent focus on governance issues at the global level has created a challenge for Bangladesh on several counts, including human rights, labour rights and safety issues, democratic space and practices, freedom of press, as well as accountability and transparency issues. The country has already had to confront some of these challenges; they also perhaps offer a preview of the future expectations from the international community. As the country inches towards a developing country status by 2026, these issues will acquire more salience, both domestically and globally (Kennedy and Hassan 2022; Hussain 2021). Beyond these visible manifestations, churning at the regional level is not less challenging either. Indeed, the growing communalisation of politics, the radicalisation of societies, the exclusionary trend in regional diplomacy, along with the prioritisation of geopolitical interests over moral or humanitarian ones as well as the tendency to look at all issues and interactions from a zero-sum game pose a new pattern of risks (Kugelman 2021).

Lessons

With Bangladesh having crossed 52 years of its existence, it would perhaps be worthwhile to look at a few lessons learnt along the way on the pattern of its engagement with the outside world. Four lessons could be noteworthy.

First, Bangladesh's diplomacy has succeeded when it has tried to build its outreach to the outside world based on its uniqueness, which revolves around the enormous sacrifice made by its people to secure its independence, the inexhaustible energy and creativity of its people and society, the strong aspirations of its citizenry for democracy, social and economic equality as well as justice, as espoused in the Proclamation of Independence and the Constitution. The future of its outreach to the world would be better served if it refines it strategy based on these expectations.

Second, modesty and professionalism have also served Bangladesh well, and in the highly crowded and competitive global environment, its image or reputation as a democratic nation will also matter more and more. This issue is particularly relevant for Bangladesh with a relatively complex and uneven stock of reputation as a nation. The idea of Bangladesh, therefore, has to be continuously enriched and updated in light of the collective expectation of its people in an uncertain global environment.

Third, yet another lesson is that the success of its diplomacy depends on creating linkages between governance and diplomacy, development and diplomacy, business and diplomacy, as well as with non-state actors. Accordingly, the development of a strategic culture inside and an appreciation of the dynamic strategic environment outside will continue to help Bangladesh in capitalizing on many unfolding opportunities in the outside world.

Lastly, Bangladesh diplomacy has been successful when it has defined its national interest from a collective perspective, not a partisan one, and in an inclusive manner, keeping in view its long-term national objectives. On the contrary, short-term and often regime-centric interpretation has not served the larger national interest of the country. This could also be a useful guide for the future engagement of Bangladesh in the outside world.

Conclusion

Despite a tough beginning, over the last 52 years, Bangladesh has immensely benefitted from its gainful engagement with the outside world. At the same time, it has also contributed proactively and responsibly towards strengthening the process of peace, progress and stability in the region and beyond. As Bangladesh achieves a different level in economic categorisation by the UN, the nature of its engagement will also change, and indeed the next 50 years could be very different (Anam 2021). Bangladesh has already emerged as a success story in economic development and has become an important geopolitical actor in South Asia and in the Indian Ocean region (Raja Mohan 2021; Riaz and Parvez 2021) as well as an important player in fighting the challenges of climate change.[39] Yet, all these are taking place at a time of multiple uncertainties, disruptions and volatilities.

Consequently, the very approach, methodology, content and style of its interaction with the outside world will also change. As the risk of uncertainties grows and the process of transformation intensifies, particularly in the post-pandemic and the post-Ukraine war situation, the nature of diplomacy will have to transcend its traditional formal and established entities and boundaries by using more creativity and agility. In this pursuit, effective and efficient utilisation of formal and informal channels and tools, such as social media, artificial intelligence, big data and other methods of digital outreach as the backbone of interactions with the multiple and varied actors of the international community could deserve more attention (Runde and Savoy 2020). Accordingly, Bangladesh diplomacy has to make urgent adjustments in terms of its understanding and approach to engaging the growing tech-savvy segments of the global population and gainfully exploring the unfolding digital economy as well as successfully navigating the emerging multipolar and multi-partner world.

Notes

1. Bangladesh war was interpreted by many as a 'civil war', which largely highlighted the statist approach and, in the process, overlooked the essence of the struggle for independence carried out by the people of Bangladesh.
2. At its birth, Bangladesh was promptly dismissed as an 'international basket case' by Ural Alexis Johnson, the US undersecretary of state for political affairs during a December 1971 meeting. US National Security Adviser Dr Henry Kissinger agreed and replied: 'But not necessarily our basket case.' Quoted in Salil Tripathi, 'Bangladesh's Long Journey from Basket Case to Rising Star', *Foreign Policy*, April 10, 2021. Even some Australian diplomats and some of their intelligence agencies had also shared this pessimistic view. For details see, Ric Smith, 'India, the United State, Australia and the Difficult Birth of Bangladesh', *Australian Institute of International Affairs*, (2019): 48–52.
3. The World Bank looks at Bangladesh as a development paradox. For details see, Harry Blair, 'The Bangladesh Paradox', *Journal of Democracy* 31, no. 4, (October 2020): 138–150; Amitava Kar, 'The Bangladesh Paradox', *The Daily Star*, February 23, 2017; Arvind Subramanian, 'The Paradoxes of Bangladesh Miracle', *The Project Syndicate*, June 11, 2021; Jyoti Rahman, 'Decoding the Bangladesh Paradox', *The Dhaka Tribune*, December 2, 2013.
4. The Proclamation of Independence, Mujibnagar, April 10, 1971.
5. The Proclamation of Independence, Mujibnagar, April 10, 1971. For details see, R. Majumder (ed.), 'Bangladesh My Bangladesh, Selected Speeches and Statements of Sheikh Mujibur Rahman (October 28, 1970 to March

26, 1971)', cited in Harun ur Rashid, *Bangladesh Foreign Policy*, Annex 1 (New Delhi, Orient Longman, 1972).
6   For details see, Harun ur Rashid, *Bangladesh Foreign Policy: Realities, Priorities and Challenges*, Fourth Revise Edition (Dhaka: Academic Press and Publishers Library, 2019), 54–55.
7   Dr Iftekhar A. Chowdhury captured this thought in his unpublished PhD dissertation at the Australian National University in 1981, citing his discussion with then then foreign minister of Bangladesh, Dr Kamal Hossain.
8   Price hike, massive smuggling at the borders, labour unrest and the rising expectations of the youth radicalised during the Liberation War created a great of challenges for the newly formed government. For details, see, Rounaq Jahan, 'Bangladesh in 1972: Nation Building in a New State', *Asian Survey* 13, no. 2, (February 1973): 199–210.
9   Ibid.
10 Author's discussion with senior colleagues at the Ministry of Foreign Affairs, Dhaka, 18 April 2022.
11 Ibid.
12 According to Economic Resources Division (ERD) an amount of $101.37 billion worth of foreign assistance has been disbursed to Bangladesh up to June 2020, of which $28.51 billion came as grant and $72.85 billion as loan. For details, see 'Foreign Assistance to Bangladesh at a Glance (1971/2-2020/2021) (Provisional)', Economic Resources Division, Ministry of Planning, Dhaka, 2021, www.erd.gov.bd (accessed on October 29, 2021).
13 Due to a massive infusion of ODA in Bangladesh since its independence, ERD under the Ministry of Finance, which coordinated the flow of aid, grew in importance, and occasionally exercised disproportionate influence in terms of Bangladesh's engagement abroad.
14 Bangladesh Krishak Sramik Awami League (BKSAL) was formed on January 25, 1975 by assuming all powers by the president, abolishing all political parties, reducing the number of newspapers and promising to create a socialist Bangladesh, among other things. For details, see Harun ur Rashid, *Bangladesh Foreign Policy* (details in endnote 6), 100–101; Probir Kumar Sarker, 'What Chairman Mujib Said About Baksal', *The Dhaka Tribune*, August 15, 2021.
15 Bangladesh won the non-permanent seat at the United Nations Security Council for the period 1979–1980 by defeating Japan, which was seen as a major victory of Bangladesh diplomacy.
16 In order to understand the dynamics of Bangladesh joining the LDC group see Nurul Islam, *Making of a Nation* (Dhaka: UPL, 2003), 360.
17 Ibid., 357–380.
18 The RMG success story of Bangladesh owes its origin to Mr Nurul Kader Khan, a former civil servant, a freedom fighter and an entrepreneur, who took advantage of the new business opening in 1978 to collaborate with South Korean Dawoo Company to produce and export RMG in volumes for the first time from Bangladesh. The government and the Bangladesh Bank had to devise new policy formulations to allow RMG sector to grow.

19 Bangladesh Prime Minister's statement on 8 May 2021. Currently, Bangladesh has offered 6,731 troops to UN PKOs. United Nation's, PKO Monthly Strength Report, www.un.org (accessed on 12 June 2021).
20 Export of manpower to Saudi Arabia in 1982 was perhaps the first formal effort to export Bangladeshi manpower to its most potential market, which now accommodates more than two million workers. The actual process of manpower export had begun in 1976. Today, around 1.3 million Bangladesh expatriate workers work in around 163 countries around the world sending around $20 billion annually. For details, see Giorgi Gigauri, 'Migrants' Contribution to the 50-Year Journey of Bangladesh', *The Daily Star*, Match 26, 2021.
21 Discussion with Ambassador Farooq Sobhan, who was Bangladesh's high commissioner in Malaysia from 1983 to 1987.
22 In October 1983 the Grameen Bank was authorised by national legislation to operate as an independent bank. It grew significantly between 2003 and 2007; 'Grameen Bank: Bangladeshi Bank', *Encyclopedia Britannica*, 2005.
23 The euphoria centring on the restoration of democracy in Bangladesh, political contest, agitation and violence continued to often paralyse the system of governance. For an excellent study on the nature of political process see, Research Directorate, 'Political Parties and Political Violence', Canada Immigration and Refugee Board, May 1, 1994.
24 For a background to the introduction of non-party caretaker government see, Zillur R. Khan, 'Bangladesh's Experiments with Parliament Democracy', *Asian Survey* 37, no. 6, (June 1997): 575–589.
25 The Security Council adopted resolution (S/RES/1325) on women and peace and security on October 31, 2000. The resolution reaffirms the important role of women in the prevention and resolution of conflicts, peace negotiations, peace-building, peacekeeping, humanitarian response and in post-conflict reconstruction and stresses the importance of their equal participation and full involvement in all efforts for the maintenance and promotion of peace and security.
26 Under the UN Security Council Resolution 1353, the council agreed to consult the Troop Contributing Countries (TCCs) regularly to address both generic peacekeeping issues relevant to the responsibilities of the Council and technical aspects of resolutions 1327 and 1353. This resolution was particularly beneficial to the troop contributing countries from the developing world, which contribute most the troops for the UN peacekeeping operations, but had little voice in the decision making process of the Security Council. Bangladesh chaired the Security Council during the adoption of those documents in March 2001.
27 Bangladesh joined the ASEAN Regional Forum in 2006.
28 For a detailed discussion on Bangladesh foreign policy during Sheikh Hasina's current regime, see A.K. Abdul Momen, 'Bangladesh Foreign Policy Compulsions, Constraints and Choices', *The Daily Star*, August 23, 2021.
29 As defined by Ross Garnaut and Peter Drysdale, it includes the use of integrative processes and regional cooperation to mutually reduce trade barriers within the Asia-Pacific region without discriminating against

outsiders. For details, see David Capie and Paul Evans, *Open Regionalism in the Asia-Pacific Security Lexicon*, Singapore: ISEAS–Yusof Ishak Institute, (online publication), October 2015.

30   India granted duty-free market access to Bangladeshi products in 2011 under both bilateral and SAFTA framework. For details see PTI, 'PM Announces Duty Free Imports from Bangladesh', *Mint*, September 7, 2011.

31   India does not yet figure out among the top five countries which invest in Bangladesh. For details, see '2021 Investment Climate Statements: Bangladesh', US Embassy, Dhaka, US Department of State, July 21, 2021; For a detailed discussion on the FDI inflow in Bangladesh until 2020, see Adam Pitman, 'Why India Must Not Allow Its Relationship to be Viewed Through Chinese Prism', *Scroll.in*, July 12, 2021.

32   Parimol Palma, 'Rohingya Repatriation: China Now Active, But Uncertainties Yet to Clear up', *The Daily Star*, May 30, 2023.

33   Press release, 'Bangladesh Must Suspend Pilot Project to Return Rohingya Refugees to Myanmar: UN Expert', Office of the High Commissioner for Human Rights, June 8, 2023; UNB, 'Momen: Many Global Actors Don't Want Rohingya to be Repatriated at This Moment, *Dhaka Tribune*, August 2, 2023.

34   Bangladesh offered $13.75 billion as part of 23 stimulus packages to ward off the adverse impact of Covid-19. For details see, Star Online Report, 'Govt Approves 2 New Stimulus Packages of Taka 2,700 Crores', *The Daily Star*, January 17, 2021.

35   Prime Minister of Bangladesh Sheikh Hasina's statement at the 77th UN General Assembly Session, September 24, 2021.

36   Ibid.

37   Diplomatic Correspondent, 'Lavrov Praises Dhaka's Stance Despite US Pressure', *The Prothom Alo*, September 8, 2023.

38   Refayet Ullah Mirdha, 'Bangladesh Moves to Join RCEP', *The Daily Star*, July 28, 2022.

39   President Biden highlighted this role of Bangladesh in this regard in a message to Prime Minister Sheikh Hasina on the occasion of its 50th anniversary of the establishment of diplomatic relations between Bangladesh and the United States. For details, see Staff Correspondent, 'Biden Hopes for Stronger Dhaka–Washington Ties', *The Daily Star*, April 5, 2022.

References

Anam, M. 'What Got Us Here Will Not Take Us There'. *The Daily Star*, March 18, 2021.

Ashrafi, S.T. 'How the Cold War Shaped Bangladesh's Liberation War'. *The Diplomat*, March 20, 2022.

Auerbach, S. 'General Defends Bangladesh Coup'. *The Washington Post*, March 25, 1982.

Azam, M.S.E. and M.Z. Alam. 'Effect of Grameen Bank Micro-Credit Program on Change in Socio-Economic Condition and Empowerment of Rural Women'. *Journal of Education and Practice* 3, no. 14 (2012).

'Bangladesh Agrees Nuclear Power Deal with Russia'. BBC, November 2, 2011.
'Bangladesh-India Joint Communiqué'. Ministry of External Affairs, Government of India, New Delhi, January 12, 2010.
Biswas, A. 'Bangladesh Defies US Pressure, Russian Aided Nuclear Plant Work on'. *Northlines*, March 16, 2022.
Bhattacharjee, J. 'A Landmark in India-Bangladesh Ties'. *Business Line*, January 23, 2018.
Bhattacharya, P. 'Economic Diplomacy Top Priority, Momen'. *The Daily Star*, February 10, 2019.
Bhuiyan, H.K. 'Bangladesh Makes Desperate Diplomatic Efforts to Get Covid-19 Vaccines'. *The Dhaka Tribune*, May 22, 2021.
Butt, A.I. 'Looking Back at the Geopolitics Behind Pakistan's Genocidal Split of 1971'. *The Wire*, December 28, 2017.
Chakma, B. 'Bangladesh-India Relations: Sheikh Hasina's India-Positive Policy Approach'. RSIS Working Paper, 252. S. Rajaratnam School of International Studies, Singapore, November 12, 2012.
Chattopadhyay, S. 'Role of Foreign Aid in Bangladesh'. *The Daily Star*, July 12, 2018.
Chatzky, A. and J. McBride. 'China's Massive Belt and Road Initiative'. Council on Foreign Relations, January 28, 2020.
Chowdhury, K.R. 'The Ganga Treaty: Ainun Nishat on How India, Bangladesh Signed a Historic Deal'. *The Third Pole*, September 20, 2018.
Constance, J. 'Bangladesh, India Court Awards Control of Maritime Region'. US Library of Congress, July 15, 2014.
'Flow of External Resources into Bangladesh'. Economic Relations Division, Ministry of Finance, Government of Bangladesh, 4–7, February 10, 2019.
Ford, L. 'The Trump Administration and the 'Free and Open Indo Pacific'. Brookings Institute, May 2020.
Franda, M. 'Ziaur Rahman and Bangladeshi Nationalism'. *Economic and Political Weekly* 16, nos 10/12, (March 1981): 357–380.
'Full Text of PM Sheikh Hasina's Speech at UNGA'. Bangladesh Sangbad Sangstha (BSS), September 24, 2022.
Gay, D. 'What LDC Graduation Will Mean for Bangladesh's Drugs Industry?' United Nations, LDC Portal, 2017.
Gong, L. 'Non-Traditional Security Concerns in the New Normal'. Webinar at S. Rajaratnam School of International Studies, June, 2021.
Hanasz, P. 'Sharing Waters vs. Sharing Rivers: The 1996 Ganges Treaty'. The Australian National University, July 28, 2014.
Hasan, M.D. 'Foreign Aid Dependency in Bangladesh: An Evaluation'. *The Chittagong University Journal of Business Administration* 26, (2011): 281–294.
'Hasina to Call for Waiver of Covid Vaccines Patent at UNGA'. bdnews24.com, September 16, 2021.
Heydarian, R.J. 'Biden's China Policy Gets ASEAN Cold Shoulder'. *Asia Times*, July 21, 2021.
Hossain, B. 'Poverty Reduction During 1971–2013 Periods: Success and Its Recent Trends in Bangladesh'. *Global Journal of Human Social Science: E Economics* 14, no. 5, (2014): 38–47.

Hossain, D. 'The UNGA Resolution on the Situation in Myanmar: Why Was the Rohingya Issue Neglected?' *Modern Diplomacy*, June 30, 2021.

'Human Rights Abuse: US Sanctions RAB, Seven Top Officials'. *The Daily Star*, December 11, 2021.

Hussain, J. 'Bangladeshi Exports to Face EU's New GSP Rule'. *The Financial Express*, May 15, 2022.

Islam, Nurul. *Making of a Nation: Bangladesh: An Economist's Tale*. Dhaka: University Press Limited, 2003.

Jahan, R. 'Bangladesh in 1973: Management of Factional Politics'. *Asian Survey*, 125–135. February 1974.

Kennedy, K. and T. Hassan, 'US Stands Firm on Sanctions on Rights Abusers in Bangladesh'. *Asia Times*, April 13, 2022.

Khan, A.K. 'Bangladesh Joining the RCEP Will Be a Bold and Epoch-Making Step'. *The Business Standard*, September 16, 2021.

Khandker, S.R. *Fighting Poverty with Microcredit: Experience in Bangladesh*. The World Bank, 1998.

Kibria, A. 'Bangladesh Benefits from WTO Membership'. *The Financial Express*, January 10, 2020.

Kugelman, M. 'India Faces Tests from Its Neighbours'. *Foreign Policy*, April 1, 2021.

Madan, T. *Major Power Rivalry in South Asia*. Council on Foreign Relations, October 2021.

Mirdha, R.U. 'Govt Goes All out to Sign FTAs'. *The Daily Star*, September 10, 2021.

Miti, S. 'By Executing CHT Accord Bangladesh Has Entered a Glorious Chapter of Peace Implementation'. *The Business Standard*, December 2, 2020.

Mahmood, S.A. 'Where Are the Foreign Investors Coming from?' *The Dhaka Tribune*, May 24, 2021.

Maniruzzaman, T. 'Bangladesh in 1975: The Fall of Mujib Regime and Its Aftermath'. *Asian Survey* 16, no. 2, (February 1976): 119–129.

Momen, Abdul A.K. 'Bangladesh Foreign Policy Compulsions, Constraints and Choices', *The Daily Star*, August 23, 2021.

O'Shea, B.J. *Bangladesh Bond Warehouse Regime Assessment Plus Recommendations*. World Bank Group, March 10, 2015.

Pedrosa, E. and C. Findlay. 'Why RCEP Is a Big Deal?' *East Asian Forum*, November 30, 2020.

Rabbee, S. 'Why Sri Lanka Collapse Looms Large over Bangladesh?' *Al Jazeera*, August 25, 2022.

Rahman, S.A. 'Rohingya Crisis and OIC: Assessing the Role—Analysis'. *Eurasia Review*, May 20, 2021.

Raihan, S. 'Policy Priorities for Foreign Aid Reforms in Bangladesh'. Paper Presented at an International Conference at Colombo, Sri Lanka, 2010.

Rashid, Harun ur. *Bangladesh Foreign Policy: Realities, Priorities and Challenges*. Dhaka Academic Press and Publishers Library, 2005.

Raja Mohan, C. '50 Years after Independence, Bangladesh Bursts into Geopolitics'. *Foreign Policy*, March 25, 2021.

Reich, M.R. 'Bangladesh Pharmaceutical Policy and Politics'. *Health Policy and Planning* 9, no. 2 (1994): 130–143.

Riaz, A. and S. Parvez. 'Bangladesh Has Emerged as an Important Geopolitical Actor'. *Prothom Alo*. March 18, 2021.

Robinson, G. 'The Rise and Rise of Bangladesh'. *Nikkei Asian Review*, December 19, 2018.

Runde, D.F. and C.M. Savoy. 'Post Pandemic Infrastructure and Digital Connectivity in the Indo-Pacific'. *CSIS Briefs*, November 2, 2020.

Star Online report. 'Bangladesh Contributes $1.5 Million to SAARC Covid-19 Emergency Fund'. *The Daily Star*, March 20, 2020.

'South Asia: The Spirit of SAARC'. *The Commonwealth Journal of International Affairs* 76, no. 301, (1987): 2–6.

Tajmim, T. 'Vaccine Diplomacy Success as Bangladesh Gets Most Vaccines from Covax'. *The Business Standard*, January 23, 2022.

'The Caretaker Government in Bangladesh and in Different Countries'. *The Lawyers and Jurists*, 2017. www.lawyersnjuriusts.com (accessed on June 3, 2021).

Toosi, N. and R. Heath. 'Strong Majority of Countries Rebukes Russia at UN'. *Politico*, October 12, 2022.

Tran, V.H. 'WTO Membership for China and Its Impact on Growth, Investment, and Consumption: A New Flexible Keynesian Approach'. University of Wollongong, January 2020.

'Treaty of Peace and Friendship between the Government of India and the Government of the People's Republic of Bangladesh, Government of India'. Mea.gov.in, Ministry of External Affairs, March 19, 1972.

Tribune Desk. 'PM Showcases 5-Point Proposal at Summer Davos to Make Indo-Pacific Initiatives a Success'. *The Dhaka Tribune*, July 2, 2019.

———. 'PM: Rohingyas a Threat to National, Regional Security'. *The Dhaka Tribune*, November 11, 2019.

———. 'Bangladesh Abstains from UN Resolution Criticizing Russian Invasion of Ukraine'. *The Dhaka Tribune*, March 3, 2022.

United News of Bangladesh (UNB). 'Bangladesh Pins Hopes on Various Trade Deals After LDC Graduation'. *The Dhaka Tribune*, December 12, 2020.

———. 'Bangladesh Urges IORA Member States to Enhance Economic Cooperation'. *The Financial Express*, 17 June, 2021.

'UN Resolution on Rohingyas Asks Myanmar to Address Crisis'. *The Business Standard*, November 18, 2021.

Wang, J.Y.L.Y. 'China's Integration with the World Development as a Process of Learning and Industrial Upgrading'. Report, The World Bank Development Economics Vice Presidency and World Bank Institute for Finance and Private Sector Development Division, December 2008.

Warren, A. and D. Nag, D. 'Advancing the BBIN Agenda to Promote Sub-Regional Trade'. The Asia Foundation, April 27, 2016.

Whisson, I., R. Haque, J. Kedroske, M. Sulaiman, et al. *The State of Economic Inclusion Report 2021: The Potential to Scale*. Report, The World Bank Group, 2021.

6

SMALLER STATES IN A MULTIPOLAR ASIA: THE CASE OF BANGLADESH

Johannes Plagemann

Introduction

For long, Bangladesh was considered as a quintessentially 'weak' state in international affairs. A major aid recipient situated uncomfortably between its much larger Indian neighbour and an impoverished and politically unstable Myanmar, Dhaka's foreign policy since independence was preoccupied with managing its vulnerabilities—from its dependency on Western aid to a favourable international trading environment for its few export products, or the fallout from Indian domestic politics with often little concern for Bangladesh's needs.

More recently, however, the picture has changed significantly. After two decades of sustained economic growth and improving social indicators, Bangladesh in 2021 found itself in the position to extend its own foreign aid to another country for the first time in its history. Indeed, the extension of a $200 million loan to Sri Lanka in June 2021 signals a change in self-conception that had been in the making for years. Shedding previous notions of Bangladesh as a weak power, foreign observers have begun referring to 'rising Bangladesh' as 'an important Indo-Pacific middle player' (Brewster 2021), indicating a changing international image too.

What explains Bangladesh's changing status both externally and internally and where do we find limits to this? This contribution continues by outlining some of the central tenets from the literature on weak states in international relations that Bangladesh for long illustrated. It proceeds by way of detailing some empirical observations that indicate changes in the international status Bangladesh enjoys before also discussing some (novel) restrictions on Dhaka's foreign affairs that a multipolar system maintains. The fundamental argument here is that the tense multipolarity we observe in Asia today accrues a greater bargaining power in bilateral relations to secondary and tertiary states such as Bangladesh. At the same time, multipolarity severely restricts the collective power of weak states through coalitions in multilateral settings.

Weak States in International Relations (IR) Theory

A key feature of international affairs is asymmetry. Nation states vary enormously according to their population size and their economies as well as other resources that determine state capacities— from the strength of its institutions to natural resource wealth. The literature on weak states in international affairs typically refers to either the nature of countries' vulnerabilities to the outside world, a small population, GDP, and/or state capacities relative to other states (see Katzenstein 2003; Thorhallsson and Steinsson 2017). Smallness in the latter senses usually (but not necessarily) indicates weakness. In any case, what matters more to IR literature (and this chapter) than the objective size of a state's territory or its population is the relative strength a state maintains vis-à-vis its neighbours, friends and adversaries. As Keohane in his classic review essay from 1969 outlines, states can be categorised along their leaders' perceptions regarding their countries capabilities to affect the international system—from system determining, system influencing, system affecting and system-ineffectual states, which includes great, secondary, middle and small powers (Keohane 1969, 295–296). On all these accounts, Bangladesh for long was widely described as a 'weak' state.[1] A state's assessment of its vulnerabilities and weaknesses is a key determinant of its foreign policy as it foregrounds a country's relations with major powers as well as international institutions.

Typically, weak states' foreign policies include three defining features. First, due to their dependency on the goodwill of a select group of major powers, weak states invest heavily in bilateral relations with them. The asymmetry in power is thus paralleled by an asymmetry in attention: whereas weak states closely follow relevant major powers' domestic as well as foreign policies, major powers note weak states only at the margins. The same logic of specialisation applies to foreign policy areas that are of particular importance to individual weak states. Often reliant on a select set of export products, weak states focus their foreign and trade expertise on these areas, thereby potentially matching major powers' proficiency, who themselves must consider many other, often domestically more relevant, foreign policy and trade considerations. As the case of Bangladesh shows, heightened political attention may come along with a strong sense of politicisation of specific foreign policy issues or bilateral relations that is not paralleled in the respective major powers' domestic debates. In sum then, ignorance is a luxury weak states cannot afford.

Second, and relatedly, given weak states' general self-understanding of being unable to affect the international system and the desire to safeguard their own autonomy, they tend to privilege benign relations with all major powers rather than aligning themselves with one major power against another. IR literature refers to a 'multivector foreign policy' (Vanderhil et al. 2020, 975–993; Tan 2020, 138), or 'omni-enmeshment' (Goh 2008, 113–157) to capture weak states' attempts in establishing pragmatic and beneficial relationships with all major powers while trying to pacify major power conflicts that threaten their autonomy. Moreover, a self-understanding of being system-ineffective may inform a reactive foreign policy outlook designed to shield itself against malign foreign forces, rather than the proactive development of international initiatives. Here, too, specialisation may come along with specific benefits. As illustrated by numerous historical episodes from secondary and tertiary countries, weak states may become highly adept at balancing competing major power demands to their own benefit—in terms of aid, investments, military or political support.

Third, weak states typically endorse international institutions enthusiastically. Across the developing world, the UN and its formalisation of the principles of sovereign states and non-interference have been read as a defence of weak states' independence from the postcolonial period onwards. Moreover, international institutions allow for reducing transaction costs in international affairs; for instance, rather than having to establish expensive embassies across the world, weak states' UN ambassadors can meet their counterparts in New York to resolve bilateral as well as multilateral matters. Many international institutions also provide technical expertise that weak states would find hard to develop on their own. And perhaps most importantly, multilateralism allows for building coalitions of partners with the possibility to, at times, overrule individual major powers' interests. Indeed, according to recent studies, weak states within international institutions can be surprisingly effective by creatively engaging in global agenda-setting (Theys and Rietig 2020, 20; Brannagan and Giulianotti 2018). Likewise, the World Trade Organization (WTO) offers numerous examples of weak states actively engaging in coalition management to counter the dominance of the world's major trading countries. More fundamentally, a multilateralism that is at least formally based on the equality of sovereign states allows weak states the same voice as it does for strong ones.

Besides these three defining characteristics, history is replete with a variety of weak states' foreign policies. Moreover, none of the above suggests that the foreign policy of weak states will be particularly successful. Pressures from the international system affect their room to manoeuvre more profoundly than it does for states that have the power to mould the system on their own. And specialisation cannot easily undo the vulnerabilities stemming from their respective geographical locations, terms of trade or the domestic politics in more powerful states. Another major problem for small and weak states in the developing world continues to be a lack of foreign policy capacity, an underfunded and ineffective diplomatic bureaucracy or a generally defunct political system (Hey 2003, 190). However, states may change their own roles within the international system, moving up the ladder of hierarchy of states, and thereby finding a new combination of weak states' strength with middle power benefits. Bangladesh today seems to be an example of just that, as illustrated in the next section.

Accounting for Bangladeshi Autonomy over Time

Although the Covid-19 pandemic starkly exposed Bangladesh's continuing dependencies on the outside world, the past decade has profoundly changed the country's self-understanding as well as its image amongst foreign powers. First, consider Bangladesh's dependence on and relations with donor countries. In fact, dependency on foreign aid, for long a characteristic of one of the world's poorest nations, has changed considerably. From independence onwards, Bangladesh's relation to Western donor countries and the international institutions dominated by them were enormously important. In the 1970s, Bangladesh's annual development programme (ADP) was funded via foreign aid entirely. Moreover, the group of important donors was small and cohesive, including the World Bank, the Asian Development Bank as well as a few major Western donor states, such as the US, UK and Germany. Consequently, and despite anti-American sentiments amongst some parts of the Bangladeshi society and political elite, relations with the US as well as major European countries occupied a central place in Bangladesh's foreign relations. By the mid-2000s, this picture had changed significantly. Sustained economic growth, a vigorous export sector and growing remittances from Bangladeshis abroad significantly decreased its budget dependency on aid, which today is only a fraction of what it used to be. In all that time, overall aid expenditures increased further in absolute terms. As a result, for Bangladesh's Western partners, project aid and most other grants practically ceased to be effective instruments of political pressure (Plagemann 2022).

At the same time, as the relative importance of aid declined, the composition of donor countries also became more diverse. Today China, India, Japan and the Asian Infrastructure Investment Bank matter more. Nonetheless, individual donor countries together only cover roughly 50 per cent of the overall aid to Bangladesh, with multilateral lenders covering the other half (ERD 2020). A higher number of donors and a more even distribution amongst country and multilateral donors significantly reduces Dhaka's dependency on any single donor. Notably, this new scenario also allows for replacing one donor with another, in case of friction. In fact, this has happened repeatedly in the recent past.

As outlined in more detail in Plagemann (2022), Bangladesh has endorsed Chinese infrastructure funding all the while welcoming other donors' investments. Diplomatically, Sheikh Hasina personally welcomed competing connectivity schemes from China's Belt and Road Initiative to India's Act East or the Japanese Free and Open Indo-Pacific Strategy. Facing problems with one donor, Dhaka succeeded in replacing it with another in some of its major road construction projects, including the Padma River Bridge project (Plagemann 2022). Likewise, in its geo-economically important port development, Bangladesh included several donor countries through the establishment of international consortia (Rafee 2019), despite pressures both from China and other countries to adopt a strictly bilateral funding strategy. Incidences such as these illustrate that Bangladesh today can reach out in different directions.

By contrast, the country's approach to regional and global institutions over the past decade primarily exhibits the continuing appreciation of multilateral processes that is typical for weak states. As a founding member, Dhaka has been a major supporter of the—however ineffective—SAARC. An analysis of Bangladeshi news sources on the WTO, the G20 and the Asian Infrastructure Investment Bank (AIIB) from 2008 to 2019[2] also shows a deeply held preference for inclusive, global multilateral agreements over more exclusive, regional or bilateral agreements in trade and elsewhere. Albeit welcoming the AIIB as a new source of infrastructure investments and recommending membership, media sources also pointed to the risk of Chinese dominance and the alienation of Western partners. Thus, we found further evidence of Bangladesh's deeply held desire to walk the thin line between major powers without falling into either camp. Media sources on the WTO were instructive too, typically emphasising that Bangladesh had profited immensely from its membership and its status as a least-developed country. The WTO's inclusive multilateral set-up was repeatedly contrasted with plurilateral or mega-regional alternatives in which individual major powers dominated. Moreover, the WTO helped in overcoming capacity constraints, which hindered Bangladesh in bilateral and regional trade relations, and it allowed for effective coalition building, another advantage absent in bilateral negotiations. Opinion pieces and reporting about the G20, in turn, expressed deep disappointment over world leaders' inability to revive global trade talks while pointing out that inclusion of smaller developing countries' perspectives were needed to increase the G20's legitimacy as well as effectiveness as a body of global economic governance. The adoption at G20 summits of issues beyond global economic cooperation—from Syria to the US–China trade war—was described less as a reform of multilateralism and more as a threat to it. Indeed, the critique was that instead of finding conversion over matters of global trade or climate change, G20 members agreed on infringing on multilateral principles of the WTO.

Limitations to Bangladesh's foreign policy autonomy, its persistent dependencies and vulnerabilities can also be found elsewhere. Bangladesh's proximity to India and the profound vulnerability to India's domestic politics demands for a deeper engagement than is possible in this contribution (see, for instance, Riaz 2019; Datta 2008). Despite fierce Bangladeshi pressure, a sustainable river water sharing agreement between the two countries is still beyond sight and one reason for this lies in India's domestic politics with the opposition in power in the crucial state of West Bengal (Plagemann and Destradi 2015). The BJP's Hindu nationalist agenda continues to irk Bangladeshis while the absence of any substantive support from the Indian side regarding the resolution of the Rohingya crisis with neighbouring Myanmar is another strain on bilateral relations with roots in India's domestic politics.

Nonetheless, it is worth pointing out that the Modi government's Hindu nationalist agenda notwithstanding—and in contrast to previous episodes—ties between the two countries are remarkably close today. Senior diplomats celebrate a 'golden era' in bilateral relations, governments have signed dozens of bilateral agreements over connectivity, trade and other issues since 2008, and India has begun exporting electricity to Bangladesh (Riaz 2019, 56). More substantively perhaps, the two countries resolved a long-simmering conflict over land boundaries in 2015 and Bangladesh received a series of major lines of credit, turning the former into India's largest individual aid recipient. The two countries also concluded a tripartite pact for civil nuclear cooperation with Russia—against opposition from Western states. Meanwhile, in a recent interview with *The Wire*, a Bangladeshi representative of the Hindu minority there lamented that following anti-Hindu violence in Bangladesh, 'India did not condemn the incidents of violence or give any stern message to the Bangladesh administration. Instead, India's foreign ministry statement was sugar coated and it congratulated the Hasina government for taking appropriate action'. Neither have, according to the interviewee, leaders of India's ruling party BJP, or other Hindu nationalist outfits such as the Rashtriya Swayamsevak Sangh (RSS) or the Vishva Hindu Parishad (VHP) come to help persecuted Hindus in Bangladesh (*The Wire* 2021). At the very least, this insinuates a sense of realpolitik on behalf of the Modi government, that privileges friendly relations with a geopolitically important regional ally over the politicisation of religious divides that we have seen in India's domestic politics in recent years.

Foreign Policy Autonomy in a Multipolar Asia and Its Limits

The above examples illustrate the characteristics of the foreign policy of weak states. While reducing its dependency on traditional donors, Bangladesh successfully sought friendly relations with all major powers active in the region, from vastly improving its traditionally strained relations with neighbouring India to deepening relations with China through infrastructure investments and military procurement, amongst others. Despite the intensification of global tensions between India, the US and other Western partners, on the one hand, and China as well Russia, on the other, Bangladesh's foreign partnerships appear healthier and more robust than at any time in its history since independence. In fact, democratic backsliding notwithstanding (see, for instance, Fair 2019), the run-up to the 2018 election showed how virtually all major powers, including Western ones, were invested in the Awami League (AL) and Sheikh Hasina personally, rather than the opposition. Four years later, the situation has changed. Amid violent opposition protest and the ongoing oppression of free speech, US and EU representatives have more vigorously called for fair elections than previously. Nonetheless, the state of Bangladesh's foreign relations with major powers thus suggests two things. For one, the political leadership appears to have a clear understanding of major partners' foci providing it with the 'finesse' an independent foreign policy requires (Keohane 1971, 171). Ostensibly, the past decade's political stability, including continuity in key foreign policy leadership posts, benefitted the country's foreign policy establishment's capacities and the diplomatic apparatus' (bargaining) skills.

Besides factors pertaining to a weak states' agency—a key determinant of their foreign policy success that is sometimes overlooked in structural IR theorising (also see Köllner 2021, 24)—systemic factors have benefitted Bangladesh's foreign policy. A multipolar Asia allows for a new menu of partners with diverging strengths and weaknesses. For instance, according to a UNDP report, Indian infrastructure funding fills 'the necessary investment gap in the transport sector that traditional donors, including the World Bank and the Japan International Cooperation Agency, had been skeptical about filling' (UNDP 2016, 36). As is the case elsewhere in the developing world, countries with a history of dependency on Western aid celebrate the emergence of China and other new donors less concerned with political and human rights than OECD member states. As a result, Western donors, including multilateral ones, have lost much of their leverage—a fact that the case of Bangladesh illustrates starkly. Moreover, as geopolitical tensions rise, competing connectivity initiatives—from China's Belt and Road Initiative to its Japanese, US or Indian equivalents—infused new energy into infrastructure investments across the Global South. In their desire to hold on to old or win new partners, major powers have become more willing to take Bangladeshi considerations into account–as visible in Bangladesh's successful insistence on consortia of international partners in several key infrastructure projects. Thus, the ongoing multipolar competition in Asia increases recipient countries bargaining power in infrastructure, aid and beyond (Plagemann 2022). The more extra-regional powers see a strategic advantage in engaging with Bangladesh, for instance through the ongoing refocus on the 'Indo-Pacific' in the US and Europe, the more negotiating power Dhaka has—provided its hedging strategy remains intact.

However, the empirical glimpses in the previous section also point to a dimension of multipolarity that is not in the weaker powers' interests. A multipolar international system, as it stands, complicates finding multilateral agreements globally and this has profound implications for weak states' 'collective power' (Long 2017). The WTO is exemplary. Now largely defunct, it continued to be hailed in Bangladeshi news sources, as well as elsewhere in the developing world, as a unique body through which weak powers can overcome major power dominance. Nowhere has this been more obvious than in its conflict resolution mechanism. In more than one case, weaker powers from South Korea to Brazil have secured important rulings against the US, China or the EU—results that are inconceivable to reach through bilateral negotiations that tend to favour the strong over the weak or the autonomous (large market) over the vulnerable (small market). It was a WTO ruling 2005 that resolved a bitter trade dispute over Indian anti-dumping duties on lead acid batteries from Bangladesh in Dhaka's favour. From the perspective of Bangladesh, the G20 as a global institution, coupled with bilateral or regional agreements, is a poor supplement. In fact, the G20 in many ways entrenches major power dominance over small and weaker powers, who do not even have a seat at the table and thus must rely on major powers advocating for them. Given the WTO's prolonged deadlock, Bangladesh has become more open to second-best alternatives regionally. However, South Asia's dismal record of intra-regional trade, its poor neighbours, and a natural dominance of major regional powers in the negotiations dampen enthusiasm for this. In particular, the more recent history of regional relations clearly showed that any such scheme not only excludes Bangladesh's major extra-regional trade partners—a major downside in the first place—but also one of the two major competitors for regional dominance, India or China. In fact, with the sole exception of the AIIB, India pursues its regional schemes, from the Bay of Bengal Multi-Sectoral Technical and Economic Cooperation (BIMSTEC) to Bangladesh, Bhutan,

India, Nepal (BBIN), deliberately without China. By contrast, the BCIM, a connectivity corridor originally envisaged by China's Yunnan province in the late 1990s, that would have included all of Bangladesh, China, India and Myanmar, never found the necessary support from India fearful of Chinese intrusion into its South Asian neighbourhood (Plagemann et al. 2021). Another, more inclusive regional trade agreement, the Regional Comprehensive Economic Partnership (RCEP), includes China, Japan, South Korea as well as ASEAN member states and Bangladesh but not India. The result is a fragmented landscape of often specialised regional schemes with varying sets of partners that undermines one of the rationales for engaging in international institutions in the first place: the reduction of transaction costs.

This is both important and lamentable, from the perspective of Bangladeshi interests. A connectivity scheme involving China and India would, on the one hand, help Dhaka in balancing major powers' interests and aligning them with its own perspectives. On the other, there are strong functional arguments for inclusive integration schemes over connectivity, investments rules and other matters. Also, countries with a history of foreign aid are acutely aware of the bureaucratic costs that the maintenance of diverging partners each with its own administrative procedures, languages and political foci entails. A multipolar Asia seems unable to help, major powers' habitual calls for a seamless, integrated and connected South Asia notwithstanding.

Conclusion

Bangladesh's foreign policy posture today is emblematic of the wider changes in the international system. Clearly not a 'weak' state anymore, Bangladesh's development from aid dependency to—however tepid—donor country epitomises the resurgence of the Global South more widely. Like other geopolitically valuable states in the Global South, Dhaka succeeded in turning its hedging strategy into a multi-vector foreign policy with major benefits for its infrastructure development domestically and autonomy externally. Clearly, in a multipolar world, advantages conventionally associated with weak states also benefit those climbing up the ladder of the international hierarchy, such as Bangladesh. Accepting Bangladesh's claim of being 'system ineffectual' (Keohane 1971, 162), major powers have so far refrained from forcing Dhaka to choose sides, thereby allowing it to reap the benefits from engagement with all sides simultaneously.

Such advantages, however, primarily pertain to bilateral relations. In fact, rivalries of today's major powers in a multipolar setting make the kind of inclusive, multilateral arrangement that weak and secondary states stand to benefit from the most highly unlikely. Instead, as the G20 illustrates, major powers seek to resolve gridlocks in global governance by way of bilateral and mini-lateral negotiations in exclusive clubs, rather than institutions with strong rules. Moreover, there is little to suggest that countries such as Bangladesh can rely on major powers to advocate on their behalf. Instead, outside strong regional organisations such as the EU, indications are that the remaining multilateral bodies, such as the OECD and the UN, remain non-major powers' best bet for advancing their interest globally—a perspective that raises further doubts about the prospects for Bangladeshi interests.

Notes

1   In academic writings, such notions have been encapsulated in titles such as *Bangladesh in International Politics: The Dilemmas of the Weak States* (Huq 1994), or *Foreign Policy of Bangladesh: A Small States Imperative* (Ahamed 2004).
2   Colleagues and I collected almost 400 articles on the three organisations from the *Dhaka Tribune*, the *Financial Express* and *The New Nation* in the context of the DFG-funded research project *Legitimate Multipolarity*. For more information on this, see https://www.giga-hamburg.de/en/projects/legitimate-multipolarity/.

References

Ahamed, E. *Foreign Policy of Bangladesh: A Small States Imperative*. Dhaka: Kamol Kuri Prokashon. 2004.

Brannagan, P.M. and R. Giulianotti. 'The Soft Power–Soft Disempowerment Nexus: The Case of Qatar'. *International Affairs* 94, no. 5, (2018): 1139–1157.

Brewster, D. 'A Rising Bangladesh Starts to Exert Its Regional Power'. Lowy Institute, 2021. https://www.lowyinstitute.org/the-interpreter/rising-bangladesh-starts-exert-its-regional-power (accessed on 25 October 2021).

'Concessional Financial Flows among Southern Countries'. UNDP, 2016. https://www.undp.org/content/dam/undp/library/development-impact/SS%20Research%20Publications/11873%20-%20Concessional%20Financial%20Flows%20Among%20Southern%20Countries_Op%2008_Web%20Version(1).pdf (accessed on 25 October 2021).

Datta, S. 'Bangladesh's Relations with China and India: A Comparative Study'. *Strategic Analysis* 32, no. 5, (2008): 755–772.

Fair, C. 'Bangladesh in 2018: Careening Toward One-Woman Rule'. *Asian Survey* 59, no. 1, (2019): 124–132.

'Flow of External Resources into Bangladesh 2019–2020'. ERD, 2020. https://erd.gov.bd/site/page/565de360-e511-4758-a966-459d0dc1acfa/Flow-of-External-Resources-2019-20 (accessed on 25 October 2021).

Goh, E. 'Great Powers and Hierarchical Order in Southeast Asia: Analyzing Regional Security Strategies'. *International Security* 32, no. 3, (2008): 113–157.

Hey, J. 'Refining Our Understanding of Small State Foreign Policy'. In *Small States in World Politics*, edited by Jeanne A.K. Hey, 185–195. Boulder: Lynne Rienner. 2003.

Huq, M.H. *Bangladesh in International Politics: The Dilemmas of the Weak States*. New Delhi: Sterling Publishers. 1994.

'Interview: "Bangladesh Hindus Deeply Upset with India's Response on Violence"': Community Leader'. *The Wire*, New Delhi, 20 October 2021, New Delhi. https://thewire.in/communalism/interview-bangladesh-hindus-deeply-upset-with-indias-response-on-violence-community-leader (accessed 20 October 2021).

Katzenstein, P. 'Small States and Small States Revisited'. *New Political Economy* 8, no. 1, (2003): 9–30.

Keohane, R. 'Lilliputians' Dilemmas: Small States in International Politics'. *International Organization* 23, no. 2, (1969): 291–310.

———. 'The Big Influence of Small Allies'. *Foreign Policy*, no. 2, (1971): 161–182.

Köllner, P. 'Australia and New Zealand Recalibrate Their China Policies: Convergence and Divergence'. *The Pacific Review* 34, no. 3, (2021): 405–436.

Long, Tom. 'Small states, great power? Gaining influence through intrinsic, derivative, and collective power'. *International Studies Review* 19, no. 2, (2017): 185–205.

Plagemann, J. 'Small States and Competing Connectivity Strategies: What Explains Bangladesh's Success in Relations with Asia's Major Powers?' *The Pacific Review* 35, no. 4, (2022): 736–764.

Plagemann, J. and S. Destradi. 'Soft Sovereignty, Rising Powers and Subnational Foreign Policy-Making: The Case of India'. *Globalizations* 12, no. 5, (2015): 728–743.

Plagemann, J., S. Datta, and S. Chu. 'The Paradox of Competing Connectivity Strategies in Asia'. *Third World Quarterly* 42, no. 10, (2021): 2265–2281.

Rafee, A.A. 'March 1. Bangladesh's Tryst with China's BRI: Economic Boom or Debt Trap?' *South Asian Voices*, 2019. https://southasianvoices.org/bangladeshs-tryst-with-chinas-bri-economic-boom-or-debt-trap/ (accessed on 25 October 2021).

Riaz, A. 'Indo-Bangladesh Relationship: "Saath Saath" (Together) or Too Close for Comfort?' *Indian Politics & Policy* 2, no. 1, (2019): 53–75.

Tan, S. 'Consigned to Hedge: South-East Asia and America's "Free and Open Indo-Pacific" Strategy'. *International Affairs* 96, no. 1, (2020): 131–148.

Theys, S. and K. Rieti. 'The Influence of Small States: How Bhutan Succeeds in Influencing Global Sustainability Governance'. *International Affairs* 96, no 6, (2020): 1603–1622.

Thorhallsson, B. and S. Steinsson. 'Small-State Foreign Policy'. In *The Oxford Encyclopedia of Foreign Policy Analysis*, edited by Cameron Thies. Oxford: Oxford University Press. 2017.

Vanderhill, R., S.F. Joireman, and R. Tulepbayeva. 'Between The Bear and the Dragon: Multivectorism in Kazakhstan as a Model Strategy for Secondary Powers'. *International Affairs* 96, no 4, (2020): 975–993.

7

FROM THE BAY OF BENGAL TO THE INDO-PACIFIC: EXTRA-REGIONAL POWERS VYING FOR BANGLADESH'S ATTENTION

Sreeradha Datta

Bangladesh extended a $200 million loan to Sri Lanka in June 2021, signalling a change that had been in the making for years. It had finally shed the previous notions of Bangladesh as a weak small state, especially given its struggle for independence and as a weak economy during the early 1970s. Today there are many references to Bangladesh as 'Rising Bangladesh', the 'New Asian Tiger', an important 'Indo-Pacific Middle Player' (Brewster 2021). Such changes indicate a changing international image of a South Asian nation that completed 50 years of its advent and has travelled a path filled with several milestones.

The recent growth story of Bangladesh has been much discussed and much analysed for the past few years. Primarily because of its cumulative achievements that led to the country's dual graduation—graduation from low-income country to lower-middle-income country (according to the World Bank criteria), attained in 2015, and eligibility for graduation from the group of least-developed country (LDC) to developing country (DC) status in 2018, set for 2026, according to the UN criteria is fascinating (Rahman 2020). In its 15th year, Bangladesh has achieved a five-time growth trajectory and reached $320 billion in 2021, up from $302.57 billion in 2019 (Asian Development Bank 2022). Bangladesh is one of the fastest growing economies in Asia (2023) with a GDP that has been standing at a growth rate of 6.15 per cent for the past two decades.[1] Its South Asian neighbours have recognised Bangladesh as a reliable partner with many of them enjoying various sectoral cooperation with Dhaka. The extra-regional actors are finding greater relevance in seeking to engage and build a partnership with Bangladesh. Undoubtedly, the country's economic progress has captured the imaginations of the world putting it in a very enviable position with all major powers building strong bilateral ties with Dhaka. Through its various infrastructural and developmental projects, including its growth pattern, Bangladesh is experiencing a growing importance in the South Asian region, which is contributing to the further emergence of strategic interests of the Indo-Pacific. As C. Raja Mohan puts it, 'Today, Bangladesh is on the cusp of a second liberation—one that would end its relative isolation and allow Dhaka to play a stronger role in the region and beyond, seeking new maritime possibilities in the Indo-Pacific' (Raja Mohan 2021). Indeed, the growth trajectory of Bangladesh has contributed to making it the most sought-after partner by international players.

In this context, this chapter examines the factors that have led to Bangladesh playing a stronger role in international affairs beyond its long-held small state and South Asian identity. It highlights Bangladesh's sustained economic growth that has propelled it to greater international recognition, opening up the scope for greater trade and economic engagement with major powers. The chapter also argues how Bangladesh's geographical location plays a distinct role in its growing outreach and how the contemporary political environment looming over this geography has lent it greater relevance. With the ongoing refocus on the 'Indo-Pacific', the extra-regional powers see a potential strategic advantage in engaging with Bangladesh, especially when the strategic asset of the Indo-Pacific is seeing powers big and small engaging with each other. Undoubtedly, the contemporary strategic developments in the region and outside have coincided with Bangladesh's growth to ensure its pivotal role in the region. At the same time, it has been able to take advantage of an atmosphere of competitive power-mongering to establish itself as a reliable partner.

The chapter studies the new developments taking place in the Indo-Pacific strategic construct and how a confident and growing Bangladesh is being coveted by all the powers in the region. It traces through three sections how Bangladesh has assumed an unprecedented significance. The first section examines the significance of its economic growth and location that has now graduated into the Indo-Pacific contour.

The second section deals with Bangladesh's important partners including India, China, Japan, Russia and the US, and analyses the contest among them to keep Bangladesh on its side. It highlights how Dhaka navigates its relationship with major and smaller powers in the region, and its ability to work with a variety of actors has given way to an interesting power mix in the Bay of Bengal (BoB) region as well as in the larger strategic space.

The third section deals with the significance of regionalism in Bangladesh's foreign policy outreach and its aspirations to act as a gateway between two regions of South and Southeast Asia.

Growth and Growing Recognition

Bangladesh is projected to be among the top 30 economies by 2030, and given the complex international milieu existing around the region, the country has received significant attention in international politics. Despite its difficult beginning of 1971, the periodic political instability has prevailed along with the recurring environmental and climate challenges it faces. It has made great strides from its difficult beginning, now having become a food- sufficient nation from a food-deficient one and also one of the largest contributors to the UN Peacekeeping Forces. However, Bangladesh's rising GDP and sustained economic growth over the last decades have been a considerable achievement, and this has lead to greater attention from regional and extra-regional players. Undoubtedly, the present international recognition of the country's strategic role reflects not only its economic growth and development but has also created a conducive environment for Dhaka to leverage its geographical position effectively. With the BoB assuming greater salience and the Indian Ocean becoming a focal point for the jostling of major powers, Bangladesh's ability to effectively use its geographical position has contributed positively to its foreign policy initiatives (Datta 2022).

Amidst these significant changes in the geo-strategic landscape, a rapidly growing economy changed one of the critical components of Bangladesh's diplomatic engagement. For a long time, seeking aid was one of the most important factors in Bangladesh's foreign policy endeavour. As the economy grew, however, its dependency on aid has not only decreased but its nature has also reversed from the earlier trends. From bilateral aid, Bangladesh has now moved to over 65 per cent being covered by multilateral funds in 2018. What is also noteworthy is that since the early 2000s, multilateral donor agencies (World Bank, ADB and various UN agencies) have been providing 70 per cent total aid, on an average while bilateral donors have contributed to remaining 30 per cent (Hasan 2011). This reflects the Bangladesh government's relative success in mobilising domestic resources (Light Castle Analysis Wing 2021).

While it has been argued that Bangladesh's location and growth trajectory has made it an attractive Asian power, the faith of external powers is not high, if the FDI flows data is taken into consideration. There has certainly been a distinct rise with FDI flows at 2.56 in 2021 (of which China contributed to 14 per cent). However, the rate of FDI inflows is around 1 per cent of its GDP (Haider 2021). There are several factors that have been a hindrance to Bangladesh being an attractive for investment climate but there is no denying that politically, there is a distinct change in how others perceive Dhaka.

It has been argued that India and China are Bangladesh's two most important neighbours. At the same time, Dhaka has been able to establish an international appeal acquired through leveraging its unique geography, showcasing its growth story and its plans to move into a knowledge-intensive society beyond apparel manufacturing (Narayan and Datta 2020). Dhaka seems suitably poised to make a long-term contribution to global politics and appears an attractive power for regional and extra-regional powers to engage with politically.

Bay of Bay Bengal to Indo-Pacific

The existing tense and multipolar political landscape in Asia and beyond offer Bangladesh a greater bargaining power in its pursuit of foreign policy goals. The dynamics of the power struggle between and among the regional and extra-regional powers allow Bangladesh a greater space to maintain ties with all major powers. China is a predominant Asian power and has heavily invested in Bangladesh, Japan has carved a niche role and India is positioning itself as an emergent Asian power with deepening linkages with its neighbour. Their clear need to have Bangladesh on their side lends Dhaka with a distinct manoeuvring choice. In the past, it would have been easier to argue that India and China were likely to continue to be the sheet anchor of Bangladesh's foreign policy. On the contrary, however, it is evident that a broader vision has been acquired (Narayan and Datta 2020).

With the growing competition over connectivity, investment flows in the South Asian region, competing connectivity initiatives—from China's Belt and Road Initiative to its Japanese, or Indian equivalents—infused new energy into infrastructure investments across this region, much of which has worked in Bangladesh's favour. It is also possible to suggest that Bangladesh has facilitated the deeper diffusion by external powers into this political mosaic, alongside others. Arguably, the lack of successful multilateralism in the region has also contributed to putting Bangladesh in a better position in the region. Such examples can be found across the globe where powers similar to Bangladesh are able to manoeuvre more effectively in their global bargain.

Not possessing a decisive military power or distinct economic leverage, Bangladesh's 'friendship with all and enmity with none' mantra was adopted and popularised by its first Prime Minister Bangabandhu Mujibur Rahman. It has subsequently been followed by all other leaders. Hence, Bangladesh was able to exert a considerable influence over its bilateral ties. Given the competitive international milieu, other powers also sought its partnership in a bid to strengthen their position.

In the immediate neighbourhood of the Bay of Bengal, geopolitical rivalry, clashing power interests, trade imbalances and debt crisis, state incapacities and failures guarantee a distinct role for a stable Bangladesh. A motley group of rising powers and smaller powers will influence the dynamics in this region and Bangladesh may contribute to this by shaping many of the policy choices by virtue of its location, growth and market access, and through the pursuit of a robust foreign policy.

The Bay of Bengal connects Bangladesh, India, Myanmar, Sri Lanka and Thailand. Historically, it served as the natural bridge between the subcontinent and the abutting regions to the east right up to the southern coast of China. It connects South Asia to Southeast Asia, blending into the Andaman Sea and from there into the mouth of the Strait of Malacca. The 19th century saw intense competition among the European powers for the resources and markets of the region. Its resource richness led the external powers to colonise the Bay of Bengal territories and beyond.

As argued by Raja Mohan, the BoB disappeared from the geopolitical and geo-economic scenario in the second half of the 20th century (Raja Mohan 2020). He suggests that it was only at the turn of the new millennium that the bay would regain some of its strategic significance. The opening up of Myanmar across the littoral and its integration into Southeast Asian structures has provided the basis for the re-imagination of the bay as a sea bridge between different regions in the Eastern Indian and Western Pacific Oceans. 'As the new spatial concept of the Indo-Pacific gains traction, it is not difficult to see the re-emerging geographic centrality of the Bay of Bengal' (Raja Mohan 2020). Since about one-quarter of the world's traded goods, 70 to 80 per cent of China's energy imports, and 90 per cent or more of South Korea and Japan's energy imports flow through the Strait of Malacca, the southern end of the Bay (Frost 2019). Therefore, securing these energy and trade routes essentially drives the geopolitical ambitions in this geography.

From the economic perspective, the potential of the BoB is extremely significant. Although estimated to possess vast deposits of hydrocarbon resources and mineral wealth, the bay is the least explored area for oil and gas reserves, let alone prospecting for and suitably harvesting mineral nodules (Karim 2021). This has made it more attractive to not only to states in the region but also to the extra-regional powers. Indeed, for Bangladesh, the prospects of the blue economy in the region make it an active actor with 450 miles of coastline with 200 nautical miles of exclusive economic zone. Interestingly, the country harvests only 0.70 million tonnes of the BoB's estimated 8 million tonnes of fish stock. Dhaka could also extract oil and gas resources worth about $1.2 billion. The 'blue economy' contributes over $6 billion to Bangladesh's

GDP (Karim 2021). The trade prospects have led to an increased and pressing presence and attention of extra-regional actors in the bay, resulting the interstate rivalry and competition.

Extending beyond the Bay of Bengal is the Indian Ocean and Indo-Pacific strategic construct that is broadly understood to include both the Indian and Pacific Oceans. In 2011, US Secretary of State Hillary Clinton used the term 'Indo-Pacific' to refer to the region that stretches from the Indian Ocean to the Pacific Ocean, noting its significance in terms of strengthening the US positions in the region (Denisov 2021). In 2017, Japan and the US worked on maps that represented their idea of the 'Free and Open Indo-Pacific Strategy', one that drew India into the strategic construct (Detsch 2021). The term first gradually gained popularity in political and academic discussions in India, the US, Japan and Australia (Denisov 2021). Subsequently, the Indo-Pacific strategy became a major preoccupation for the leaderships in the US, India, Australia, Japan, the Association of Southeast Asian Nations (ASEAN) and China. Gradually, they have all developed their perspectives on the Indo-Pacific. While there is some amount of consensus amongst most actors, China views the construct through a contrarian lens.[2] The growing economic, political and social ties in the Indo-Pacific inevitably lead to the emergence of new problems in terms of regional governance requiring to develop a political architecture with a suitable governance system (Denisov 2021). The US and India are two major players in this geography. While India is said to hold the genuine power in the Indian Ocean Region (IOR), it still plays a minor role compared to the US and its naval capability and ambition in the region (Ramadhani 2015).

In the last one decade, there has been a greater focus on the IOR and Indo-Pacific region from regional and global powers intending to solidify their presence in some way. For instance, the Chinese presence in the IOR is primarily based on its need to secure the International Shipping Routes (ISR), and it is noteworthy that within a very short span of 10 years, China is in a position to dominate the shipping lanes and assert its presence politically (Ramadhani 2015). As a result, China's growth and its significant regional presence had led to a strategic consensus, led by the US and Japan to counter China. Subsequently, the formation of the QUAD, consisting of the US, Japan, Australia and India has led to a distinct strategic contour to the geographical construct which has resulted in strong reactions from China.

Apart from establishing bilateral ties, China, India and Japan are trying to establish connectivity networks to leverage their positions in Asia individually as well as along with other partners. Beginning with cross-border transport and infrastructural development, China, India and Japan enjoy a robust engagement with Bangladesh. Japanese

Defence Minister Taro Kono, touching upon the Japan–Bangladesh Summit Meeting in May 2019, conveyed Tokyo's intention to work with Dhaka to promote principles such as freedom of navigation, rule of law and market economy (Ministry of Foreign Affairs of Japan).

On the other hand, China, US and other major powers have a greater impetus to engage with Bangladesh. The big power rivalry has increased Bangladesh's importance for all. Thus, the re-emergence of the Indo-Pacific region including the Bay of Bengal has accorded Bangladesh a greater regional presence. The geo-strategic and economic factors have created competition amongst all the major powers, drawing in the smaller powers into their theatre. Also, given the phenomenal domestic growth and transformation alongside following successful foreign policy relations in the last decade, ensuring free sea lanes and an open Indian Ocean is vital to Bangladesh's interests too. The growth trajectory of Bangladesh has led to its greater recognition within the region. And given the power rivalry in the extra-regional space, Bangladesh was an expected centre of the contemporary developments due to Western nations efforts to woo Dhaka. Therefore, it is also possible to suggest that Bangladesh has facilitated the deeper penetration by external powers into this political mosaic, given its need to seek developmental partnership. The dynamics of the power struggle allow Bangladesh greater space to maintain ties with all the major powers.

The tense multipolar political landscape that exists in Asia has offered a greater bargaining power in bilateral relations with Bangladesh. The ongoing reality where China is a predominant Asian power, Japan having carved a niche role and India positioning itself as an emergent Asian power, their need to have Bangladesh on their side lends Dhaka with distinct manoeuvring choices.

The geopolitical rivalry, clashing power interests, trade imbalances and debt crisis, state incapacities and failures, and questionable intent of the major powers has put Bangladesh into a critical space. The US has clearly stated that geostrategic location and continuous economic growth and stability of Bangladesh make it more attractive (*The Daily Star* 2022).

Similarly, Japan has been open in its assessment of Bangladesh's role in the Indo-Pacific region.

> The recent involvement of the great powers in the Indo-Pacific region has led to geopolitical uncertainties in this region which often engendering greater concern among the littorals of the Bay of Bengal and the Indian Ocean region. Bangladesh as the gateway to South and Southeast Asia remains geographically central to the Bay of Bengal which allows it to play a pivotal role in regional and

interregional trade and commercial activities. (Embassy of Japan in Bangladesh 2022)

In defining this phenomenon in a theoretical sense, it can be argued that in certain circumstances, small states may affect the behaviour of bigger/great powers in a way that mitigates the latter's rivalry. It appears that the small states act as a pivot, and may choose from a range of strategies including balancing, joining the bandwagon, leaning towards a third power, staying neutral or hedging risks to sustain their survival as an independent unit (Efremova 2019). Similarly, Plagemann argues that the tense multipolarity we observe in Asia today accrues a greater bargaining power in bilateral relations to secondary and tertiary states, such as Bangladesh (Plagemann 2021). Indeed, the growth of regionalism, rising state ambition and competitiveness amongst some of the major powers has meant each of them are vying to partner with Bangladesh.

Bangladesh recently (May 2023) launched its Indo-Pacific Outlook. Timed just ahead of PM Hasina's visit to Japan, the UK and the US there was a distinct messaging integral in this initiative that was a 'vision of a free, open, peaceful, secure and inclusive Indo-Pacific for the shared prosperity for all' (MOFA 2023). Upcoming elections, sounds of disapprovals from Washington about the state of governance, attempts to engage Japan more robustly while managing its Asian powers all would be a factored in while formulating a policy with contemporary geo-strategic relevance. The guiding principles and objective have laid out a broad framework for Bangladesh's engagement in the Indo-Pacific but much would also depend upon Dhaka joining the Pacific Economic Framework for Prosperity (PEFP) an economic initiative that hold promise for greater economic interaction amongst the 14-plus countries that have already joined this initiative.

Growing Ties between Bangladesh and Its Asian Neighbours

Bangladesh has developed sound ties with many of the Asian neighbours. Undoubtedly India and China are the two that are perceived as closest. The bilateral engagement spanning across many sectors reflects the depth Dhaka that enjoys with Delhi as well as Beijing.

India
India–Bangladesh bilateral trade stands close to $20 billion at present (2022) and continues to grow. It is for the first time that Bangladesh exports to India may reach worth $2 billion this year, largely in the apparel and clothing sector. Bangladesh also remains the highest recipient of India's Line of Credit, accounting $8 billion in total and

much of this has been used for the energy and transport sector. The benefits emanating from such cooperation between Bangladesh and India will directly help the people in Bangladesh. Apart from bilateral developmental cooperation, India and Japan have come together to collaborate in building the mass transit transport in Dhaka for the first time. It will essentially serve the common people and Bangladesh has signed bigger deals, covering trade and defence, with China as well. Today, Beijing has grown to be Dhaka's trusted partner despite their belated start in 1975 and has positioned itself as a bipartisan player. Despite being distant neighbours and missing ancient connections, Bangladesh and China have travelled miles. Seen from a distance, India and China seem to be competing for Dhaka's attention. Yet, a new momentum seems to be unfolding on the economic and development front which expands to building ports, roads, railways, bridges and economic zones. However, China's overwhelming role as Bangladesh's defence partner is rather evident.

China

The Belt Road Initiative's (BRI's) announcement by Chinese President Xi Jinping in 2013 and its formal launch with great fanfare in 2017 attracted global attention. The Chinese themselves have engaged in a massive propaganda blitz to promote Xi's image and hail the initiative as a win-win outcome (Datta 2021). According to China, 'in pursuing the Belt and Road Initiative, we should focus on the fundamental issue of development, release the growth potential of various countries and achieve economic integration and interconnected development and deliver benefits to all' (Belt and Road Forum for International Cooperation 2017). Bangladesh has maintained close relations with China over the past four decades. The bilateral cooperation straddles a wide spectrum of activities, including a series of infrastructure projects. Thus, when China decided to map out its One Belt and One Road (now BRI) network of transport corridors, it would have counted on Bangladesh to join the network considering growing trade and development cooperation with the latter. As per some reports, Bangladesh will receive $26 billion for BRI projects and $14 billion for joint venture projects, together totalling a $40 billion package (*The Daily Star* 2019). However, not much of the promised funds have flown in as yet. Attracting loans and investments from China has witnessed a certain political consensus in Bangladesh and as yet there have not been many concerns regarding the financial model that China employs in Bangladesh (Datta 2021). Beginning from the H.M. Ershad period (1982–1990), China has also emerged as the largest player in the FDI sector in Bangladesh. The latter has keenly encouraged both public and private sectors in China for introducing modern technology and develop its communication infrastructures. In terms of defence cooperation, with nearly $20 billion in bilateral trade, Dhaka is second only to Pakistan in buying arms from China. As the world's eighth-largest country by population, Bangladesh is likely to remain an important market for Chinese investors and exporters. Therefore, given the burgeoning youth population, Bangladesh is likely to contribute to the global workforce in the days ahead.

Khusru aptly sums up Bangladesh's ties with its two large neighbours.

> While China has strengthened its economic ties with Bangladesh by bankrolling development projects, India has the benefit of a shared history, values, culture and connectivity with Bangladesh. The onus is now on the two giants to prove whose strategic objectives are more aligned with the long-term interests of Bangladesh. For now, the country can enjoy the attention it gets from the two rivals. (Khusru 2021)

Interestingly, Bangladeshi Prime Minister Sheikh Hasina has urged India to join the BRI, despite knowing India's reservations emanating from the so-called China–Pakistan Economic Corridor which passes through long-disputed territories between India and Pakistan (Ministry of External Affairs 2019). Bangladesh argues that 'being such a big country and big economy, India should not worry about it [OBOR]. Rather, they can also join so that all the countries can benefit economically' (*The Daily Star* 2019). Such advocacy from Bangladesh exhibits that while it has been wooed by all the major powers, it has south to balance its relations with China, the US and India. It may be noted that when the US and Bangladesh signed their draft Defence Cooperation Agreement, Prime Minister Hasina also inaugurated a China-funded power plant, which once completed will be Bangladesh's largest one (Anwar 2022). Aptly put by an analyst, Bangladesh has 'robust ties' with the US, 'blood ties' with the US-empowered partner India, 'strategic ties' with the US arch-rival China, and 'historic ties' with the US arch foe Russia (Shovon 2022). Bangladesh is indeed striking a fine balance between its interstates and ongoing power rivalry/contest/competition in the region and around.

The US

US Deputy State Secretary Stephen Biegun, during his visit to Dhaka in October 2021, mentioned that Bangladesh should be a partner to the Indo-Pacific Strategy (*The Daily Star* 2022). Similar interest has also been echoed by Gowher Rizvi, the international affairs adviser to the prime minister of Bangladesh who argues that Bangladesh is 'very much willing to be a partner in the Indo-Pacific initiative' (IISS 2021). To that end, the US has promised to persuade American companies to invest in Bangladesh. Further, if the US also allows duty-free access of their garment products to their market, Bangladesh's economic dependence on China might reduce and a new strategical alignment might emerge. The US undersecretary for political affairs Victoria Nuland also mentioned that the US will be happy if Bangladesh joins most of the areas of this initiative, which include economic, security and technological elements in the Indo-Pacific Strategy (*Prothom Alo* 2022).

However, there exist some irritants in Bangladesh–US bilateral ties, especially in the context of US-led sanctions against Bangladesh on Rapid Action Battalion (RAB) as well as over the US not extending an invite to Dhaka for the Summit for Democracy (2021). Bangladesh has also been requesting the US for a long time for the restoration of the generalized system of preference (GSP) facilities for Bangladesh, which the US suspended in 2013 (citing serious shortcomings in labour rights and workplace safety.) In the US–Bangladesh Partnership Dialogue concluded in March 2022, Foreign Secretary Masud Bin Momen described the cooperation between the two countries as 'the beginning of a rejuvenated robust engagement with our US friends' (Palma 2020). These sentiments were reciprocated towards Bangladesh by US ambassador to Bangladesh Peter D. Haas, who added, 'the United States is ready to hit the gas to enhance our partnership and realize the great potential of our relationship. We are ready to move as quickly as you are' (US Indo-Pacific Command 2022).

Japan

Japan and Bangladesh have maintained rather close and cordial ties since 1972. For decades, the former has been one of Bangladesh's largest development partners and a vital source of aid. Interestingly, Japan offered a $1.5 billion loan package for developing several major projects, including a coal power plant and a rapid transit system in the capital Dhaka in 2016 and again in November 2016, coinciding with the focus of the international community on the Indo-Pacific region. Besides other ongoing financial support, Bangladesh received an annual official development assistance loan package from Japan worth $3.2 billion in 2020 for the development of seven large projects, including the Dhaka Mass Rapid Transit, the Jamuna Railway Bridge and the Hazrat Shahjalal International Airport expansion (Rahman 2020). Japan and Bangladesh have also entered a petroleum sector joint venture firm (Allen-Ebrahimian 2017). Japan has emerged as a strong developmental partner, with its collaboration in the construction of a new deep-sea port at Matarbari that is underway; it is set to have a

16.5-metre draft all through the year unlike any other port facilities that presently exists in Bangladesh. More importantly, under the strategic Bay of Bengal Industrial Growth Belt scheme, Japan sees Bangladesh as a gateway to South and Southeast Asia (Allen-Ebrahimian 2017). In a more recent and significant development, Japan and India also working together with Bangladesh in some of the infrastructural projects in the country.

The QUAD

In March 2021, a high-level delegation from the US administration visited Dhaka for bilateral discussions as well as issues covering the security of the Bay of Bengal and the Indo-Pacific region. Bangladesh conveyed is more interested in economic and infrastructure development, and wished to stay away from the strategic alignment, the US interest was apparent (*Dhaka Tribune* 2021). While Dhaka has not evinced any interest to engage with QUAD, China's warning to Bangladesh to not join the QUAD reflects growing insecurity in Beijing about the developing regional equation (Datta 2021). In a rather unusual outburst, Chinese ambassador to Bangladesh Li Jiming said in a virtual official programme that Beijing–Dhaka ties would be 'substantially damaged' if it joins the QUAD (*The Daily Star* 2021). Not only that, *the Global Times* largely seen as the mouthpiece for the Chinese government, further cautioned that 'if the country falls into the geopolitical trap of the Quad, its economic prospects will accordingly be at risk (Zongyi 2021). The Bangladesh government reacted strongly to the Chinese envoy's statement to 'maintain decency and decorum' (Krishna 2021). While the QUAD may not be a choice for Dhaka at the moment, it has pointed at its strategic ties with Beijing. At the same time, QUAD has also evinced greater interest in supporting a developmental partnership with Bangladesh. Indeed, while Australia's ties with Bangladesh have been limited, there is a new interest emerging about this South Asian economy. Their bilateral trade (in 2019–2020) grew to over $2.6 billion, with agricultural products forming Australia's top exports to Bangladesh, while Dhaka exports clothing and textiles to Canberra. In the aftermath of Covid-19, Australia has expressed interest to pursue new opportunities to promote trade and investment. It has conveyed that private sector opportunities in growth industries, such as information technology, will be supported through Australia's new Emerging Markets Impact Investment Fund, the Business Partnerships Platform and the Commonwealth Scientific and Industrial Research Organisation (Australia Department of Foreign Affairs and Trade n.d.).

In the wake of the ongoing Ukraine crisis, Dhaka–Washington relations may stretch a bit. It is well known that since 1972, Russia has been a steadfast partner to Bangladesh in providing economic support. The former Soviet Union had thrice vetoed the US-backed resolutions to intervene in Bangladesh's War of Independence against Pakistan in 1971. Apart from military ties, Moscow is assisting Dhaka in building a 2,400 MW nuclear power plant in Rooppur—the first of its kind in Bangladesh. In the current scenario, the financial and payment sanctions against Russia would make disbursements from them a considerable challenge (Hassan 2022). According to Russian diplomats, the project is 'being carried out on schedule'. However, the joint US–European embargo would make procuring the relevant materials for implementing the second unit of the project very difficult (Chowdhary 2022, Mavis and Hossain 2022).

During 2020–2021, Bangladesh exported goods worth $665.31 million to Russia and imported goods worth $466.70 million (Shovon 2022). The Ukraine crisis has revealed Bangladesh's nuanced position on the developing situation as well as its loyalties. Bangladesh was one of the 35 countries to abstain from the voting on the US-backed resolution (condemning Russia), along with India and China (Tiezzi 2022). Bangladesh (explained its abstention by saying that it calls on 'all parties concerned to exercise maximum restraint, to pursue dialogue through all channels, including diplomatic means to contain the situation, to prevent it from further escalation and to see peaceful resolution in accordance with international law and the UN Charter' (Shovon 2022). While there is a domestic murmur against this policy on Russia as expressed in a few media pieces including one, 'Russian leader Vladimir Putin's invasion has now killed a Bangladeshi, wrecked a state-owned ship, raised fuel and wheat prices on Bangladeshis, and called into question Russia's most notable contribution to Bangladesh's future, a nuclear power plant project, Bangladesh has its justifications' (Pitman 2022). While this position would be upsetting to Washington, it is also testing other powers including Russia, China and India, and own its ability to withstand any pressure from others while maintaining balance in all its bilateral ties with all the major powers in the Indo-Pacific. Prior to PM Hasina undertaking travel to Japan, the UK and the US (May 2023), Bangladesh announced an Indo-Pacific Outlook strategy. It has been pointed out that while the document highlights its attempts to keep peace and security in the region while engaging with all the Indo-Pacific states, it has stopped short of clearly explain how it intends to achieve its aims (Asia Pacific Foundation of Canada 2023). Apart from this, Bangladesh's deft foreign policy management has allowed it to maintain balance while engaging with the big powers. This is applicable not only bilaterally but also through the regional groupings that Bangladesh has shown its intention to work with others.

Partnering Regionalism Initiatives

Bangladesh is also a regional partner in the Bay of Bengal Initiative for Multi-Sectoral Technical and Economic Cooperation (BIMSTEC), ASEAN Regional Forum apart from being a South Asian Association for Regional Cooperation (SAARC) member. As is well known, the idea of a regional grouping in South Asia, SAARC was first mooted by Bangladesh President Ziaur Rahman in the early 1980s. Bangladesh did not allow past animosity and present differences to be hurdles in seeking and developing friendlier relations with Pakistan. In March 2022, the Bangladesh–India–Nepal (BIN) Pact was signed. The BIN will essentially provide seamless movement across the countries through the Motor Vehicle Act for facilitating trade and commerce within the sub-region and outside. The Transit and Trade Agreement signed with India has not only given quicker access to India's Northeast region but has also enabled Bangladesh to develop economic corridors and create linkages to bring South Asia and Southeast Asia closer. The possibility of energy trade that is now under discussion between Bangladesh and Nepal looks promising for regional integration. While both neighbours are examining the technical aspects of using Indian transmission lines for trading electricity, it has been a longish journey to even reach this point. Bangladesh is also strengthening ties with many Southeast Asian and East Asian countries and has a huge number of Bangladeshi workers employed in Singapore and Malaysia. Further, Bangladesh has used the ASEAN Regional Forum to urge collective action by members to address the cause of millions of Rohingyas that Bangladesh has sheltered for a long (*New Age* 2021).

It has been suggested that Bangladesh should actively seek a dialogue partnership with ASEAN and this is possible for all its practical reasons. For instance, if pursued effectively, ASEAN could be persuaded to grant Bangladesh a Sectoral Dialogue status with ASEAN, which has similar dialogue partnerships with some countries, including Pakistan. India is one of the very few countries that enjoy a comprehensive dialogue partnership with ASEAN. If such a partnership can be achieved, it will give Bangladesh greater visibility and a place in the greater Asia-Pacific canvas (Choudhury 2020). That apart, Bangladesh can contribute to ASEAN as a consumer market as well as provide production facility (Tanzim 2022). Bangladesh enjoys bilateral ties with all ASEAN countries and this engagement can be significantly increased through a regional dialogue.

Through its Look East Policy, Bangladesh has been focusing on some Southeast Asian and East Asian countries. It was also part of the Bangladesh–China–India–Myanmar Initiative, which was essentially a 2,800-km-long trade route connecting Kolkata, India, to Kunming, China, via Bangladesh. However, beyond the trial car journey, this grouping did not make any headway in the face of rising Indo-China tensions. Despite this, Bangladesh has established itself as a useful partner for the region (Datta 2022). It assumed the chairmanship of the Indian Ocean Rim Association (IORA) Council of Ministers Meeting and hosted the 21st Meeting (17 November 2021). Additionally, it has reiterated its sustained efforts to strengthen regional cooperation and sustainable development within the Indian Ocean region (IORA News 2021).

Bangladesh is also part of the Asian Development Bank's proposed Asian Highway and Trans-Asian Railway. Through this route, Bangladesh will provide the main transit for South and Southeast Asian nations. Dhaka has expressed its desire to be linked with the India-Myanmar-Thailand Trilateral Highway underway. With adequate hard and soft infrastructure in place, Bangladesh will be able to connect the two emerging regions very effectively and act as an important bridge. It will eventually put Dhaka in the mainstream leadership role in the Asian region. However, currently, the Asian Highway projects have been critiqued for lack of implementation.

While Bangladesh has made great strides in its foreign policy it has a few concern areas. Since the mid-1900s, periodic outbreaks of hostility and violence have led large numbers of Rohingya refugees from Myanmar to seek safe refuge in neighbouring countries. Bangladesh has been one of the favoured destinations as it shares a 271-km border with Myanmar. In August 2017, when violence broke out in Myanmar, the Myanmar army launched an offensive against the Rohingya in response to Muslim insurgents' attacks on the armed forces. Amongst them, a large number of Rohingyas found shelter in Bangladesh. While most host nations have extended humanitarian assistance to persecuted Rohingyas, their inability to condemn or compel the Myanmar government to address this internal conflict points to the existing political dilemma faced by South Asian countries. Interestingly, Bangladesh is disappointed at India's refusal to offer asylum to the forcibly displaced Rohingya population in favour of building houses in the Arakan province and at China's verbal assurance, none of which has changed the ground scenario, which has forced Bangladesh to house millions of Rohingyas (Datta 2021). The February 2021 coup in Myanmar made the situation worse as Bangladesh was discussing repatriation policies with the earlier government. It was desperate to make some headway with the military leaders and did not officially condone the coup. Pertinently, Bangladesh declined to endorse a non-binding UN General Assembly resolution on Myanmar that condemned the military junta as it did not reflect the Rohingya issue more emphatically (Bhuiyan 2021). Not only that, Bangladesh was among only eight countries that sent their defence attaché to attend the Myanmar Armed Forces Day parade in Naypyitaw in March 2021, a month after the coup. Bangladesh's participation in the parade offered a certain validity to the new military regime in Myanmar with the hope that Naypyitaw will see Dhaka as a potential ally (Bhuiyan 2022). While Bangladesh has been unhesitant in engaging with Myanmar irrespective of who heads Naypyitaw, given the instability in Myanmar, Bangladesh has reasons to be wary about the state of Rohingyas and its ties with the region. Especially when it has not found any support from within the region or outside. While the Rohingya issue remains a problem for Bangladesh as they are hosting over one million of them, Bangladesh has been lauded for its humanitarian efforts but without any international move towards resolving this problem, Dhaka continues to grapple with the ongoing matter. Notwithstanding this political problem, Dhaka has been able to build bilateral partnerships and regional cooperation.

Conclusion

Bangladesh has emerged as a stable economy in the past decade, despite the present concerns surrounding its state of democracy. Its scope and range of economic interactions have led to it being perceived as a viable trade partner. It has made its presence felt, especially in the US and Europe, through the success of its ready-made garment industry. Predictions of its sustained growth, despite the setback caused by the pandemic, reflect the strength of its economic growth as its service sector that continues to grow to become the largest contributor to the economy. The global attention on the Indo-Pacific has catapulted Bangladesh's geographical location to greater significance. The proximity Bangladesh enjoys with China and India has made it more attractive as a regional power to engage with more robustly. Bangladesh's adroit management of its ties with all its bilateral partners ensures that Dhaka enjoys popularity with all the powers engaged in the region. Dhaka's sensitive handling of an incident in India, which evoked a string reaction from the Gulf countries as it was seen as an insult to the Prophet, reflects both the importance of India to Bangladesh as well as its ability to stand apart from the other Islamic nations, despite its very high dependence on the remittance that occurs from many of these Gulf nations. While there is much to applaud Bangladesh for pursuing an effective foreign policy, the domestic trends have not been very encouraging. Not only is Bangladesh pursuing hybrid democracy and exhibiting tendencies to centralise authority in the absence of any strong opposition, the pillars of democracies, the judiciary, the parliament and the media have been deliberately weakened. The recent sanctions by the US on the Rapid Action Battalion for its human right abuse is instructive to some unhealthy trends underway in Bangladesh. Given the growing global interest in Bangladesh, its human rights and liberty record will also come under the radar of Western democracies and is likely to reverse the international gains it has made in recent times. Pertinently, Bangladesh has not come so far thanks to a strong, intolerant, centralised government, but rather due to the lack of one (*The Economist* 2021). The country has shown growth in social and economic sectors, and attention to some of its domestic developments would enhance its position tremendously. For Bangladesh, economic growth, political stability and social freedom are necessary factors that can contribute comprehensively to Bangladesh's growing recognition and relevance in global affairs.

Notes

1 During the pandemic, Bangladesh recorded a 5.24 per cent growth in 2021 with its average per capita income. For details, see "Bangladesh Economy Shows Early Signs of Recovery: WB," *Prothom Alo*, April 12, 2021, https://en.prothomalo.com/business/bangladesh-economy-shows-early-signs-of-recovery-wb

2 The so-called "Indo-Pacific strategy" devised under the pretext of "the China threat". What the US says in its "Indo-Pacific strategy" is different from what it is actually doing. The US claims to advance "freedom and openness" in the region, but is in fact forming an exclusive clique through AUKUS and QUAD. It asserts to strengthen regional security, but is generating grave nuclear proliferation risks that would undermine regional peace and stability. It professes to promote regional prosperity, but is stoking opposition and confrontation between regional countries which undercuts the ASEAN-centred regional cooperation architecture that has formed over the years, and poses a serious threat to regional cooperation outcomes and development prospects. (Official Remarks of the Spokesperson of the Chinese Ministry of Foreign Affairs, https://bit.ly/3le9Qyq)

References

'21st IORA Council of Ministers Meeting on 17 November 2021. Held by the People's Republic of Bangladesh'. Press Release, *IORA News*, November 17, 2021. https://www.iora.int/en/events-media-news/news-updates-folder/official-press-release-21st-iora-council-of-ministers-meeting-on-17-november-2021-held-by-the-peoples-republic-of-bangladesh.

Allen-Ebrahimian, B. 'China Scoops Up Chevron's Gas Fields in Bangladesh'. *Foreign Policy*, April 24, 2017. https://foreignpolicy.com/2017/04/24/amid-scramble-for-influence-china-scoops-up-chevrons-gas-fields-in-bangladesh/.

'Ambassador Haas's Remarks at BIISS Seminar on U.S.–Bangladesh Relations'. U.S. Ambassador in Bangladesh, Peter Haas, US Indo-Pacific Command, April 25, 2022. https://www.pacom.mil/Media/News/News-Article-View/Article/3009775/ambassador-haass-remarks-at-biiss-seminar-on-us-bangladesh-relations/.

Anwar, A., G. Macdonald, D. Markey, and J. Siddiqui. 'Bangladesh's Balancing Act Amid the U.S. Indo-Pacific Strategy', Unites States Institute of Peace, April 1, 2022. https://www.usip.org/publications/2022/04/bangladeshs-balancing-act-amid-us-indo-pacific-strategy.

'Australia's Development Partnership with Bangladesh: How We Are Helping, Department of Foreign Affairs and Trade', Australia Department of Foreign Affairs and Trade. https://www.dfat.gov.au/geo/bangladesh/development-assistance/development-assistance-in-bangladesh.

'Bangladesh's Growth Has Been Remarkable, But Is Now at Risk'. *The Economist*, May 27, 2021. https://www.economist.com/leaders/2021/03/27/bangladeshs-growth-has-been-remarkable-but-is-now-at-risk.

'Bangladesh Important in US-Indo Pacific Strategy'. *The Daily Star*, October 15, 2022. https://www.thedailystar.net/country/news/bangladesh-important-us-indo-pacific-strategy-us-deputy-secretary-during-visit-1978445.

'Bangladesh Officially Releases Its First Indo-Pacific Outlook', Asia Pacific Foundation of Canada, May 5, 2023. https://www.asiapacific.ca/publication/bangladeshs-first-indo-pacific-outlook-aims-friendship.

'Belt and Road Initiative: Perspective from Bangladesh'. *The Daily Star*, August 7, 2019. https://www.thedailystar.net/round-tables/news/belt-and-road-initiative-perspective-bangladesh-1782928 (accessed on March 17, 2020).

Bhuiyan, H.K. 'Bangladesh Abstains from UNGA Resolution on Myanmar'. *Dhaka Tribune*, June 19, 2021. https://archive.dhakatribune.com/bangladesh/rohingya-crisis/2021/06/19/bangladesh-abstains-from-unga-resolution-on-myanmar.

Bhuiyan, P.S. 'Bangladesh Engages with the Myanmar Military Regime Because of Strategic Interests'. *Mizzima*, April 18, 2022. https://www.mizzima.com/article/bangladesh-engages-myanmar-military-regime-because-strategic-interests.

Brewster, David. 'Kickstarting a New Strategic and Defence Partnership with Bangladesh'. *The Strategist,* June 8, 2021, at https://www.aspistrategist.org.au/kick-starting-a-new-strategic-and-defence-partnership-with-bangladesh/.

Choudhury, Shamsher Mobin. Email interview with author. May 10, 2020.

Chowdhary, S.I. 'Russia Seeks Alternatives to SWIFT for Bangladesh Deals'. *New Age*, March 24, 2022. https://www.newagebd.net/article/166323/russia-seeks-alternatives-to-swift-for-bangladesh-deals.

Datta, S. 'Surely Not a Faux Pas: China Warns Bangladesh against Joining the QUAD'. *VIF Commentary*, June 1, 2021. https://www.vifindia.org/2021/june/01/surely-not-a-faux-pas-china-warns-bangladesh-against-joining-the-quad.

———. 'Bangladesh and Belt Road Initiative: Unfolding Possibilities'. *National Security* 4, no. 3, (July–September 2021).

———. 'The Rohingya Exodus: South Asia's Predicament'. *South Asian Voices*. September 8, 2021. https://southasianvoices.org/the-rohingya-exodus-south-asias-predicament/.

———. 'Bangladesh-Growing Regional Presence,' *Journal of International Relations*, Special Issue, Vol. 15, No. 1–2, 2022. DOI: https://www.doi.org/10.56312/DUJIR15e1n2e5.

Datta, Sujit. 'The Making of a Chinese Global Plan'. *National Security* 4, no 3, (July–September 2021): 3.

Denisov, Igor, Oleg Paramonov, Ekaterina Arapova, and Ivan Safranchuk. 'Russia, China, and the Concept of Indo-Pacific'. *Journal of Eurasian Studies* 12, no. 1, (2021): 72–85.

Detsch, Jack. 'How the US stopped Worrying about Pacific and Loved the Indo-Pacific'. *Foreign Policy*, July 31, 2021. https://foreignpolicy.com/2021/07/30/biden-pacific-china/.

'Dhaka Conveys Coolness Towards Security Cooperation with Washington'. *Dhaka Tribune*, March 2, 2021. https://archive.dhakatribune.com/bangladesh/foreign-affairs/2021/03/02/dhaka-conveys-coolness-towards-security-cooperation-with-washington.

'Economic Indicators for Bangladesh'. Asian Development Bank Asian Development Outlook. April 2022. https://www.adb.org/countries/bangladesh/economy.

Efremova, K. 'Small States in Great Power Politics: Understanding the "Buffer Effect"'. *Central European Journal of International and Security Studies* 13, no 1, (March 2019): 100–121.

'Foreign Aid to Bangladesh: A Thing of the Past?'. Light Castle Analysis Wing, June 21, 2021. https://www.lightcastlebd.com/insights/2021/06/evolution-of-development-assistance-to-bangladesh-part-2-2001-2020/.

'Foreign Minister Seeks ARF Support in Solving Rohingya Crisis'. *New Age*, August 6, 2021, Bangladesh Sangbad Sangstha. https://www.newagebd.net/article/145629/foreign-minister-seeks-arf-support-in-solving-rohingya-crisis.

Frost, Ellen. 'It's Time to Deepen Integration Around the Bay of Bengal'. *Carnegie India*. 31 May 2019. https://carnegieindia.org/2017/05/31/␣s-time-to-deepen-integration-around-bay-of-bengal-pub-70128.

'Full Text of President Xi's Speech at Opening of Belt and Road Forum'. Belt and Road Forum for International Cooperation. May 14, 2017. http://www.beltandroadforum.org/english/n100/2018/0306/c25-1038.html.

Geopolitics of Indo-Pacific and Reconnecting the Bay of Bengal Littorals'. Bangladesh Institute of International and Strategic Studies (BIISS) and

Embassy of Japan in Bangladesh. February 28, 2022. https://www.bd.emb-japan.go.jp/itpr_en/11_000001_00501.html.

Haider, A.A. 'Why is Foreign Direct Investment So Low in Bangladesh and How to Increase It?' *The Daily Star*, August 23, 2021. https://www.thedailystar.net/views/opinion/news/why-foreign-direct-investment-so-low-bangladesh-and-how-increase-it-2158151.

Hasan, M.D. 'Foreign Aid Dependency of Bangladesh: An Evaluation'. *Chittagong University of Business Administration Journal*, no. 26, (2011): 281–294.

Hassan, Ahmed Shovon. 'US-Bangladesh Partnership Dialogue: What Next?'. *The Diplomat*, 29 March 2022. https://thediplomat.com/2022/03/us-bangladesh-partnership-dialogue-what-next/.

'If Dhaka Joins Quad, It'll Harm Ties with Beijing, Says Chinese Ambassador Li Jiming'. *The Daily Star*, May 11, 2021. https://www.thedailystar.net/frontpage/news/beijing-wants-dhaka-not-join-quad-2091529.

'India–Bangladesh Relations: Prospects and Challenges'. IISS, March 23, 2021. file:///C:/Users/hp/Downloads/India-Bangladesh%20relations%20-%20 prospects%20and%20challenges%20-%20IISS%20webinar%20transcript.pdf.

'India Shouldn't Worry about China-Led One Belt One Road'. *The Daily Star*, January 23, 2020. https://www.thedailystar.net/frontpage/news/india-shouldnt-worry-about-china-led-one-belt-one-road-1691632 (accessed on March 17, 2020).

'Indo-Pacific Outlook of Bangladesh'. Press Release, Ministry of Foreign Affairs, Bangladesh, April 24, 2023. https://mofa.gov.bd/site/press_release/d8d7189a-7695-4ff5-9e2b-903fe0070ec9.

'Japan Bangladesh Foreign Minister's Dinner'. Ministry of Foreign Affairs of Japan, July 30, 2019. https://www.mofa.go.jp/s_sa/sw/bd/page3e_001056.html.

Karim, Tariq. 'Importance of the Bay of Bengal as a Causeway between the Indian and Pacific Oceans'. *Asia Pacific Bulletin*, no. 557, (2021). https://www.eastwestcenter.org/publications/importance-the-bay-bengal-causeway-between-the-indian-and-pacific-oceans.

Khusru, S.M. 'Why China, India Wooing Bangladesh'. *The Daily Star*, July 3, 2021. https://www.thedailystar.net/views/opinion/news/why-china-and-india-are-wooing-bangladesh-2122206.

Krishna, A. 'Bangladesh Rebuffs China on Quad Warning'. *The Hindu*, May 12, 2021. https://www.thehindu.com/news/international/bangladesh-rebuffs-china-on-quad-warning/article34542373.ece.

Liu Zongyi, L. 'Wooing Bangladesh to Quad against China Not to Help Bangladesh Devt'. *Global Times*, May 11, 2021. https://www.globaltimes.cn/page/202105/1223193.shtml.

Mavis, M. and S. Hossain. 'No Immediate Impact on Bangladesh, but Businesses Wary of Oil and Food Price Hike'. *Dhaka Tribune*. February 27, 2022. https://www.dhakatribune.com/business/2022/02/27/no-immediate-impact-on-bangladesh-but-businesses-wary-of-oil-and-food-price-hike.

'Ministry of External Affairs', Response to Question No. 849 One Belt and One Road Initiative in the Lok Sabha (Lower House of the Parliament)'. June 26, 2019. https://bit.ly/3LpbYhe.

Narayan, S. and S. Datta. 'Introduction', *Bangladesh at 50: Development and Challenges*. Orient BlackSwan: New Delhi, 2020.

Palma, P. 'US Bangladesh Relationship: What's in the Feast'. *The Daily Star*, March 24, 2020. https://www.thedailystar.net/news/bangladesh/diplomacy/news/us-bangladesh-relationship-whats-the-feast-2989131.

Plagemann, J. 'Small States and Competing Connectivity Strategies: What Explains Bangladesh's Success in Relations with Asia's Major Powers?'. *The Pacific Review*, May 6, 2021.

Pitman, A. 'Russia Is Not Bangladesh's Friend'. *Dhaka Tribune*, March 27, 2022. https://www.dhakatribune.com/op-ed/2022/03/27/russia-is-not-bangladeshs-friend.

Rahman, M. 'A Journey of Dual Graduation and the Attendant Challenges'. In *Bangladesh at 50: Development and Challenges*, edited by S. Narayan, Sreeradha Datta. New Delhi: Orient BlackSwan, 2020.

Rahman, S.A. 'Deepening Japan–Bangladesh Relations'. *East Asia Forum*, September 17, 2021. https://www.eastasiaforum.org/2021/09/17/deepening-japan-bangladesh-relations/.

Raja Mohan, C. 'The Bay of Bengal in the Emerging Indo-Pacific'. Issue Briefs and Special Reports, Observer Research Foundation, October 27, 2020. https://www.orfonline.org/research/the-bay-of-bengal-in-the-emerging-indo-pacific.

———. '50 Years after Independence Bangladesh Bursts into Geopolitics'. *Foreign Policy*, March 25, 2021. https://foreignpolicy.com/2021/03/25/bangladesh-independence-anniversary-geopolitics-india-china-pakistanindo-pacific-quad/.

Ramadhani, E. 'China in the Indian Ocean Region: The Confined "Far-Seas Operations"'. *India Quarterly* 71, no 2, (2015): 146–159.

Shovon, H.A. 'US–Bangladesh Partnership Dialogue: What Next?' *The Diplomat*, March 29, 2022. https://thediplomat.com/2022/03/us-bangladesh-partnership-dialogue-what-next/.

———. 'Decoding Bangladesh's Response to the Ukraine Crisis'. *The Diplomat*, March 25, 2022. https://thediplomat.com/2022/03/decoding-bangladeshs-response-to-the-ukraine-crisis/.

Tanzim, N. 'Bangladesh's Biggest Focus Should Be Getting into ASEAN'. *The Business Standard*, March 7, 2022. https://www.tbsnews.net/features/panorama/bangladeshs-biggest-focus-should-be-getting-asean-381070.

Teizzi, Shannon. 'How Did Asian Countries Vote on the UN's Ukraine Resolution?'. *The Diplomat*, March 3, 2022. https://thediplomat.com/2022/03/how-did-asian-countries-vote-on-the-uns-ukraine-resolution/.

'US Wants Bangladesh to Join IPS'. *Prothom Alo*, March 23, 2022. https://en.prothomalo.com/bangladesh/us-wants-bangladesh-to-join-ips.

Zahid, H. 'No One Immune from the Impact of Russia–Ukraine Conflict'. *The Daily Star*, March 3, 2022. https://www.thedailystar.net/business/economy/news/no-one-immune-the-impact-russia-ukraine-conflict-2974496.

8

THE EVOLVING DYNAMICS IN BANGLADESH AND SOUTHEAST ASIAN RELATIONS: A LONG ROAD OF CONSTRAINTS AND OPPORTUNITIES

Don McLain Gill

From its humble beginnings in the post-1971 independence era, Bangladesh has now positioned itself as an emerging middle power, given its growing economic, demographic and diplomatic capacity. The South Asian state's graduation from a least-developed country (LDC) status has also added more impetus to its geopolitical significance not only in its immediate geographic neighbourhood, but also beyond. Traditionally speaking, Bangladesh's external engagements were significantly concentrated within South Asia's geopolitical and economic dimensions. However, as it continues to grow, Dhaka has congruently been able to expand and enhance its relations with other key regions of the world. Among them are the burgeoning ties between Bangladesh and the Association of Southeast Asian Nations (ASEAN).

Since the dawn of the 21st century, Bangladesh has sought to deepen bilateral cooperative relations with Southeast Asian states. The strengthening of the relationship seems to be a logical and inevitable progression, given the expanding and increasingly interconnected nature of their economies, brought by a globalising international political–economic landscape. Hence, economics is often understood as the driving force for closer relations. However, other key areas also remain vital behind this level of regionalisation. Similarly, ASEAN also seeks to bolster engagements with a wide array of emerging states—of which Bangladesh is part. Moreover, as its material capacity continues to improve, Dhaka has equally endeavoured to reinvigorate its partnership with Southeast Asian states at the bilateral, multilateral and institutional levels.

Bangladesh laid the foundations for deeper relations with Muslim-majority states Indonesia and Malaysia based on shared values, religion and culture. From the desire to strengthen connectivity, trade and commerce, both Southeast Asian states have recently expressed their willingness to deepen ties with Bangladesh given the latter's expanding economic trajectory (*Dhaka Tribune* 2022; Rashid 2022 and Izzuddin 2020). The relationship between Bangladesh and Cambodia have also witnessed an upswing since both states decided to establish a joint commission for bilateral relations in 2010. Seven years after the agreement, Bangladesh and Cambodia signed 10 forward-looking deals that aimed to broaden and deepen the bilateral partnership based on a long-term and multidimensional framework for cooperation.

Moreover, both states have not only bolstered their engagements in the agriculture sector but have also improved coordination in labour laws to manage and maximise the growing migration of workers (Samean 2022). Furthermore, Bangladesh and Cambodia are also in talks to sign a Free Trade Area (FTA) agreement to add momentum to bilateral trade (Kunmakara 2022). Similar growth trajectories can also be seen with Bangladesh's ties with Singapore, Vietnam, Thailand and the Philippines (*The Daily Star* 2022; Saptaparna 2022 and Rahman 2022). Bangladesh has also been pivotal in positively contributing towards health and counterterrorism with regional states like Myanmar.

Dhaka continues to cooperate with its Southeast Asian neighbours through sub-regional arrangements such as the Bay of Bengal Initiative for Multi-Sectoral Technical and Economic Cooperation (BIMSTEC), with the inclusion of Thailand and Myanmar as members, and the Indian Ocean Rim Association (IORA) with Indonesia, Malaysia, Thailand and Singapore. Additionally, while Bangladesh became a member of the ASEAN Regional Forum (ARF) in 2006, talks are underway for the elevation of the South Asian state as ASEAN's sectoral dialogue partner.

However, while Bangladesh's foreign policy trajectory towards Southeast Asia is generally positive, the ability to maximise its potential continues to be hampered by the unaddressed challenges brought by the Rohingya refugee crisis. The Rohingya refugees face a great and ongoing uncertainty amid the political shifts taking place in Myanmar and the relative unwillingness of ASEAN to play a more active role in pressuring and holding the leadership in Myanmar accountable. With such turbulence, Bangladesh maintains a central position as it continues to shelter over 10,00,000 refugees despite constrained and limited resources (Ansar and Khaled 2021).

Apart from the humanitarian aspect of the Rohingya crisis, the geopolitical dimensions that come along with it also create significant challenges for stable and peaceful inter-state relations in the region. Accordingly, Bangladesh and the nine other member states of ASEAN are positioned in the immediate geographic periphery of Myanmar and are thus more directly impacted by the crisis in terms of its political, social, and economic contexts. However, while Bangladesh and ASEAN member states seek to stabilise the situation, both sides currently diverge in their approaches, thus creating complications in forwarding a coordinated, holistic and robust cooperative framework between Bangladesh and Southeast Asian states.

While the international community and various activist groups around the world continue to voice their concerns about the crisis and focus on providing relief and assistance to the Rohingya in Bangladesh, the most pragmatic framework for a potential settlement will eventually revolve around the joint efforts between Bangladesh and ASEAN. This chapter argues that at a time when Bangladesh seeks to enhance its geopolitical position in the world and expand its engagements with Southeast Asia, the ongoing Rohingya refugee crisis presents a critical challenge for Dhaka's foreign policy calculations and interests. Thus, this chapter does not only seek to assess the constraints faced by Bangladesh vis-à-vis its bilateral ties with Myanmar and ASEAN in the context of the crisis, but it also attempts to highlight a way forward in forging proactive levels of engagement with its Southeast Asian neighbours. Furthermore, given the inconsistent attention from extra-regional powers towards the crisis, it will be practical and necessary for Bangladesh to maintain the momentum behind its push to forge closer relations with ASEAN, given the shared concerns both sides have regarding their immediate neighbourhood.

Bangladesh–Myanmar Relations under the Shadow of the Rohingya Crisis

Myanmar and Bangladesh are immediate geographic neighbours that share an estimated 271-kilometre border. Geographically speaking, both countries also serve as geopolitical fulcrums between South and Southeast Asia. Hence, to maintain a proactive and inclusive framework for inter-regional connectivity and integration, the participation of both these countries is paramount. However, despite the conditions for robust bilateral engagements, Bangladesh–Myanmar relations continue to be marred with complexities, most especially due to the unfolding Rohingya crisis. Such an evolving impediment continues to impact the potential of the bilateral ties in several dimensions.

The Rohingya have been at an uncertain juncture in Myanmar for several decades brought by discriminative and oppressive policies by the leadership towards them since the 1970s.

Operation Naga Min under the leadership of General Ne Win in 1978, drove out approximately 2,00,000 Rohingya to Bangladesh. Consequently, as a move by the nationalist regime in the Southeast Asian state to harness Burmese ethnic power, the Burma Citizenship

Act of 1982 was established, which provided citizenship to individuals residing in the state and who could trace their family residency before 1983. However, the act explicitly identified 130 communities that are eligible to obtain citizenship status, with the Rohingya community being left out, thus resulting in their statelessness. Furthermore, another major campaign called Operation Pyi Thaya in 1991–1992, also led to a mass movement of at least 2,50,000 Rohingya to find refuge in the South Asian state (Finnigan 2019 and Congressional Research Service 2017). While a repatriation process took place with the participation of the UN from 1992 to 1997, which saw the return of approximately 2,36,000 Rohingya to Myanmar, a study conducted by the Médecins Sans Frontières highlighted that 63 per cent of the refugees were not willing to return to Myanmar, and 65 per cent were unaware of their right to refuse repatriation (Médecins Sans Frontières-Holland 2002). Given the continuous persecution of the Rohingya, the flow of outward movement from Myanmar to Bangladesh persisted, with large-scale movements taking place in 2012 and 2016.

Hence, the most contentious issues between both states revolve critically around the Bangladesh–Myanmar border. Although the maritime boundary dispute between Bangladesh and Myanmar was eventually settled in 2012, the continuous escalation of security challenges remains interlinked with the cross-border movement of the Rohingya and the unavailability of legal frameworks and mechanisms to address this in both bilateral and multilateral formats. The constant movement of refugees inevitably became a significant component in defining and understanding the bilateral relationship between the two countries involved, which eventually spilled over towards other critical areas of cooperation.

The lack of political will, particularly in Myanmar, to address the proliferating situation in a pragmatic and efficient manner adds more strain to the overarching bilateral relationship of both states. Since the 1970s, the leadership in Myanmar has been reluctant and aloof towards the possible resettlement of Rohingya refugees back to Myanmar. This is parallel to the unwillingness of the refugees a return to Myanmar due to the tumultuous conditions that continue to plague the state at their expense. Hence, a practical and systematic solution to alleviate the crisis in that period was largely non-existent. However, in the 1990s, both states sought to navigate the situation of the Rohingya refugees through a potential legal framework. The period witnessed a series of paperwork and agreements signed, such as the 1992 Memorandum of Understanding (MoU) between both states to set the parameters for a repatriation process with limited participation from the UN. A similar MoU was signed the following year between Bangladesh and the UN Human Rights Commission (UNHCR) regarding the protection of the Rohingya refugees, as well as the prioritisation of a voluntary repatriation method without the utilisation of coercive approaches (UNCHR 1993). In the same year, a similar MoU was also signed between the Myanmar government and the UNHCR. However, despite such attempts throughout the 20th century, no effective solution was achieved due to the lack of political will in Myanmar and the complications brought by external geopolitical forces in the region and the greater international system.

In 2009, a revitalised attempt between both states to address the ongoing crisis was witnessed with the restart of negotiations, which highlighted the necessity and importance of resolving the Rohingya crisis. This was then followed by a firm statement by the Bangladeshi foreign minister during his visit in Myanmar two years after, stating that the South Asian state is constrained and limited in its capacity to accommodate and shelter the growing influx of refugees from Myanmar, despite the insistence of the international community for the borders to remain open (Relieweb 2009). What resulted from these series of developments was a mere symbolic gesture and acknowledgement by the Myanmar elites stating that they seek to review the refugees' list to evaluate their eligibility and citizenship status. However, the most controversial movement took place in 2017, when 7,50,000 Rohingya were driven out of Myanmar through a counter-insurgency operation conducted by the Myanmar military (Albert and Maizland 2020).

Given the unaddressed status of the issue, the porous border also continues to be an avenue for illicit activities, including drug and human trafficking. The border with Myanmar has been constantly identified by the Department of Narcotics Control of Bangladesh as a critical entry for illegal drugs, and arrests are continuously made. In fact, among these arrests, several drug traffickers were displaced Rohingya (Banerjee 2020). Human trafficking of the Rohingyas also serves as a notorious thorn in the side of the border security. Furthermore, Rohingya militant groups based in Myanmar create more insecurity in the border area, given that they also have sympathisers in Bangladesh's refugee camps (Banerjee 2020). Hence, the nexus between the ongoing exodus of the Rohingya refugees and the exacerbating drug- and human-trafficking routes inevitably create serious security challenges for both states. The undeniable spill over of such complexities has restricted the desire of both states to forge more enhanced levels of physical connectivity.

While such crucial infrastructure could have developed the tourism and commercial industries of Bangladesh and Myanmar, the fear of having more insecurity due to the potential free flow of non-state actors using such modes of connectivity trumps the desire to maximise economic gains. However, current developments between both sides including the agreement between both countries' border police forces to work jointly and cohesively to prevent the spill over and movement of illegal activities by traffickers and militants is an optimistic step in the right direction (Chowdhury 2022). Much work still needs to be done in order to effectively create a stabilising and long-term solution for the security dynamics in the bilateral relationship for more sustainable Bangladesh–Myanmar ties.

The turbulent relationship between Myanmar and Bangladesh, particularly in the context of the exacerbating Rohingya refugee crisis, not only illustrates the lack of political will to do anything significant about it but also points to the limits of sub-regional frameworks such as BIMSTEC, given their lack of legal mechanisms to deal with the issue of displaced people. Therefore, this limitation has also cost the development potential of both states for a more robust inter-regional cooperative framework between South Asia and Southeast Asia, due to impediments in the development of vital infrastructure projects, such as the Asian Highway and the BCIM (Bangladesh, China, India, Myanmar) Corridor, which is supposed to run through Myanmar's Rakhine State.

Given the clear constraints in the bilateral relationship, both states are not able to effectively leverage their ties to proactively address the exacerbating conditions that come with the refugee crisis. The spill over has gone beyond both states and reached regional and international dimensions. As a result, there have been attempts by extra-regional and regional states to resolve the unfolding issue. However, such attempts have often stopped short of providing a robust and long-term resolution that banks on a legal mechanism that will hold the current leadership in Myanmar accountable, to pressure it in order to repatriate refugees and ease the socio-economic and political constraints that Bangladesh continues to face.

The Limits of Bangladesh's International Outreach

Six years since the major 2017 exodus of Rohingya refugees from Myanmar, and two years since the 2021 coup, Bangladesh continues to shelter over 9,00,000 refugees due to the unavailability of any effective solution to address the ongoing crisis. Moreover, Myanmar continues to downplay and overlook Dhaka's attempts to initiate an effective and long-term resolution for repatriation and political accountability. As a result, Dhaka has sought to engage with extra-regional powers with the hope of achieving a sustainable short-term and long-term solution for the crisis, given the limitations of national resources and the exacerbating conditions in the refugee camps brought by the Covid-19 pandemic and the escalating political and economic impact of the Russia–Ukraine war. Additionally, such factors have also added more complex layers of bureaucratic restrictions that, in turn, create more pressure towards granting access to the limited foreign aid and actors that seek to contribute positively vis-à-vis the crisis.

During her address to the United Nations General Assembly (UNGA) in 2022, Bangladeshi Prime Minister Sheikh Hasina pointed to how Bangladesh's economic, security and socio-political stability continues to be compromised by the unwillingness of international and regional states to forge a legal framework for accountability towards the crisis (Ahmed 2022). In fact, before her UNGA speech, she also outlined important elements that needed to be incorporated in an equation for a long-term resolution of the crisis: (*i*) to financially and politically support the Rohingya people, (*ii*) support and uphold legal trials conducted in the International Court of Justice (ICJ) and International Criminal Court (ICC) to collectively pressure and hold Myanmar accountable, (*iii*) apply the commitments of Myanmar in the context of ASEAN's Five-Point Consensus[1] and (*iv*) ensure that there is uninterrupted access for humanitarian assistance (Ahmed 2022).

Additionally, in order to systematically address the assistance gap, an annual joint response plan (JRP) was established between the UN and Bangladesh to organise and strategically evaluate and enumerate various objectives, gaps and funding plans within the year. It is important to note that since 2018, the JRP began putting great emphasis on the protection and assistance of not only for the refugees but also for the host communities (UNHCR 2018). This has resulted in a notable recalibration of JRP objectives since 2018 that also encompass a holistic approach towards collective development, and not only restrained and limited to humanitarian assistance. However, the realities on the ground paint a different and less congruent picture from the policies that have been encouraged on paper. While the protection and safety of the vulnerable continue to be at stake, the number and scale of emergencies that have been recently occurring (for example, landslides, flash floods, fires and other calamities) are seen to have exponentially intensified (Ahmed 2021). In terms of foreign funding, an objective analysis of the JRP highlights how in 2020, 60 per cent of the objectives were fulfilled, while in 2022, only 45 per cent of the programmes were funded (UNOCHA 2022).

The US has by far been the largest single donor contributing towards the alleviation of the Rohingya crisis. This is followed by the UK, the EU and Japan. In fact, since the launch of the 2021 JRP, the US has pledged over $155 million, while during the 2022 JRP launch, US ambassador to Bangladesh Peter Haas announced over $152 million in the form of additional humanitarian assistance for the Rohingya refugees in Bangladesh and other countries that are critically affected (*Dhaka Tribune* 2022). This brings US total assistance to more than $1.7 billion since August 2017. In addition, Julieta Valls Noyes, US state department assistant secretary of state for population, refugees, and immigration, announced that Washington is considering a resettlement and rehabilitation programme for Rohingyas in the US from Bangladesh—similar to programmes previously done with the Malaysian and Thai governments (US Department of State 2022).

However, a critical evaluation of the overall framework and operationalisation of funds provided by the international donor community indicates critical gaps due to their inconsistent engagement and coordination with the government of Bangladesh to create a broader framework for protection, relocation and sustainable socio-economic programmes to benefit the Rohingya refugees and the affected Bangladeshi communities. Moreover, while the US resettlement programme will allow more flexibility in Bangladesh, it is still in its initial stages of planning. Hence, delays and domestic miscoordinations can occur.

Beyond the US, other states have also taken measures to address the crisis and the events that have been taking place since the 2021 coup. For instance, the African state of Gambia brought Myanmar before the ICJ based on the allegations that the Myanmar military committed genocide in the Rakhine State (ICJ 2022). Gambia's action, in turn, gained support among members of the Organisation of Islamic Cooperation (OIC). Moreover, the ICC also authorised an investigation on the crimes against humanity committed against the Rohingya community. The US, the UK, Canada and the EU have also imposed sanctions on the senior leaders of the junta and other and key military organisations, such as the Myanmar Economic Corporation (MEC) and Myanmar Economic Holdings Limited (MEHL).

However, the impact of these sanctions to put pressure on the military and constrain its capacity to procure funds to bankroll its operations and defence purchases remains limited, especially since there is no consensus at the international level to sanction the vast foreign oil and gas profits. Moreover, other key states like Japan and Australia have also stopped short of imposing heavy individual sanctions on the military of Myanmar. Meanwhile, at an organisational level, the UN Security Council continues to lack much-needed consensus, particularly among its permanent members, to forge and collectively agree on a long-term and action-based framework to tackle the enduring Rohingya crisis and the role played by the Myanmar military.

While Dhaka has also sought China's assistance to act as a mediator between Bangladesh and Myanmar, it is still unclear how Beijing can effectively persuade the Myanmar leadership to responsibly repatriate the refugees. China has been continuously engaging with the Myanmar regime on various levels to safeguard its economic and security interests. In fact, China also classifies the crisis as a domestic issue (Lambert 2022). Its position indicates its support for non-interventionist policies that will not infringe on the sovereignty of Myanmar. Moreover, Beijing also continues to thwart any potential resolution and action in the UN that seeks to take a larger and more active step against the leadership in Myanmar (Lambert 2022). On the other hand, China has also been supplying sophisticated weapons to the armed groups in Myanmar, including the Arakan Army— Naypyitaw-designated terrorist group (*The Times of India* 2020).

However, among Bangladesh's major Asian development partners, Japan has illustrated significant humanitarian support for Dhaka's response towards the Rohingya refugees. In fact, since 2017, Tokyo has provided over $175 million to the United Nations Population Fund (UNFPA) and other relevant UN agencies and non-governmental organisations in Bangladesh to improve living conditions of the refugees in the South Asian state (Sakib 2022). Moreover, while remaining largely quiet on sharing the burden of Bangladesh through the accommodation of more Rohingya refugees, Tokyo eventually broke its silence in December 2022 with Japanese Ambassador to Bangladesh Ito Naoki stating that his country is considering the resettlement of Rohingyas to Japan upon Dhaka's constant request (*The Daily Star* 2022). However, despite the noteworthy statement by the ambassador, no concrete framework for repatriation to Japan has been made yet. Moreover, given the role of geography, Japan seeks to maintain functional relations with Myanmar, despite UN experts and human rights organisations pressing Tokyo to apply more pressure on the Southeast Asian state (UN News 2023). This intricate equation creates challenges for Japan's capacity to play a larger role in addressing the escalating issue.

Hence, despite Bangladesh's outreach towards extra-regional powers to forge a lasting solution for the crisis, their responses have been inconsistent and marred with delays and gaps given the role of geography and their varied degrees of interest towards the unfolding issue vis-à-vis their strategic priorities. This has led to a revitalised realisation in Dhaka regarding the significance of Bangladesh's relations with ASEAN states. While ASEAN has also maintained a careful position regarding the Rohingya issue, its significance for a potential alleviation (and even resolution) of the crisis is undeniable, particularly in Bangladesh's strategic calculus. Against the backdrop of limited extra-regional responses, the next section magnifies the need for Bangladesh to continue proactively deepening its engagements with ASEAN despite current shortcomings in addressing the Rohingya crisis.

Challenges and Opportunities in the Bangladesh–ASEAN Dynamics

The primary regional institution in Southeast Asia, ASEAN serves as the most crucial avenue for Southeast Asian member states to practically address and deal with issues that challenge regional peace and stability. Recognising this, Bangladesh has been pushing for ASEAN to play a more proactive role amid the crisis by taking a more legal approach towards holding the Myanmar military more accountable while looking for a lasting solution to repatriate the displaced Rohingya.

Bangladesh Foreign Minister A.K. Abdul Momen has emphasised how Southeast Asian states must take an active role in cooperating with his nation to resolve the spiralling crisis by bringing the Myanmar leadership into the picture for robust negotiations (Bala 2021). Such negotiations will be necessary not only to apply pressure on Myanmar but also to create conducive conditions for an unhampered process of repatriation for the Rohingya. However, ASEAN's unwillingness to intervene through the bloc's multilateral format creates further frustrations in Dhaka.

While the UN and major extra-regional powers have contributed towards humanitarian assistance, the scope and depth of these responses have been limited given the inconsistent momentum surrounding them and the inability to put pressure on Myanmar. Moreover, the geopolitical reality of international politics can also explain how such efforts by extra-regional states continue to dwindle, given the fluctuations in their immediate strategic calculations. While it is in ASEAN's best interest to resolve the Rohingya refugee crisis and stabilise relations with Myanmar, it is necessary for Dhaka to understand the motivations behind ASEAN's response in order to look for a more practical middle ground where Bangladesh and its Southeast Asian neighbours can more effectively collaborate to address the unfolding crisis.

As a regional bloc, ASEAN has been maintaining a position of constructive engagement based on the very nature of its membership and structure. Its 10 member states cooperate based on shared interests and concerns without compromising each member's sovereignty and national interests. Hence, the ASEAN Way is crucial to understand the Southeast Asian bloc's position vis-à-vis Myanmar. It banks on a series of norms that include respect for sovereignty and non-interference. Accordingly, such defining norms thereby also illustrate the limits of ASEAN to take coercive and assertive measures against its members, given the discouragement towards intervening in another state's domestic affairs.

Thus, it is understandable how ASEAN opts for a quieter diplomacy. The ASEAN Way of inter-state engagement is also seen in the bloc's manner of addressing the Rohingya crisis. Despite the continuation of the crisis and the stark violations of human rights, ASEAN has carefully refrained from taking aggressive measures against the regime in Myanmar, while maintaining the importance of backdoor negotiations and inclusive diplomacy. Such methods have resulted in fairly positive results such as the confirmation of the Myanmar military to allow international aid to get to the people.

Furthermore, as ASEAN's key mechanism for fostering coordinated responses for disaster management and emergencies, the ASEAN Coordinating Centre for Humanitarian Assistance (AHA Centre) has also been playing a vital role in the humanitarian response and assistance to the Rohingya in the Rakhine state since 2017. However, such a mechanism is also constrained due to its emphasis on engaging based on the supervision and agreement of the affected state—in this case, the regime in Myanmar (AHA Centre 2018). Similarly, while the ASEAN Intergovernmental Commission on Human Rights was initially tasked to protect human rights and freedom, its capacity is also restrained not only because of the limitations imposed by the ASEAN Way, but also because there is no explicit mandate that allows and empowers it to take robust actions to secure human rights (Barber and Teitt 2021).

Given such a situation, it may be arduous for Bangladesh to push ASEAN to recalibrate its approach to play a bigger role immediately. ASEAN's adherence to the importance of non-interference, respect for sovereignty and constructive diplomacy may undermine Dhaka's desire to push for a collective, legal and robust strategy to put significant pressure on Myanmar, while also ensuring a consistent and unhampered repatriation process of the refugees back into the Southeast Asian state. However, while the overarching significance of the ASEAN Way is a defining attribute in the bloc's institutional engagement, scholars and analysts of the Southeast Asian bloc have pointed to the flexibility of such adherence by ASEAN member states.

Matthew Davies explained how the way ASEAN engages is not always monotonous and strictly adherent to the ASEAN Way; rather, it is subject to the interests of the member states (Davies 2016). Given that ASEAN is not structured like a supranational institution that requires member states to cede a portion of their sovereignty for collective action, the Southeast Asian bloc is a less rigid arrangement where its members seek to cooperate and take collective action based on issues that all can loosely agree upon vis-à-vis their individual interests. Nesadurai makes a similar assessment by highlighting how ASEAN can depart from rigidly pursuing particular agreed-upon norms without ignoring the rest for specific issues (Nesadurai 2017). Such an observation also draws from the state-led format of ASEAN, where states may engage in a particular way based on their strategic interests.

Jurgen Haacke provided an interesting case to support these observations by drawing on ASEAN's ability to take a more interventionist stance against Myanmar between the years 2005 and 2009, due to the fear among ASEAN states of losing US and Western support in economic development and security at a time when China continued to deepen its political-economic clout in the region, along with its growing assertiveness and expansion (Haacke 2010). A similar logic can be applied to ASEAN's recent actions towards the current leadership in Myanmar. While the 2021 ASEAN Summit saw the inclusion of the military representative of Myanmar in the name of inclusive diplomacy, the latter was banned from attending the 2022 ASEAN Summit due to the regime's inability to create a conducive environment in Myanmar for the return of the Rohingya. Hence, while such actions may not be considered strong, it still points to the ability of ASEAN to deviate from the agreed-upon norms to a certain extent.

Recognising this, Bangladesh must seek to consistently deepen engagements with ASEAN member states to be able to find alternative shared areas of concern, which can result in the recalibration of policies towards the crisis. Moreover, Bangladesh must continue to use its growing relevance on the world stage bringing other key players to the negotiating table along with ASEAN. While it is prudent not to expect the regional bloc to instantly shift its position, constant negotiations and dialogue may pave the way for more practical options that can alleviate the concerns of both Bangladesh and the ASEAN member states. Amid this attempt, Bangladesh must also continue to maintain its foreign policy momentum throughout the region to deepen and broaden other areas of cooperation. Such a positive outlook between Bangladesh and its southeastern neighbours can foster more conducive conditions to take on more sensitive issue areas. Given the unpredictable shifts in the international geopolitical landscape, it is a pragmatic necessity for both Bangladesh and ASEAN members to enhance and expand their ties. Only such forms of cooperation may result in a long-term solution, given the immediate geopolitical implications the crisis has on Bangladesh and ASEAN member states.

Conclusion

Bangladesh's rise as an emerging middle power in the international system has catalysed a reinvigorated foreign policy. In the past few years, Bangladesh's desire to forge closer relations with Southeast Asian states has been largely welcomed by the region due to the expanding economic potential that can be leveraged by both sides.

However, the Rohingya refugee crisis continues to serve as a critical obstacle to effectively maximise Bangladesh's relations with the members of ASEAN. Given Myanmar's lack of accountability and ASEAN's cautious responses, Bangladesh has pushed extra-regional powers to be involved in alleviating the crisis. Unfortunately, the responses of extra-regional states have been limited to an inconsistent humanitarian approach brought by the divergences in their strategic interests.

However, despite the regional bloc's constructive approach, pragmatism emphasises the need for Bangladesh to continue strengthening its ties with ASEAN and its member states, especially given their geopolitical positions vis-à-vis the crisis. While the adherence to the ASEAN Way is often seen as an impediment for a more pragmatic Bangladesh–ASEAN joint response towards the crisis, it must be understood that ASEAN, a group of states that put emphasis on cooperation based on the convergence of interests and respect for sovereignty, has the potential to forward actions that may not rigidly adhere to the agreed-upon norms in their entirety. Hence, the need for Bangladesh and ASEAN states to consistently engage and negotiate on common or alternative grounds for cooperation and a way forward will be crucial, not only for the future of the crisis but also the overall partnership between both sides.

Note

1   The five points include: an 'immediate cessation of violence in Myanmar', a 'constructive dialogue among all parties concerned', a 'special envoy of the ASEAN Chair shall facilitate mediation of the dialogue process', 'ASEAN shall provide humanitarian assistance through the AHA Centre' and 'the special envoy and delegation shall visit Myanmar to meet with all parties concerned' (ASEAN 2021).

References

'10 Years for the Rohingya Refugees in Bangladesh: Past, Present and Future'. Médecins Sans Frontières-Holland, July 1, 2002.

'2018 Joint Response Plan for Rohingya Humanitarian Crisis.' UNHCR, March–December 2018.

Ahmed, K. 'At Least Six Rohingya Refugees Killed as Floods Hit Camps in Bangladesh'. *The Guardian*, July 29, 2021.

Ahmed, K.U. 'Hasina's Pitch for Solving the Rohingya Crisis'. *The Diplomat*, October 11, 2022.

Albert, Eleanor and Lindsay Maizland. 'The Rohingya Crisis', Council on Foreign Relations, 23 January 2020. https://www.cfr.org/backgrounder/rohingya-crisis

Ansar, A. and A.F. Md. Khaled. 'From Solidarity to Resistance: Host Communities' Evolving Response to the Rohingya Refugees in Bangladesh'. *Journal of International Humanitarian Action* 6, no. 16, (2021).

'Application of the Convention on the Prevention and Punishment of the Crime of Genocide (The Gambia v. Myanmar)'. International Court of Justice, 2022.

'ASEAN-Emergency Response and Assessment Team (ASEAN-ERAT) 2018'. AHA Centre, 2018.

Bala, S. 'Bangladesh Calls on Southeast Asia to Pressure Myanmar to Take Back the Rohingya Refugees'. CNBC, April 19, 2021.

Banerjee, S. 'The Rohingya Crisis and Its Impact on Bangladesh–Myanmar Relations'. Observer Research Foundation, 26 August 26, 2020.

'Bangladesh May Hold Talks with ASEAN Countries to Sign FTA: Philippine Envoy'. *The Daily Star*, May 12, 2022.

'Bangladesh Urges Myanmar to Help Repatriate Rohingya Refugees'. Relieweb, May 16, 2009.

Barber, R. and S. Teitt. 'Legitimacy and Centrality Under Threat: The Case for an ASEAN Response to Human Rights Violations against the Rohingya'. *Asian Politics & Policy*, no. 13, (2021): 471–492.

'Burma's Brutal Campaign Against the Rohingya'. Congressional Research Service, September 26, 2017.

'China Supplying Weapons to Arakan Army Armed Group to Weaken India, Myanmar: Report'. *The Times of India*, July 2, 2020.

Chowdhury, K.R. 'Bangladesh, Myanmar Border Police Agree to Work Jointly against Militant Groups'. *Radio Free Asia*, November 29, 2022.

Davies, M. 'A Community of Practice: Explaining Change and Continuity in ASEAN's Diplomatic Environment'. *The Pacific Review* 29, no 2, (2016): 211–233.

Finnigan, C. 'Rohingya Refugees in Bangladesh: How the Absence of Citizenship Rights Acts as a Barrier to Successful Repatriation'. LSE Blogs, June 12, 2019.

Haacke, J. 'The Myanmar Imbroglio and ASEAN: Heading Towards the 2010 Elections'. *International Affairs* 86, no 1, (2010): 153–174.

'Indonesia Seeks to Bolster Ties with Bangladesh'. *Dhaka Tribune*, August 17, 2022.

Izzuddin, M. 'Rebooting Bangladesh–Malaysia Relations'. ISAS Insights, March 23, 2020.

'Japan Considers Rohingya Resettlement'. *The Daily Star*. December 15, 2022.

Kunmakara, M. 'Hopes High for Bangladesh FTA'. *Phnom Penh Post*, October 9, 2022.

Lambert, R. 'Hidden Parallels: The Impact of Beijing's Policies on the Rohingya Crisis'. Wilson Center, January 18, 2022.

Nesadurai, H.E.S. 'ASEAN During the Life of the Pacific Review: A Balance Sheet on Regional Governance and Community Building'. *The Pacific Review* 30, no. 6, (2017): 938–951.

Rahman, S.A. 'Fifty Years of Singapore–Bangladesh Ties: Shared Past, Robust Future'. *Australian Outlook,* March 29, 2022.

Rashid, M. 'Indonesia Seeks Direct Air Link with Bangladesh'. *New Age,* December 24, 2022.

'Resettlement Initiative for Vulnerable Rohingya Refugees in Bangladesh'. US Department of State, 13 December 13, 2022.

'Rohingya Humanitarian Crisis Joint Response Plan 2022'. UNOCHA, 2022.

Sakib, S. 'Japan, UN sign $3.7M assistance to Rohingya.' Anadolu Agency. November 23, 2022.

Samean, L. 'Bangladesh, Cambodia Strengthening Labour Ties'. *The Phnom Penh Post,* July 1, 2022.

Saptaparna, S. 'Boosting Bangladesh–Vietnam Bilateral Trade: The Way Forward'. *Financial Express,* November 14, 2022.

UN News. 'UN expert urges Japan to 'step up pressure' on Myanmar junta.' UN News. April 28, 2023.

'UNCHR Activities Financed by Voluntary Funds'. UNHCR, 1993.

'US Ambassador Haas Announces $152 Million in New Assistance for Rohingyas,' *Dhaka Tribune,* March 30, 2022.

Part III

INTRODUCTION

Not bogged down by ideological moorings, Dhaka forged partnerships based on a pragmatic assessment of its own needs during its most critical period. Mujibur Rahman as the first prime minister attempted to reach out far and wide, which the subsequent governments emulated despite different political moorings. Interestingly, while Mujib did not hesitate to reach out to hostile powers like China that did not receive its recognition during his term, the turnaround of bilateral ties that Bangladesh and China have had in the post-Mujib phase has been extraordinary.

Sino-Bangladesh bilateral ties, initiated in 1975, soon ranged across a broad scope of economic, trade, commerce, military, education and social ties. Unlike some other South Asian powers, Bangladesh has not faced a debt trap problem vis-à-vis China. Although in recent times, the funding has not poured in as promised by Beijing, the partnership remains strong. Remarkably, Bangladeshi leaders have ensured their deepening relationship with its other larger neighbour, India, did not come in the way of Sino-Bangladesh partnership.

Dhaka's ties with New Delhi saw a breakthrough with a change in guard in Dhaka in 2009 and the scope of the bilateral ties has leapfrogged to unprecedented heights ushering in what is widely referred to as a *shonar adhaya* (golden period). China has been for long supportive of infrastructure development in Bangladesh, and it is only in the post-2010 period that Indo-Bangladeshi ties have witnessed substantial developmental partnerships, including through the building of several cross-border infrastructure enabling border connectivity and robust energy trade. From defence cooperation to medical, education to cultural events, the collaborations have virtually covered every aspect between the two neighbours. While India offered Bangladesh the largest lines of credit it has ever given to any other bilateral partner, Dhaka's forthright support to addressing India's core security concerns and allowing for transit and use of ports and other trade facilities opened up vistas of collaborative endeavours.

While Dhaka has maintained regular periodic ties with China and other major powers, Bangladesh's ties with India and Pakistan shift depending on the government in power in Dhaka. Given the history of the subcontinent, the cause of the East Pakistan–West Pakistan breakup and the festering of many of the outstanding bilateral issues, Bangladesh, specifically the Awami League government, has shown reservations about its ties with Pakistan. At the same time, given the past linkages, there are some sectors that are keen to work closely. With an Awami League government in Dhaka, the Bangladeshi-Pakistani bilateral ties have been nominal, interspersed with some tense moments too.

Bangladesh's ability to establish strong bilateral ties in the region and outside makes for an interesting study of the evolution of its ties not only with its neighbours but also with powers outside the region. While the US was initially dismissive about Bangladesh and its prospects, it slowly warmed up to country. Subsequently, the US has been very forthcoming with aid support and the two countries have worked well together over the past few decades. However, the US's scepticism over some of the Bangladeshi governance issues has led to recent tensions. In 2022, the US sanctioned a few Rapid Action Battalion officers for failing to uphold principles of human rights while dispensing their official duty. It has also publicly advocated for free and fair multiparty elections which has not earned Washington much popularity with Dhaka.

Bangladesh, with its economic growth story, has created a niche for itself as a knowledge-based economy for long-term economic sustainability. Its Vision 2041 is a strategic plan to further improve its socio-economic conditions. Through this and many other contributing factors, Bangladesh exudes an appeal that even those located geographically far away are turning their attention towards Dhaka. The country's presence within the Indo-Pacific is gradually growing and with greater political and economic stability, Bangladesh will be a land of opportunities for many across the globe.

9

BANGLADESH AND INDIA: AN EVOLVING RELATIONSHIP

Deb Mukharji

From the heady, uncertain and blood-soaked days of 1971 when India stood beside Bangladesh in her quest for identity and independence, relations between Bangladesh and India have oscillated between cordial to indifferent to near hostile. The logic of geographical proximity and shared natural resources have not always informed their approach to bilateral relations. Their shared past, or perceptions of the past, have at times been a restraining rather than a cementing element in bilateral relations. Understanding the complexities of this relationship is important if pitfalls are to be avoided. Happily, recent years have shown a steady positive trend in economic relations and some understanding of mutual core concerns, even if some issues continue to remain unaddressed.

Meanwhile, the signal success achieved by Bangladesh in economic growth and social policy indicators has given her an international stature which would give her greater confidence in pursuing her national interests, including in her relationship with India.

Indian Prime Minister Narendra Modi has described the present as a golden chapter in Indo-Bangladesh relations (*The Economic Times* 2018). And so might it be considered, particularly as seen in the context of the recent past, the only yardstick by which we can compare.

The India–Bangladesh Boundary

The ratification by the Indian parliament in 2015 of the 1974 Indira–Mujib Land Boundary Agreement, and the subsequent exchange of enclaves, drew the final curtain on a sorry episode that started with the anomalies of the line drawn by Cyril Radcliffe, the efforts of the Nehru–Noon Agreement of 1958 and the 1974 Land Boundary Agreement (LBA) notwithstanding. It was finally made possible by the painstaking joint surveys which determined the precise areas to be exchanged, without which ratification was not possible. The entire episode remains a sad commentary on the two governments not moving quickly on demarcation, thus consigning to uncertainty, lack of civic amenities or medical facilities, with around 90,000 people residing in enclaves surrounded by a foreign country. While given the offer of retaining their citizenship and moving to their mother country, or staying with their land and acquiring the new citizenship, a large majority chose the latter option. The unanimity in ratification demonstrated in the Indian parliament was a reflection of the esteem in which Bangladesh had come to be regarded.

The maritime boundary between India had remained unsettled despite several rounds of negotiations between the two. It was necessary to find a resolution of the issue, the continental shelf and the exclusive economic zone (EEZ). In 2009, Bangladesh approached the United Nations Convention on the Law of the Sea (UNCLOS) for arbitration with India's concurrence. The award favouring Bangladesh and granting her nearly 80 per cent of the contested area was announced in 2014 and accepted without demur by India. The maturity displayed by both sides reflected a new paradigm in their bilateral relations.

New Paradigm in Bilateral Relations

A new template for bilateral relations had been put in place during Bangladesh Prime Minister Sheikh Hasina's visit to India in January 2010 after her electoral return a year earlier. During this visit, India offered Bangladesh a credit of $1 billion, and there were agreements in diverse fields from fighting terrorism, providing access to Bhutan and Nepal, supply of electricity, etc. Agreements apart, what was of lasting significance was the commitment of the prime ministers

> to put in place a comprehensive framework of cooperation for development between the two countries, encapsulating their mutually shared vision for the future, which would include cooperation in water resources, power, transportation and connectivity, tourism and education. They agreed on the need to operationalise the various areas of cooperation at the earliest. (Ministry of External Affairs 2010)

If a new template had been put in place during this visit, it was reaffirmed and enlarged during Indian Prime Minister Manmohan Singh's visit to Dhaka in September 2011. A vision of cooperation was spelt out that had not been seen since the days of Indira Gandhi and Sheikh Mujib. The importance of cooperation on security issues was underlined and a Framework Agreement on Cooperation for Development envisaged meaningful cooperation in the development of water resources, trade and investment, transport connectivity by land and water, disaster management, scientific and educational exchanges and co-operation, generation and transmission of electricity (including physical connectivity and joint development of projects) and protection of the environment.

Details aside, and even though a conclusion on sharing the Teesta River waters was stymied at the last moment, it would be a fair assessment to conclude that subsequent projects and proposals stood a greater chance of being considered on merits than being subject to considerations of political constraints, as had frequently been the norm. In the years that followed, despite significant political changes in India, the plethora of agreements and MOUs signed during successive prime ministerial visits (PM Narendra Modi to Bangladesh in 2015 and 2021 and PM Sheikh Hasina to India in 2017 and 2019) bear witness to this.

Economic Partnership and Connectivity

Following India's unilateral grant of duty-free access to a wide range of Bangladeshi products in 2012, besides growth in trade, the balance of trade with India has become far less adverse for Bangladesh. As Sreeradha Datta points out, 'Bangladesh enjoys a far greater trade balance with India than with China, a point that is often overlooked' (Datta 2020). To fully optimise the potential of bilateral trade, however, greater facilitation and reduction of transport and handling costs would need to be addressed.

As Pinak Ranjan Chakravarty states,

> Energy cooperation has reached a new high.... Over 3600 MW of power projects are under implementation by Indian companies. FDI (Foreign Direct Investment) from India into Bangladesh has reached US$3.2 billion (as of 2021), with a potential to increase to US$9 billion, as per the statement of the Bangladesh Minister of Industries. Bangladesh-India Development Cooperation is valued at around US$10 billion, consisting of grants and Lines of Credit. (Pant 2021)

Sreeradha Datta's image of the movement of goods through Bangladesh would have appeared a mirage not too long ago when Bangladesh declined to participate in an Asian highway project as it might have been a pretext for the movement of goods from the mainland to the northeast of India across Bangladesh.

Sreeradha Datta further notes that despite the domestic preoccupation with the pandemic, the transhipment of cargo through a multimodal system, including railways, surface and waterways, as well as coastal shipping between India and Bangladesh, has gained momentum during that phase and progress has been evident in all the sectors, including the signing of a memorandum of understanding on inland water transport that would complement the existing bilateral inland waterway agreement and, in the process, increase the proposed inland river ports to five locations (Datta 2020). This agreement (20 May 2020), allowed India to access its northeastern state of Tripura and the proposed inland water protocol route from the lower segment on the Gomati river between Sonamura (Tripura, India) and Daudkandi (Comilla, Bangladesh) was going to increase the interdependence between India's northeast and Bangladesh as well provide greater access to mainland India. 'This proposed inland water route between the Ashuganj river port in eastern Bangladesh and Sonamura in Sipahijala district of Tripura through Gomati and Meghna rivers will facilitate cargo movement between Tripura and Bangladesh through a short distance of 60 kilometres, skirting the long route via Siliguri' (Datta 2020).

This may also be applied to the Coastal Shipment Agreement and cross-border container-train movement. Significant movement has taken place in developing communications between both countries, and its importance should be seen in the background of earlier reluctance of Dhaka to engage in this field in any manner whatsoever. While India may not have unrestricted connectivity to its northeastern states, some ground has been covered. What is also important is that the focus has widened from connectivity between two parts of India to connectivity as well for mutual benefit and enhancement of commercial possibilities. There has been a long-standing MoU between the two countries for the use of Bangladeshi ports for movement of goods to India, confirmed by a cabinet decision in Bangladesh in 2018. During the April 2022 visit of the Indian External Affairs Minister S. Jaishankar to Dhaka, Bangladesh Prime Minister Sheikh Hasina reiterated the offer of the use of Chittagong port for transporting goods to Northeast India. The implementation of this offer by both sides could bring about significant advantages to the northeastern states.[1]

Factors Binding Indo-Bangladesh Relations

As we see the graph of positive developments in Indo-Bangladesh relations over the past few years and hope for this trend to continue, it would be useful to take a look back and try to analyse elements of the relationship so that the past may not again cloud the future.

Track II dialogues are most productive when relations between states are sluggish or in hibernation. This was the state of Indo-Bangladesh relations in the period 2005–2007, when a track II dialogue took place with several sessions in either country with the participation of eminent citizens from all walks of life. The conclusions of this dialogue, both as general principles and specific suggestions, remain valid today. The first conclusion stated, 'Lack of political will and direction has stood in the way of closer collaboration between India and Bangladesh. Necessary to have frequent interaction at the political level. Cooperation provides win-win situation for both' (Mukharji 2011). This truism underlies Indo-Bangladesh relations from the earliest days.

It is often assumed in Bangladesh, and at times reflected in India, that the relations between them are not so much governed by the yardstick of national interests but by the party in power. The Bangladesh Nationalist Party (BNP) rarely lets by any opportunity to accuse the Awami League (AL) of subordinating the nation's interests to that of India's. India has consistently demonstrated a national consensus of positivity towards Bangladesh over the past three decades and across governments, whether it is the Indian National Congress or the Bharatiya Janata Party (BJP), and under leaderships of different hues. Admittedly, however, India may have a greater comfort level in dealing with an AL government in Dhaka, though her stamina in pursuing issues could merit improvement.

Rehman Sobhan had been a close associate of Sheikh Mujib and one of the co-authors of the famous Six Points of the AL, which had led inexorably to the 1971 war. After liberation, Sobhan was assigned high posts for the economic regeneration of a shattered economy. In the recently published second volume of his *Untranquil Recollections* dealing with this period, he notes,

> in the immediate aftermath of liberation, it was believed within the leadership of both India and Bangladesh that mutual self-interest originating in our shared struggle for national liberation would serve as the driving force of our relationship. This turned out to be a rather shortsighted perception of the shape of things to come. (Sobhan 2021)

As Sobhan further explains that the 'close intimacy during the course of the liberation war could not obliterate attitudes and perceptions inherited over three decades of relations or lack of them with India during the era of Pakistani rule when adversarial attitudes to India constituted one of the cornerstones of national politics.' (Sobhan 2021). For years the fears of Indian domination had been ceaselessly embedded in all Pakistanis including the Bengalis. The armed forces were particularly susceptible to this propaganda ... those who challenged this were described as 'mediocre minions of a foreign power' (Sobhan 2021, 233).

More notably, he says, 'if one examines the public statements of the regime after 1971, it is significant that apart from the PM's ritual commitment to Indo-Bangladesh friendship, there is no evidence of any move at any level to actually confront the propaganda which had polluted the political climate' (Sobhan 2021, 236). Clearly, even Sheikh Mujib at the height of his authority was unable to move beyond 'ritual' commitments to Indo-Bangladesh relations. His inability to confront the vicious propaganda, supported even by some members of his own party, had tragic consequences. As Sobhan continues,

> For this reinterpretation of history to be accepted, an image of Bangladesh had to be created of Bangladesh being a satellite of India ... the AL as a comprador regime whose every thought, word and deed was at the behest of India.... India was depicted as plundering Bangladesh ... inflation, production shortfalls, famine and economic dislocation were, thus directly attributable to the insatiable appetite for plunder by India. (Sobhan 2021, 237)

Sobhan's comments explain why adequate political will to promote closer economic relations between India and Bangladesh has so often been absent.

What may have been covert or subliminal in the Mujib years blossomed freely after his assassination under the patronage of subsequent military and quasi-military governments, as I saw both from my assignment at the time in the Indian High Commission in Dhaka and subsequently the Bangladesh desk in the Indian Ministry of External Affairs. Later, the elected BNP government fell into the same ideological mould.

Many years later, late Justice Muhammad Habibur Rahman, the former chief justice and head of the caretaker government that oversaw the fraught 1996 elections—also a noted scholar on Tagore—noted my concern as the relations were not moving forward. In 1971, even during the Pakistan army crackdown, he said the people of East Pakistan could probably be divided in three equal categories. A third which wanted an independent Bangladesh, a third which had remained largely cowed and indifferent and a third which continued to believe in a united Pakistan. And, he may have added, each has continued to influence governments.

These observations from two eminent persons may not be welcome to many in India and perhaps also Bangladesh. But they do need to be appreciated in order to ensure an objective understanding of Indo-Bangladesh relations. It would be a mistake to assume that with the passage of years, yesterday's concerns and convictions no longer exist.

There is a running theme of self-satisfaction in India that the emergence of Bangladesh had buried the two-nation theory. It was nothing of the sort. In fact, but for the role of the Bengali Muslim, there may not have been a Pakistan at all, and their struggle in the years that followed was for their economic and linguistic rights within the framework of Pakistan. Any other interpretation is self-serving and an affront to the history of Bangladesh.

What these observations do underscore for us is that a certain degree of anti-Indianism lies in the substratum of the consciousness of many Bangladeshis that can be excited by interested parties, internal or external. The leader of the BNP, Begum Khaleda Zia, had told me, then the Indian high commissioner, in the months following the Ganga Waters Agreement, that India would make a mistake if it believed that Indo-Bangladesh relations would improve under an AL government. Any movement for such improvement could be stymied by public agitation by her party, which alone was seen as the upholder of the national interests of Bangladesh. It is to the great credit of Prime Minister Sheikh Hasina that she has decided in the past years to overcome these concerns for what she believes is the greater good of the country. With the passage of time and visible benefits of bilateral cooperation, one may hope that the mental barriers of the past may become increasingly irrelevant. But for this to happen, sensitivity and care would have to be exercised with regard to mutual core concerns and sensitivities. These may be summarised as follows:

From the Indian perspective, security has always had the highest priority. Right from the 1960s, Pakistan and China have taken an interest in insurgent movements in India's Northeast and provided sanctuary and material support to such outfits. Following the emergence of Bangladesh and some stabilisation in Sino-Indian relations, as also the resolution of some of the internal issues, there was a period of relative calm, during the 1970s. From the 1980s, however, first with quasi-military governments and then an amenable BNP in power, Pakistan's Inter-Services Intelligence (ISI) had a free hand assisting disaffected insurgent elements. With the active involvement of Bangladesh security agencies, space was provided for sanctuary and training. Meanwhile, Dhaka charged Delhi with encouraging the Shanti Bahini, a group of Chakmas who were compelled to flee Bangladesh and living in camps in Tripura.

Sanctuary and assistance to Indian insurgent groups ceased with the coming to power of the AL in 1996, though the intelligence agencies would have continued to have elements engaged in support to Indian insurgents, facilitating a complete reversal with the advent of the BNP in 2001. Even though prior to the 2001 elections, BNP had assured India of desisting from such activities, an accidental arms haul off Chittagong in April 2004 blew the lid off the ongoing collusion between the United Liberation Front of Assam (ULFA) and the Bangladesh government at the highest levels. Despite initial efforts of the BNP government to suppress and sidetrack the case, it was pursued subsequently by the caretaker government and, later, the AL government. Among others, the then state minister for home affairs, and the directors general of the armed forces intelligence and the national security intelligence were found guilty by the courts and sentenced to death, and await the final outcome in prison.

Such blatant involvement of senior government functionaries, including ministers, in gun running to assist insurgent groups in a neighbouring country with which good neighbourly relations ostensibly prevailed was odd enough, but the government turning a blind eye to the growth of jihadists in the country was inexcusable, even from a purely Bangladesh point of view. This was the time when the BNP was in a coalition government with the Jamaat-e-Islami. Jihadi groups were spawned in Jamaat stables and concerned commentators wondered if Bangladesh was headed the Afghanistan way. Over the years, there have been a spate of bomb attacks on cultural functions and prominent individuals. A corollary to the collaboration between the government and jihadi elements was the grenade and sniper attack on an AL rally in August 2004 that targeted Sheikh Hasina. Though she narrowly escaped, the concerted attack left 24 dead and over 300 injured. The state minister of home affairs later acquired a second death sentence for his involvement in the attempted assassination.

Since her election in 2008, and subsequent re-elections, Sheikh Hasina has been successful in containing jihadi elements, though there have been instances like the July 2016 carnage at the Holey Artisan Bakery. India is fully supportive of these efforts at curbing jihadi terrorism. The firmness with which sanctuary or support to Indian insurgent groups has been terminated has also created a degree of mutual confidence where information and intelligence can be shared.

India's Security Interests/Concerns

India's security concern vis-à-vis Bangladesh is twofold. There is the traditional concern with regard to cross-border assistance to disaffected groups in the Northeast. But in the longer term, there would be the far greater concern about a radicalised and hostile Bangladesh embedded in a sensitive part of India. The efforts of the Bangladesh government to strive towards a liberal, inclusive society should be a matter of profound interest to India.

Ever since the emergence of Bangladesh, the issue of sharing of river waters has been high on the agenda of Bangladesh's security concerns. For many years, the unresolved issue of the sharing of Ganga waters at Farakka subsumed movement on any other bilateral issue. With respect to this issue, Dhaka charged Delhi with the desertification of Bangladesh. Farakka goes back a long way, when the colonial government had decided that future navigability of the Calcutta port would depend on flushing the Hooghly River with water diverted from the main branch of the Ganga at Farakka in the Murshidabad district of Bengal. Thus, when India was partitioned, Muslim-majority Murshidabad was awarded to India in lieu of the Hindu-majority district of Khulna. As India proceeded with plans for the construction of the barrage, Pakistan objected, citing possible adverse effects downstream in the Padma, as the Ganges is called in erstwhile East Pakistan (Bangladesh). Importantly, several rounds of discussions between the ministries of water resources and external affairs of the two countries produced no results.

Following the independence of Bangladesh, discussions continued. The barrage was commissioned in 1975; in 1976, Bangladesh took the issue to the UN, which asked the two countries to arrive at a fair solution. In November 1977, the two countries signed an interim sharing arrangement for five years. This was subsequently renewed for short periods until 1989. The story of the flows at Farakka reflected the nature of the relations between the two countries.

The no-agreement regime after 1989 was unacceptable to Bangladesh and all possible and less possible ills were attributed to Farakka. It was, as I later discovered, a curious situation where there were vested interests, even within governments, that did not want a resolution and wanted Farakka to continue as an albatross, an insoluble problem, to become, so to say, the Kashmir of Indo-Bangladesh relations and ever ready fodder to agitate people against India.

The BNP government at the time would have wanted an agreement on its own terms to win plaudits at home while India also wanted an agreement, realising the damage being caused to its image in the public eye (the issue of Ganga waters had indeed permeated people's consciousness at all levels. I recall driving in the Kushtia area when a farmer, noticing my flag, asked me plaintively to restore normal flows of the Ganga). This was my understanding when I arrived in Dhaka in end March 1995 to take charge as high commissioner of India to Bangladesh. Within days, I was discussing with the Bangladesh foreign office the contours of a new agreement for a longer term. At the time, the idea was that this could be a quid pro quo for transit facilities to India's Northeast, as had been suggested in an earlier non-paper from Bangladesh. I was shortly summoned by Foreign Minister Abu Saleh Mohammad Mustafizur Rahman who told me that while his government appreciated my enthusiasm to find a solution to Farakka, the fact was that general elections were due in a year and whatever might be decided would have political repercussions, which were best avoided at the moment. He promised that when his party returned to power the following year, a resolution of Farakka would be high on its agenda.

Both governments dealt with Farakka in all seriousness after a change of government in both countries, with the AL and the coalition with Deve Gowda as prime minister coming to power in Dhaka and Delhi respectively in June 1996. Besides discussions between the foreign offices and exchange of ministerial visits, Chief Minister Jyoti Basu of West Bengal was kept informed and consulted. Views of Track II members who had earlier addressed the issue were obtained. Basu visited Dhaka in November and the discussions between ministers Buddhadeb Bhattacharya and Ashim Dasgupta with the Bangladesh team led by the principal secretary to the prime minister laid the groundwork for the Farakka agreement, which was concluded when Prime Minister Hasina visited Delhi the following month. There was a consensus in Delhi that the issue should be negotiated on merits without reference to any transit facilities.

The 30-year Farakka Agreement was important in itself for laying to rest a long-standing and bitter controversy and opening up the possibilities of future bilateral engagement and cooperation. Given the extreme emotions aroused over the water of the Ganga in Bangladesh and the opposition to an agreement with India from some quarters, signing the agreement was an act of singular political courage on the part of Prime Minister Sheikh Hasina.

Presently in limbo is an agreement on the sharing of Teesta waters. A sharing formula arrived at by the central government and agreed to by Bangladesh was stymied at the last moment by objections from West Bengal. It is agreed by all parties that that there is a shortage of water in the lean season. West Bengal's refusal to share the shortage should be unacceptable. It needs to be recalled that a Kaurava-like attitude eventually resulted in a far larger share of the Ganga waters to Bangladesh than had been sought by Pakistan in the 1960s.

There are 54 rivers of various sizes that flow from India to Bangladesh, several with origins in, or major contributions from, Nepal, Tibet and Bhutan over whose management of water resources neither Bangladesh nor India have any control. As a middle riparian, India shares some of the concerns of Bangladesh as a lower riparian. In the absence of any binding international agreement on the sharing of common rivers, it is necessary for India to share all data and the waters available in a spirit of justice and fair play. Unfortunately, since its early days, Indo-Bangladesh discussions have always centred on the sharing of the waters of individual rivers; a dialogue on the development of water resources with mutual benefit has been absent. The Joint Rivers Commission (JRC) emerged from a decision of the Indo-Bangladesh Treaty of Peace and Friendship of 1972 which stated, inter alia, 'The high Contracting Parties further agree to make joint studies and take action in the fields of flood control, river basin development and the development of hydro-electric power and irrigation' (Ministry of External Affairs 1972). Unfortunately, these expectations were never addressed. The JRC could not fulfil its potential and remained confined to endless discussions on the sharing of river waters where neither side was able to see any merit in the views of the other. The absence of dialogue was reflected in the construction of barrages on the Teesta River within miles of each other. In the long run, the answer to these issues will lie in regional collaboration where all rivers are seen as common property and their use and development a common responsibility. However, with present Chinese attitudes, this appears a distant possibility. Meanwhile, given the sensitivities and genuine requirements of Bangladesh as a nation dependent on rivers in multiple ways, India has to tread cautiously. A declaration about linking the Himalayan rivers to those of South India with no prior discussion with Bangladesh could only be calculated to arouse severe concerns. Free sharing of data on river flows and planning can also create mutual confidence.

One takeaway from the 1996 agreement on sharing the Ganga waters is that while experts have to be relied upon for data and technical advice, these should be evaluated critically and independently by the foreign ministry and submitted for political direction. Experts run the risk of trying to prove their professional prowess with an inability to acknowledge alternative points of view, invariably failing to give due weightage to the needs of the other party. Serious and sustained political engagement and direction are required from all countries concerned.

Migration and Conflict

Alleged illegal migration from Bangladesh has been at times a major point of contention between the two countries. Prior to 1971, there had been spurts of Hindu migration following communal riots, notably in the early 1950s and 1960s. The Nehru–Liaquat Pact of April 1950 to prevent an exchange of population as in the west of the subcontinent had only partially succeeded. The percentage of Hindus in erstwhile East Pakistan (Bangladesh) dropped from 27 per cent at Partition to about 13 per cent in 1971. At present, it is around 9 per cent. Hindu migration has been for both economic reasons as also reasons of security. In terms of actual migration, the major factor may have been the enemy/vested property act lingering from the 1965 Indo-Pak War. This was finally struck down in 2010 and its results could be reflected in the next census. Muslim migration into India was for economic reasons, and, at times, seasonal. Strictly speaking, the welfare of Hindus in Bangladesh should not be India's concern. But ground realities of kinship and public sentiment cannot be ignored. While India was willing to turn a blind eye to Hindu migration, treating it as a consequence of Partition, it was not willing to accept Muslim migration, more so as it was feared to alter the demographic balance in Assam and West Bengal, particularly in border districts. Among the complicating factors was that there had been substantial Bengali Muslim migration from Mymensingh to the Brahmaputra valley in the 1930s with active government encouragement to cultivate land lying fallow. In Bihar, there were instances of reverse migration of Muslims who had fled as refugees to East Pakistan.

This issue had been flagged to the Bangladesh government at regular intervals from the mid-1970s. Dhaka's consistent response was a denial of such migration. It was also very well known that major political parties in Assam and West Bengal had provided identity documents to many illegal migrants in order to enlarge their vote bank. Owners of orchards in Meghalaya, which is otherwise rigid about outsiders, found Bangladeshi labour a less expensive option.

The porous border also did not hinder illegal movement of people. The expression by some political elements in Bangladesh looking on northeastern India as their *lebensraum* was not calculated to create confidence in India. Meanwhile, in 2005, the Indian Supreme Court considered illegal migration from Bangladesh to be an act of aggression.

In fulfilment of the 1985 Assam Accord and the directives of the Supreme Court, an exercise to determine the citizenship of residents was carried out in Assam. The exercise caused great hardship and was kept in abeyance presumably after it was found not to support the theory of large numbers of illegal Muslim migrants on which the exercise was largely predicated. Since the illegal migrants also included Hindus, the government of India passed the Citizenship Amendment Act (CAA) 2019, by which Hindus were to be accorded fast-track citizenship. The constitutional validity of the act has been challenged in the Indian Supreme Court.

Through this entire process, two separate issues have come together, which could complicate and impact Indo-Bangladesh relations negatively in the time to come. The issue of illegal migrants from Bangladesh is not new. But the emphasis placed on it, the large numbers mentioned and an undertaking to eliminate these 'termites' is, of course, offensive both to the government and the people in Bangladesh. The CAA could be considered a decision internal to India. But since it implies relief to Hindus deemed to have suffered persecution in Bangladesh, it also becomes a reflection on that country. At a time when, for 10 years the government of Bangladesh has taken demonstrable steps to provide security to minorities, the CAA, implying their insecurity, has been found unacceptable by Bangladesh even if their public reaction has been restrained. Most importantly, by accepting Hindus in Bangladesh as a specially favoured category for immigration, their loyalty to their motherland is being brought into question. The consequences of this do not seem to have been thought through.

Surprisingly and unfortunately, despite the goodwill at the government level, there have been many occasions when derogatory comments have been made about Bangladesh and its citizens by senior members of the Indian government in the recent past. This, together with reports of persecution of Muslims in India, has affected public opinion in Bangladesh. As the Bangladesh foreign minister said recently, in a democracy public opinion cannot be ignored. One unfortunate fallout was several people being killed in demonstrations against the recent visit to Bangladesh by Prime Minister Narendra Modi as chief guest on the occasion of the golden jubilee of the independence of Bangladesh.

There are many instances round the world where a change in government impacts a nation's foreign policy, even though national interests remain constant. But in the case of Bangladesh, changes in government have brought into question the very essence of the nation. As Riaz and Parvez succinctly put it,

> The context of religion was implicated with the national identity of Bangladesh's citizens in such a manner, as if there is a conflict between the anthropological Bengali identity and adherence to the Islamic faith. Yet the multidimensional identity of Bengalis is evident down the ages of history. (Riaz and Parvez 2021)

Many other contradictions arose from the effort to mould Bangladesh in the image of the 1940 Lahore Resolution after Mujib's assassination, while perforce extolling the war of liberation. One direct victim of these contradictions has been relations with India, as reflected in Rehman Sobhan's comments on the early days.

The two extremes of Bangladesh polity came face to face in the spring of 2013 at Shahbag and Shapla Chottor in Dhaka. The former comprised large numbers of apolitical students demanding accountability for those guilty of war crimes in 1971 and by implication, endorsing the liberal and secular values at the founding of the nation. The latter demanded punishment for 'atheist bloggers', their term for the students, under the banner of the Islamist Hefajet-e-Islam. Subsequent disturbances cost many lives. Shahbag was followed by a spate of killings of liberal intellectuals, publishers and members of minority communities, culminating in the horrific carnage in the Holey Artisan Bakery in 2016. There are reports of Islamic State association with jihadis in Bangladesh (Crisis Group 2018). The government's response appears to have been effective so far.

The preceding paragraphs would show why there has been an absence of political will, as mentioned earlier in the chapter, in taking Indo-Bangladesh relations forward. The relationship is directly affected by the latter's still-evolving socio-political dynamics. Fortunately, there is congruence today between Indian interests and views with regard to territorial security as well as growth of radical Islam in Bangladesh and the views of the Bangladesh government. But the views of the only alternative ruling party in Bangladesh, which has been elected twice to governance, the BNP, remains unclear. There are reports of internal churning within the party, trying to move it away from the Jamaat and its rigid Islamist views towards at least a neutral view on the country's relations with India.

Conclusion

While the future parameters of Bangladesh society and polity would continue to evolve, presently there is a 'golden chapter' in Indo-Bangladesh relations. This would need to be nurtured and hopefully will help create an effective economic and cultural lobby in favour of stronger relations with India. On India's part, negativity, be it with regard to river waters, or careless statements made in the context of our internal politics, but its fallout in Bangladesh needs to be carefully monitored and cannot be ignored. The rise of the political right in India with an anti-Muslim bias would have its own impact and is inevitably an encouragement to its counterparts in Bangladesh. But these internal developments cannot be tailored, and Bangladesh would have to meet the challenge as best as it can. While adopting an uncompromising attitude towards jihadi elements, the Bangladesh government has sought accommodation with moderate Islamic parties, drawing criticism from secular liberal elements. Sheikh Hasina's adoption of the Prophet of Islam's Medina charter in 2014 is an interesting development, affording as it then did protection to minorities. The imperatives of political accommodation cast its shadow when the Awami League found it expedient to enter into an arrangement with the Bangladesh Khelafat Majlish in December 2006, prior to the aborted general elections of the following year. This had included acceptance of the right of clerics to issue fatwas and a veiled rejection of Ahmediyas as Muslims. One must hope that such compromises would not surface again as the 2024 elections approach. As history has repeatedly shown, concessions on religious issues become almost impossible to subsequently rectify. A positive trend in Bangladesh that requires note, even if its impact on relations with India can only be indirect, is that despite many years of contrary state indoctrination, the youth of Bangladesh, far removed from 1971, still value the sacrifices and cherish the values that underpinned the war of liberation.

Note

1   Northeast India is connected to the mainland only through a 11 km-corridor. The route is very circuitous, making the cargo more expensive given the longer time taken to travel. The cargo from other parts of India would reach Northeast India in lesser time through Bangladesh.

References

'Countering Jihadist Militancy in Bangladesh International Crisis Group'. Crisis Group, February 38, 2018. https://www.crisisgroup.org/asia/south-asia/bangladesh/295-countering-jihadist-militancy-bangladesh, downloaded on March 2, 2018.

Datta, S. 'Bangladesh the Much-Coveted Neighbour'. ISAS Insights, August 5, 2020. https://www.isas.nus.edu.sg/papers/bangladesh-the-much-coveted-neighbour/.

'Golden Chapter in Indo-Bangladeshi ties: Narendra Modi'. *The Economic Times*, May 26, 2018. https://economictimes.indiatimes.com/news/politics-and-nation/golden-chapter-in-indo-bangladesh-ties-narendra-modi/articleshow/64327017.cms.

'Joint Communiqué Issued on the Occasion of the Visit to India of Her Excellency Sheikh Hasina, Prime Minister of Bangladesh'. Ministry of External Affairs, January 12, 2010. https://mea.gov.in/bilateral-documents.htm?dtl/3452/Joint+Communiqu+issued+on+the+occasion+of+the+visit+to+India+of+Her+Excellency+Sheikh+Hasina+Prime+-Minister+of+Bangladeshm.

Mukharji, D. 'India and Bangladesh: A New Phase in Bilateral Relations'. *Indian Foreign Affairs Journal*, 6, no. 4, October–December 2011.

Pant, H. 'Bangladesh: A Golden Chapter in Bilateral Ties'. In *Politics and Geopolitics—Decoding India's Neighbourhood Challenge*, edited by Harsh Pant, 101–105. New Delhi: Rupa Publications, 2021.

Riaz, A. and S. Parvez. 'A Return of Religion to Politics'. *Prothom Alo*, March 20, 2021. https://en.prothomalo.com/opinion/op-ed/a-return-of-religion-to-politics.

Sobhan, R. *Untranquil Recollections: Nation Building in Post-Liberation Bangladesh*, 233. Delhi: Sage Publications, 2021.

'Treaty of Peace and Friendship'. Ministry of External Affairs, March 19, 1972. https://www.mea.gov.in/bilateral-documents.htm?dtl/5621/Treaty+of+Peace+and+Friendship.

10

CHINA-BANGLADESH RELATIONS: REVIEW AND PROSPECTS

Li Jianjun

Introduction

This chapter briefly reviews the history of China-Bangladesh relations from 1971 to 1991, and discusses the current situation of the bilateral relations from the political, economic and trade, security and people-to-people contact perspectives. It makes an analysis of China's Bangladesh policy covering six aspects: politics, economy, security, culture, international cooperation and proper management of China-India-Bangladesh relations. It also offers a discussion on the future prospects of the bilateral relationship between China and Bangladesh.

China-Bangladesh Relations:
A Brief Historical Review (1971–1991)

The contemporary exchanges between China and Bangladesh can be traced back to the 1950s. The founding father of Bangladesh, Sheikh Mujibur Rahman, paid two important visits to China in 1953 and 1957, as a minister. When Chinese Premier Zhou Enlai visited Dhaka in 1956, he was warmly greeted with a bouquet of flowers presented to him by Rahman and his daughter, none other than Sheikh Hasina, the current prime minister of Bangladesh. As Chinese President Xi Jinping conveyed to Bangladesh leaders, 'this is a much-told tale of the friendship between China and Bangladesh passed down from generation to generation' (Chenzhi 2016).

The quadrilateral relationship between China, Pakistan, Bangladesh and India has been the main factor affecting the engagement between China and Bangladesh. In the four years since Bangladesh declared its independence in March 1971, China did not establish diplomatic relations and refused its attempt to join the UN. The Chinese government had its own considerations. First, China and Pakistan always maintained traditional friendly relations and advocated the maintenance of Pakistan's unity; Second, China's relationship with India and the Soviet Union broke down given that Bangladesh's independence was supported by the latter two nations (Luo 2016).

Beginning in 1974, as Bangladesh and Pakistan began to reconcile, Sino-Bangladesh relations began to thaw. In February of that year, Pakistan recognised Bangladesh, Bangladesh, Pakistan and India signed a tripartite agreement on the repatriation of prisoners of war and civilian internees, at New Delhi on 9 April 1974. Pakistani Prime Minister Zulfikar Ali Bhutto visited Bangladesh two months later, on 27 June. The bilateral relations between the two countries started to improve and progress.

The obstacles to the establishment of diplomatic relations between China and Bangladesh no longer exist as it buried the hatchet with Pakistan. China immediately voted for Bangladesh's bid to join the UN. In July, Bangladeshi Commerce Minister Khandakar Mushtaq Ahmed visited China.

The year 1975 was an important turning point in Sino-Bangladesh relations. Bangladesh took part in the Canton Trade Fair in China and signed four trade agreements. In August, China provided relief worth RMB4 million for the flood-affected people in Bangladesh. On 15 August, the Awami League (AL) government was overthrown and Sheikh Mujibur Rahman was killed. Ziaur Rahman, after consolidating military and political power, declared the pursuit an independent and non-aligned foreign policy emphasising friendship with all countries, especially with Islamic countries in particular. On 3 October, Pakistan established diplomatic relations with Bangladesh. On 4 October, China and Bangladesh formally signed the communiqué on the establishment of diplomatic relations. The decision to establish diplomatic relations between the two countries was a win for both nations. Bangladesh used the strategic relationship between China and Pakistan to ease relations with Pakistan, strengthen its presence as a new country and its influence in the third world. For China, the establishment of diplomatic relations with Bangladesh has expanded its all- round diplomacy in South Asia.

Since the establishment of diplomatic relations to the end of the Cold War, Bangladesh was in a period of seeking new and reliable partners. Sino-Bangladesh relations have experienced the reigns of Ziaur Rahman and Hussain Muhammad Ershad. The acting leaders had promoted a continuous policy towards China, which laid a solid foundation for friendly relations between the two countries.

Ziaur Rahman's administration opened the door to the normalisation of relations between the two countries. On 9 September 1976, when Chairman Mao Zedong passed away, the Bangladeshi government ordered the cessation of all festive activities, and the main buildings flag at half-mast. The Bangladeshi army included a portrait of Chairman Mao in the album *Bangladesh Army Marching* published in November that year and wrote in the editor's note that 'the Bangladeshi army and people will always remember Chairman Mao's outstanding contributions' (Xinhua News Agency 1977). In January 1977, Ziaur Rahman visited China, the first time that the highest leader of Bangladesh had visited China. The two countries signed the first intergovernmental cooperation agreement—the Economic and Technical Cooperation Trade and Payment Agreement between the Government of the People's Republic of China and the Government of the People's Republic of Bangladesh. In March 1978, Vice Premier Li Xiannian visited Bangladesh. This, in turn, was the first visit to Bangladesh by a high-level Chinese leader since the establishment of diplomatic relations between the two countries in 1975. In November 1979, the two countries signed the China–Bangladesh Government Cooperation Agreement, which further strengthened the cooperation between the two governments and furthered the development of bilateral relations. In July 1980, Ziaur Rahman and his wife visited China and notably, during this visit, Khaleda Zia appeared for the first time in the vision of China's diplomacy.

Ershad's government continued and deepened Ziaur Rahman's China policy, and the political mutual trust between the two countries increased. Ershad visited China six times, during which time the Chinese leader Deng Xiaoping met him in November 1982 and July 1987. Deng Xiaoping reiterated the friendly ties between China and Bangladesh. They can exchange hearts with each other and share the same views on a series of major issues (Cang 1987). In mid-November 1989, Premier Li Peng visited Bangladesh. This happened to be the first visit by a high-level Chinese leader after China experienced political turbulence earlier that year and was sanctioned by Western countries. The Ershad's government gave the warmest welcome in Bangladesh's history for Premier Li Peng's visit, and gave China firm diplomatic support, which strengthened the mutual political trust between the two countries.

Contemporary China Bangladesh Relations (1991–present)

Political Relations between China and Bangladesh: Strategic Partners

Since 1991, Sino-Bangladesh relations have gone through two Khaleda Zia administrations, a caretaker government and four Sheikh Hasina administrations. Politically, the mutual trust between the two countries has been constantly sublimated, as China today regards Bangladesh as an 'all-weather friend'.[1]

Prime Minister Zia's visit to China in December 2002 was a significant landmark in bilateral relations, with the signing of three treaties and an MoU covering military, economic and technological cooperation. Furthermore, to commemorate the 30th anniversary of Sino-Bangladesh diplomatic relations, 2005 was declared as 'China Bangladesh Friendship Year'. During Chinese Premier Wen Jiabao's visit to Bangladesh in April 2005, a 13-point joint communiqué on further strengthening of bilateral relations along with five agreements and two MoUs were signed. The two countries announced the establishment of a 'long-term friendly, equal and mutually beneficial comprehensive cooperative partnership' (Cang 1987).

In March 2010, when Hasina visited China, the two sides signed four major documents: (*i*) an Agreement on Economic and Technical Cooperation; (*ii*) Framework Agreement on Providing Preferential Loan; (*iii*) the Protocol on Remitting the Bangladesh Interest-Free Loan due in 2008 and (*iv*) the Exchange of Letters on the Construction of the Seventh Bangladesh-China Friendship Bridge. The two countries also announced the establishment and development of a closer comprehensive cooperative partnership.

In June 2014, during Hasina's visit to China, the two countries publicised a joint statement on deepening the closer comprehensive cooperative partnership. In October 2016, President Xi Jinping's visit to Bangladesh ushered in a new chapter for the friendly relations between China and Bangladesh, which had important historical significance for the development of bilateral relations. During this visit, the joint statement on the establishment of a strategic partnership was issued (*Xinhua Net* 2016). So far, the relationship between China and Bangladesh has scaled up and upgraded to a strategic level.

There are three connotations in Sino-Bangladesh strategic partnership: firstly, the two countries are partners, not rivals; secondly, the core of bilateral relations is political mutual trust, which has broad common interests and common positions; and thirdly, the partnership is a strategic significance-based effort covering cooperation on politics, economy, military, security, culture and other fields.

There are several reasons why China and Bangladesh have formed a strategic cooperative partnership. First, there is a convergence of national interest and development planning. This is reflected in the Golden Bengal Dream and the 2030 Long-Term Development Goals, which are consistent with the Chinese Dream and the Two Centennial Goals. This can be translated into the willingness and action of the two countries to connect each other's development strategies in the process of pursuing their respective development paths. Second, the two countries actively practice the five principles of peaceful coexistence in foreign exchanges, respect and support each other's development path and domestic and foreign policies. Since 2015, China has always prioritised its neighbouring countries in its diplomatic initiatives and paid more attention to the integrity and balance of its policy towards South Asia, thus enhancing its partnership with Bangladesh. In 2002, the BNP-led four-party coalition government in Bangladesh adopted a 'Look East' policy to maximise economic and strategic gains that could emerge from closer relations with eastern countries, especially China (Aneja 2006). Third, China attaches great importance to the importance of Bangladesh's geo-strategic position. The latter is an important country for China's land access to the Indian Ocean. Hence, it is very important for China to stabilise its surrounding areas, maintain the security of southwest frontiers, and protect the supply of strategic resources.

The strategic cooperative partnership between China and Bangladesh was gradually formed in the diplomatic practice of the two countries. On 12 May 2008, after the Wenchuan earthquake in the Sichuan Province of China, the Bangladesh government declared 21 May 2008 as a national day of mourning and sent special planes to deliver relief materials to the disaster-hit areas (Hossain 2010). The Yarlung Zangbo River is the only geographical link between China and Bangladesh. On 16 September 2008, an MoU was signed between the Ministry of Water Resources of China and the Ministry of Water Resources of Bangladesh, upon the provision of hydrological information of the Yarlung Zangbo/Brahmaputra River in the flood season by China to Bangladesh in the Great Hall of the People in Beijing.

According to the memorandum, in the flood season, China would provide hydrological information from three hydrological stations along the main stream of the Yarlung Zangbo River to Bangladesh. This will further enhance the bilateral cooperation in the water sector between the two countries and help Bangladesh to strengthen flood control and disaster relief in the Brahmaputra River Basin (Ministry of Water Resources China 2008).

Bangladesh is one of the first countries in South Asia to support the Belt and Road Initiative (BRI), and it is also an active supporter and participant in the construction of the Bangladesh–China–India–Myanmar Economic Corridor (BCIM). In October 2016, the two countries signed an MoU on cooperation under the BRI. The document is of iconic significance—its signing will not only promote mutually beneficial cooperation between China and Bangladesh under the BRI framework but will also play a positive role in promoting the construction of the BCIM (The State Council Information Office of

China 2016). Under the BRI, the two countries have made significant progress in infrastructure sector cooperation. The construction of important transportation pivot projects such as the Padma Bridge in Bangladesh has greatly improved the level of connectivity in the country. During President Jinping's visit in 2016, China promised to give $24 billion in economic assistance to Bangladesh, primarily as lines of credit for 24 projects (Bhattacharjee 2018).

As of 2020, among the South Asian partners of the BRI, Chinese investment in Bangladesh is second only to Pakistan. In June 2020, when China and India faced fierce physical clashes in the strategically sensitive Galwan Valley, Bangladesh adopted a neutral stance and called for a peaceful settlement of contentious issues (Bastola 2021).

China–Bangladesh Security Relations: Pragmatic Low-Level Cooperation

China–Bangladesh security relations are largely reflected by defence and regional security cooperation. Defence cooperation is one of the important pillars of bilateral relations. In December 2002, Zia visited China and signed a Defence Cooperation Agreement with Beijing (Chowdhury 2010). It was the first such agreement signed by Bangladesh with a foreign country, and it helped to institutionalise and codify the existing accords in the defence sector. It further provided a comprehensive framework for cooperation in personnel training, equipment maintenance and some areas of production (Aneja 2006). The agreement not only emphasises the need to further deepen the existing close relations between the two countries but also enhances Bangladesh's defence capabilities through a bilateral defence cooperation mechanism (Luo 2016).

In June 2009, Xi Jinping visited Bangladesh, when the latter hoped to discuss the issue of the developing its first deep-water port. It is particularly worth mentioning that the purchase of weaponry from China is also under discussion. Dipu Moni, Minister of Education in the Bangladesh government, said, 'our cooperation with China is multifaceted, including the military. We have a lot of arms purchases from China, so we will definitely talk about it this time' (Yan 2015). This means that China and Bangladesh cooperate closely in defence and military affairs. Bangladesh depends on China to provide weapons and equipment (Yan 2015). In May 2014, Xu Qiliang, vice chairman of China's Central Military Commission, visited Bangladesh and attended the signing ceremony of four China–Bangladesh military agreements to provide Bangladesh with military equipment and technical support and train its military personnel to enhance Bangladesh's defence capabilities.

In 2016, China and Bangladesh signed Article 16 of the Joint Statement on the Establishment of Strategic Cooperation Partnership between China and Bangladesh, and both sides agreed to maintain and strengthen exchanges and cooperation at all levels of the two militaries and deepen the areas of personnel training, technology, and UN peacekeeping cooperation (Chinese Embassy in Bangladesh 2016).

The defence cooperation between the two countries is pragmatic but at a low level. China is currently the number one supplier of military equipment to Bangladesh. About 86 per cent military hardware used by the Bangladesh armed forces is of Chinese origin, which includes two refurbished submarines inducted in 2017 and naval warships (Shukla 2021). According to data from the Stockholm International Peace Research Institute in Sweden, since 2010, China has provided Dhaka with 5 maritime patrol ships, 2 light cruisers, 44 tanks, 16 fighter jets, as well as surface-to-air missiles and anti-ship missiles (Cui 2016). As part of the Bangladesh navy's modernisation efforts, on 14 November 2016, China delivered the first batch of submarines to the Bangladeshi navy—two modified Type 035- (Ming-) class diesel-electric submarines. General Nizamuddin Ahmed, Bangladesh's chief of naval staff, led a delegation to attend the delivery ceremony, which marked the formation of a broad military bond between China and Bangladesh (Ren and Tan 2016).

This low-level relationship in this sector is mainly reflected in the fact that the defence cooperation between the two countries is still in the realm of high-rank dialogues, delegation visits, equipment and technology cooperation, personnel training, joint exercises and joint training. In April 2014, a Bangladeshi frigate arrived at Qingdao Port to participate the 14th Western Pacific Naval Symposium (WPNS) and joint maritime exercises. In January 2016, the 21st batch of the Chinese navy escort fleet arrived in Chittagong, Bangladesh. This was the first visit to Bangladesh by the Chinese navy escort fleet. In May 2017, the Chinese navy's voyage visit formation and the Bangladeshi navy held a joint maritime exercise in the waters of the Bay of Bengal. In July 2017, the first round of China–Bangladesh maritime cooperation dialogue was held in Beijing, and the two parties communicated on strengthening cooperation in the maritime field. In February 2020, the 33rd escort fleet of the Chinese navy arrived in Chittagong and conducted a five-day friendly visit to Bangladesh.

On the whole, due to the complex geopolitics of South Asia, China–Bangladesh defence cooperation, although pragmatic and effective, is still at a low level and has not made major breakthroughs. In this field, there has not been a regular mutual visit mechanism or a defence security consultation mechanism. At present, the joint military exercises are small in scale and fragmented, and defence cooperation has not been institutionalised and integrated. However, since the two countries do not have a fundamental conflict of interest and can benefit more from cooperation, it is likely that both sides will further strengthen their defence cooperation in the future.

In terms of security cooperation, the two countries are jointly committed to regional stability. On 20 May 2014, Bangladesh's Minister of Foreign Affairs Abul Hassan Mahmood Ali signed the document on Bangladesh's accession to the Conference on Interaction and Confidence-Building Measures in Asia (CICA), making the country the 26th member state of this body. After signing, Abu Hassan Ali said that Bangladesh is willing to play its role in Asian security cooperation, and at the same time expressed gratitude to China, Turkey and Kazakhstan for their support (Pei et al. 2014). In August 2017, the Rohingya crisis broke out on a massive scale in Myanmar. In November of the same year, Chinese Foreign Minister Wang Yi visited Bangladesh and Myanmar, held consultations with the two countries, and proposed a 'three-step approach' to resolve the Rohingya issue in Rakhine State. The first step is to achieve a ceasefire and restore stability and order; the second step is to find a feasible way to solve the problem as soon as possible through equal and friendly negotiations between Myanmar and Bangladesh; the third step is to explore a permanent solution (*Cankaoxiaoxi* 2017).

China–Bangladesh Economic and Trade Relations: Rapid and Unbalanced Development

At present, China is Bangladesh's largest trading partner, and largest source of imports, while the latter is China's third largest export market in South Asia. China–Bangladesh trade started in 1975 when the volume was at only $3.06 million. By 2020, the trade volume reached $15.86 billion. Among them, China's exports to Bangladesh were at $15.06 billion while imports from Bangladesh were at $800 million. Chinese companies have invested $320 million directly in Bangladesh, while Bangladesh has invested $270,000 in China. Additionally, Chinese companies have signed a contract value of $13.17 billion in Bangladesh (Ministry of Commerce China 2021). As China becomes the second-largest economy in the world and Bangladesh graduates from the UN's list of least-developed countries, the dependence of the Bangladeshi economy on China might increase substantially, as the trade volume between the two countries is expected to further increase.

However, the other side of that relationship is that for a long time, China has had a huge trade surplus with Bangladesh. The imbalance in the economic and trade relations between the two countries continues to widen with the increase in trade volume, and it is developing unfavourably for Bangladesh. This has become a critical issue that needs to be addressed. Bangladesh has strong opinions on the huge long-term trade deficit between the two countries and hopes that China will take measures to change the trade imbalance.

But this long-standing unresolved problem does have its objective reasons. First, considering the distribution structure of foreign trade target countries for both nations, it can be observed that the EU, the US and other developed countries predominantly serve as markets. This is determined by their own economic conditions and development stages, and there will be no fundamental changes in the short term, which generally limits the scale of trade between the two countries. Second, considering the import-and-export commodity structure, the competitiveness is far greater than the complementarity. Chinese products, such as electronic products, mechanical and electrical products, chemical products, and light industrial products are generally cheap and of high quality. As a result, they are competitive in the Bangladeshi market and are suitable for the country's consumption level. While Bangladesh's exports to China are mostly raw materials with low added value, such as raw hemp, fertilisers, jute products, marine products, knitwear, bulk tea. China has adopted various measures to resolve the issue of trade imbalance and, in recent years, even made efforts to increase its imports from Bangladesh. Starting from 1 September 2022, China has applied a preferential tax rate of zero to 98 percent of products from Bangladesh, involving 8,786 tax items (Ministry of Commerce China 2022). The adjustment involves a variety of commodities including textile fabrics, textile, aquatic and leather products and so on.

China–Bangladesh People-to-People Bounds: Strange Neighbours

The people-to-people relationship between China and Bangladesh is an integral part of the exchanges between the two ancient civilisations. Eminent Chinese monks Fa Xian and Xuan Zang travelled west to learn Buddhist knowledge while the eminent Bangladeshi monk, Venerable Atisha, went to China to preach. The great Chinese navigator Zheng He (active in the early Ming Dynasty) visited Bangladesh region twice, leaving a great record in the history of people-to-people contact. However, it is understandable that due to geographical separation, people of the two regions have not had intensive contact in history. They have neither strong cultural interests nor motivation to understand each other.

First, there are certain problems in the channels through which the people of the two countries understand each other with limited first-hand channels. The main source for the Bangladeshi people to understand

China is to learn about it from Western media reports. It is therefore difficult to ensure that the Bangladeshi people have a comprehensive and objective understanding of China. On the other hand, Chinese people obtain information about Bangladesh through the Chinese official media's journalist station in Bangladesh. Second, people-to-people exchanges between the two countries are more active in economic and trade exchanges at present. In other social fields, they still rely on various government-led exchange programmes, while spontaneous non-governmental exchanges are still far from sufficient, including tourism. Third, the development of China–Bangladesh relations is currently dominated by government channels. With the joint efforts of the two governments, some programmes to strengthen the exchanges have been well implemented. These are welcome steps. However, such bilateral engagements are guided by politics. This, however, is not in line with the essence of non-governmental engagements, as such engagements should encourage people of both sides to develop a strong interest to understand each other. Importantly, it needs to be distanced from political engagement.

Additionally, the media can play a more active role in shaping public opinion and image on both sides. In recent years, the media of both countries have reported more objective and positive news about each other, and this has played an important role in shaping people's perceptions. In the coming years, this will have a further positive effect on the development of people-to-people relations between the two countries.

China's Strategy for Bangladesh

China's foreign policy towards Bangladesh is a three-fold matrix focusing on the friendship between the two countries, expansion of all-round cooperation, and consolidation of the strategic cooperative partnership. Its main targets are to enable Bangladesh to gradually possess independent strategic capabilities and become an important force in maintaining the balance of power in South Asia. The overarching objective is to prevent Bangladesh from being controlled by regional or global powers to ensure the security of China's southwest border and energy security channel.

Enhance Political Mutual Trust

China aims to strengthen high-level strategic dialogue and policy communication with Bangladesh. Under the guidance of the Five Principles of Peaceful Coexistence, China adheres to the friendly neighbour policy of kindness, sincerity, benefit and tolerance, and tries to deepen diplomatic consultations, economic and trade, maritime cooperation dialogues and consular-level consultations through high-level exchanges, ministerial meetings and senior officials. China is working hard to connect the Chinese Dream, the Two Centenary Goals, the Golden Bangladesh Dream, and the Development Goals of the 2030 vision, to build greater consensus and promote the development of China and Bangladesh.

China's policy towards Bangladesh is persistent with its preference for resolving disputes through dialogue, resolving differences through consultation and carrying out cooperation on the basis of equality and mutual benefit to consolidate the traditional friendship between the two countries. The Chinese side fully understands the considerations of Bangladesh's non-aligned, diversified and balanced foreign policy. It is important for China to properly handle the China, Bangladesh and US relationship, the China, Bangladesh and India ties and other multilateral relations, and take a new path of state-to-state exchanges that involves dialogue without confrontation, and partnerships without forging alliances.

Deepen Security Cooperation

The China–Bangladesh defence cooperation has been gradually institutionalised and both sides are working to deepen it further. They are committed to establish a mechanism for regular mutual visits of the highest-level military leaders, and establish an intergovernmental military technology cooperation committee led by the minister of defence to coordinate related matters. Another focus is the institutionalisation and normalisation of routine military exercises between the two countries, and the increase in the number of visits to Bangladesh by the Chinese naval fleet. China is also working towards deepening personnel training and establishing a long-term officer training mechanism with Bangladesh. The two countries have also agreed to expand military trade and shift from traditional goods trading to cooperation on military equipment and military technology.

In the field of non-traditional security, pragmatic cooperation has been carried out in combating terrorism, transnational crime, humanitarian assistance, climate change, disaster response, and global health. As always, China will play a constructive role in properly resolving the Rohingya crisis in accordance with the Three Steps of anti-violence, repatriation and development, and provide constructive assistance to support Bangladesh and Myanmar in seeking proper solutions to promote the repatriation of people who have escaped to Bangladesh (Ministry of Foreign Affairs 2018).

Expand Economic Integration

China has decided to speed up the joint research work on the China–Bangladesh Free Trade Agreement by starting negotiations as soon as possible. China has also decided to implement zero-tariff treatment for 98 per cent of Bangladesh's products, and further encourage the export of its products to China.

China has also enhanced its effort for coordination of policies, rules and standards with Bangladesh. Beijing decided to promptly negotiate or amend treaties or agreements such as bilateral investment, consular protection, judicial assistance and facilitation of personnel exchanges to provide favourable conditions for corporate investment. China is actively considering strengthening the integration of infrastructure construction planning and quality and technology systems, and promoting the integration of policies, plans and standards.

The interconnection of infrastructure is another policy priority. The Chinese side supports its enterprises to participate in Bangladesh's railway, highway, airport, port, bridge, telecommunications and other infrastructure development programmes. It is willing to accelerate the development of the BCIM and to encourage production capacity investment cooperation. Through development assistance, economic and trade investment, and infrastructure cooperation, Chinese companies receive government support to participate in the construction of Bangladesh's 100 economic zones, blue economy, and Digital Bangladesh, including Payra coal-fired power plant, the Chittagong China Industry Park, to enhance the international competitiveness of the Bangladesh industry.

Cooperation between financial institutions and financial markets is encouraged as well. Give full play to the role of platforms such as the Asian Infrastructure Investment Bank and the Silk Road Fund to explore cooperation in RMB financing and bond issuance. The two countries can deepen cooperation on capital and securities markets. Further, the Shenzhen Stock Exchange, the Shanghai Stock Exchange Consortium and the Dhaka Stock Exchange can be encouraged to strengthen cross-border equity cooperation as soon as possible. Strategic cooperation between digital giants such as Ant Financial and Bangladesh's largest mobile payment company Bkash is also favourable.

Expand People-to-People Exchange

The two countries can develop multilevel platforms to jointly promote exchanges in the fields of education, science and technology, culture and health. China will continue to deepen exchanges and cooperation in areas such as poverty reduction, urban and rural governance, tourism, archaeology and heritage protection. The two sides can also explore cooperation in new media, news, film and television, and forge a favourable environment for BRI. China is interested in promoting the development of Confucius Institutes in Bangladesh, increasing opportunities for exchanges between Chinese and Bangladeshi students, and promoting cultural exchanges and educational advancement between the two sides through scholarships and overseas study exchange programmes. Both countries can encourage scientific research cooperation and exchanges between scientific research institutions in the field of humanities and social sciences. Mass media and new media can be employed to promote the positive image of each other.

Navigating the Trilateral Relations between China, Bangladesh and India

Over the years, Bangladesh has always adopted an independent foreign policy to seek a balance among the big powers. This 'big power balance' strategy has restricted the distance between Bangladesh's bilateral relationships with China, India and the US. Bangladesh does not want to damage its ties with China due to developing relationships with the other two countries, with which it has been even more difficult to establish alliances.

However, the geopolitical reality determines that it is difficult for the Bangladeshi government to bypass India in its diplomatic activities. Even under the strong leadership of the Hasina government, it is still difficult to get rid of the shackles of Indian factors. For example, due to India's opposition and concerns, Bangladesh did not agree to the Chinese conditions on the construction of the Sonadia deep-sea port in 2014 (Bhattacharjee 2018). Therefore, Bangladesh's balance policy has always been characterised by limited neutrality. Since Hasina took office, Bangladesh–India relations have a made significant breakthrough. The Modi government has also actively improved relations with Bangladesh and increased its investment and assistance. The rapid development of ties between the two nations has restricted its strategic options inclusive of cooperation with China. Fortunately, China's policy towards Bangladesh has been relatively cautious and restrained.

Bangladesh's active participation to the BRI has become a concern for India, with the latter cautious of the China–Bangladesh defence cooperation, especially in the maritime sector. In order to alleviate India's concerns, Bangladesh's leaders have repeatedly emphasised that its participation in the BRI cooperation is purely an economic issue. In February 2018, when an Indian media delegation visited Bangladesh, Prime Minister Hasina said during the meeting that India does not need to worry about the growing relations between Bangladesh and China since the cooperation with Beijing is only for economic development (Lin 2018). Despite this, India interprets China's influence in Myanmar, Bangladesh, Nepal, Central Asia and the Persian Gulf as a strategy to encircle India. Therefore, the rapid development of Bangladesh–China relations has become a factor affecting the country's relationship with India.

At present, the trilateral relationship between China, Bangladesh and India has formed a delicate and relatively dynamic balance. China should carefully handle the trilateral relations between China, Bangladesh and India. While formulating a specific strategy towards Bangladesh, China must take into account Indian factors but not be dominated by India; it must not only reasonably meet the latter's interests and needs, but also pay careful attention to threats from India. Even as it opposes India's hegemonic behaviour, China should not overly demonise India.

Importantly, the improvement or deterioration of China–India relations will not sacrifice Bangladesh–China ties, as they are all-season partners.

Strengthen China–Bangladesh Cooperation on International Platforms

China and Bangladesh need to make full use of multilateral cooperation mechanisms such as the Conference on Interaction and Confidence-Building Measures in Asia (CICA), the Asian Infrastructure Development Bank, the Silk Road Fund, and the Bay of Bengal Multi-Field Technical and Economic Cooperation Initiative (BIMSTEC) to explore the cooperation model of China-Bangladesh Cooperation. Incorporating Bangladesh into multilateral mechanisms initiated by China, such as the Shanghai Cooperation Organisation, might be instrumental in this regard. The two countries need to abide by international rules, standards and market rules on the one hand while encouraging all countries to jointly establish new mechanisms and formulate new rules for emerging areas such as the ocean, the internet, outer space and climate change, on the other hand.

Prospects of China-Bangladesh Relations

The formation, maintenance and development of the traditional friendship between China and Bangladesh benefits from China's active practice of the five principles of peaceful coexistence in its foreign exchanges, the two countries respect and support for each other's development path and domestic and foreign policies, and display a willingness to collaborate in the pursuance of their respective development goals. The cornerstone of Bangladesh's

China policy is to maintain the same friendly relations with China, India, the US and other partner countries. At the same time, with the help of China, Bangladesh seeks to reduce its dependence on India and US, and obtain economic benefits from the competition between China, India and the US in the long run. The China factor has become an important tool for Bangladesh to balance India and the US. Ultimately, as long as Bangladesh's future China policy remains friendly and neutral, the long-term prospects of their relations will continue to develop steadily.

Due to its unique geographical location, Bangladesh has attracted the attention of major powers both inside and outside the region. In order to curb China's rise and offset its growing influence in South Asia, the US might have a consideration in asking Bangladesh to play a role in the US-led Indo-Pacific strategy. China–Bangladesh relations will stagnate or even regress if Bangladesh deviates from its neutral policy and joins the QUAD security dialogue mechanism—comprising the US, Japan, India and Australia—to contain China.

Note

1 The phrase was used by Chinese Foreign Minister Yang Jiechi during his visit to Bangladesh on 24–25 April 2008, when he was hosted by the author, then foreign advisor (foreign minister) of the Bangladesh caretaker government.

References

Aneja, U. 'China–Bangladesh Relations an Emerging Strategic Partnership?' IPCS Special Report 33, November 2006.

'Announcement of the Customs Tariff Commission of the State Council on Granting Zero Tariff Treatment to 97% of the Products of the People's Republic of Bangladesh'. Ministry of Commerce of the People's Republic of China, June 18, 2020. http://gss.mof.gov.cn/gzdt/zhengcefabu/202006/t20200618_3534450.htm.

Bastola, E.R. 'Bilateral Relations between Bangladesh and China Have Widened in Various Dimensions: Dr. Islam'. *Khabarhub*, February 25, 2021. https://english.khabarhub.com/2021/25/165290/.

Bhattacharjee, J. 'Forget Pakistan. China-Bangladesh Is the One to Watch'. *Daily O*, June 29, 2018. https://www.dailyo.in/politics/decoding-china-bangladesh-relationship-pakistan-defence-partnership/story/1/25183.html.

'Both Bangladesh and Myanmar support China's three-stage solution to the Rohingya crisis'. *Cankaoxiaoxi*, November 21, 2017. http://www.cankaoxiaoxi.com/china/20171121/2244111.shtml.

'Brief Introduction of China–Bangladesh Economic and Trade Cooperation from January to December 2020'. Ministry of Commerce of the People's Republic of China, March 25, 2021. http://www.mofcom.gov.cn/article/tongjiziliao/sjtj/yzzggb/202103/20210303042323.shtml.

Cang, L. 'Deng Xiaoping Telling Al Shad, Wherever Reform and Opening up Are Carried Out, It Is Successful, and the Pace of Reform and Opening up Is Bigger, and China Will Develop Faster'. *People's Daily* (electronic edition), July 4, 1987. https://new.zlck.com/rmrb/news/KM0CXATY.html.

Chenzhi, H.X. '6 Touching Details of President Xi Jinping's Trip to Asia'. *Xinhua Net*, October 18, 2016. http://www.xinhuanet.com/world/2016-10/18/c_129326988.htm.

'China and Bangladesh Signed MOU for Hydrological Information Exchange'. Ministry of Water Resources, September 19, 2008. http://www.mwr.gov.cn/english/news/200809/t20080919_102801.html.

'China and Bangladesh Sign Intergovernmental Memorandum of Understanding on Cooperation under the Belt and Road Initiative'. The State Council Information Office the People's Republic of China, October 18, 2016. http://www.scio.gov.cn/ztk/wh/slxy/31200/Document/1494484/1494484.htm.

Chowdhury, I.A. 'Bangladesh–China: An Emerging Equation in Asian Diplomatic Calculations'. ISAS Working Paper 105, no. 31 (March 2010).

Cui, J. 'India Keeps a Close Eye on Bangladesh's Defense Cooperation with China. Why Is It So Sensitive?' *Global Times*, May 26, 2016. https://world.huanqiu.com/article/9CaKrnJVEHu.

Hossain, M.S. 'Sino-Bangladesh Relations: Friendship Unbounded'. *The Independent*, October 22, 2010.

'Joint Statement of the People's Republic of China and the People's Republic of Bangladesh on the Establishment of a Strategic Cooperative Partnership'. Chinese Embassy in Bangladesh, October 14, 2016. http://bd.china-embassy.org/chn/zmgx/zywj/t1460487.htm.

'Joint Statement of the People's Republic of China and the People's Republic of Bangladesh on the Establishment of a Strategic Cooperative Partnership'. *Xinhua Net*. October 15, 2016. http://www.xinhuanet.com/world/2016-10/15/c_1119721775.htm.

Lin, M. 'The Belt and Road Initiative Boosts Bangladesh's Economic Development'. *World Affairs Pictorial* 20, (2018): 74. https://www.fx361.com/page/2018/1121/4512572.shtml.

Luo, S. 'On Sino-Bangladesh Relations Since 1975'. *Indian Ocean Economic and Political Review* 5 (2016): 792.

Noor Mohammad Sacker, N.M. 'Bangladesh–China Relationship at the Dawn of the Twenty-First Century'. *Peace and Security Review* 6, no. 11 (2014 First Quarter): 88.

Pei, G., C. Zhao, and M. Zhang. 'Bangladeshi Foreign Minister: China Has Made Important Contributions to Peace and Security in Asia'. *People's Daily*, May 21, 2014. http://world.people.com.cn/n/2014/0521/c1002-25044195.html.

Ren, X. and L. Tan. 'India Will Upgrade Its Defense Cooperation with Bangladesh. Indian media: To Contend China'. Global Network, November 16, 2016. https://world.huanqiu.com/article/9CaKrnJYDJX.

Shukla, R. 'China, Bangladesh and Quad: What Should India do?' *Financial Express*, May 28, 2021. https://www.financialexpress.com/defence/china-bangladesh-and-quad-what-should-india-do/2260801/.

'The Full Text of the Speech by Ambassador Zhang Zuo at the Seminar on China–Bangladesh Relations: Foreseeing the Future'. Ministry of Foreign Affairs of the People's Republic of China, December 12, 2018. https://www.fmprc.gov.cn/web/dszlsjt_673036/t1621193.shtml.

Xinhua News Agency. 'The Long History of the Sino-Bangladesh Friendship'. *People's Daily* (electronic edition), January 6, 1977. https://new.zlck.com/rmrb/news/IHGCJ008.html.

Yan, Y. 'A Study on China–Bangladesh Relations in the View of Power Transition (1974–2014)'. Unpublished Master's Thesis, Yunnan University, May 2015.

11

BANGLADESH–PAKISTAN RELATIONS: OLD AND NEW DIMENSIONS

Amna Ejaz Rafi

The year 1971 is the darkest chapter in history of Pakistan (Hashmi 2016). Fifty-one years have been passed since the dreadful episode but still the memories are alive, especially for those Pakistanis who have lived in East Pakistan, present-day Bangladesh. The factors that led to the dismemberment of former East Pakistan can be traced back to the 1970 general elections. Although the elections are still regarded as the fairest (Ahmar 2020), the failure was the lack of political will to accept the outcome (Rafi 2022, 4). The Pakistan People's Party and Awami League (AL) were the two lead political parties of the time. The AL won 160 out of 162 seats in former East Pakistan while the Pakistan People's Party secured 81 out of 138 seats in West Pakistan (mainly in Punjab and Sindh) (Agha 2021, 83). The voting pattern reflected peoples' varied outlooks in East and West Pakistan (Rafi 2022, 3). But, it was a democratic decision and should have been taken that way. The equating of election results with division provoked hate sentiments and it weakened the prospects of a political solution. Whether it was being done deliberately or it just happened in the lust of power, the outcome was civil unrest and loss of peace for the people of Pakistan.

Awami League leader Sheikh Mujib said in the statement he made post the win:

> The election, for the people of Bangladesh, was above all a referendum on the vital issue of full regional autonomy on the basis of Six Points, and the eleven-point programme. Therefore, a constitution securing full regional autonomy on the basis of "Six Point Programme" has to be framed and implemented in all respects. (Agha 2021, 85)

As per the democratic rule, Pakistan People's Party was second in election run and principally should have sat on opposition benches.

However, party head Zulfikar Ali Bhutto's statement, 'No constitution could be framed nor could any government at the Centre be formed, without my party's (Pakistan People's Party) cooperation', was a negation of AL's overall win. Zulfikar Ali Bhutto was popular for his slogan 'roti, kapda, makan' but his actions reflected more of a feudalistic approach (Agha 2021, 86). This adamant posturing of the lead political parties stretched the electoral divide into an internal strife (Ahmar 2020). No breakthrough seemed possible between Dhaka and Larkana (Zaidi 2017). On 19 December, Sheikh Mujib issued a statement, 'I warmly thank the people for having given a historic verdict in favour of our "Six Point Programme". We pledge to implement this verdict. There can be no constitution except one which is based on the Six Point Programme' (Agha 2021, 85). Sheikh Mujib's election campaign rhetoric was centred on Bengali 'deprivation', which he employed to win over Bengali sentiment (Agha 2021, 37). G.W. Choudhury, a central minister in the cabinet of President General Yahya Khan writes in his book, *The Last Days of United Pakistan*, 'Mujib's election campaign and strategy were to carry the gospel of Bengali nationalism and the ideal of Bangladesh' (Ahmar 2020). Earlier, during the days of United Pakistan, Mujib was implicated in the Agartala Conspiracy Case (but was later freed) (Zaidi 2017). Mujib's 'Six Points Programme' (1966) was seen as a demand for an independent country (Ahmar 2020). However, within a span of five years, the demand became a central issue in Pakistan's politics. The gist of the 'Six Points' was: (*i*) there should be a Federation of Pakistan on the basis of the 'Lahore Resolution', (*ii*) the federal government should be limited to defence and foreign affairs, (*iii*) two separate currencies for the two wings, (*iv*) the centre should have no tax raising powers, (*v*) a separate external trade account for each federating state and (*vi*) States to have constitutional authority to maintain para-military or territorial force (Agha 2021, 37).

The situation deteriorated post the 1970 general elections (Datta 2022). Denying the Bengali population their majority vote hurt Bengali sentiment. A plausible scenario of the 1970 general election would have been a cooperative approach by the lead political parties of the time. They should have sorted out their concerns through talks.

On 21 November 1971, Indian troops entered the sovereign territory of East Pakistan. Around 3,00,000 Indian troops were stationed there, while the strength of the Pakistani troops in East Pakistan was 34,000 (Hashmi 2021). Over all, three million people lost their lives in 1971 war (Janjua 2021). On the role of the Pakistan army in 1971, the military's intervention had been to safeguard the country's frontiers against Indian-trained Mukti Bahini. In his book, *Inside RAW: The Story of India's Secret Service*, Asoka Raina has said that 'during the Indian Army's Dhaka campaign, Mukti Bahini and the Indian Army fought shoulder to shoulder together in the final battle' (Raina 1981, 90).

Qutubuddin Aziz, a former diplomat, journalist and chairman of the National Press Trust in his book, *Blood and Tears*, has documented '170 eye-witness accounts of the atrocities committed on Biharis[1] and other non-Bengalis across 55 towns in East Pakistan by Awami League militants and other rebels in March-April, 1971' (Aziz 1974).

In the aftermath of war, on 9 April 1974, India, Pakistan and Bangladesh signed a Tripartite Agreement in New Delhi. The agreement was an initiative undertaken to forego the past mistakes and step up efforts towards enhanced cooperation (Hashmi 2016, 203–204).

The AL formed the government on 16 December 1971 in Dhaka, Bangladesh. Sheikh Mujibur Rahman became the prime minister of Bangladesh. Mujib's takeover was widely supported by India (Siddiqi 2018, 39). Mujib was called Bangabandhu, which meant 'Father of the Bangladeshi Nation' (Agha 2021, 389). However, it was only a few years later that resentment started building among the people of Bangladesh, to the extent that Bangabandhu was ruthlessly gunned down in a military coup on 15 August 1975 (Agha 2021, 389). In the words of Anthony Mascarenhas:

> Few men in history have betrayed the aspirations of their people as did the first leaders of Bangladesh.... Once the darling of the independence movement in whose magic name all things are done; Sheikh Mujib as Prime Minister and President became the most hated man in Bangladesh within three short years of its founding. (Hashmi 2016, 209)

After the 1971 war, half a million Bengalis were in Pakistan as political hostages. Bangladesh also held prisoners of war (POWs) from West Pakistan (Mehmood et al. 2015). Indonesia and the UK offered to mediate between the two countries but to no avail, and the deadlock between them continued. It was in 1972 that an agreement over the POWs was reached under the Shimla Accord (Mehmood et al. 2015). This paved the way towards normalisation of bilateral ties. Resultantly, in February 1974, Pakistan and Bangladesh recognised each other as sovereign states (Hashmi 2016, 12).

In his remarks on the recognition of Bangladesh, Pakistan Prime Minister Zulfikar Ali Bhutto said:

> The country (Pakistan) was dismembered, the unity was sundered and a yawning gap was opened between you and us. In a sense, it may be too late to cry on what happened already, but it is never too late to repent, to say Tauba (repent before Allah, the Creator), from the depth of our hearts. The people of Pakistan respect your decision; they and the Government of Pakistan recognize and respect (the)

sovereignty and independence of Bangladesh. More than that, we wish you rapid progress and prosperity. We extend to you all our goodwill and we are prepared to cooperate with you to the extend that you desire. (Hashmi 2016, 12)

In February 1974, Bangladesh Prime Minister Sheikh Mujib visited Pakistan and attended the Organisation of Islamic Countries (OIC) summit in Lahore (Khan 2022). This was followed by Prime Minister Bhutto's visit to Bangladesh. Bhutto was warmly welcomed by the Bengali people. Late J.N. Dixit, who was the then Indian ambassador to Dhaka at the time, has narrated the Bengali enthusiasm in his book *Liberation and Beyond: Indo-Bangladesh Relations* (1999), where he writes: 'Bhutto arrived in Dhaka. I drove to the airport through dense crowds lining both sides of the road all the way from the Tejgaon airport Banga Bhavan, resounding with slogans like Bangladesh-Pakistan maitri (friendship) Zindabad' (Agha 2021, 387–388).

Bangladesh–Pakistan Relations: Various Dimensions

Pakistan's diplomatic mission in Dhaka was established in 1976 (Hashmi 2016, 12). The period from 1977 to 1996 witnessed growth in the relationship between the two countries. Bangladesh President Ziaur Rahman visited Pakistan in December 1977. In 1989, Pakistan was Bangladesh's second-largest trading partner after the US (Ahmar 2022, 163–167). That decade also saw cooperation on the defence front with Pakistan exported F6 aircraft and some tanks to Bangladesh in the 1980s (Hafeez 2021). Pakistan also provided training to the Bangladeshi army personnel on its indigenously produced Al-Khaled tank (Hashmi 2016, 200).

There have been ups and downs between Bangladesh and Pakistan but the perception that the ties have remained hostile throughout is not correct altogether. In this regard, the statement of former foreign minister of Bangladesh Muhammad Shamsul Haq is significant:

Bangladesh and Pakistan were bound by many common ties rooted in a shared history and culture, which was overshadowed but not obliterated by the tragic happenings of 1971. The Bengalis' role in (the) creation of Pakistan (is) also a historical fact. The original Pakistan resolution was moved by Abdul Kasem Fazlul Haq, a Bengali Muslim leader, and of the Muslim majority provinces of British India, Bengal was the only province where the Muslim League was voted to power, thus providing the Muslim League with a political power base. (Ahmar 2022)

Awami League's Rule and Its Relationship with Pakistan

In Bangladesh, the two major political parties on stage are the AL and the Bangladesh Nationalist Party (BNP). Both claim to be the custodians of the 1971 war of liberation. The AL head Sheikh Hasina is the daughter of Sheikh Mujib, which makes the party a dynastic-led political group. Notably, AL has maintained a close relationship with India, also signing a 'Treaty of Peace and Friendship' with India in 1972 (Kumar 2014). The present-day AL regards India as a 'true friend' (Hashmi 2021). On its relations with Pakistan, the AL is adamant over 'apology, reparations and division of assets' from the Government of Pakistan (Hashmi 2016, 203–204). In 2009, Prime Minister Hasina Wajed (Sheikh Hasina as she is popularly known) resumed the 1971 trial of 'war crimes' (Syed 2020). Resultantly, in 2016, Bangladesh executed several leaders of Jamaat-e-Islami for their participation in such crimes. The executions were condemned by Pakistan, and 'labelled as politically motivated action' (Bhanu 2023). In response, Bangladesh called Pakistan's condemnation an 'interference in the internal matters of Bangladesh' (Bhanu 2023).

The 1971 trial of war crimes brought the bilateral ties to the lowest ebb. The diplomats from each other's country were asked to leave (Hassan 2021). Bangladesh also imposed visa restrictions on Pakistani nationals (Ahmar 2021). The relationship remained strained for about seven years, from 2013 right up to 2019. It was in November 2019 that Bangladesh accorded approval to the appointment of Pakistani High Commissioner, in Dhaka. This led to the resuming of Pakistan's diplomatic ties with Bangladesh (Chowdhury 2020, 5). Afterwards, in July 2020, the telephonic conversation between Prime Minister Imran Khan and Prime Minister Hasina saw the discussion of bilateral ties and cooperation on the regional front (ANI 2020). Prime Minister Khan called for 'enhanced regional cooperation' (Syed 2020). The leadership of both countries also deliberated upon the safety measures taken against Covid-19 pandemic. Prime Minister Khan extended an invite to Prime Minister Sheikh Hasina to visit Pakistan (Syed 2020).

Prime Minister Hasina responded heartily and sent a gift of mangoes—an act that has been referred to as 'mango diplomacy' (Bhanu 2023). The Khan–Hasina telephonic conversation could be termed as a step towards political exchange. In March 2021, on Bangladesh's 50th Independent Anniversary Celebrations, Dhaka invited leaders of India, Nepal, Bhutan, Maldives and Sri Lanka to participate in the celebrations. However, no invitation was extended to Pakistan. Despite that, then Prime Minister Imran Khan sent a congratulatory video message to Bangladesh's leadership (Hassan 2021) and invited Prime Minister Hasina to visit Pakistan. Prime Minister Hasina also reciprocated in kind (Hafeez 2021).

While diplomatic links have been resumed between Bangladesh and Pakistan, there are loopholes in the way of a cooperative relationship. The insistence by Bangladesh that Pakistan should extend a formal apology for the events of 1971 is a major impediment towards a fruitful interaction. Bangladeshi Foreign Minister A.K. Abdul Momen's statement merits consideration in this regard. The statement categorically points towards 1971:

> the country has not forgotten Pakistan's gruesome killings of some 30 lakh (300,000) Bangladeshi and rape of hundreds of thousands of women during the liberation war in 1971. Pakistan has not yet apologized for the genocide it committed during the liberation war. We want to maintain friendship with everyone but how is that possible if they could not make an apology. (ANI 2020)

The apology issue continues to be a bone of contention in the relationship between the two nations. Should both the countries continue to view each other from the 1971 prism or is there a way out? Seeing the apology issue in the context of the 'Tripartite Agreement for repatriation of war prisoners, back then Sheikh Mujib had agreed that in the interest of regional peace, no one would be put to trial' (Malik). However, in later years, the Awami League government has initiated a war tribunal (25 March 2010). This act was in contrast to the vision held by AL's founding father. Many of the convicts tried in tribunal were members of opposition. The war tribunal was questioned by Jamaat-e-Islami and Bangladesh Nationalist Party (BNP) (Habib 2010).

There existed a perception that AL had solidified the 1971 sentiment, and the war tribunal was a politically motivated tactics to squash the opposition. The Bangladesh–Pakistan ties in the prevalent scenario requires a redressal by both countries. As regional players, both nations need to reorient their foreign policies towards regional integration. The divide of 1971 should be bridged with economic cooperation and political consonance.

An important angle in the Bangladesh–Pakistan relationship is the government in power in Dhaka. During AL's tenure, the ties primarily revolve around 1971. Whereas, during BNP's tenure, a sense of warmth is apparent in the country's dealings with Pakistan. Late President Pervez Musharraf's visit to Bangladesh in July 2002 is a testament to this fact. President Musharraf visited the National Martyrs Memorial (outside Dhaka) and expressed deep regrets to the loss of lives in 1971. President Musharraf said, 'Your brothers and sisters in Pakistan share the pains of the events of 1971. The excesses committed during the unfortunate period are regrettable' (*The Dawn* 2002). Prime Minister

Khaleda Zia accepted Musharraf's gesture and thanked him in a state banquet for his words (Ahmar 2022).

Diversified Societal Outlook of Bangladeshi Society

Other than the AL and BNP, another political representative is the Jamaat-e-Islami. The party contested the 1979 elections as part of the Islamic Democratic League and secured six seats (Pattanaik 2020). The diversity in the political parties of Bangladesh points to a varied societal structure. Thus, the society of Bangladesh is divided into different socio-political ethos. In Bangladesh, 'Bishwa Ijtema' is also held annually in Dhaka. The Tablighi Jamaat organises the event that sees the participation of Muslims from the world over (Kamruzzaman 2021). In the backdrop of the religious orientation of Bangladeshi society, Islam can be a common factor in strengthening relations between Bangladesh and Pakistan.

At the time of the freedom struggle, what was then Pakistan (both East and West) was a collective struggle; in fact, Sheikh Mujib was a political worker for the All-India Muslim League, which was born in Dhaka in 1906 (Hafeez 2021). The argument that the historical baggage wherein the civil unrest continues to dominate the psyche of many Bengalis will never let cordiality prevail between Pakistan and Bangladesh is also a reality. However, there are instances in world where countries have overcome the past and move forward with new goals and aspirations. The example of Britain's legacy in South Asia is a case in point. Great Britain had once ruled the land that included present-day India, Pakistan and Bangladesh. The South Asian countries now have cordial ties with Britain.

Bangladesh and Pakistan are independent countries, and both need to work- towards a cooperative partnership. Bilateral ties need to be developed in line with the emerging regional realities. Both the countries can enhance cooperation in countering challenges of poverty, extremism and climate change (Hafeez 2021). In this regard, the regional countries can learn from each other's experience. For instance, Pakistan is fighting militancy and is still stable. Despite the shortcomings because of the economic situation, the country continues to move forward. Likewise, Bangladesh has a success story when it comes to economic growth. The country's socio-economic indicators, in particular the considerable decline in poverty are reflective of Bangladesh's upward march (Hasan 2020). The improved literacy rate in Bangladesh with 98 per cent school children attaining primary level education is also a success story (Siddiqi 2018). Moreover, Bangladesh has managed to balance the population growth against the agricultural production (Quibria 2019). Thus, both Pakistan and Bangladesh have encountered challenges in one way or the other, and have come up strong. The countries can learn from each other's experience. For instance, Pakistan can follow the footsteps of Bangladesh in the context of population growth and literacy rate. Other areas where Bangladesh and Pakistan can cooperate and head towards a better future are discussed below.

Common Areas of Cooperation between Bangladesh and Pakistan

The commonality between Pakistan and Bangladesh is religion and culture. These two factors can be a strength in promoting the bilateral relations, particularly the cultural interaction. Cultural diplomacy with Bangladesh therefore needs to be ramped up through the appointment of diplomats with Bengali connections and cultural affinity. The people of Pakistan who have lived in erstwhile East Pakistan and have memories attached to the land need to be encouraged to share their experiences in the media. Through such exchanges, the 'sohni dharti of Pakistan' and the 'sonar Bangla of Bangladesh' can lead to a fusion of soils and souls (Jabbar 2020).

Prospects of film and drama collaboration is another area that needs to be explored. Pakistani dramas can be aired in Bangladesh, likewise, the Bengali dramas can be shown in Pakistan. This soft power can set the stage for people-to-people contact between the two countries. Meanwhile, the collaboration between the film industries of both countries needs to be promoted. This art and cultural interaction will open doors for friendly ties.

At the school level, sports events between Bangladeshi and Pakistani students need to be encouraged. Visiting each other's country for sports will help generate goodwill feelings on both sides.

The positive image building between the two brotherly Muslim countries is important. For that, the role of academia is significant. There is a need to engage academically with the schools of Bangladesh. Pakistan has set up educational institutions in Bangladesh, including the Beaconhouse and the City Schools in Dhaka (Hashmi 2016, 200). To further the idea of people-to-people contact, student-exchange programmes with Bangladesh educational institutions should also be encouraged.

On the travel policy between Bangladesh and Pakistan, it is indeed a pity that there is no direct air link between the two countries (Hafeez 2021). There is a need to ease the business and travel visa regimes. This will facilitate businessmen in both countries to explore economic opportunities in each other's countries. Importantly, with economic interests, the political cooperation will likely move forward.

Pakistan also needs to step up political exchanges with Bangladesh. The lack of interaction between the two governments will further create vacuum and provide space for others to fill in. Thereby, to avoid such a situation, Pakistan needs to reach out to Bangladesh's political leadership for a cooperative partnership.

Bangladesh and Pakistan Can Gain by Growing Economic Ties

Bangladesh-Pakistan bilateral trade is only $600–700 million currently, which is far below the desired potential. During the fiscal year July–November 2022–2023, Pakistan's exports to Bangladesh stood at $365.290 million while the imports from Bangladesh during the same period were $35.622 million (Haque 2023).

Pakistan's lead exports to Bangladesh are 'cotton (which accounted for 73.3 per cent of total exports), salt, sulphur, earth and stone, plastering materials, lime and cement, edible vegetables, raw hides and skins, machinery, inorganic chemicals, man-made staple fibres, plastics, tanning or dyeing extracts and edible fruits and nuts' (Gulzar 2022). As for Pakistan's lead imports from Bangladesh, they include 'vegetable textile fibres (which accounted for 77.5 per cent of total imports)' (Gulzar 2022). According to the Pakistan Business Council (PBC) data, Pakistan can enhance exports to Bangladesh by focusing more in sectors like 'textiles, agriculture, chemicals, base metals, plastics, salt and cement products' (Council). Pakistan also imports raw jute from Bangladesh (Gulzar 2022). In fact, in the 2020–2021 budget, the government of Pakistan removed the additional customs duty on jute import (Khan 2020).

To proceed with the idea of enhanced trading ties, there needs to be a direct shipment of goods between Bangladesh and Pakistan; at present, Pakistan's cargo is shipped via Singapore or Colombo to Chittagong (Gulzar 2022).

The prospects of joint ventures in sectors like agriculture, IT and textiles can be explored between the two countries. Bangladesh's apparel industry has expanded and Bangladesh currently is the second-largest apparel exporter after China (2020). It is pertinent to mention that 'Soorty Textile (BD) Limited is the single largest apparel company with investment from a Pakistani group and is 100 per cent export oriented with more than 6,000 employees' (2020). Thus, the prospects of a Bangladesh–Pakistan joint clothing industry certainly has promise.

In the field of agriculture, Syngenta Bangladesh Limited exports vegetable seeds to Pakistan (Haque 2023). Bangladesh and Pakistan can expand agricultural cooperation, in particular, the agricultural practices can be utilised for provision of diversified crop seeds.

'Blue economy' is another area that can be explored for strengthening trade cooperation. In this regard, Pakistan's coastal belt from Karachi to Gwadar offers the scope for 'marine transportation, fisheries, extraction of hydrocarbons, seabed minerals, fish processing and eco-tourism' (2023).

Free Trade Agreement (FTA)

A 'Bangladesh–Pakistan FTA' was initially proposed in 2002. Later, in 2004, the idea was discussed at the SAARC summit. Bangladesh's demand was free access to Pakistan's markets within one year of signing the FTA. At present, its economic outlook offers the scope for an FTA. Dhaka will be out of the least-developed country (LDC) status by 2026. Given this, Bangladesh has been trying to enhance export revenues and access to newer (improved) markets. The 'Bangladeshi government is reviewing the possibility of trade agreements with forty-four countries, including Preferential Trade Agreements (PTAs)' (Gulzar 2022). Islamabad needs to capitalise upon this opportunity and try to ink an FTA or a PTA with Dhaka (Gulzar 2022).

Joint Mechanism to Safeguard Supply of Water

Bangladesh and Pakistan are both dependent on external sources of water. For Pakistan, a major portion of water is drawn from India and some degree comes from Afghanistan and China. For Bangladesh, the situation is almost similar—the country is dependent on outside water from China (Brahmaputra) and India (Ganga). Given this, both countries could evolve a joint mechanism to safeguard the supply of water from outside sources. In the words of Dr Saleem H. Ali, Professor of Energy and Environment at the University of Delaware, USA, 'Bangladesh and Pakistan, both are dependent on water from outside sources. Both the countries can collaborate on the water dependency issue. The cooperation could be a way by which Bangladesh and Pakistan can have a joint negotiation strategy to deal with both India and China. Pakistan has better relations with China and Bangladesh has better relations with India and may be there is an opportunity for some hydro-diplomacy around this issue. It will be a good win-win prospect for both the regional countries (Ali 2021).

Regional Dimension and Prospects of Cooperation

Pakistan's policy towards bridging the differences with Bangladesh should not entirely rely on the bilateral spectrum. The focus should rather be on the region. Pakistan's former foreign ministry spokeswoman, Aisha Farooqui has said the following about the relationship with Bangladesh:

> We have a very strong historical connection and we want to have cooperative relations between us. As founding members of (the) South Asian Association of Regional Cooperation (SAARC) and for mutual objective of forward movement towards economic prosperity and fulfillment of development goals of the people of South Asia we believe both Pakistan and Bangladesh can play an important role to strengthen SAARC processes for regional cooperation. (Kamruzzaman and Latif 2020)

The cooperation between them towards a secured water channel can also open up prospects of cooperation in other non-traditional security areas, like climate change (Hafeez 2021).

Bangladesh and Pakistan's Strategic Convergence in the Region

Bangladesh's Regional Significance

Bangladesh is located between the Himalayan foothills in the north and the Bay of Bengal in the south. Bangladesh's immediate neighbours are India, and Myanmar. During the Mughal period, the fertile landmass of the Bhati region, present-day Bangladesh was an economic powerhouse. The Mughal Empire accounted for one-fourth of the world's Gross Domestic Product (GDP) till the 17th century (Taufiq-E-Faruque 2018, 4–5). The seaports along the river of Bengal facilitated regional and trans-regional maritime trade of jute, textiles, sugar, indigo, tea and spices to Persia, Middle East and Europe (Taufiq-E-Faruque 2018, 5).

In the prevalent era, Bangladesh's proximity with Southeast Asia makes the country a natural gateway for regional connectivity between South Asia and ASEAN (Association of Southeast Asian Nations) region. In the emerging trans-regional economic cooperation amidst the connectivity by the Belt and Road Initiative (BRI), the seaport of Chittagong along the Bay of Bengal is likely to play a significant role. Likewise, the Gwadar seaport will be a trading hub for Central, South and East Asia. Pakistan and Bangladesh, both are part of the regional connectivity endeavour. This convergence of interest between the two South Asian countries and China needs to be exploited.

South Asia is one of the least integrated regions of the world, in a 'transnational sense' (Kugelman 2023). The region's politics are led by bilateral disputes and confrontational politics. India and Pakistan are the major regional countries. India is about three-quarters of the South Asian region. The frontiers of India meet the borders of all the regional countries. Pakistan is the second largest country in region. Although smaller in size but being a nuclear power, it nevertheless is substantially strong than other South Asian countries. The India-Pakistan relations have failed to progress. The two countries have fought three wars (1948, 1965, 1971) and a limited war at Kargil (1999). Both the countries have divergent political outlook on terrorism. Due to the India-Pakistan conflictual ties, the region's political environment remains tense. The region's economic vehicle—SAARC has failed to deliver economic cooperation and better political ties. South Asia has also been a victim of terrorism, and the wars fought in neighbouring Afghanistan have impacted the region's political security. Resultantly, 'polarization, intolerance, border disputes, economic stress and climate change' have badly impacted the region's peace (Kugelman 2023). While comparing South Asia with other regions of the world, in particular ASEAN, it is evident that the latter has progressed owing to a peaceful regional environment. ASEAN countries have conflicting claims in South China Sea with China but through economic engagement, the regional countries interest is towards collective growth and progress. The net outcome is economic progress that is in the larger interest of region.

Seeing the development of ASEAN, South Asia can also tread the path towards economic progress. However, to become a developed region, the political will of regional countries is needed. The South Asian countries will need to give up shortsightedness and adopt an inclusive approach to ensure holistic regional growth.

In the recent past, the South Asian countries have started to align their political outlook with economic security and connectivity. In this regard, the electricity-sharing arrangements involving India, Nepal and Bangladesh, and the rail projects involving Pakistan, Afghanistan and Uzbekistan are efforts directed towards connectivity and energy cooperation (Kugelman 2023). The building of seaports (Gwadar, Chittagong, Hambantota, Sittwe) is yet another positive move towards integration and trade cooperation. The trading links will open up the region to neighbouring countries and enhance the prospects of South, Central and East Asia connectivity. This will provide South Asia with an opportunity to improve its prevailing poor socioeconomic indicators.

With the operation of the China–Pakistan Economic Corridor (CPEC), the influx of new political players in the region is expected. In particular, China's growing role in South Asia, as apparent from seaports and corridors, will make it an active player in the region. The

CPEC is an integral part of the larger Belt Road Initiative or BRI (which will link 80 countries). Geographically, CPEC will commence from the deep seaport of Gwadar and terminate at Kashgar in the Xinjiang province of China, and from there, it will fan out into Central Asia. Clearly, CPEC is an economic dividend for South Asia. However, to translate regional connectivity into political gains, a regional approach is needed. Observing Pakistan and Bangladesh's regional outlook in view of the emerging economic corridors, both countries appear to be on the same page. Bangladesh has 'formalized its participation' in BRI (15 October 2016) (Gulzar 2022). Anand Kumar, associate fellow at the Manohar Parrikar Institute for Defence Studies and Analysis sees the evolving ties between Bangladesh and China as being geo-strategically driven (Kumar 2014, 652–667). China's submarine base in the Bay of Bengal (Hannan 2020) and access to seaports of Chittagong and Mongla merit consideration in this regard (Singh 2022). The Chittagong seaport is a major pivot through the Indian Ocean and China needs the seaport to activate the Silk Road Economic Belt and the 21st Century Maritime Silk Road (Taufiq-E-Faruque 2018). Besides this, through the land-based connectivity with Bangladesh, the oil and gas pipelines from Chittagong seaport to Kunming (Myanmar territory) will ease the transport of energy resources in southwestern China (Taufiq-E-Faruque 2018, 7).

Bangladesh is part of the Bangladesh–China–India–Myanmar (BCIM) bloc as well (Taufiq-E-Faruque 2018, 7). Its economic growth is also laudable, seeing as it is the 35th largest economy in the world ['Bangladesh Invites Pakistan's Businessmen to Explore Investment Opportunities', PkRevenue.com (*Pakistan Revenue*), March 10, 2023. https://pkrevenue.com/bangladesh-invites-pakistans-businessmen-to-explore-investment-opportunities/]. Shijin Chan, the former vice president of the Asian Development Bank (ADB), says that Bangladesh is one of the fastest-growing economies in the region. Notably, the poverty level in the country has reduced to 24.6 per cent (Chowdhury 2021).

Bangladesh's economic growth and geographic proximity with ASEAN region are important in terms of South and East Asia connectivity. Bangladesh can be a bridge between South Asia and ASEAN. Moreover, Bangladeshi businesses through the regional corridors like CPEC can explore the markets of 'West and Central China, Central Asia and the Middle East' (Gulzar 2022). These credentials merit consideration in Bangladesh's role in regional connectivity. More importantly, Bangladesh also has an opportunity to develop its relationship with China in the regional domain as it will enhance the former's position. Economic cooperation with China ideally brings Pakistan and Bangladesh on the same page in terms of regional connectivity—Pakistan's Gwadar seaport can be an attractive destination for Bangladeshi businesses to reach out to the adjoining regions (Hassan 2021). Against this backdrop, Bangladesh and Pakistan can be the lead players in regional connectivity, resulting in a shared strategic consonance. Both countries need to tune their economies in line with regional connectivity trends (Rafi 2022).

With regional connectivity, the South Asian countries economic engagements with adjoining regions'/countries will enhance. In particular, China is likely to emerge as an active player in region. China's economic growth in region will have acceptability from some countries like Pakistan, Bangladesh and Sri Lanka. Whilst, some regional quarters will be opposed to China's enhanced role in region. In particular, India will not support China's presence in Arabian Sea and Bay of Bengal. As this will shift the balance of power more towards the East Asian player. However, to grow in an era of trans-regionalism, economic connectivity is a must, and South Asia needs to connect with other regions of the world. Thereby, to materialize regional connectivity and reap economic dividends, cooperation at regional level is essential. Both Bangladesh and Pakistan being littoral states along the Indian Ocean are significant countries in regional connectivity. Thus, it is high time that both Bangladesh and Pakistan take a lead role in enhancing their connectivity and economic integration.

Bangladesh-Pakistan maitri (friendship) Zindabad.

Note

1 Migrants from the Indian state of Bihar, the Bihari population came to East Pakistan in 1947. They were an educated and well-to-do community. In the aftermath of 1971, however, Biharis lost their social status. Bengalis took them as enemies and at present, around 3,00,000 of them are living in relief camps in Bangladesh. In 1974, Pakistan accepted 1,70,000 Bihari refugees. The repatriation process has since stalled (Bashir 2023).

References

Agha, K.A. *Witness to Carnage 1971*. Islamabad: Print-X Pvt Limited, 2021.
Ahmar, M. 'How 1970 Elections led to the Break-up'. *The Express Tribune*, December 11, 2020.
———. 'Pakistan-Bangladesh Relations—Prospects and Way Forward'. *IPRI Journal* 12, no. 1, (2022): 163–167.

Ali, S.H. 'Is Climate Change Going to Drive National Security?' IPRI Lecture Series, 2021.

ANI. 'Pakistan's Attempt to Reconcile with Bangladesh Will Fall Flat'. *The Times of India*, July 27, 2020.

Aziz, Q. *Blood and Tears*. Karachi Publications Division: United Press of Pakistan Ltd, 1974.

'Bangladesh Invites Pakistani Investment in Export Industries'. *The News International*, January 29, 2020.

'Bangladesh Invites Pakistan's Businessmen to Explore Investment Opportunities'. *Pakistan Revenue*, March 10, 2023.

Bashir, Faizan. 'Ignoring Those Who Stood by Pakistan'. *The Dawn*, August 13, 2023.

Bhanu, M. 'Significance of Momen-Khar Meeting'. *Daily Times*, February 7, 2023.

Chowdhury, J. 'Why and How Bangladesh is Moving Forward?' *Pakistan Today*, December 24, 2021. https://www.pakistantoday.com.pk/2021/12/24/why-and-how-bangladesh-is-moving-forward/#:~:text=Bangladesh%20is%20moving%20from%20a,employment%20for%2020%20million%20people.

Chowdhury, I.A. 'Bangladesh-Pakistan: A Palpable Thaw'. *Institute of South Asian Studies (ISAS)* 637, no. 5 (2020).

Datta, Sreeradha. *India-Bangladesh Bonhomie at 50: 1971 and the Present*. p. 5. Vivekananda International Foundation, New Delhi, 2022. https://www.vifindia.org/sites/default/files/India-Bangladesh-Bonhomie-at-50-1971-and-the-Present.pdf.

'Friend and Neighbour: On India-Bangladesh Virtual Summit'. *The Hindu*, December 19, 2020.

Gulzar, N. 'Revitalizing Pakistan-Bangladesh Trade Cooperation in Pursuit of Free Trade Agreement'. Atlantic Council, February 15, 2022.

Habib, Haroon. 'New Liberation War'. *Himal Southasian*, August 1, 2010.

Hafeez, J. 'Healthy Pakistan-Bangladesh Ties Will Help Both Countries'. *Arab News*, December 24, 2021.

Hannan, A. 'Too Woo and Entice'. *Dhaka Tribune*, October 21, 2020.

Haque, E. 'Pakistan, Bangladesh Can Boost Ties Through Seed Diplomacy', March 12, 2023.

Hasan, M.T. 'Numbers Do Not Lie (But They Hide)'. *Dhaka Tribune*, September 5, 2020.

Hashmi, A.M. *1971: Fact and Fiction Views and Perceptions in Pakistan, India and Bangladesh*. Islamabad: Khursheed Printers Pvt Limited, 2016.

———. 'Pakistan Should Not Apologise to Bangladesh on 1971 (Islamabad considers the issue settled and fully resolved, with the conclusion of the Bangladesh-India-Pakistan Agreement of 9 April 1974)'. *Academia*, September 18, 2021.

Hassan, P. 'A Golden Chance for Pakistan'. *Pakistan Today*, October 31, 2021.

'How to Positively Transform Ties with Bangladesh?' *The Express Tribune*, December 26, 2021.

Independent News Pakistan (INP). 'Truth Must be Told about 1971 Genocide of Bengalis'. *The Express Tribune*, November 16, 2021.
E-International Relations. 'Interview – Michael Kugelman', written by Nachiket Midha, March 4, 2023. https://www.e-ir.info/2023/03/04/interview-michael-kugelman/.
Jabbar, J. 'From 1971 to 2021'. *The Dawn*, December 16, 2020.
Janjua, H. 'Should Pakistan Apologize to Bangladesh for the 1971 War?'. DW, March 30, 2021.
Kamruzzaman, M. and A. Latif. 'Bangladesh's No Foe Diplomacy Grows Ties with Pakistan'. *Politics, World, Asia-Pacific*, July 30, 2020.
Kamruzzaman, M. 'Bishwa Ijtema Opens Income Streams for Bangladeshis'. *Politics, World, Asia-Pacific*, January 20, 2021.
Khan, M.Z. 'Plan Evolved to Boost Export of Processed Jute'. *The Dawn*, July 23, 2020.
Khan, N. 'Veteran Journalists Recall 1974 OIC Lahore Summit Where Pakistan Finally Recognized Bangladesh'. *Arab News*, March 21, 2022.
Kumar, A. 'Domestic Politics of Bangladesh and India-Bangladesh Relations'. *Strategic Analysis, Routledge Taylor and Francis Group*, (September 2014): 652–667.
Malik, R.H. 'Bangladesh-Pakistan Relations: A Beacon of Hope for Regional Prosperity'. *Muslim Institute*, n.d.
Mehmood, A., S. Farooq, and N. Awan, 'Bangladesh-Pakistan Relations: A Hostage to History'. *American International Journal of Contemporary Research* 5, no. 2 (2015): 68.
'Mukti Bahini: The Forgotten Terrorists'. *Voice of East*, December 13, 2022.
'Pakistan, Bangladesh Agree to Strengthen Ties, Pakistan Today'. *Pakistan Today*, October 25, 2021.
Pattanaik, S.S. 'Hefajat-e-Islami and the Politics of Islamism in Bangladesh'. Manahar Parrikar Institute for Defence Studies and Analysis (IDSA), December 11, 2020.
'President Regrets 71 War Excesses: Trade Accords to be Signed Today', *The Dawn*, July 30, 2002. https://www.dawn.com/news/50327/president-regrets-71-war-excesses-trade-accords-to-be-signed-today.
Quibria, M.G. *Bangladesh's Road to Long-Term Economic Prosperity: Risks and Challenges*, 5–7. Switzerland: Palgrave Macmillan, 2019.
Rafi, A.E. 'Pakistan and Bangladesh Strategic Consonance'. *The Express Tribune*, January 6, 2022.
———. 'Pakistan-Bangladesh Relations'. Focus, Institute of Regional Studies (IRS) (2022).
Raina, A. *Inside RAW: The Story of India's Secret Service*, 90. New Delhi: Vikas Publishing House. 1981.
Rehman, T. 'From Revolutionaries to Visionless Parties: Leftist Politics in Bangladesh'. Carnegie Endowment for International Peace, September 6, 2022.
Saikia, Y. *Women, War and the Making of Bangladesh Remembering 1971*, 41. Durham: Duke University Press, 2011.

Saleem, F. 'Mukti Bahini, the Forgotten Terrorists'. The News International, March 14, 2016.
Sehgal, I. 'Pakistan and Bangladesh'. *Daily Times*, December 10, 2020.
Siddiqi, B. *Becoming Good Muslim*, 39. Singapore: Springer Nature Singapore, 2018.
Singh, A.I. 'Is India Slipping Behind? Bangladesh Reveals India's Challenged Pre-eminence in the Bay of Bengal'. *The Times of India*, October 20, 2022.
Syed, Baqir Sajjad. 'In Rare Call to Hasina, Imran Urges Closer Ties with Bangladesh', *The Dawn*, July 23, 2020.
Taufiq-E-Faruque. 'Sino-Indian Geostrategic Competition: Bangladesh Perspective'. *ELK Asia Pacific Journal of Social Sciences* 5, no. 1, (2018): 4–5.
'Trade and Investment Opportunities in a Pakistan–Bangladesh FTA'. The Pakistan Business Council, n.d.
Yasmin, L. 'Bangladesh-India Tussles'. Quarterly *Magazine of South Asian Journalists and Scholars,* (July–September 2004): 91–93.
Zaidi, S.K.A. 'Special Report: The Breakup of Pakistan, 1969-1971'. *The Dawn*. December 16, 2017.

12

BANGLADESH–US BILATERAL RELATIONS

Nilanthi Samaranayake

Since Bangladesh's independence in 1971, the country's relationship with the US has developed significantly. Washington was not supportive of Bangladesh's independence due to its concern about 'the dismemberment' of Pakistan and 'allied commitments' to Pakistan's defence (Raghavan 2013). The context of the Cold War meant Washington viewed the 1971 war between India and Pakistan through the lens of competition with what was then the Soviet Union, regardless of the implications for Bangladesh. Even in 2022, memories about the early years of the relationship are not distant, as seen in recent comments by the Awami League's (AL) General Secretary Obaidul Quader, 'We have bitter experiences with the US. We saw their role in 1971 and 1975. Despite all these incidents, we want good relations with the US' (*Dhaka Tribune* 2022).

Following the establishment of diplomatic relations in 1972, the two countries have largely cultivated a positive relationship across multiple areas of cooperation. Prominent examples from previous decades include the US conducting two major disaster-response operations after cyclones struck the country in 1991 and 2007. Meanwhile, Bangladesh provided important diplomatic and military support to the US-led coalition after Iraq's invasion of Kuwait in 1990 (Uddin 2021).

More recently, the eighth US-Bangladesh Partnership Dialogue was concluded in March 2022 and continues to span critical areas of trade and investment, security cooperation, and democracy and governance. Even beyond those areas, bilateral cooperation can be seen in a new resettlement initiative to help alleviate Dhaka's burden of hosting more than one million Rohingya refugees on Bangladesh's territory (US Department of State 2022). Furthermore, in response to the Covid-19 pandemic, the US provided Bangladesh with 61 million vaccine doses—the most to any country from Washington (US Embassy in Bangladesh 2022).

This chapter considers US–Bangladesh interactions in the realms of economics, security and diplomacy, highlighting both areas of cooperation and potential issues that could complicate the trend of positive ties between the two countries. The conclusion then focuses on how both countries are increasingly diverging on democratic governance and will need to manage this area carefully in order to enable cooperation to grow in other areas of the relationship.

Economics

Given its difficult origins, Bangladesh was known for years for its poverty and challenging environmental circumstances. However, the country has made significant progress over the years to reduce poverty and raise human developmental indicators. Widely viewed as an economic and development success story, Bangladesh is expected to graduate from the status of least developed country (LDC) in 2026 and seeks to reach upper-middle-income status by 2031 (World Bank 2022).

A key to Bangladesh's economic growth has been the striking success of its garments industry, which has constituted roughly 80 per cent of the country's total exports (CIA 2022). Of note, the US consistently ranks as the top export market for Bangladesh. In 2019, it received 15 per cent of the country's exports (CIA 2022), thereby making this $10 billion bilateral trade relationship critical to the success of Bangladesh's economy (United States Trade Representative 2022). Moreover, the United States Agency for International Development (USAID) has had a large programme in Bangladesh, therefore illustrating the importance of the country's development to the US (Association for Diplomatic Studies and Training 2014). Within Bangladesh, USAID has been characterised as 'an essential partner in promoting transparency and accountability in the public sector Bangladesh, along with its mandated work as a vital development partner in Bangladesh's growth' (Khan 2021) Since 1972, the US has provided roughly $8 billion in development assistance, making Bangladesh the largest recipient of American assistance in Asia (US Department of State 2022; Haas 2022).

Labour rights have been a priority in US policy, including towards Bangladesh. An additional interest is that women make up a majority of Bangladesh's garments workforce, with estimates ranging from 58 per cent to 80 per cent (Frayer 2022; ADST 2014). In fact, Washington suspended Bangladesh's benefits under the Generalized System of Preferences (GSP) in 2013 due to concerns about worker safety following deaths and injuries in two major industrial accidents, the Tazreen Fashions fire in 2012 and the Rana Plaza building collapse in 2013. Bangladesh continues to seek restoration of GSP status, most recently in December 2022 during a meeting of the US–Bangladesh Trade and Investment Cooperation Forum Agreement Council.

In terms of foreign direct investment (FDI), the US is the largest source of FDI to Bangladesh (*Prothom Alo* 2022). In 2021, the US Chamber of Commerce launched the US–Bangladesh Business Council to advance investment and trade ties between the two countries. The following year, a delegation of US business leaders headed by Jay R. Pryor, vice president of business development for Chevron Corporation, visited Bangladesh to explore opportunities across various sectors. However, concerns about worker safety have extended beyond trade relations to impede development financing from the US Development Finance Corporation (DFC). In May 2022, US officials explained that Bangladesh will not receive DFC funding due to these labour concerns (*Prothom Alo* 2022).

Despite these setbacks, the outlook for bilateral economic relations appears strong as seen by efforts to expand trade and investment activities. Still, the combined effects of the Covid-19 pandemic, Russia's war in Ukraine and climate change have increased the headwinds for Bangladesh in its path out of the LDC list and into upper-middle-income status. Similar to Pakistan and Sri Lanka in 2022, Bangladesh requested assistance from the International Monetary Fund (IMF) as it became concerned about troubling decreases in its foreign exchange reserves. Dhaka reached a staff-level agreement with the IMF in November 2022 for $4.5 billion: $3.2 billion under the Extended Credit Facility and the Extended Fund Facility and $1.3 billion under the Resilience and Sustainability Facility.

Nevertheless, Bangladesh maintains a resilient and growing economy. Its economic ties with the US can be augmented through greater coordination and advancements on worker safety to unleash more American investment. Bangladesh Foreign Minister AK Abdul Momen observed that most US investment in the country has gone towards the energy sector but suggested considering other sectors (US Department of State 2022). Development of Bangladesh's infrastructure could be a next-step goal in economic relations, as experts have observed the lack of US investment in infrastructure in their country (Khan 2021).

Security

Although Bangladesh is not a US treaty ally, cooperation between the two countries on security is strong in several areas. In the past decade, Bangladesh has taken significant steps to enhance its national security. The country resolved its maritime delimitation dispute with India in 2014 through international arbitration and concluded a land boundary agreement with India the following year. Bangladesh has also taken steps to expand and modernise military platforms under its Forces Goal 2030 project (Samaranayake 2016). For example, the navy has contracted with a Canadian firm to design landing craft tanks that will be built domestically, and is developing an undersea force after purchasing two submarines from China. Bangladesh is taking steps to improve its military cooperation with other countries as well, including through cooperation with the US as a partner to augment its security.

The country has historically ranked among the top contributors to UN Peacekeeping Forces. As of July 2023, Bangladesh contributed 7,279—the most troops and police of any country (UN Peacekeeping 2023). As a result of this deep commitment, Washington has paid particular attention to Bangladesh (ADST 2014). This includes providing roughly $44 million since 2005 to support its peacekeeping capabilities (US Department of State 2022). Both countries' militaries participate in training and exercises. Examples include the Tiger Shark and Joint Combined Exchange Training exercises between their special operations forces in 2022. The Bangladesh navy participates in the US Cooperation Afloat Readiness and Training (CARAT) exercise. Beginning in 2011, it became the first South Asian navy to participate in this exercise series. The US has also transferred excess defence articles, including two retired US coastguard cutters serving as the Bangladesh Navy's largest ships, as well as donated patrol boats to the Bangladesh army, coast guard and navy (US Department of State 2022; *New Age* 2021). Finally, senior US military officials sometimes pay visits to Bangladesh to support its leadership in promoting international security. In 2016, the commander of the US Pacific Fleet Admiral Scott Swift travelled to Dhaka when the Bangladesh navy chaired the Indian Ocean Naval Symposium, and Admiral Harry Harris, commander of US Pacific Command, visited Bangladesh in 2017 for the dedication of the Bangladesh Institute of Peace Support Operations Training (BIPSOT), a new multinational facility for training peacekeepers in UN Peace Support Operations.

As the Biden administration executes the US Indo-Pacific Strategy, Bangladesh will remain an important non-allied partner for the US in the coming years. As an example of its commitment to legal norms, Bangladesh sought to resolve its maritime delimitation disputes with both Myanmar and India through the use of international legal venues. As a result of these efforts and the ensuing decisions from 2012 and 2014, Bangladesh helped make the Bay of Bengal a model of international order for the rest of the Indian Ocean and the wider Indo-Pacific region (Samaranayake 2022). The US ambassador to Bangladesh, Peter Haas, even commented on Bangladesh's alignment with the US regarding the latter's Free and Open Indo-Pacific approach:

Bangladesh has made important contributions to this cause. For instance, by committing to the peaceful resolution of its land and maritime border disputes, Bangladesh has made the Bay of Bengal an example for the world to follow. (US Embassy in Bangladesh 2022)

By complimenting Bangladesh on its efforts to seek dispute resolution, Washington is casting a spotlight on behaviour that it seeks to support in the broader region—especially by a non-treaty allied partner.

To operationalise this strategic-level alignment between their military forces, the US is seeking Bangladesh's signature on two foundational defence agreements: the General Security of Military Information Agreement (GSOMIA) and the Acquisition and Cross-Servicing Agreement (ACSA) (US Embassy in Bangladesh 2022). The GSOMIA permits the two governments to set terms for sharing military information, and the ACSA enables the exchange of logistics such as food and fuel between the two countries' militaries. Within South Asia, the US has concluded both agreements with India (2002 and 2016, respectively), and has concluded ACSAs with Sri Lanka and Maldives (2017 and 2010, respectively) (US Department of State 2020). Bangladesh is reportedly reviewing the proposed agreements (*The Business Standard* 2022).

Regarding US security assistance to Bangladesh, the state department has provided $78.45 million for Foreign Military Financing (FMF) and $14.5 million for International Military Education and Training (IMET) since 2014 (US Department of State 2023). Beyond the $54.8 million in bilateral FMF assistance, the state department has developed a Bay of Bengal Initiative with $23.6 million for the FMF to build regional security capacity as well. This activity suggests the ongoing importance that multiple administrations have placed on the relationship with Bangladesh and the security of the Bay of Bengal as part of the US strategy of engaging the Indo-Pacific region.

Finally, the US has played a significant role in addressing the non-traditional security threats confronting Bangladesh. These include vulnerability to cyclones, flooding, climate change and earthquakes. Washington has provided relief after major cyclones struck Bangladesh. In 1991, when Cyclone Marian struck, the US military provided the largest disaster response through Operation Sea Angel. Later in 2007, when Cyclone Sidr struck Bangladesh, the US military again provided relief under Operation Sea Angel II (Samaranayake et al. 2014). Beyond disaster response operations, Washington has funded the construction of coastal crisis management centres and cyclone shelters throughout Bangladesh (Samaranayake et al. 2014). More recently, Washington donated the most vaccine doses to Bangladesh than any other country during the Covid-19 pandemic (US Embassy in Bangladesh 2022).

The outlook of Bangladesh–US security relations thus appears to be strong and growing. The two countries continue their operational exchanges and cooperation on defence platforms. Meanwhile, Bangladesh has increased its capacity to withstand environmental crises such as cyclones and floods, and has even become a provider of relief to the smaller South Asian neighbours, Sri Lanka and Maldives (Samaranayake 2022).

Diplomacy

Whereas Bangladesh–US ties are strong in terms of economics and security, diplomatic relations overall have seen lows and highs during the past 50 years. The US support for Pakistan before Bangladesh's independence strained the foundations for the superpower's relationship with Bangladesh, which was formally established in 1972 (Ali 2010). Yet, both countries' ties had improved under the presidency of General Hussain Muhammad Ershad, who built support over the years for his leadership in Washington, according to former foreign secretary Hemayet Uddin (2021). Bangladesh's support in 1990 to a US-led coalition in the Persian Gulf, including its diplomacy among six Muslim countries to resolve the Iraq–Kuwait crisis, was recognised personally by then President George H.W. Bush in a conversation with President Ershad (Uddin 2021).

In the contemporary era, the US emphasis on 'mutual respect for the rule of law, democracy, and human rights' in its relationship with Bangladesh has posed complications for diplomatic relations (US Department of State 2022). After the 2014 general election, which was boycotted by most of the country's opposition parties, Washington called for an additional election process:

> The United States is disappointed by the recent Parliamentary elections in Bangladesh. With more than half of the seats uncontested and most of the remainder offering only token opposition, the results of the just-concluded elections do not appear to credibly express the will of the Bangladeshi people. While it remains to be seen what form the new government will take, United States commitment to supporting the people of Bangladesh remains undiminished. To that end, we encourage the Government of Bangladesh and opposition parties to engage in immediate dialogue to find a way to hold as soon as possible elections that are free, fair, peaceful, and credible, reflecting the will of the Bangladeshi people. (Harf 2014)

Washington even diverged with New Delhi in its communications leading up to Bangladesh's elections and about the result (Samaranayake 2014). This was notable at a time when the US was focused on actively building a strategic partnership and joint security approach with India in the wider Indo-Pacific region (Biswal 2014).

Then US ambassador Dan Mozena received criticism within Bangladesh in 2014 (bdnews24 2014). In an oral history reflecting on her tenure in Dhaka nearly a decade earlier, former ambassador Patricia Butenis provides insight into the challenge of representing US policy interests in the context of Bangladesh's heated politics:

> Our growing concern during my time was the increasing violence that accompanied election campaigning and voting. Each party had what they called "muscle men", basically their own thugs, young men who would attack opposition members, intimidate people, extort support, etc. So to the extent I had any marching orders, they were to urge both parties to eschew violence and to have what we called free, fair, credible elections in 2007. (ADST 2014)

The topic of democratic governance has increased as a flashpoint in the relationship. Since 2021, there has been a deterioration of bilateral ties in this area due to the heightened focus on democracy under the Biden administration, which is evident in key strategy documents (The White House 2022; US Department of Defense 2022).

The effects have already been seen in US policy toward Bangladesh. For example, Washington did not extend an invitation to Bangladesh in November 2021 to participate in the Summit for Democracy the following month. Given the overall positive state of US–Bangladesh relations and with more than 100 invited participants, this was a noteworthy omission (US Department of State 2021). In response, Bangladesh Foreign Minister Abdul Momen downplayed the lack of invitation:

> We will ensure that none dies in any election in the future. If we have any weaknesses, we will try to overcome them. So, there is nothing to worry about if we are invited to the democracy conference or not. (*The Business Standard* 2021)

Shortly after this dent in relations, Washington made a more consequential decision. In December 2021, the US Department of the Treasury's Office of Foreign Assets Control imposed sanctions on Bangladesh's Rapid Action Battalion and seven current and former officials for human rights abuses (US Department of the Treasury 2021). The sanctions were criticised at the highest level of the Bangladeshi government. Prime Minister Sheikh Hasina characterised this move as 'very much an abominable act' (*Dhaka Tribune* 2022).

Diplomatic relations became even more strained in 2022. In April, with the sanctions still a heated topic of discussion, the state department was critical of Bangladesh in its annual Country Reports on Human Rights Practices. In its first paragraph, the report assesses Bangladesh's December 2018 election:

> Bangladesh's constitution provides for a parliamentary form of government that consolidates most power in the Office of the Prime Minister. In a December 2018 parliamentary election, Sheikh Hasina and her Awami League party won a third consecutive five-year term that kept her in office as prime minister. This election was not considered free and fair by observers reportedly due to irregularities, including ballot-box stuffing and intimidation of opposition polling agents and voters. (US Department of State 2021)

The report also discussed former prime minister and opposition party leader Khaleda Zia in its section on 'Political Prisoners and Detainees', citing experts' conclusion about 'a political ploy to remove the leader of the opposition from the electoral process' (US Department of State 2021). In response to the report, Bangladesh's Home Minister Asaduzzaman Khan Kamal asserted that the US 'misrepresented the facts in its report' and took issue with its methodology (*The Daily Star* 2022).

The US representation within Bangladesh has also emphasised democratic governance. In early December 2022, Ambassador Haas discussed US concern about killings and political violence in Bangladesh (US Embassy in Bangladesh 2022). In response, the Awami League general secretary Obaidul Quader advised the US representative, 'Do not make unwanted comments or interfere in any issue of Bangladesh', and then spoke about election fraud in the US (*Dhaka Tribune* 2022). Quader emphasised Bangladesh's desire for positive ties with the US.

Towards the end of 2022, US concerns became far more serious, expanding beyond the fairness of Bangladesh's elections and political violence to include the safety of US embassy personnel. After a trip to a missing opposition leader's home, the US ambassador ended his meeting early due to deteriorating security and when 'protestors surrounded the Ambassador's vehicle', according to the US Embassy in Dhaka (2022). As a result of concern for the US ambassador's safety, US Assistant Secretary of State Donald Lu reportedly discussed the topic with Bangladesh's ambassador to the US Muhammad Imran in Washington (*The Daily Star* 2022). A week later, Deputy Secretary of

State Wendy Sherman conveyed concerns about 'the safety and security of U.S. embassy personnel' to Bangladesh's state minister for foreign affairs Shahriar Alam (US Department of State 2022).

The upcoming general election, planned for January 2024, has the potential to present additional challenges for the US–Bangladesh relationship after an already difficult period. Further deterioration of the diplomatic relationship over the issue of democratic governance could undermine relations in other areas, including economic and security cooperation.

Conclusion

This chapter has examined three major realms of activity between the US and Bangladesh: economic, security and diplomatic relations. The two countries continue to build their economic and security ties. Bangladesh seeks to resume full trade benefits via GSP status with its top export partner. Furthermore, greater US FDI especially beyond the energy sector represents another goal. The US is also seeking out Bangladesh's partnership and stability in the Bay of Bengal under the US Indo-Pacific Strategy. A next-step goal towards this objective appears to be receiving Bangladesh's final signature on a foundational defence agreement: GSOMIA.

Beyond these areas of cooperation, there will continue to be areas where the two countries' interests and actions do not always align. This includes Washington's condemnation of Russia's February 2022 invasion of Ukraine and Bangladesh's abstention on the March 2022 UN General Assembly resolution criticising the invasion. Meanwhile, Dhaka has sought greater assistance from the US on managing the one million Rohingya refugees from Myanmar on Bangladesh's soil. But these differences are not significant enough to disrupt the bilateral relationship.

As both countries implement their foreign policy visions in line with their national interests and work to build bilateral cooperation, democratic governance remains the most challenging issue for Bangladesh and the US to navigate. Along the way, they will need to be mindful of each other's redlines. The Biden administration's heightened focus on democracy under the new era of strategic competition with non-democracies like China and Russia has brought this issue to the forefront in its relations with other states, including Bangladesh (The White House 2022). At the same time, actions such as police firing on protestors and arresting opposition leaders and activists have heightened international scrutiny of Bangladesh's democratic institutions (Rahman 2022; Hasnat and Mashal

2022). As Bangladesh's January 2024 elections approach, Washington has raised the temperature on Dhaka through high-level visits; statements on human rights, freedom of expression and democratic elections; and new policy. In particular, Secretary of State Antony J. Blinken announced a visa policy in May 2023 to restrict the entry of Bangladeshi citizens who undermine the election process. Meanwhile, Sheikh Hasina publicly criticised the US for its emphasis on democracy and human rights in Bangladesh, suggesting bias for an opposition party. At the time of this writing, there is much uncertainty about the conduct of the forthcoming elections and potential implications for bilateral relations.

Consequently, democratic governance is the issue that both countries will need to address as they collaborate on other areas of national interest. As policymakers in Dhaka and Washington examine bilateral ties at the 50-year mark, they should work to ensure that disputes in the diplomatic sphere do not reverse progress towards achieving economic and security goals that are mutually beneficial for the US and Bangladesh.

References

'2021 Country Reports on Human Rights Practices: Bangladesh'. US Department of State, April 12, 2022. https://www.state.gov/reports/2021-country-reports-on-human-rights-practices/bangladesh.

Ali, S.M. *Understanding Bangladesh*, 82–83, 85, 93, 110. London: C. Hurst & Co. 2010.

'Ambassador Haas's Remarks at BIISS Seminar on U.S.–Bangladesh Relations'. Bangladesh Institute for International and Strategic Studies (BIISS) Seminar on Bangladesh and the United States Relations: Moving Towards Enhanced Cooperation and Partnership, US Embassy in Bangladesh, April 24, 2022. https://bd.usembassy.gov/bangladesh-and-the-united-states-relations-moving-towards-enhanced-cooperation-and-partnership.

'Bangladesh'. The CIA World Factbook, December 13, 2022. https://www.cia.gov/the-world-factbook/countries/bangladesh/.

'Bangladesh Not Eligible to Receive DFC Funding from the US'. *Prothom Alo*, May 12, 2022. https://en.prothomalo.com/bangladesh/bangladesh-not-eligible-to-receive-dfc-funding-from-the-us.

'Bangladesh–US Security Dialogue in Washington on Wednesday'. *The Business Standard*, April 4, 2022. https://www.tbsnews.net/bangladesh/bangladesh-us-security-dialogue-washington-wednesday-396770.

Biswal, N.D. 'U.S. Foreign Policy in South Asia: A Vision for Prosperity and Security'. Assistant Secretary, Bureau of South and Central Asian Affairs, Harvard University, Kennedy School of Government, Cambridge, April 16, 2014. https://2009-2017.state.gov/p/sca/rls/rmks/2014/224914.htm.

Butenis, Patricia A. Interview by Charles Stuart Kennedy. Association for Diplomatic Studies and Training, Foreign Affairs Oral History Project, September 11, 2014. https://adst.org/OH%20TOCs/Butenis.Patricia.pdf.

'Deputy Secretary of State Sherman's Call with State Minister for Foreign Affairs of Bangladesh Shahriar Alam'. US Department of State, December 22, 2022. https://www.state.gov/deputy-secretary-of-state-shermans-call-with-state-minister-for-foreign-affairs-of-bangladesh-shahriar-alam.

Frayer, L. 'How Bangladesh Went from an Economic Miracle to Needing IMF Help'. National Public Radio, November 9, 2022. https://www.npr.org/2022/11/09/1134543648/bangladesh-economy-imf-loan.

Haas, P. '50th Anniversary of the U.S.–Bangladesh Partnership: Looking Forward to the Next 50 Years'. April 4, 2022. https://bd.usembassy.gov/27675.

Harf, M. 'Parliamentary Elections in Bangladesh'. Deputy Department Spokesperson, Office of the Spokesperson, US Department of State, Washington, DC. January 6, 2014, https://2009-2017.state.gov/r/pa/prs/ps/2014/01/219331.htm.

Hasnat, S. and M. Mashal. 'Bangladesh Arrests Opposition Leaders as Crackdown Intensifies'. *The New York Times*. December 9, 2022. https://www.nytimes.com/2022/12/09/world/asia/bangladesh-protests-election.html.

Khan, S.E. 'The Bangladesh–US Bilateral Relations: Rethinking through the Blurring Space between Geopolitics and Geoeconomics in the Indo-Pacific Region'. *The AmCham Journal* 15, no. 3, (July–September 2021): 22–23.

'National Defense Strategy of the United States of America'. US Department of Defense, October 27, 2022. https://media.defense.gov/2022/Oct/27/2003103845/-1/-1/1/2022-NATIONAL-DEFENSE-STRATEGY-NPR-MDR.PDF.

'National Security Strategy'. The White House, October 12, 2022. https://www.whitehouse.gov/wp-content/uploads/2022/10/Biden-Harris-Administrations-National-Security-Strategy-10.2022.pdf.

'Nothing to Be Worried for Not Invited to US Democracy Summit: FM'. *The Business Standard*, November 26, 2021. https://www.tbsnews.net/bangladesh/nothing-be-worried-not-invited-us-democracy-summit-fm-335047.

'PM Hasina Slams Sanctions on RAB, Says It's "Abominable Move"'. *Dhaka Tribune*, March 28, 2022. https://www.dhakatribune.com/bangladesh/2022/03/28/pm-hasina-slams-sanctions-on-rab-says-its-abominable-move.

'PM Hasina Urges US Companies to Boost Investment in Bangladesh'. *Prothom Alo*, May 10, 2022. https://en.prothomalo.com/bangladesh/government/pm-hasina-urges-us-companies-to-boost-investment-in-bangladesh.

'Quader to Envoy: Do Not Undermine US–Bangladesh Ties with Comments on Local Politics'. *Dhaka Tribune*. December 9, 2022. https://www.dhakatribune.com/foreign-affairs/2022/12/09/quader-to-envoy-do-not-undermine-us-bangladesh-ties-with-comments-on-local-politics.

Raghavan, S. *1971: A Global History of the Creation of Bangladesh*, 243, 250. Cambridge: Harvard University Press. 2013.

Rahman, S.A. 'Bangladesh Arrests Thousands of Political Activists ahead of Opposition Protest'. *Voice of America*, December 7, 2022. https://www.

voanews.com/a/bangladesh-arrests-thousands-of-political-activists-ahead-of-opposition-protest/6867314.html.

'Remarks by U.S. Ambassador Haas at Bay of Bengal Conversations Panel on Untangling the Myriad of Multilateral Frameworks in the Indo-Pacific'. Pan-Pacific Sonargaon Dhaka, US Embassy in Bangladesh, November 21, 2022. https://bd.usembassy.gov/28844.

'Resettlement Initiative for Vulnerable Rohingya Refugees in Bangladesh'. US Department of State, December 13, 2022. https://www.state.gov/resettlement-initiative-for-vulnerable-rohingya-refugees-in-bangladesh.

Samaranayake, N. 'U.S., India's Goals Diverge in New Delhi's Near Abroad'. *World Politics Review*, May 13, 2014. https://www.worldpoliticsreview.com/u-s-india-s-goals-diverge-in-new-delhi-s-near-abroad.

———. 'Bangladesh's Submarines from China: Implications for Bay of Bengal Security'. RSIS Commentary, CO16295, S. Rajaratnam School of International Studies (RSIS). December 6, 2016. https://www.rsis.edu.sg/rsis-publication/rsis/co16295-bangladeshs-submarines-from-china-implications-for-bay-of-bengal-security.

———. 'Bay of Bengal as a Microcosmic Model for Law of the Sea in the Indian Ocean'. *CBoBS Journal* (August 1, 2022): 51–53.

Samaranayake, N., C. Lea, and D. Gorenburg. 'Improving U.S.–India HA/DR Coordination in the Indian Ocean'. *CNA*, (July 2014): 18–22. https://www.cna.org/archive/CNA_Files/pdf/drm-2013-u-004941-final2.pdf.

'Secretary Antony J. Blinken and Bangladeshi Foreign Minister Abdul Momen before Their Meeting'. US Department of State, April 4, 2022. https://www.state.gov/secretary-antony-j-blinken-and-bangladeshi-foreign-minister-abdul-momen-before-their-meeting.

'Summit for Democracy: Invited Participants'. US Department of State, 2021. https://www.state.gov/participant-list-the-summit-for-democracy.

'The World Bank in Bangladesh'. The World Bank, October 6, 2022. https://www.worldbank.org/en/country/bangladesh/overview.

'Treasury Sanctions Perpetrators of Serious Human Rights Abuse on International Human Rights Day'. US Department of the Treasury, December 10, 2021. https://home.treasury.gov/news/press-releases/jy0526.

'Treaties in Force: A List of Treaties and Other International Agreements of the United States in Force on January 1, 2020'. US Department of State, 202, 283, 419, August 2020. https://www.state.gov/wp-content/uploads/2020/08/TIF-2020-Full-website-view.pdf.

'Troop and Police Contributors: Ranking of Contributions by Country'. United Nations Peacekeeping, October 31, 2022. https:// peacekeeping.un.org/en/troop-and-police-contributors.

Uddin, H. *Diplomacy in Obscurity: A Memoir*, 86–89, 196. Dhaka: The University Press Limited, 2021.

'United States and Bangladesh Convene 6th Meeting of the U.S.–Bangladesh Trade and Investment Cooperation Forum Agreement Council'. United States Trade Representative, December 6, 2022. https://ustr.gov/about-us/policy-offices/press-office/press-releases/2022/december/united-states-

and-bangladesh-convene-6th-meeting-us-bangladesh-trade-and-investment-cooperation.

'US Ambassador Haas's Statement on Political Violence in Dhaka'. US Embassy in Bangladesh, December 8, 2022. https://bd.usembassy.gov/28948.

'U.S. Ambassador Peter Haas's Remarks at the International Conference on Moving Forward in the Indo-Pacific'. International Conference on Moving Forward in the Indo-Pacific: Bangladesh's Role in Fostering an Open, Resilient, and Interconnected Bay of Bengal and Beyond, Independent University Bangladesh (IUB), US Embassy in Bangladesh, March 31, 2022. https://bd.usembassy.gov/u-s-ambassador-peter-haas-remarks-as-prepared.

'US–Bangladesh Ties to Grow Further: Mozena'. bdnews24, 20 December 20, 2014. https://bdnews24.com/bangladesh/us-bangladesh-ties-to-grow-further-mozena.

'US Donates 20 Patrol Boats to Bangladesh Navy, Coast Guard'. *New Age BD*, September 10, 2021. https://www.newagebd.net/article/148705/us-donates-20-patrol-boats-to-bangladesh-navy-coast-guard.

'US Embassy Spokesperson Statement on December 14 Mayer Dak Meeting'. US Embassy in Bangladesh, December 19, 2022. https://bd.usembassy.gov/29047.

'US Human Rights Report on Law Enforcers Misrepresents Facts: Home Minister'. *The Daily Star*, April 13, 2022. https://www.thedailystar.net/news/bangladesh/news/us-human-rights-report-law-enforcers-misrepresented-home-minister-3004316.

'US Reiterates Its Concerns over Haas's Security'. *The Daily Star*, December 19, 2022. https://www.thedailystar.net/news/bangladesh/crime-justice/news/us-reiterates-its-concerns-over-haass-security-3199471.

'US Relations with Bangladesh'. US Department of State, July 19, 2022. https://www.state.gov/u-s-relations-with-bangladesh.

'U.S. Security Cooperation with Bangladesh'. US Department of State, September 1, 2023. https://www.state.gov/u-s-security-cooperation-with-bangladesh.

13

BANGLADESH: AUSTRALIA'S BLIND SPOT

Andrew Hunter

Introduction

The lack of Australian attention on Bangladesh is anomalous with its current geo-economic objectives and inconsistent with the approach taken by its regional partners. Australia is concerned about its economic reliance on an increasingly assertive China but pays little attention to a country with a population of over 160 million, an impressive, sustained pre-Covid-19 economic growth of 6 per cent, located in an area of geo-strategic significance. Bangladesh is an Australian blind spot even as its Quadrilateral (Quad) partners—India, Japan and the US—for different reasons and with different approaches and objective circumstances, deepen their engagement.

Australia was the second country to recognise Bangladesh. Under Prime Minister Robert Menzies, Australian policy was to maintain a neutral position between Pakistan and India. At the time, India enjoyed friendly relations with the Soviet Union, thus limiting the potential for strategic alignment with Australia. The latter was sympathetic to the cause of East Pakistan's secessionists and became only the second country to recognise Bangladesh (Gyngell 2017). This position was inconsistent with that of the US—an Australian ally—which supported Pakistan in the Bangladesh war of independence. Its then a senior US State Department official, Ural Alexis Johnson, had predicted that Bangladesh would turn into a 'basket case'. However, Bangladesh is no longer a basket case; it has realised an economic transformation over a short period of time and under incredibly challenging circumstances. Such challenges remain. Bangladesh is susceptible to social, political and ecological volatility. The possibility of dramatic changes in circumstances may explain Australia's hesitancy to engage wholeheartedly. But Canberra also understands it is not immune to downstream effects of changing circumstances within Bangladesh, including ecological disaster, a less tolerant form of Islam or shifts in popular attitudes towards India.

Bangladesh's rise gives it greater salience to the broader Bay of Bengal community, which occupies an important position in Indo-Asia, now the geo-strategic focus of the great powers. Circumstances may partly explain the attention Bangladesh now attracts. Its position in the Bay of Bengal, between reawakened giants India and China, makes it the subject of growing strategic competition. But its prominence is also the result of its economic progress, which draws comparisons with earlier Asian 'tiger economies' (Hong Kong, Singapore, South Korea and Taiwan) and has been similarly described as an 'economic miracle', with its potential for further growth. Engagement with Bangladesh is now actively pursued by the US, which, for the first time under a president from the Democratic party, is pursuing an Indo-Pacific rather than transatlantic foreign policy agenda. China, India and Japan are each seeking to deepen engagement through a range of means, including foreign direct investment (FDI), defence and security cooperation, and areas where there are shared interests in another country. Despite Bangladesh's improved circumstances and clear strategic importance, Australia has yet to show serious intent with respect to its bilateral relationship. Dhaka is clearly of growing regional importance but remains on the periphery of Australia's strategic vision. Although Canberra increasingly sees the world through the prism of great power competition between China and the US, it appears happy to leave the geo-strategic heavy lifting to fellow members of the Quad. It may be time for Australia to reconsider the nature of its engagement with Bangladesh.

Economic Progress and Rising Geo-Strategic Importance

At its outset, Bangladesh stood in the middle of cul-de-sac of endemic poverty and strategic irrelevance and for much of its history, has punched below its weight. It was seen by the world as a poor backwater, a view easily resolved by its own introspection, timidity and focus on internal culture wars. Bangladesh is now rising beyond the endemic poverty for which it was initially characterised and increasingly understands its own strategic significance.

From humble economic beginnings, Bangladesh's recent economic performance has inspired comparisons with the paths taken by other Asian 'tigers'. Dr David Brewster, a senior research fellow at the National Security College in Canberra, has taken the position that Australia should do more with a country which boasts a population of 160 million and a booming, export-oriented economy (Brewster 2021a), which has grown at an annual average of about 6 per cent for two decades, and now boasts a per capita GDP ($2,227) that is higher than India's ($1,947) and much higher than its former master's, Pakistan ($1,543) (Brewster 2021b).

Brewster also cites other measures of progress. Bangladesh is exceeding its South Asian neighbours in social indicators including health, life expectancy, birth rates and employment of women (Brewster 2021a). It is well known that Bangladesh is a global garment-manufacturing powerhouse, a strength which is often associated with poor labour standards. Yet, it is important not to overlook the transformative, positive power of the most significant industry of an Islamic, male-dominated society that is wholly reliant on women participating in its workforce. When the bell rings to bring an end to another shift, women spew out of stores, talking and shopping together.

Bangladesh's progress has also been expressed in other ways. It recently provided aid to Sri Lanka, marking the first time it gave financial assistance to another country. The $200 million currency swap indicates a treasury in rude health, with foreign reserves of $45 billion (Brewster 2021b). These are important, and for countries such as Australia, a surprising development for a country that has throughout its history remained in the shadow of India, which surrounds it on three sides.

This reversal in economic fortune has coincided with a shifting geo-strategic environment. Bangladesh is located at the fulcrum of the Bay of Bengal, between India and China, and is the subject of growing strategic competition between them. It holds the key to the re-establishment of a long, dormant historic trade route between the rising giants of the 21st century and providing China access to the Bay of Bengal and the larger Indian Ocean (Kaplan 2010). Bangladesh has successfully leveraged its place as a metaphorical and literal crossroad, courting infrastructure investment from a range of countries which have come to understand its geo-strategic value.

Challenging Circumstances

The Australian diplomats and business leaders spoken to in preparation for this chapter all mentioned, with admiration, that Bangladesh's rise is more impressive because it has been achieved in a distinctly challenging context. National unity was born of linguistic nationalism when a people refused the imposition by West Pakistan of Urdu as the national language. Language—rather than religion—was initially the organising social principle. It was born of abject poverty, and throughout its existence, has tilted on the precipice of climate disaster. Such circumstances, one would assume, could only be overcome with unparalleled social harmony but, like many countries, different social dynamics lead to inter-city rivalries; for example, between the larger cities of Chittagong and Dhaka which boast different characters. The latter is Bangladesh's capital and largest city, whereby Chittagong's history is more defined by the Bay of Bengal and the larger Indian Ocean world (Kaplan 2010). It is Bangladesh's politics, however, where divisions are sharpest and most fiercely contested.

The historic rivalry between the Awami League (AL) and the Bangladesh Nationalist Party (BNP) has shaped Bangladesh's politics since its inception. Each of the various Australian diplomats who in the past served in Dhaka mentioned the country's pervasive, high-stakes politics which American writer Robert D. Kaplan described as darkly Shakespearean and driven by personal vendetta, much like Pakistan (Kaplan 2010). The character of Bangladesh's politics has implications for its place in the world. For instance, although Sheikh Hasina has served as prime minister since 2009, a change in government could result in significant upheaval and a shift in policy direction. This could also include shifting allegiances, although Bangladesh has demonstrated a capacity to intelligently balance its respective relationships with India and China, prioritising its national interest. The AL is left-leaning and generally inclined to India, whereas the BNP is closer to the military, and more favourably disposed to China.

A weak central government leaves gaps in service delivery, in a country in which need is acute. Thousands of local non-governmental organisations (NGOs) help fill the void between a remote, badly functioning central government and village communities (Kaplan 2010). Such NGOs have historically played a positive role in the country. The late Sir Fazle Hasan Abed KCMG, for example, was the founder of one of the world's largest non-governmental organisations, the Bangladesh Rehabilitation Assistance Committee (BRAC). The increased politicisation of NGOs is unfortunate, and they now operate in a hotly contested space. As we will see, an organised Islam has for decades worked to address this gap in service delivery. This has provided refuge for many people, and a grassroots network that provides a strong foundation for an influential political movement that could exert an influence on both domestic politics and foreign policy.

The Subject of Geo-Strategic Competition

Australia is now increasingly viewing the Indo-Pacific through a geo-economic lens. The AUKUS initiative (a trilateral security pact between the US, the UK and Australia) announced in 2021 makes apparent its strategic alignment with the US and the UK, despite the economic importance of Australia's trading relationship with China, which is increasingly seen by some analysts more as a strategic risk rather than economic benefit. According to former secretary of Australia's Department of Foreign Affairs and Trade (DFTA), Peter Varghese, AUKUS represented, 'a strategic fault line down the middle of the Indo-Pacific, with Southeast Asia—our strategic hinterland—uncomfortably trying to straddle the strategic fence' (Varghese 2021).

In this context, Australia's lack of engagement should be considered alongside the efforts of other important Indo-Pacific actors. Let us briefly consider how Bangladesh's bilateral engagement has simultaneously grown with each, to identify gaps, complementarities or potential collaborations that could bring new impetus to Australia's bilateral relationship with Bangladesh.

India

Bangladesh remains politically close to India, despite growing resentment. This is a pragmatic reflection of Bangladesh's geographic realities. Shyam Saran described the defining feature of South Asia as asymmetry; India is the largest country in terms of area, population, economy and military, and shares significant ethnic, linguistic and cultural features with its neighbours that they do not share with each other. Young Bangladeshis, for example, love the Bangla language, and literature and Rabindra Sangeet help correct misconceptions and deepen ties through culture (Saran 2018). Bangladesh is far down India's cultural and geo-strategic gravity well, a situation from which it benefits.

But Bangladesh is also important to India. The existence of Bangladesh effectively condemned India's Northeast to relative isolation, and it still forms a political barrier to India's seamless linking with Southeast Asia. This barrier will only be overcome with ongoing improvements to the bilateral relations (Saran 2018), which are increasingly strained by the seeming incompatibility of Modi's India with a sense of fraternity many Bangladeshis feel with fellow Muslims beyond its borders. In 2019, the then president of the Bharatiya Janata Party (BJP) and Home Minister Amit Shah, referred to illegal immigrants from Bangladesh as 'termites' and said his party would 'throw them into the Bay of Bengal (Ghoshal 2021). Comments such as these, as well as concerns over the Modi government's treatment of Indian Muslims, has hardened popular anti-Indian sentiment in Bangladesh. This has added to concerns that India treats Bangladesh as a subservient, lesser partner in a long-standing relationship.

Recent engagements have been marked by violence and tragedy. In October 2019, a student named Abrar Fahad was beaten to death in Dhaka on the campus of the Bangladesh University of Engineering and Technology, allegedly by cadres of the Chhatra League, the student wing of the ruling AL, who had reportedly taken offence at a Facebook post in which Fahad had voiced his concerns about the seemingly unilateral nature of the bilateral agreements Bangladesh Prime Minister Sheikh Hasina had signed with India during her trip across the border days earlier (BBC 2019). Then, in the days prior to the visit of Indian Prime Minister Narendra Modi in March 2021, the conservative orthodox group Hefazat-e-Islam Bangladesh ('safeguarding Islam in Bangladesh') protested the mistreatment of Muslims in India. The visit was part of the 50th anniversary of Bangladesh's independence. The protests were violently suppressed by AL supporters, who were actively supported by police. Four Hefazat-e-Islam Bangladesh protesters were shot dead in Chittagong (Hasan 2021).

Overall, if the Hasina government is unable to develop a defter approach to addressing the concerns of an organised and increasingly political Islam, or if it loses power, there may be a further shift in favour of the 'other' giant in the neighbourhood, which continues to court better relations.

China

China shares with Bangladesh and other South Asian countries threats to national security, including international terrorism, national separatism and international drug trafficking. In this sense, regional security and development are two sides of the same coin (Zhang 2013). For a long time, these shared challenges gave rise to deep consideration of arrangements that would serve to deepen positive cooperation between China and South Asia. Economic cooperation between Bangladesh, China, India and Myanmar (BCIM), which would have effectively created a continental bridge between China's southwest regions and neighbouring regions of South and Southeast Asia, was contemplated since the first half of the 20th century, until it was framed as part of Xi Jinping's Belt and Road Initiative (BRI), rendering the concept unpalatable from an Indian perspective (Chen 2013).China nonetheless continued to increase its investment in infrastructure, although this has proved problematic in more recent times. China withdrew funding for BRI infrastructure projects in Bangladesh after the recipient country re-evaluated the programmes and downwardly revised their costs (Islam 2021). At least two rail projects are now uncertain at the time of writing, and last year Bangladesh's Finance Minister Mustafa Kamal warned developing countries against taking Chinese loans through the BRI.

China's engagement with Bangladesh has risen as the incumbent Hasina government seeks to balance India's influence. China is currently the major defence supplier. According to the Stockholm International Peace Research Institute, Bangladesh has spent $2.59 billion on military equipment from China since 2010 (Amas 2020). Further, Bangladesh is inclined to support China in multilateral institutions, including on sensitive issues such as the treatment of Uighurs. China has deftly filled India's traditional aversion to multilateralism, the latter preferring the flexibility of bilateral, and the potential to exercise leadership through mini-lateral arrangements such as the Bay of Bengal Initiative for Multi-Sectoral Technical and Economic Cooperation. This leaves a gap that China will continue to work on to develop deeper engagement in Bangladesh. There are circumstances—increased popular anti-Indian sentiment or a change of government to a more China-friendly BNP—in which Bangladesh will take steps in China's direction. But Bangladesh will continue to cultivate a careful balance, in its national interest, between a range of actors, not least of with Japan.

Japan

Japan's presence in South Asia is not a recent development. Japan and India believe they share fundamentally similar civilisational moorings, the focus on which was accentuated under the respective leaderships of Abe Shinzo and Narendra Modi. A joint statement made by the two leaders in November 2016 affirmed the 'two Prime Ministers appreciated the deep civilisational links between the people of the two countries, including the common heritage of Buddhist thought' (Government of India 2016). The growing promotion of the civilisational affinity between the two countries has been complemented by an increasing alignment in the respective foreign policy frameworks: the Arc of Freedom and Prosperity, the Quad and Asia's Democratic Security Diamond. Japan's Free and Open Indo-Pacific (FOIP) and India's Act East Policy and Security and Growth for All in the Region (SAGAR) initiative are complementary frameworks that create scope for the two countries to deepen their collaboration in the region (Banerjee and Basu 2021).

Further, Japan and India have started to collaborate in third countries, including Bangladesh, in the context of their shared outlook towards the Indo-Pacific. Both countries have invested heavily in Bangladesh from India and Japan in 2019—$115.9 million in FDI from India and $72.3 million from Japan in 2019 (Banerjee and Basu 2021). Japan's increasing investment in Bangladesh is also motivated by its broader diversification strategy, which has prompted it to decrease the concentration of its manufacturing interests in China (Bloomberg 2021). Bangladesh has gratefully welcomed Japan's increased interest. In 2016, it supported Japan's bid for a permanent seat in the United Nations Security Council. As with other bilateral relationships, Bangladesh continues to play its hand well, deploying an omnidirectional foreign policy to strike a cautious balance between regional actors increasingly aware of its importance to a broader geostrategic balance of powers. The US now also figures amongst its suitors.

The US

Unlike Australia, the US opposed the creation of Bangladesh and wanted Pakistan to prevail in any conflict involving India, as the alternative scenario would diminish it in China's eyes. Indeed, the US sent its aircraft carrier, the *USS Enterprise*, into the Bay of Bengal, in a barely disguised effort to threaten India (Saran 2018). Despite its opposition to Bangladesh's independence, Kaplan described the local population as positively disposed to America, particularly when it is considered alongside the UK (a former colonial power) or either China and India, which frequently seek to impose their will on it, and certainly when compared to Pakistan with which it has a lingering hostility. The one issue which diminishes this positive image of the US is the latter's indifference to climate change, which as we have seen is an existential issue in Bangladesh (Kaplan 2010).

This issue has to some extent been addressed under the Biden administration, which uses multilateral platforms including the Quad arrangements to encourage its partners to work with it to address the climate crisis. Time is no longer on our side. With aligned perspectives on the immediacy of the ecological threat, the US is extremely well placed to deepen its engagement with an 'emerging ally', with an initial focus on building defence ties (Amas 2020). The US is another country increasing the overall 'demand' for Bangladesh's attention, in what has become a seller's market.

An Australian Perspective on Bangladesh

Australia cannot compete with Japan's prolonged engagement with Bangladesh, or the proximity and intermingled historic experience of China and India. However, it does not share India's political baggage or seek favour through support in multilateral institutions for contentious behaviour. Any indication that Australia, the second country to recognise Bangladesh, intends to deepen its engagement in Bangladesh, would no doubt be welcomed.

But, Bangladesh struggles to penetrate the Australian consciousness. No Australian foreign minister visited Bangladesh between 1997 and 2019, when (then) Foreign Minister Marise Payne's visit was the product of her oversight of Australia's significant humanitarian assistance to the Rohingya crisis (Brewster 2021a). Previous foreign ministers maintained a watching brief, but did not see Bangladesh as a strategic opportunity, let alone a priority. The level of focus in Australia will likely increase in the coming years, driven by strategic and economic imperatives, as well as an active and increasingly visible diaspora.

From the writer's viewpoint in Perth, Australia's 'Indian Ocean capital', a greater focus on Bangladesh is imminent. The vice chancellor of the University of Western Australia, Amit Chakma, was born in the Chittagong Hill Tracts. Western Australians of Bangladeshi heritage have been particularly active during the recent pandemic, raising their profile. The number of Bangladesh-born Australians, which according to the most recent Census is now over 40,000—an increase of around 50 per cent from the 2011 Census—have a deep emotional commitment to Australia, complementing a natural tie to their country of origin (Australian Government 2018). Members of the local community have noticed the dramatic elevation of the Australia and India bilateral relationship and hope this illuminates a path to a similar elevation of Australia's relationship with Bangladesh.

The volume of bilateral trade continues to increase and there are ample opportunities for further growth with the fastest-growing South Asian economy, with which Australia's economy has complementary features. There is an appetite in Bangladesh for what Australia reduces, and the prospect of growing demand for tourism and education ultimately prompted serious consideration and reflection. There are grounds for optimism. Bangladesh's striking economic growth trajectory has recently captured Canberra's attention. The Australia-Bangladesh Trade and Investment Framework Arrangement (TIFA) was concluded on 15 September 2021. Though largely symbolic, the Australia–Bangladesh TIFA is a belated but welcome sign that Australia now recognises the economic opportunity that others identified some time ago (Augustin 2021). When seen in the context of the circumstances which now inform Australia's economic, diplomatic and security settings, a closer relationship with Bangladesh makes sense.

Trade diversification is a necessary response to the shifting geostrategic context, all of which warrant a more active engagement with Bangladesh. As former minister for foreign affairs, Stephen Smith, recently wrote:

> Less than a decade ago, Australia's post-war experience, life, the region and future economic prosperity all seemed relatively straightforward. The nation seemed on track for continuous ongoing economic prosperity in an environment of peace and stability, with well understood international and regional frameworks: China as the leading trading partner, the United States as security provider, and no need to choose between the two. (2021)

That certainly has, in a short space of time, been removed. Smith continues:

> The set of post-war dynamics ... has now been the subject of significant disruption. And this disruption has yet to see the full consequences of an aggressive and assertive China, an uncertain US, climate change and COVID-19. All of these features may, in a remarkably short period of time, become deeply significant ongoing features of the Indo-Pacific .... (Smith 2021)

China has recently deployed economic instruments as a means of applying pressure to Australian foreign policy. In 2020, China blocked or disrupted Australian exports including beef, wine, barley and coal, further signalling the arrival of an era of geo-economics (Laurenceson 2021). Although these trade restrictions were lifted in mid-2023, these shifting conditions have added significance to the northeast Indian Ocean, and from an Australian perspective, it adds weight to arguments in favour of economic diversification, as well as defence and security engagement with Bangladesh.

For at least a decade, Australia has rightly concentrated on its partnership with India, and analysts such as Brewster suggest that it is now time to broaden that strategy to include other countries in that region, which laments the negligible existing defence and security engagement with Bangladesh. Official military visits are very rare, and the last visit by the Australian navy was in 2014. There is no resident defence representative. Australia currently provides no material assistance to the Bangladesh armed forces. No Bangladesh military officers receive professional military education in Australia (Brewster 2021c). Further, Brewster points to greater attention from Bangladesh. Official visits to Australia in 2019 by senior Bangladesh officers, Lieutenant General Mohammad Mahfuzur Rahman (head of the Armed Forces Division) and Admiral Aurangzeb Chowdhury (the chief of naval staff), flagged Bangladesh's interest in developing a closer defence and security relationship as part of a more comprehensive relationship with Australia. Dhaka sees countries like Australia and Japan as valuable and benign regional partners that can potentially mitigate some of those pressures and add further ballast to Bangladesh's regional relationships (Brewster 2021c).

Changing geo-strategic realities are complemented by a range of other shared challenges. Smith referred to the shared immediate challenges of climate change and Covid-19, to which one may also add drug smuggling, refugees and the risk of Islamic extremism, which may increase following the Taliban's return to power in Afghanistan. Australia may not be able to directly assist in alleviating these risks but will likely suffer the downstream effects of them. If the experience of climate change is only now becoming grudgingly apparent to a broader Australian population, in Bangladesh, overcrowding gives every ounce of land an existential value. As Kaplan once described, millions of lives in Bangladesh are affected by the slightest climactic variation, let alone more dramatic impacts of global warming (Kaplan 2010). Australia and Bangladesh have a shared stake in addressing climate change, even though both countries have historically had a different experience of its impact. The same could be said of other problems for which Australia is susceptible to downstream effects, including drug trafficking and human movement, caused by a yearning for better economic opportunities or the need to find asylum. Over one million refugees have crossed the border from Myanmar to Bangladesh in recent years, presenting a significant crisis for the latter, and for those who have been displaced from their homes.

A closer look at one of these significant threats faced in Bangladesh illustrates why Australia should take more interest. A proliferation of Islamic orphanages, madrassas and cyclone shelters have long provided refuge from ecological upheaval, poverty and lack of other service provision (Kaplan 2010). This strong grassroots network is now complemented by a stronger political presence, providing a platform for conservative Islamic views. According to Kaplan, Islam arrived late to the region now recognised as Bangladesh, at the beginning of the 13th century with Delhi-based Turkish invaders. Modern Bangladesh has had a more moderate, syncretic form of Islam, which, more recently, started giving way to a more assertive Wahabist tradition (Kaplan 2010). Bangladesh has seen a recent increase in terrorist activity, focused on foreigners, activists and religious minorities (Hardig 2020). The implications of a politically active, well-organised Islam has implications that will not be confined to Bangladesh's domestic affairs. It has, for example, contributed to a growing anti-India mindset in Bangladesh. An active, organised, politicised and internationally aware Islam could shape Bangladesh foreign policy and thus the geo-strategic landscape. This reality should pique the interests of Australia's foreign policy establishment, already aware that a fundamentalist, violent expression of discontent will not necessarily be confined within near-national boundaries. July 2021 marked the fifth anniversary of the Holey Artisan Bakery attack, in which young men who had studied in Australia, Canada, the US and UK, came together to kill 20 innocent people in Dhaka.

There are solid grounds for a closer collaboration with Bangladesh on a range of matters, but Australia, for the moment, appears content with its partners doing the heavy lifting, increasing their influence and reaping the economic rewards. Will the geo-strategic lens through which Australia increasingly sees the Indo-Pacific also be applied to opportunities to deepen its bilateral relationship with Bangladesh, which it recognises as an increasingly capable regional actor? Bangladesh continues to invest in defence capacities commensurate with its growing economy, and its defence portfolio is now overseen by Prime Minister Sheikh Hasina. The country no longer limits itself to traditional suppliers, China and Russia, and now also acquires from the likes of Turkey, which has sold more than US$750 million (approximately in armoured vehicles and rocket launchers (Brewster 2021b).

Australia's pursuit of deeper strategic engagement with Bangladesh could encompass several 'no regrets' steps, according to Brewster. These could also include the appointment of a defence advisor in Bangladesh, the establishment of military education opportunities and targeted exchanges, a naval visit to Bangladesh and assistance to build its maritime capacity in selected areas (Brewster 2021a). These represent sensible steps Australia may well take, even if it has demonstrated little inclination thus far to match Bangladesh's enthusiasm for a deeper relationship. Even acknowledging the economic and geostrategic importance of Bangladesh, Canberra evidently believes Dhaka remains at the periphery of its sphere of interest. Thus, it is comfortable allowing its QUAD partners to balance China's interests in, and influence over, the country.

Conclusion

Despite the centrality of the Indo-Pacific in Australian foreign policy, Bangladesh is currently a second-order priority for Australian policymakers. In one sense, it appears on the periphery of Australia's sphere of interest, and although few would dispute Dhaka's growing strategic importance, Canberra would be satisfied that its QUAD partners—India, Japan and now the US—are sufficiently engaged to balance China's influence.

When Canberra, aware of its extraordinary rise, finally decides to make Dhaka a greater focus, there are attractive options for further engagement. The recently signed TIFA may lead to further interest in economic engagement, which could include trade and investment in sectors including garments, international education, agriculture, and mineral resource and energy exports. Energy clearly is a critical issue for Bangladesh, which has an interest in renewables, rooftop solar and micro-grids, especially for village use. With respect to security engagement, Brewster states that Australia is 'a potential supplier in niche defence technologies or surplus equipment in light of Bangladesh's military modernisation' and proposes military education to senior Bangladeshi officers (Brewster 2021a).

The current level of Canberra's engagement in Bangladesh does not diminish the admiration held for its rapid rise, which was achieved under fundamentally adverse circumstances. It also does not suggest an ignorance of Bangladesh's geo-strategic importance, but more so an acknowledgement that its QUAD partners are more enmeshed and better placed to exert influence. But, irresistible economic and strategic forces are such that it is only a matter of time before Australia sharpens its focus on Bangladesh.

References

Ahmed, I. 'In Bangladesh, a Student's Murder Opens a Window on Rising Anti-India Sentiment across the Border'. *Scroll.in*, October 10, 2019. https://scroll.in/article/939979/in-bangladesh-a-students-murder-opens-a-window-on-rising-anti-india-sentiment-across-the-border.

Amas, A.Z.M. 'US Uses Defence Diplomacy to Woo Bangladesh Away from China. *Nikkei Asia*. September 22, 2020. https://asia.nikkei.com/Politics/International-relations/US-uses-defense-diplomacy-to-woo-Bangladesh-away-from-China.

Augustin, B. 'Australia–Bangladesh: A Booster Dose for Trade Diversity?' Australian Institute of International Affairs, September 24, 2021. https://www.internationalaffairs.org.au/australianoutlook/australia-bangladesh-a-booster-dose-for-trade-diversity/.

Banerjee, S. and P. Basu. 'India and Japan Partnership in Third Countries: A Study of Bangladesh and Myanmar'. Observer Research Foundation Issue Brief No. 460, 2021. https://libguides.library.usyd.edu.au/ld.php?content_id=38859760.

'Bangladesh Born Community Information Summary'. Australian Government (Department of Home Affairs), 2018. https://www.homeaffairs.gov.au/mca/files/2016-cis-bangladesh.PDF.

BBC. 'Abrar Fahad: Bangladesh police charge 25 over murder'. BBC. November 13, 2019. "https://www.bbc.com/news/world-asia-50409831" \t "_blank" Abrar Fahad: Bangladesh police charge 25 over murder - BBC News.

Bloomberg. 'Japanese Companies Move from China to Bangladesh.' *Taipai Times*. Wednesday, February 17, 2021. "https://www.taipeitimes.com/News/biz/archives/2021/02/17/2003752372" \t "_blank" Japanese companies move from China to Bangladesh - Taipei Times.

Brewster, D. 'Kick-Starting a New Strategic and Defence Partnership with Bangladesh'. *The Strategist*, June 8, 2021a. https://www.aspistrategist.org.au/kick-starting-a-new-strategic-and-defence-partnership-with-bangladesh/.

———. 'A Rising Bangladesh Starts to Assert Its Regional Power'. *The Interpreter*, June 10, 2021b. https://www.lowyinstitute.org/the-interpreter/rising-bangladesh-starts-exert-its-regional-power.

———. 'New Indo-Pacific Partnership: Building Australia-Bangladesh Security Ties.' ANU National Security College Policy Options Paper, No. 20, June 2021c. https://nsc.crawford.anu.edu.au/sites/default/files/publication/nsc_crawford_anu_edu_au/2021-06/nsc_policy_options_paper_bangladesh_web_1.pdf.

———. 'Bangladesh Finance Minister warns developing nations of Chinese loans strapped with debt-trap'. *The Economic Times,* August 10, 2022. China Loans: Bangladesh Finance Minister warns developing nations of Chinese loans strapped with debt-trap - *The Economic Times* (indiatimes.com)

Chen, J. 'The BCIM Trade Corridor and its Development'. In *Across the Himalayan Gap: A Chinese Quest for Understanding India*, edited by Tan Chung, Zhang Minqiu and Ravni Thakar, 283–290. New Delhi: India International Centre, 2013.

Ghoshal, D. 'Amit Shah Vows to throw Illegal Immigrants into Bay of Bengal'. 2021. "https://www.reuters.com/article/india-election-speech/amit-shah-vows-to-throw-illegal-immigrants-into-bay-of-bengal-idINKCN1RO1YD/" \t "_blank" Amit Shah vows to throw illegal immigrants into Bay of Bengal | Reuters. Reuters. April 13, 2019.

Government of India, Ministry of External Affairs, 'India-Japan Joint Statement during the Visit of Prime Minister to Japan,' November 11, 2016. https://mea.gov.in/bilateral-documents.htm?dtl/27599/IndiaJapan+Joint+Statement+during+the+visit+of+Prime+Minister+to+Japan.

Gyngell, A. *Fear of Abandonment: Australia in the World since 1942*. Melbourne: La Trobe University Press, 2017.

Hardig, A.C. 'Conservative Islamic Views Are Gaining Ground in Secular Bangladesh and Curbing Freedom of Expression'. *The Conversation*, February 19, 2020. https://theconversation.com/conservative-islamic-views-are-gaining-ground-in-secular-bangladesh-and-curbing-freedom-of-expression-128692

Hasan, M. 'Understanding Bangladesh's Most Potent Religious Opposition'. *The Interpreter*, March 31, 2021. https://www.lowyinstitute.org/the-interpreter/understanding-bangladesh-s-most-potent-religious-opposition.

'India–Japan Joint Statement during the Visit of Prime Minister to Japan'. November 11, 2016. https://mea.gov.in/bilateral-documents.htm?dtl/27599/IndiaJapan+Joint+Statement+during+the+visit+of+Prime+Minister+to+-Japan.

Islam, S. 'Belt and Road Projects in Limbo as Bangladesh Cuts Budget'. *Nikkei Asia*, June 28, 2021. https://asia.nikkei.com/Spotlight/Belt-and-Road/Belt-and-Road-projects-in-limbo-as-Bangladesh-cuts-budgets.

'Japanese Companies Move from China to Bangladesh'. *Taipai Times*, February 17, 2021. https://www.taipeitimes.com/News/biz/archives/2021/02/17/2003752372.

Kaplan, R. *Monsoon: The Indian Ocean & the Battle for Supremacy in the 21st Century*. Melbourne: Black Inc, 2010.

Laurenceson, J. 'Why Pushing for an Economic "Alliance" with the US to Counter Chinese Coercion Would Be a Mistake.' *The Conversation*. September 13, 2021. https://theconversation.com/why-pushing-for-an-economic-alliance-with-the-us-to-counter-chinese-coercion-would-be-a-mistake-167629.

Saran, S. *How India Sees the World: Kautilya to the 21st Century*. New Delhi: Juggernaut Books, 2018.

Smith, S. 'Expectations Disrupted: Lesson's for Australia's Indo-Pacific Future'. National Security College Futures Hub, 2021. https://futureshub.anu.edu.au/expectations-disrupted-lessons-for-australias-indo-pacific-future/.

Varghese, P. 'AUKUS Is Our Plan B for China, But Let's Not Barrack for Cold War 2.0'. *Australian Financial Review*, 2021. https://www.afr.com/policy/foreign-affairs/aukus-is-our-plan-b-for-china-but-let-s-not-barrack-for-cold-war-2-0-20210920-p58ta8.

Zhang, G. 'China's South Asia Policy: The Role of Balance and Stability.' In *Across the Himalayan Gap: A Chinese Quest for Understanding India*, edited by Tan Chung, Zhang Minqiu and Ravni Thakar, 283–290, New Delhi: India International Centre, 2013.

Epilogue

THE ROAD AHEAD FOR BANGLADESH— PROSPECTS TO EMERGE AS THE 'NEXT FRONTIER' OF ASIA

Ramita Iyer

Bangladesh is at the cusp of an important shift in the international system with a well-poised advantage to grow and further increase its relevance globally. There has been an intensification in the geopolitical competition in the Indo-Pacific region with several regional and extra-regional powers vying for the attention of the smaller states located here. And Dhaka is uniquely placed to reap significant economic and strategic gains. At the same time, however, the country faces several challenges, such as having to manage foreign relations, sustain economic growth and handle domestic political and social compulsions, including upholding the rule of law and ensuring communal harmony.

Bangladesh in a Dynamic Global System

Bangladesh is situated favourably at the mouth of the Bay of Bengal, a region that is witnessing increased attention among bigger powers. Located between India and Myanmar, the country also acts as a land-connectivity bridge between South Asia and Southeast Asia. With direct access to both regions, Dhaka can use its position as a strategic wedge in influencing the economic and political engagements between countries. In addition to the geographical contiguity, the growing competition between India and China also significantly plays into Bangladesh's foreign political calculations. Both Delhi and Beijing have been undertaking decisive steps to increase their foothold in Dhaka, clearly reflected in their inclination to view Bangladesh not only through the prism of bilateral ties but also by situating it within the growing regional framework (Datta 2019). Both sides have markedly increased their engagements with Bangladesh through an increase in trade, economic aid and connectivity, as well as advancements in humanitarian assistance and the conduction of state and ministerial-level diplomatic visits.

For long, international relations scholars and policymakers alike feared that rising competition between bigger powers in the region would result in smaller countries of South Asia (including Bangladesh) being embroiled in the rivalry, with little room for bargaining or manoeuvre. In this regard, with time, it has become rather evident that the rising geopolitical and geo-economic contestation, with states from both within and outside South Asia seeking to increase their regional footprint, could potentially render significant benefits to smaller countries like Bangladesh. Multipolarity has helped increase their leverage as they are now able to choose between options, diversify the sources of aid in order to avoid over-reliance on any single partner, and set their own terms for economic engagement.

Bangladesh seems to have effectively navigated such competition over the past decade, securing its interests and at the same time managing bilateral and regional ties. As a country whose foreign policy was predominantly preoccupied with managing its own internal and external vulnerabilities in the initial years, the economic and social developmental journey over the last two decades appears to have contributed to a change in its foreign policy posturing and ability to forge meaningful ties with countries. One of Bangladesh's successes in this regard is evident in the dealings pertaining to China's Belt and Road Initiative (BRI) (Raja Mohan 2023). Unlike other South Asian loan-recipient nations such as Pakistan or Sri Lanka, Bangladesh has been calculative about negotiating suitable terms with China, ensuring that it does not find itself in a position of defaulting on foreign debt repayment (Rahman 2021). Given this favourable trend in the country, it will be in Bangladesh's interest to proceed with the same selective and prudent measures in its future dealings with foreign loans, especially those concerning infrastructure development. Bangladesh's extension of a $200 million loan to Sri Lanka in 2021 was another important milestone in its newfound self-conception, moving beyond an identity of being a 'small' and 'weak' state to one that is more proactive and outward looking. The emergence of Bangladesh as a net provider also marked an important shift in the structural dynamics of South Asia, with smaller countries demonstrating comprehensive engagement, without relying on India as the primary provider in the region.

However, it is important to note that the geopolitical world that Bangladesh finds itself in today is starkly different from the international system not only during its early years of independence but even that which existed two decades ago. Multipolarity, while increasing bargaining power, also makes it more complex to manage several seemingly beneficial relationships. Bangladesh will also have to be wary of the implications of events such as the Covid-19 pandemic and the spill over effects of the Russia–Ukraine war that have tested the country both politically and economically.

Pivot to the Indo-Pacific Region

While the India–China rivalry is undoubtedly carving the contours of the present regional landscape, another factor that will potentially determine Bangladesh's future trajectory is the increasing interest among developed (both Western and East Asian) countries towards the region. This has been evident in the fact that several nations have, in recent times, released their Indo-Pacific strategies. The strategic pivot of the US towards the Asia-Pacific region since 2011 has undoubtedly been one of Washington's moves in response to the growingly confrontational nature of Sino-US ties. Articulated first as a concept by Japan when then Prime Minister Shinzo Abe outlined the 'Indo-Pacific' framework in a speech in the Indian Parliament in 2007, several countries have quickly followed suit by strategically prioritising the region in their foreign policies, predominantly based on the principles put forth by the US (Ministry of Foreign Affairs of Japan 2007). The idea of advocating for a 'Free and Open Indo-Pacific' has gained considerable traction and apart from announcing initiatives at the country level, players have also been engaging with each other through various mini-lateral forums such as the Quadrilateral Security Dialogue (Quad) comprising Australia, India, Japan and the US, and more recently, through the US-led 14-member Indo-Pacific Economic Framework (IPEF).

In an interesting development in April 2023, Bangladesh unveiled its Indo-Pacific Outlook (IPO), which spells out the country's interests in the region. The Bangladesh Ministry of Foreign Affairs press release clearly laid down the IPO's basis in Dhaka's central foreign policy principle of embracing 'friendship towards all, malice towards none'. It emphasises issues such as regional connectivity, economic growth through trade and investment, peace and stability, technology, innovation and the environment. With the aim of boosting socio-economic regional engagement while also securing the country's geopolitical and geo-economic interests, the IPO highlights the importance of the stability and prosperity of the Indo-Pacific for Bangladesh to achieve its 'Vision 2041' goal of building a 'modern, knowledge-based developed country' by 2041 (Ministry of Foreign Affairs Bangladesh 2023). However, given that it is an 'outlook' rather than a 'strategy', there are concerns over Bangladesh's formal approach to the region stopping short of providing any clarity on the country's central policy priorities (Muniruzzaman 2023).

Nonetheless, at a time when the relationship between Washington and Dhaka has not been optimal due to multiple issues including recent statements by the US on human rights violations in Bangladesh, as well as a perception in the Western world of Dhaka's growing overdependence on China, the release of the IPO is timely. The emphasis of the document on issues pertaining to maritime security and combating terrorism and piracy evidently echoes the US strategy for the Indo-Pacific (Ahmed 2023). In this regard, as a large and successful economy that is eagerly working towards being recognised as a maritime nation, Bangladesh appears to be using the opportunity to come out with its own ideas of what constitutes the 'Indo-Pacific'. While some experts have coloured Bangladesh's IPO as an attempt to merely placate concerns in China and the US (Asia-Pacific Foundation of Canada 2023), the opportunities presented to small countries from big-power geopolitical contestation reveal that the IPO can potentially be used as an effective tool to hedge bets and secure Dhaka's interests while productively engaging with partners. Moreover, the release of Bangladesh's IPO also reflects an attempt by the country to shift its perception beyond the comparatively limiting South Asian paradigm to one having a broader Indo-Pacific identity.

At the same time, the usage of the term 'outlook' instead of 'strategy' may also indicate Bangladesh's hesitancy to commit entirely to the idea of the 'Indo-Pacific' as espoused by the US (Rahman 2023). While the release of the IPO implies Dhaka's recognition of the Indo-Pacific as a region of geopolitical interest and importance, the lack of a clear-cut strategy in this regard will bode well for the country to be able to comfortably work with partner countries without the alienation of China. This will be of utmost interest to Bangladesh especially given that the notion of the 'Indo-Pacific' is largely dismissed by Chinese officials as a tool of aggression and division.[1]

Managing Ties for Socio-Economic Regional Engagement

Bangladesh makes for a successful case to examine fostering and maintaining ties with several countries. While its relations with key partner countries have faced their fair share of strains, Bangladesh has largely been able to navigate these complex relationships in a manner that has ensured continuity and stability. Today, the country has forged cooperative partnerships with states both within its neighbourhood as well as with like-minded partners across geographies.

China and Bangladesh largely enjoy warm and friendly relations that comprise cooperation on economic and strategic fronts. Over the years, the increased stability and rising level of engagement between the two sides have led to Beijing being called Dhaka's 'all-weather friend' (Sakhawat 2020). China is Bangladesh's largest trading and investment partner, with more than a 17 per cent share in the country's total trade (Rahman 2022; Haroon 2022). In comparison, this is well above the second-largest trading partner, India's share of 13 per cent (Haroon 2022). Both sides also enjoy a strategic cooperative partnership. Notably, Bangladesh was one of the first countries in South Asia to embrace China's BRI and has a host of in-progress and upcoming infrastructure projects under the umbrella initiative. In the coming days, deepening security and defence ties, expanding economic integration and intensifying people-to-people exchanges will help Dhaka and Beijing take their relationship forward. While Bangladesh is proving to be a favourable destination for China to increase its presence and strategic footprint in South Asia, it will be important for Dhaka to manage Beijing's geostrategic expectations both within the subcontinent as well as the broader Indo-Pacific region.

Bangladesh–India relations are currently in what is described as a 'golden chapter' of bilateral relations. While India played an important role in Bangladesh's liberation in 1971, ties have fluctuated over the decades. Relations have also been determined by domestic political sentiments as well as the government in power in Bangladesh. Economically, India has now slipped to being Bangladesh's second-largest trading partner. However, it is noteworthy that bilateral economic engagement has increased in recent years; both sides have partnered in several developmental projects including connectivity-related ones as well as infrastructural development works. Other regional factors have also contributed to the favourable position that Bangladesh finds itself in. For one, the current Indian administration has made significant strides in overcoming the colonial strategic overhang (inherited from the British Raj) of its primacy in the subcontinent (Raja Mohan 2023). Over the past decade, it has made efforts to substantially engage with partner countries outside the region for projects in South Asian states. A recent significant example here is the Indo-Japanese trilateral connectivity initiative that aims to establish an industrial hub as well as develop supply chains (Kumar 2023). Overall, the complementing strategic location of the countries has pushed both sides to forge closer ties and further develop strategic, connectivity and people-to-people ties. Additionally, India's aspirations of being a voice of the Global South,[2] as emphasised during its G20 presidency, may also be attractive for the soon-to-be-developing country, Bangladesh. Going forward, it will be important for India and Bangladesh to reconcile issues pertaining to boundaries, river-water sharing, the sheltering and repatriation of Rohingya refugees as well as alleviating India's geo-strategic concerns about a growing China in its immediate neighbourhood.

Further West, Bangladesh's history has largely complicated its relationship with Pakistan since Dhaka's conception and liberalisation in 1971 is rooted in its independence from its former identity of East Pakistan. While both sides formally recognised each other in 1974, bilateral relations have been suboptimal through the decades. As in the case of India, Bangladesh–Pakistan ties have also hinged on domestic political sentiment and the ruling government in Bangladesh. Economic cooperation between both sides is not very comprehensive. Given China's growing role in the region and both Bangladesh and Pakistan's close ties with the country, there is scope for both sides to jointly work on extending their trade and economic cooperation, especially for intra-regional connectivity and infrastructure-based projects. People-to-people connections are another area that can be tapped into by establishing deeper links in areas of culture, tourism and education. Apart from this, there are also calls to converge ties between both nations as 'Muslim nations' working towards mutual economic progress and strategic development.

Moving beyond the neighbourhood, US–Bangladesh relations, despite the initial hiccups imposed by the Cold War dynamics, have emerged strong both politically and economically. On the economic front, the US is one of the biggest markets for Bangladeshi garments while Washington has been one of the largest sources of foreign aid and foreign direct investment (FDI) in Dhaka. Over the decades, military and security relations have blossomed; in 2022, both sides approved a draft pact on defence cooperation (PTI 2022). From a strategic lens, Washington and Dhaka have much to gain from cooperation in the Indo-Pacific region. While the relationship between the US and Bangladesh has considerably progressed under the Biden administration (*Prothom Alo* 2023), recent statements on alleged human rights violations and other issues pertaining to labour rights have caused some fissures. Given the domestic political sensitivity over such issues and the national elections in Bangladesh in early 2024, the government's inhibition towards overcoming the turbulence is expected.

Beyond the first-level primary external partnerships of Bangladesh, there are other states with whom Dhaka can potentially expand cooperation. One of the frontrunners in this respect is Australia. With the clear pivot to the Indo-Pacific in recent years and Canberra's interest in the region on account of China's growing influence, it will be of utmost importance to enhance bilateral ties on issues of economic and strategic relevance. While Australia was the second country to formally recognise Bangladesh, bilateral relations have not emerged to an optimal level. There is much scope for collaboration and cooperation in the coming years. Another key geographical region is Southeast Asia, one that is becoming increasingly interconnected with South Asia. On this front, the political tension owing to the Rohingya crisis is likely to complicate the evolution of a more comprehensive partnership with countries in the region. However, the emphasis on non-interference in domestic issues, sovereignty and ASEAN centrality[3] among Southeast Asian states will allow for a more collaborative relationship in other key areas of mutual interest and benefit.

Apart from expanding relations at the bilateral level, a key tool for Bangladesh to ensure effective management of its foreign relations while ensuring socio-economic regional development is by advancing dialogue and partnerships through institutions. Bangladesh has always championed regional organisations and initiatives, including the South Asian Association for Regional Cooperation (SAARC), the Bay of Bengal Initiative for Multi-Sectoral Technical and Economic Cooperation (BIMSTEC) and the Bangladesh–Bhutan–India–Nepal (BBIN) initiative. While Bangladesh has recorded significant development since its independence years, the country will continue to require strong partnerships and a steady flow of foreign aid in the future. Given this, multilateral seems to be a promising path for the country to tread.

The Challenges of Sustaining Economic Growth

Bangladesh has demonstrated unprecedented growth over the past few decades. This is of particular significance given the difficulties on account of the long periods of political instability faced by the country. From being described as a 'basket case' in its early days to now becoming an exemplar for its rapid progress in economic development and social indicators, Dhaka has come a long way. With a GDP growth of around 6.9 per cent, the country has consistently recorded one of the highest growth rates in the South Asian region (World Bank 2021). In this vein, Bangladesh's impressive growth story would be incomplete without mention of its massive ready-made garments (RMG) industry, which has played a crucial role in the transformation of the economy.[4] As of 2023, the RMG sector contributes to about a fifth of its GDP and more than 80 per cent of its export earnings (Fatima 2023).

Another remarkable achievement by the country is reflected in its upcoming graduation from the United Nation's list of least-developed countries (LDC) to developing country status by 2026. This watershed moment for a relatively young country like Bangladesh will render benefits such as improving credit rating, increasing foreign direct investment flows and maximising Dhaka's confidence in its engagements with international financial institutions (Rahman 2021). At the same time, however, graduation from the LDC category would also present myriad challenges such as the loss of certain preferential market access, subsidies for select industries and access to some LDC-specific funds (Rahman 2021).

Additionally, Bangladesh's economic future is also affected by the increased volatility on account of the recent global economic slowdown. Despite Dhaka recording a growth rate of over 6 per cent during the last three years, the aftermath of the Covid-19 pandemic and the implications of the Ukraine crisis on global energy and supply chain disruptions have deeply affected Bangladesh's economic position. In January 2023, Bangladesh secured a $4.5 billion loan from the International Monetary Fund (IMF) to address economic troubles (Frayer 2022). The country's foreign exchange reserves were at a seven-year low in 2023, and a fall in exports and remittances has also sparked grave concerns (Chaube 2023). Importantly, the economic situation has also directly affected the domestic population. Since mid-2022, tens of thousands of people have taken to the streets in protest against the rising living costs, food and fuel shortages, and inflation (Rahman 2022; Islam 2022). This has not only further stressed the country's already fragile economy but also sparked concerns over domestic political stability and raised fears regarding repression and violence by the government (Islam 2022). In this light, it will be important for the country to not only take short-term measures to ease the day-to-day living of its domestic constituents but also ensure economic policy course correction to meet the challenges of the LDC graduation in 2026.

Bangladesh's population of approximately 170 million and a sizeable portion of more than 65 per cent within the working age group of 15 and 64 makes it favourable for the country to tap into its demographic profile in order to further accelerate productivity and economic development (Bangladesh Bureau of Statistics 2022). While there are concerns over the fact that one-third of the youth are currently unemployed, taking effective policy measures to ensure the skilling of youth, as well as the conversion of skilled youth into remunerative employment areas, will be key to sustaining growth (Molla and Zaman 2022). Apart from this, it will also be vital for Bangladesh to take prudent economic measures to increase the flow of remittances, a key source of foreign exchange earnings.[5]

Importantly, Bangladesh is now attempting to position itself beyond the RMG industry, moving towards building and being recognised as a 'knowledge hub country'.[6] This will be a favourable move for Dhaka, especially given its impending double graduation to a developing country as well as a middle-income country. However, in the short term, especially in light of the present economic troubles that the country faces,[7] it will be beneficial for Bangladesh to capitalise on key successful sectors such as its high-performing RMG industry to play a strategic role in addressing the economic troubles.

It has become widely popular that not only China but also Bangladesh has become an inextricable component of the regional supply chain networks. With the shifting away of supply chains from China in a concerted effort by countries to reduce their risks, Bangladesh is already at the forefront of reaping its benefits (*Tex Talks* 2022; Fatima 2023). In recent times, there has been a call to 'de-risk' rather than 'de-couple' from China. This was amplified at the 2023 G7 summit where US President Joe Biden emphasised on the new approach (Toyoda and Dolan 2023). This too signals an opportunity for Bangladesh to attract more trade and investment. Dhaka has already emerged as a regional gateway for supply chains in both South Asia and Southeast Asia (Rahman 2022) and in the wake of the global supply chain disruptions, it is well positioned to influence and channelise flows towards the country and proceed further in its path of becoming a critical supply chain frontier in Asia.

The Quest for a Global Identity

Bangladesh is demonstrating a steady inclination to develop a global identity. From being a country that interacted with external players only to reap short-term economic and political benefits, Bangladesh has now transitioned into a phase of conducting its foreign policy with a long-term vision that is focused on building and enhancing meaningful partnerships. As highlighted in this volume, an effective way to achieve this would be through the development of a Bangladesh doctrine. Importantly, it is in Bangladesh's interest to have a peaceful Bay of Bengal to accelerate growth in its economic, social, political and diplomatic spheres. In this regard, a clear policy outlining the coordination of its national security policy with its development policy, and charting out the associated institutions and their roles will be of strategic significance.

Bangladesh will also require international legitimacy and support to afford more credible global recognition. Here, it is useful to reflect on the construction and reconstruction of the notion of Bangladeshi diaspora as well as the state's identity as a Muslim nation. While the notion of being a 'Bangladeshi' among the diaspora has undergone several transformations over time and varies across geographies, the large population of diaspora across the US, the UK and other countries contribute to increasing Dhaka's social and political footprint in the host countries. A study conducted by the International Organization for Migration (2022) laid down concrete policy measures to ensure the inclusion of the diaspora in Bangladesh's national development, which includes fostering trade linkages, supporting diaspora diplomacy, facilitating investment, promoting diaspora tourism and encouraging philanthropy, among others.

With respect to its identity as a Muslim nation, it is important to note that at independence, despite the country consisting of a majority Muslim population, the liberation movement was instead deeply rooted in a Bengali national identity (Ludden 2014). Over the years, however, the question of political Islam has played a prominent role in domestic politics. Islam has influenced not only the periods of military rule in the country but also driven the competition for legitimacy and authority between the Awami League and the Bangladesh Nationalist Party, during the parliamentary periods. Further, the external projection of Bangladesh as a 'secular country' versus a 'Muslim country' has had direct and severe implications on domestic politics. On the international front, pursuing a foreign policy that embraces Bangladesh as a Muslim nation has facilitated meaningful engagement with countries in the Middle East and the Gulf. Its membership in the Organisation of Islamic Cooperation (OIC) in 1974 helped grant the country granted more legitimacy and enlarged its space within the international community.

Humanitarian issues and the challenges of human security continue to test the strength and agility of Bangladeshi foreign policy and diplomacy. Since 2017, the Rohingya crisis has evolved into a central issue of regional security (*Dhaka Tribune* 2019). Hosting more than a million refugees, Bangladesh is at the core of the unfolding crisis (United Nations High Commissioner for Refugees 2023). While the international community vouched for the safe repatriation of Rohingyas back to their homeland initially, not much progress has taken place due to the lack of proper mechanisms in place to facilitate a safe return and an increased reluctance among refugees to return to Myanmar over fears of being persecuted (TBS Report 2021; Human Rights Watch 2023). Going forward, the sensitivity with which Bangladesh handles the security and humanitarian issues pertaining to the Rohingyas will determine its appeal globally.

In its pursuit of advancing a global image, Bangladesh will also have to tackle fragile global challenges like climate change. Bangladesh is one of the most climate-vulnerable countries in the world, with a high risk of natural disasters (Eckstein et al. 2021). Geography and demographic factors have compounded the catastrophic effects of climate change in the country. As examined in this book, Bangladesh has put together a set of domestic strategies to address climate change issues. These include mitigation efforts, managing energy and power usage, laying down adaptation measures, tackling food insecurity, improving community resilience and accelerating gender and economic empowerment. On the international stage, too, Dhaka has embraced clear-cut strategies. While many initiatives are in motion, others are yet to be implemented. The World Bank, in its assessment of Bangladesh's present climate concerns, has advised a three-pronged approach to tackling issues: (*i*) people-centric, climate-smart development; (*ii*) delivering development benefits with decarbonisation; (*iii*) enabling environment and institutional realignment (World Bank 2022). Climate change also presents another opportunity for Bangladesh to exert its influence among vulnerable countries in South Asia and the Indo-Pacific region. Given the advancements the country has made in carving out clear climate directions, aiding the effective implementation through knowledge and resource-sharing mechanisms in vulnerable areas could help Dhaka build global credibility.

Bangladesh as a New Asian Frontier?

With the 21st century being touted as the 'Asian century', Bangladesh is presented with a real opportunity to progress towards emerging as a new frontier in Asia. As this volume has shown, Bangladesh's relations with the 'outside world' have dramatically changed since the country gained independence in 1971. Largely, Bangladesh's growing global outreach and its quest for a global identity are inextricably woven and complementary to each other. Today, it is at the forefront in playing a decisive role in the evolution of geo-economics and geopolitics of not only South Asia but also the wider Indo-Pacific region. With effective engagements spanning across partner countries around the world on economic, geo-economic, geopolitical, geo-security and geo-energy aspects, Dhaka must ensure calculative steps going forward that help strengthen its regional and global integration.

At the same time, Bangladesh must not lose sight of the economic, social, political and diplomatic challenges that lie ahead. Its position in the world will be affected by the ongoing great-power rivalry, burgeoning economic concerns and fragile domestic politics. As a country that has only recently received appreciation and recognition on the global stage, Bangladeshi policymakers must tread carefully with proactive, forward-looking yet realistic policy goals. This will determine the success of Dhaka's foreign policy future.

Overall, the continuation of an independent and neutral foreign policy hinged on Bangladesh's first prime minister, Bangabandhu

Mujibur Rahman's ideal of 'friendship with all, enmity with none' is bound to bode well for the country's future trajectory. In the coming days, Bangladesh will have to navigate through an international arena that is exceedingly multipolar and far more geopolitically complex than ever before. Given this, it remains to be seen how the country effectively maintains internal growth and stability while capitalising on the shifting global order while managing its economic, strategic and diplomatic ties with partners in the region and beyond. The jury is out on that count.

Notes

1. Since the term gained traction, China has viewed the 'Indo-Pacific' construct as an aggressive step adopted by the US to counter Beijing's growing power and influence in Asia. The country's apprehensions have been voiced by several Chinese officials in recent years. For instance, in May 2022, State Councillor and Foreign Minister Wang Yi declared that the US Indo-Pacific strategy as a tool that attempts to contains China and create divisions, incite confrontation and undermine peace the Asia-Pacific region. See Wang, Y. 'The U.S. Indo-Pacific Strategy Is Bound to be a Failed Strategy', Ministry of Foreign Affairs of the People's Republic of China, May 22, 2022, https://www.fmprc.gov.cn/eng/zxxx_662805/202205/t20220523_10691136.html.

2. Indian Foreign Minister has consistently emphasised that it is Delhi's duty to become a voice of the Global South or the developing world. As the G20 president this year, the idea has received much traction and fanfare. In January 2023, the country also organised a Voice of the Global South Summit. For more information, see 'Voice of Global Summit', PIB, Ministry of Petroleum and Natural Gas, January 13, 2023, https://pib.gov.in/PressReleasePage.aspx?PRID=1891153#:~:text=The%20Voice%20of%20Global%20South,members%20of%20the%20global%20south.

3. ASEAN refers to the Association for Southeast Asian Nations. 'ASEAN centrality' implies that ASEAN must be the dominant regional platform to address common challenges and engage with external powers. For more information, see the ASEAN Charter available at https://asean.org/wp-content/uploads/2021/09/21069.pdf.

4. Other factors contributing to Bangladesh's economic growth are covered in the introduction chapter by Sreeradha Datta. They include the 'ability to introduce internal measures leading to the growth of agricultural output, huge export driven by readymade garments, a large number of migrant labourers outside the country bringing in considerable remittances and investment in the construction sector'.

5. For more information on prescriptive measures that Bangladesh can take to increase the inward flow of remittances in the country, see Banerjee, P.K. 'How Can We Increase Our Remittance?' *The Daily Star*, September

26, 2022, https://www.thedailystar.net/opinion/views/news/how-can-we-increase-our-remittance-3128646.
6 The goal of establishing Bangladesh as a knowledge-based country is clearly laid out in its 'Vision 2041'. See General Economics Divisions (GED) Bangladesh Planning Commission. 'Making Vision 2041 a Reality: Perspective Plan of Bangladesh 2021–2041', Ministry of Planning, Government of the People's Republic of Bangladesh, March 2020, http://oldweb.lged.gov.bd/uploadeddocument/unitpublication/1/1049/vision%202021-2041.pdf.
7 The International Monetary Fund (IMF) has expressed concerns over falling foreign reserves in Bangladesh. For more information on the IMF's worries pertaining to Bangladesh's economy, see Chaube (2023).

References

Ahmed, K. 'How Different is Dhaka's Outlook from the US Indo-Pacific Strategy?' *The Daily Star*, April 30, 2023. https://www.thedailystar.net/opinion/views/news/how-different-dhakas-outlook-the-us-indo-pacific-strategy-3308056.
'Bangladesh's First Indo-Pacific Outlook Aims for "Friendship Towards All"'. Asia Pacific Foundation of Canada, May 5, 2023. https://www.asiapacific.ca/publication/bangladeshs-first-indo-pacific-outlook-aims-friendship.
'Bangladesh: New Risks for Rohingya Refugees'. Human Rights Watch, May 18, 2023. https://www.hrw.org/news/2023/05/18/bangladesh-new-risks-rohingya-refugees.
Chaube, Y. 'IMF Flags Risks to Bangladesh Economy as Foreign Reserves Fall Further'. WION, May 8, 2023. https://www.wionews.com/business-economy/imf-flags-risks-to-bangladesh-economy-as-foreign-reserves-fall-further-590331.
'China is Losing Its Place as the Center of the World's Supply Chains, Here Are 5 Places Supply Chains Are Going Instead'. *Tex Talks,* December 28, 2022. https://textalks.com/china-is-losing-its-place-as-the-center-of-the-worlds-supply-chains-here-are-5-places-supply-chains-are-going-instead/.
'Confluence of the Two Seas'. Ministry of Foreign Affairs of Japan, August 22, 2007. https://www.mofa.go.jp/region/asia-paci/pmv0708/speech-2.html.
'Country Profile: Bangladesh. World Development Indicators Database'. World Bank, 2021. https://databank.worldbank.org/views/reports/reportwidget.aspx?Report_Name=CountryProfile&Id=b450fd57&tbar=y&dd=y&inf=n&zm=n&country=BGD.
Datta, S. 'Bangladesh: Leveraging its Locational Advantage'. Vivekananda International Foundation, January 11, 2019. https://www.vifindia.org/2019/january/11/bangladesh-leveraging-its-locational-advantage.
Eckstein, D., V. Kunzel, and L. Schafer. 'Global Climate Risk Index 2021: Who Suffers Most from Extreme Weather Events? Weather-Related Loss Events in 2019 and 2000–2019'. *Germanwatch,* (January 2021): 1–48.

https://germanwatch.org/sites/default/files/Global%20Climate%20Risk%20Index%202021_2.pdf.

Fatima, K. 'Bangladesh Ready to Topple China as Top Clothing Exporter to EU'. *Nikkei Asia*. February 17, 2023. https://asia.nikkei.com/Economy/Trade/Bangladesh-ready-to-topple-China-as-top-clothing-exporter-to-EU.

Frayer, L. 'How Bangladesh Went from an Economic Miracle to Needing IMF Help'. NPR, November 9, 2022. https://www.npr.org/2022/11/09/1134543648/bangladesh-economy-imf-loan.

Haroon, J.U. 'China Becomes Bangladesh's Top Trading Partner Again'. *The Financial Express*, August 1, 2022. https://thefinancialexpress.com.bd/trade/china-becomes-bangladeshs-top-trading-partner-again-1659319605.

Islam, S. 'Bangladesh Tea Strike Spotlights Poorest Workers' Inflation Plight'. *Nikkei Asia*, August 20, 2022. https://asia.nikkei.com/Economy/Inflation/Bangladesh-tea-strike-spotlights-poorest-workers-inflation-plight.

———. 'Bangladesh Government Digs in against Protests as Economy Teeters'. *Nikkei Asia*, December 13, 2022. https://asia.nikkei.com/Politics/Bangladesh-government-digs-in-against-protests-as-economy-teeters.

'Joint Government of Bangladesh—UNHRC Population Factsheet'. United Nations High Commissioner for Refugees, May 2023. https://data.unhcr.org/en/documents/details/101160.

Kumar, M. 'Japan Proposed Industrial Hub in Bangladesh with Links to Northeast India'. *The Japan Times*, April 12, 2023. https://www.japantimes.co.jp/news/2023/04/12/business/japan-bangladesh-hub-port-transport-india/.

Ludden, D. 'The Politics of Independence in Bangladesh'. *Economic and Political Weekly*, August 27–September 2, 2011. Vol 46, no. 35. https://www.jstor.org/stable/23017911.

Molla, M.A.M. and M.A. Zaman, 'Demographic Dividend: Are We Letting it Pass Us By?' *The Daily Star*, August 14, 2022. https://www.thedailystar.net/news/bangladesh/news/demographic-dividend-are-we-letting-it-pass-us-3094231.

Muniruzzaman, A.N.M. 'Indo-Pacific Is Lacking in Depth'. *Prothom Alo*, April 28, 2023. https://en.prothomalo.com/opinion/op-ed/qcyrobqd2a.

'Policy Brief: Ensuring Active inclusion of Diaspora in Bangladesh's National Development'. International Organization for Migration, January 2022. https://bangladesh.iom.int/sites/g/files/tmzbdl1006/files/documents/Policy%20Brief%20-%20Ensuring%20Active%20Inclusion%20of%20Diaspora%20in%20Bangladesh%27s%20National%20Development.pdf.

'Population & Housing Census 2022'. Statistics and Informatics Division, Bangladesh Bureau of Statistics, Ministry of Planning, 2022. https://drive.google.com/file/d/1Vhn2t_PbEzo5-NDGBeoFJq4XCoSzOVKg/view.

'PM Will Decide When Polls-Time Govt Will Be Formed: Law Minister'. *The Daily Star*, June 4, 2023. https://www.thedailystar.net/news/bangladesh/news/pm-will-decide-when-polls-time-govt-will-be-formed-law-minister-3337356.

PTI. 'Bangladesh, US Approve Draft Pact on Defence Cooperation'. *The Times of India*, March 20, 2022. https://timesofindia.indiatimes.com/world/rest-of-world/bangladesh-us-approve-draft-pact-on-defence-cooperation/articleshow/90339517.cms.

Rahman, M.M. 'Bangladesh's Graduation: Challenges and Imperatives to Continued International Support Measures'. ISAS Working Papers, Institute of South Asian Studies, July 22, 2021. https://www.isas.nus.edu.sg/papers/bangladeshs-graduation-challenges-and-imperatives-to-continued-international-support-measures/.

———. 'A Tough End to 2022 for Bangladesh'. South Asia Chat. 20 December 20, 2022. https://isas.podbean.com/e/episode-174-a-tough-end-to-2022-for-bangladesh/.

———. 'Growing with Two Giants—A Mixed Blessing for Bangladesh'. South Asia Scan. Institute of South Asian Studies, August 16, 2022. https://www.isas.nus.edu.sg/wp-content/uploads/2022/08/SouthAsiaScan_Complete_26082022.pdf.

Rahman, S.A. 'The BRI in Bangladesh: 'Win-Win' or a 'Debt Trap'?' *The Diplomat*, November 9, 2021. https://thediplomat.com/2021/11/the-bri-in-bangladesh-win-win-or-a-debt-trap/.

Rahman, Z. 'What's Our Priority in the Indo-Pacific Outlook?' *The Daily Star*, May 9, 2023. https://www.thedailystar.net/opinion/views/news/whats-our-priority-the-indo-pacific-outlook-3315231.

———. 'South Asia Geoeconomics'. South Asia Chat, April 28, 2023. https://isas.podbean.com/e/episode-190-south-asia-geoeconomics/

Raja Mohan, C. 'India, Japan and South Asia Geoeconomics'. ISAS Briefs, Institute of South Asian Studies, April 19, 2023. https://www.isas.nus.edu.sg/papers/india-japan-and-south-asia-geoeconomics/.

Sakhawat, N. 'China–Bangladesh Relations Stronger Than Ever before'. *The Daily Star*, October 6, 2020. https://www.thedailystar.net/opinion/news/china-bangladesh-relations-stronger-ever-1972993.

TBS Report. 'UN Resolution on Rohingyas Asks Myanmar to Address Crisis'. *The Business Standard*, November 18, 2021.

Toyoda, Y. and D. Dolan. 'Analysis: G7's Nuanced Pledge to "De-Risk" from China Reflected Concerns from Europe and Japan'. Reuters, May 22, 2023. https://www.reuters.com/world/g7-pledge-de-risk-china-reflects-concerns-europe-japan-2023-05-22/.

Tribune Desk. 'PM: Rohingyas a Threat to National, Regional Security'. *The Dhaka Tribune*, November 11, 2019.

'US Gives Importance to Its Partnership with Bangladesh'. *Prothom Alo*, January 8, 2023. https://en.prothomalo.com/bangladesh/9790ipizc9.

World Bank. 'Urgent Climate Action Crucial for Bangladesh to Sustain Strong Growth'. October 31, 2022. https://www.worldbank.org/en/news/press-release/2022/10/31/urgent-climate-action-crucial-for-bangladesh-to-sustain-strong-growth.

ABOUT THE EDITOR AND CONTRIBUTORS

The Editor

Sreeradha Datta is a professor of international affairs at the OP Jindal Global University. She is also a Non-Resident Senior Fellow with the Institute of South Asian Studies, National University of Singapore, Singapore. Prior to that, she was director, Maulana Abul Kalam Azad Institute of Asian Studies, Kolkata and held fellowships with the Institute for Defence Studies and Analyses, among other institutions. Her recent works include *India Bangladesh Bonhomie : 1971 and the Present*, edited, (Vivekananda International Foundation, New Delhi, 2023), *Act East Policy and Northeast India* (Vitasta Publication, New Delhi, 2021), *BIMSTEC: The Journey and Way Ahead* and edited (Pentagon Publishers, New Delhi, 2022), *Bangladesh at 50: Development and Challenges* (Orient Blackswan, New Delhi, 2020). That apart, she has written *Caretaking Democracy: Political Process in Bangladesh, 2006–2008* (Institute for Defence Studies, New Delhi, 2009). *Bangladesh: A Fragile Democracy* (Institute for Defence Studies, New Delhi, 2004), *The Northeast Complexities and Its Determinants* (Institute for Defence Studies, New Delhi, 2002) and edited *Changing Security Dynamics in South East Asia* (Pentagon Publishers, New Delhi, 2009) and few other monographs covering Bangladesh, Southeast Asia, Myanmar. She has also published over 160 articles in journals, edited volumes, newspapers and academic websites. Her research interests include South Asia and Southeast Asia, regionalism and cross-border issues.

The Contributors

Don McLain Gill is a Manila-based geopolitical analyst, author and the director for South and Southeast Asia at the Philippine-Middle East Studies Association (PMESA). He is also a lecturer at the Department of International Studies, De La Salle University (DLSU). He specialises in Indo-Pacific affairs, Indian and Philippine foreign policy, and India–Southeast Asian relations. He has written books, book chapters, peer-reviewed international journal articles, newspaper columns and commentary/analysis articles for major publishers such as *The Diplomat*, *The National Interest*, the East-West Center, the Stimson Center, *Japan Times*, *South China Morning Post*, the Observer Research Foundation, *Asia Times* and the Royal United Services Institute (RUSI), among others. Gill is also regularly interviewed by international news TV channels and newspapers.

Andrew Hunter is an experienced advisor to government and commercial entities on international relations, strategic development and public policy. In 2022, Andrew established Hunter&Co, a firm providing services related to strategic development and international engagement. Andrew previously served as Director at Minderoo Foundation (Minderoo International) and before that as senior advisor (international engagement) to the Premier of South Australia. Andrew holds a Masters of Philosophy (Asian Studies) from The University of Adelaide and Diploma in Languages (Japanese) from University of Canberra. Andrew also studied on a Japanese Government scholarship at the International University of Japan (International Relations School) in 2002. He is currently finishing a Doctorate of Education at The University of Melbourne.

Ramita Iyer is a research analyst at the Institute of South Asian Studies (ISAS), National University of Singapore. Her research focus is on geoeconomic and geopolitical developments in the Indo-Pacific region. She has a keen interest in South Asian politics, the intersection of policy and technology, global health and the role of small states in the Indian Ocean region. Before joining ISAS, Iyer worked with several Indian and international organisations on issues such as global mental health policies for transwomen, education and skill development and international policies on commercial sexual exploitation of children, among others. She was also a consulting editor at the Alexis Foundation, India. Iyer graduated with a master's in international affairs from the Lee Kuan Yew School of Public Policy, National University of Singapore and holds a BA (Honours) in political science from Delhi University.

Li Jianjun is an associate professor at the Institute of South Asian Studies, Sichuan University, a key research institute at Chinese universities. His research focuses on Bangladeshi economy and foreign relations. He has published one book and more than 20 research papers including 'Belt and Road Initiative Economic Study: Bangladesh' (2020), 'Food Security in Bangladesh: Current Situation, Challenges and Counter-Measures' (2020), 'Bangladesh: Its Economic Development in Recent Years and Future Scenario' (2017), 'Bangladesh's General Election and Its Trend in Political Situation' (2014) and 'An Analysis of Extremism in Bangladesh: Present Conditions, Characteristics and Counter-Measures' (2011).

About the Editor and Contributors

Ashley Johnson joined the Office of Asian Affairs at the US Department of Energy (DOE) as an international relations specialist in January 2023. In this role, she coordinates with inter-agency and international partners on DOE's work in China, Taiwan, South Korea and smaller South Asian countries. Prior to this position, she was the senior director of Energy and Environmental Affairs at the National Bureau of Asian Research (NBR), where she led NBR's research on energy security, environmental sustainability and disaster management across the Indo-Pacific. Johnson received an MA from the Johns Hopkins University School of Advanced International Studies and a graduate certificate in Chinese-American Studies from the Hopkins-Nanjing Center. She also holds a BA in international studies from Southwestern University in Georgetown, Texas.

M. Humayun Kabir, a career diplomat, retired from the government service as secretary in the Ministry of Foreign Affairs of Bangladesh in September 2010. Before his retirement, he had served as Bangladesh ambassador to the US. Earlier, he had served as the Bangladesh ambassador to Nepal and high commissioner to Australia and New Zealand. He had also served as the Bangladesh deputy high commissioner in Kolkata. He had studied in universities in Bangladesh and abroad, and began his career as a faculty member in the University of Dhaka, and currently he serves as an adjunct faculty member at the Bangladesh Institute of Governance and Management (BIGM), Dhaka. Ambassador Kabir regularly writes on professional issues, and has written several chapters in reputed publications at home and abroad. He is also a regular commentator at media outlets in Bangladesh and abroad. Currently, he is the president of Bangladesh Enterprise Institute, a think tank in Dhaka.

Michael Kugelman is the director of the South Asia Institute at the Wilson Center in Washington, DC. He leads the Wilson Center's activities and research on South Asia, with a particular focus on India, Pakistan, Afghanistan and Bangladesh, a portfolio he has managed since 2007. He is also a columnist for *Foreign Policy* magazine and writes its South Asia Brief, a weekly newsletter of news and analysis from around the region.

Deb Mukharji was a member of the Indian Foreign Service (1964–2001) and retired as India's ambassador to Nepal. He had earlier served as high commissioner to Bangladesh (1995–2000), Nigeria (1986–1989) and consul general in San Francisco (1983–1986). He is an alumnus of the National Defence College (1976). His diplomatic assignments included Switzerland (1965–1968), Pakistan (1968–1971), Germany (1971–1974) and Bangladesh (1977–1980). At the Ministry of External Affairs in New Delhi, he has headed the Bangladesh and Americas desks. After retiring from foreign service, he was the convenor of the Indo-Bangladesh Track II Dialogue (2005–2007) and anchored over a hundred TV discussions on Indo-Bangladesh relations. He is an occasional contributor to newspapers and journals. Mukharji has published four books: *The Magic of Nepal* (Rupa, 2005), *Kailash and Manasarovar: Visions of the Infinite* (Nepalaya, 2009), *Perspectives on Nepal* (ICWA, 2013) and *A Quest Beyond the Himalaya* (Niyogi, 2013). His interests include trekking, photography, reading and music.

Johannes Plagemann is a research fellow at the German Institute for Global and Area Studies in Hamburg. He works at the intersection of foreign policy analysis, international relations and comparative politics. His research interests include rising powers in international politics, the legitimacy of international organisations in a multipolar world and small states' foreign policy in between major power rivalries. Moreover, he works on populism and its consequences for foreign policy and international relations. His work has been published in, amongst others, the *British Journal of Politics and International Relations*, *Review of International Studies*, *Foreign Policy Analysis*, *International Studies Review*, *International Relations of the Asia Pacific* and *The Pacific Review*.

Amna Ejaz Rafi is a research associate at Islamabad Policy Research Institute (IPRI). Her areas of interest are the Asia-Pacific and Southeast Asia. Rafi has participated in the prestigious National Media Workshop-6, organised by the National Defence University in Pakistan, and the 10th Gansu International Fellowship Programme sponsored by the Gansu Provincial Foreign Affairs Office, China. As part of intellectual interactions with international think tanks, she has visited the RUSI, London, Centro Studi Internazionali (Ce.S.I.), Rome and the Myanmar Institute of Strategic and International Studies, Yangon, where she presented papers pertaining to the China–Pakistan Economic Corridor (CPEC). Rafi has an MA in defence and diplomatic studies from Fatima Jinnah Women University, Rawalpindi (thesis: 'India's Quest for UNSC Membership: Ramifications for South Asia') and an MPhil in International Relations from School of Politics and International Relations (SPIR), Quaid-e-Azam University, Islamabad (thesis: 'Sino-India Competition in Asia Pacific: Balancing and Rebalancing Strategies').

About the Editor and Contributors

Ali Riaz is a Distinguished Professor of political science at Illinois State University, a Non-Resident Senior Fellow of the Atlantic Council and the President of the American Institute of Bangladesh Studies (AIBS). He has served as a visiting researcher at the Varieties of Democracy (V-Dem) Institute at the University of Gothenburg, Sweden (2023) and a public policy scholar at the Woodrow Wilson International Center for Scholars at Washington, DC (2013). Dr Riaz has Ali taught at universities in Bangladesh, England and South Carolina and worked as a broadcast journalist at BBC in London. His research interests include South Asian politics, political Islam, democratisation and violent extremism. His recent publications include *Trials and Tribulations: Politics, Economy and Foreign Affairs of Bangladesh* (Dhaka: Prothoma, 2023), *More than Meets the Eye: Essays on Bangladeshi Politics* (Dhaka: University Press Limited, 2022). *Religion and Politics in South Asia* (London: Routledge, 2021) and *Voting in a Hybrid Regime: Explaining the 2018 Bangladeshi Election* (Singapore: Palgrave Macmillan, 2019).

Ali Riaz's recent publications include *Trials and Tribulations: Politics, Economy and Foreign Affairs of Bangladesh* (Prothoma, 2023), *More than Meets the Eye: Essays on Bangladeshi Politics* (University Press Limited, 2022). *Religion and Politics in South Asia* (Routledge, 2021) and *Voting in a Hybrid Regime: Explaining the 2018 Bangladeshi Election* (Palgrave Macmillan, 2019).

Nilanthi Samaranayake is an Adjunct Fellow at the East-West Center in Washington and Visiting Expert at the United States Institute of Peace. She studies Indian Ocean regional security, Smaller South Asian countries, non-traditional security, and US alliances and partnerships. Most recently, Samaranayake served as Director of the Strategy and Policy Analysis Program at CNA, where she led a team of analysts who conduct multidisciplinary research and analysis for civilian and military leaders. Before joining CNA in 2010, she analyzed public opinion for a decade at Pew Research Center in Washington and completed a fellowship at the National Bureau of Asian Research (NBR) in Seattle. Samaranayake received an MSc in International Relations from the London School of Economics and Political Science. She is lead author of *Raging Waters: China, India, Bangladesh and Brahmaputra River Politics* (Marine Corps University Press). The views expressed are solely those of the author and not of any organization with which she is affiliated.

Brigitta Schuchert is a programme officer for South Asia at the US Institute of Peace. Prior to that, she spent three years working with the

Stimson Center's South Asia Program where she served as managing editor for *South Asian Voices*, an online policy platform on South Asia's strategic and security affairs. Her research focuses on China–South Asia relations, religion and nationalism, and territorial disputes. From 2014 to 2017, Schuchert worked with New York University's international campuses in Abu Dhabi and Shanghai as a writing fellow. She received her master's in security studies with a concentration in terrorism and sub-state violence from Georgetown University in 2019, and her bachelor's in religious studies from Bryn Mawr College in 2014.

Rashed Al Mahmud Titumir is a Professor of Economics at the Department of Development Studies of the University of Dhaka, Bangladesh. He is currently chairman of the department. His career has spanned a variety of settings, including government, think tanks, international organisations and media, in addition to academia. He is the author of *Fiscal and Monetary Policies in Developing Countries: State, Citizenship and Transformation* (Routledge, 2022), *State Building and Social Policies in Developing Countries: The Political Economy of Development* (Routledge, 2022), *Why Agriculture Productivity Falls: Political Economy of Agrarian Transition in Developing Countries* (Purdue University Press, 2023) and *Numbers and Narratives in Bangladesh's Economic Development* (Palgrave Macmillan, 2021). He is also the co-author of *Natural Resource Degradation and Human Nature Wellbeing: Cases of Biodiversity Resources, Water Resources, and Climate Change* (Springer Nature, 2023), the editor of *Sundarbans and Its Ecosystem Services: Traditional Knowledge, Customary Sustainable Use and Community Based Innovation* (Palgrave Macmillan, 2022) and co-editor of *COVID19 and Bangladesh: Response, Rights and Resilience* (University Press Limited, 2021).

INDEX

A

Acquisition and Cross-Servicing Agreement (ACSA), 241
African American community, 80
Afro-Asian Solidarity Summit, 53
Agency for International Development, 15
Agreement on Economic and Technical Cooperation, 206
Aiyer, Sana, 51
All-India Muslim League, 226
Annual Development Programme (ADP), 117
Arab-Israeli war, 54
Art and cultural interaction, 227
Ashuganj river port, 190
Asian Development Bank (ADB), 10, 37, 140, 148, 162, 232
Asian highway project, 189
Asian Infrastructure Development Bank, 216
Asian Infrastructure Investment Bank (AIIB), 141, 214
Asian security cooperation, 210
Asian Youth Movement (AYM), 82
Association of Southeast Asian Nations (ASEAN), 9, 13, 145, 153, 161, 169, 230, 231
   coordinating centre for humanitarian assistance, 179
   Intergovernmental Commission on Human Rights, 179
   regional forum, 122
AUKUS, 253, 254
Australia-Bangladesh Trade and Investment Framework Arrangement, 258
Australian diplomats, 252
Australian policy, 250
Awami League, 3, 5, 50, 51, 53, 57–62, 66, 143, 201, 222, 237, 244
Awami League Rule, 224–226
Aziz, Qutubuddin, 222

B

Bangladesh
   armed forces, 4
   award favouring, 188
   China relations, 216
   constitution, 20
   constitution of, 22
   Delta Plan, 95, 99
   desire for a cultural identity, 3–5
   dynamic global system, 265–267
   economic growth, 238
   economic partnership and connectivity, 189
   educational institutions, 227
   foreign policy, 19
   geographic proximity, 232
   government, 194, 204
   growth story, 1–3
   and India, 215
   India Development Cooperation, 189
   new Asian frontier, 275–276
   paradox, 3
   plethora of agreements and MOUs, 189
   policy, 11
   politics, 65
   ports for movement of goods, 190
   rapid action Battalion, 243
   refugees, 117
   security agencies, 193
   signal success achieved by, 187
   Society, 226–227
   and strategic convergence in the region, 230–233
   strategy, 32
   trade relations, 35
   trilateral relations, 215

US security relations, 242
War of Independence, 160
youth approach, 82
youth association, 82
Bangladesh Advancing Development Growth through Energy (BADGE), 102
Bangladesh Aid Group, 10
Bangladesh–Bhutan–India–Nepal (BBIN), 271
Bangladesh-China-India–Myanmar Economic Corridor (BCIM), 207, 214
Bangladesh Climate Change Strategy and Action Plan (BCCSAP), 95
Bangladesh Climate Change Trust Fund, 95, 98
Bangladeshi market, 211
Bangladesh–India–Nepal (BIN) Pact, 161
Bangladesh Krishak Sramik Awami League, 4
Bangladesh Nationalist Party (BNP), 4, 5, 7, 51, 57–62, 59, 61, 62, 191, 193, 194, 195, 200, 224, 253
 led four-party coalition government, 207
Bangladesh Rehabilitation Assistance Committee, 253
Bangladesh Rice Research Institute (BRRI), 97
Bangladesh Rural Advancement Committee, 120
Bangladesh University of Engineering and Technology, 255
Bangladesh Welfare Organization, 81
Bangladesh Youth Front (BYF), 82
Bangladesh Youth League (BYL), 82
Bangladesh Youth Movement (BYM), 82
Basu, Jyoti, 196
Bay of Bengal, 29, 30, 40, 144, 149, 152, 159, 230, 232, 245, 251, 254
Bay of Bengal Multi-Field Technical and Economic Cooperation Initiative (BIMSTEC), 2, 9, 144, 161, 169, 216, 256, 271

Belt and Road Initiative (BRI), 34, 156, 207, 232, 255
Bharatiya Janata Party (BJP), 191, 254
Bhattacharya, Buddhadeb, 196
Bhutto, Zulfikar Ali, 3, 221, 222
Bilateral relations
 new paradigm in, 188–189
Blood and Tears, 222
Bose, Neilesh, 51
Brahmaputra River, 207
Brahmaputra valley, 198
British-Bangladeshi community, 84
Bush, H.W., 58

C
Calcutta port, 195
Cargo movement, 190
Chakravarty, Pinak Ranjan, 189
Chief Election Commissioner, 7
China–Bangladesh defence cooperation, 209, 213
China–Bangladesh Economic and Trade Relations, 210–211
China–Bangladesh Free Trade Agreement, 214
China Bangladesh Friendship Year, 206
China–Bangladesh Government Cooperation Agreement, 205
China–Bangladesh military agreements, 208
China–Bangladesh People-to-People Bounds, 211–212
China–Bangladesh security relations, 208
China–India relations, 216
China–Pakistan Economic Corridor (CPEC), 231
China policy, 14, 205
China's Central Military Commission, 208
China's foreign policy, 212
China's Strategy for Bangladesh, 212–213
Chinese Exclusion Act, 79
Chinese products, 211
Chittagong China Industry Park, 214

Chittagong port, 190
Chittagong seaport, 232
Citizenship Amendment Act (CAA), 198, 199
Climate Change and Gender Action Plan for Bangladesh, 95
Climate Risk Index, 91
Climate Vulnerable Forum, 99
Coastal Shipment Agreement, 190
Cold War, 15, 19, 24, 29, 32, 49, 53
Commonwealth Head of Government Conference, 116
Community Climate Change Project, 95
Comprehensive and Progressive Agreement for Trans-Pacific Partnership (CPTPP), 128
Confidence-Building Measures in Asia (CICA), 216
Construction of the Seventh Bangladesh-China Friendship Bridge, 206
Covid-19, 2, 10, 23, 25, 124, 125–126, 140, 224, 237, 260
Cross-border container-train movement, 190

D

Dasgupta, Ashim, 196
Datta, Sreeradha, 13, 189, 190
Defence Cooperation Agreement, 208
Department of Foreign Affairs and Trade (DFTA), 254
Department of Narcotics Control of Bangladesh, 173
Dhaka International Islamic Bank Limited, 10
Dhaka Mass Rapid Transit, 158
Dhaka Stock Exchange, 214
Dhaka Tribune, 2, 67, 103, 237
Digital Security Act, 6, 66
Doklam Plateau, 39

E

Economic and Technical Cooperation Trade and Payment Agreement, 205

Electronic products, 211
Energy and Power Mix, 94
Ershad, H.M., 119, 121
European Union (EU), 121
Exclusive economic zone (EEZ), 40, 188
Extended Credit Facility, 239

F

F6 aircraft, 223
Farakka Agreement, 196
Farakka subsumed movement, 195
Farooqui, Aisha, 230
Federation of Bangladeshi Youth Organisations (FBYO), 82
Five Principles of Peaceful Coexistence, 212
Foreign direct investment (FDI), 2, 240, 251
Foreign Military Financing (FMF), 241
Forest Investment Plan (FIP), 98
Framework Agreement on Cooperation for Development, 189
Framework Agreement on Providing Preferential Loan, 206
Free Trade Agreement (FTA), 123, 229

G

Galwan Valley, 39, 208
Gandhi, Indira, 19, 188
Ganga Waters Agreement, 193, 195, 197
Ganges River, 122
Ganges Water Sharing Agreement, 122
Generalized system of preference (GSP), 158
General Security of Military Information Agreement (GSOMIA), 241
Geopolitics and Digital Economy, 127–128
Global War on Terror (GWOT), 59, 87
Golden Bangladesh Dream, 213

Golden Bengal Dream, 206
Gomati rivers, 190
Green Climate Fund (GCF), 95, 101
Greenhouse gas, 93
Gross Domestic Product (GDP), 230
G20 summit, 64
Gulf Cooperation Council, 64
Gulf War, 57, 85
Gwadar seaport, 233

H

Hasina, Sheikh, 20, 50, 51, 57, 122, 141, 157, 188, 190, 193, 194, 196, 205, 224, 244, 246
Hazrat Shahjalal International Airport expansion, 158
Hefazat-e-Islam, 5
Himalayan rivers, 197
Hindu migration, 198
Holey Artisan Bakery, 200
Holey Artisan Bakery attack, 261
Hooghly River, 195
Houthi missile attacks, 63
Hunter, Andrew, 15
Hydropower, 94

I

Independent Anniversary Celebrations, 224
India–Bangladesh bilateral trade, 155
India–Bangladesh Boundary, 187–188
Indian External Affairs Minister, 190
Indian High Commission, 192, 193
Indian Ministry of External Affairs, 192
Indian National Congress, 191
Indian Ocean Region (IOR), 40, 113, 153, 207, 232
Indian Ocean Rim Association (IORA), 124, 162
India's Act East Policy, 256
India Skills Report, 35
Indira–Mujib Land Boundary Agreement, 187
Indo-Bangladesh discussions, 197

Indo-Bangladesh relations, 187, 191, 193, 199
Indo-Bangladesh Treaty of Peace and Friendship of 1972, 197
Indo-Pacific nations, 35
Indo-Pacific Outlook (IPO), 8, 267
Indo-Pacific Strategy, 24
Indo-Pak War, 198
Inland river ports, 190
Inside RAW: The Story of India's Secret Service, 221
Intergovernmental cooperation agreement, 205
Intergovernmental military technology cooperation committee, 213
Intergovernmental Panel on Climate Change, 91
International Association of Genocide Scholars, 3
International Court of Justice (ICJ), 175
International Criminal Court (ICC), 175
International Military Education and Training (IMET), 241
International Monetary Fund (IMF), 2, 239
International Organisations, 99–101
International Relations (IR) Theory, 138–140
International Shipping Routes (ISR), 153
Inter-Services Intelligence (ISI), 193
Islamic Development Bank, 10
Islamic State association, 200
Islamic Youth Movement (IYM), 82
Islami Oikya Jote (IOJ), 58
Islamist Hefajet-e-Islam, 200
Iyer, Ramita, 15

J

Jaishankar, S., 190
Jamaat-e-Islami, 5, 57, 194, 225
Jamuna Railway Bridge, 158
Jatiya Party, 4, 5
Jihadi groups, 194

Index

Johnson, Ashley, 12
Joint Rivers Commission (JRC), 91, 197
Joint Statement on the Establishment of Strategic Cooperation Partnership, 209

K
Karim, Tariq A., 101
Kashmir of Indo-Bangladesh relations, 195
Khan, Yahya, 53, 221
Krishak Praja Party, 52
Kuwaiti investors, 56

L
'Lahore Resolution', 221
Lahore summit, 55
Land Boundary Agreement (LBA), 187
Liberation and Beyond: Indo-Bangladesh Relations, 223
Liberation War, 4, 11, 14, 21, 113

M
Manohar Parrikar Institute for Defence Studies and Analysis, 232
Mascarenhas, Anthony, 222
Meghna rivers, 190
Modi, Narendra, 187, 199, 256
Momen, Abdul, 243
Momen, A.K. Abdul, 178
Motor Vehicle Act, 161
Mughal Empire, 230
Mujib, Sheikh, 188, 191, 192, 220, 221, 223, 225
    election campaign, 221
Muslim League, 52
Muslim-majority nation, 53
Myanmar Economic Corporation (MEC), 176
Myanmar Economic Holdings Limited (MEHL), 176

N
Nationally Determined Contribution (NDC), 93
National Martyrs Memorial, 225
National Policy for Development Cooperation, 100
National Press Trust, 222
Nehru–Liaquat Pact of April 1950, 197
Nehru–Noon Agreement of 1958, 187
Nehru–Noon Agreement of 1974, 187
Nikkei Asian Review, 113
Non-Aligned Movement (NAM), 53
    summit, 54
Non-Aligned Summit, 116
non-traditional security, 213
North Atlantic Treaty Organization (NATO), 23

O
Official Development Assistance (ODA), 117
Open Indo-Pacific approach, 240
Organisation of Islamic Cooperation (OIC), 10, 55, 60, 61, 116, 223
Organisation of the Islamic Conference, 54

P
Pacific Economic Framework for Prosperity (PEFP), 155
Pacific Oceans, 40
Padma Bridge, 2
Padma River Bridge project, 141
Pakistan Business Council (PBC), 228
Pakistani military machine, 114
Pakistan Welfare Organization, 81
Palestinian Liberation Organization (PLO), 54
Paris Club, 118, 119
Plagemann, Johannes, 12
Political mutual trust, 212–213
Pragmatic cooperation, 213
Preferential trade agreements (PTAs), 123, 229
Progressive Youth Organization (PYO), 82
Protocol on Remitting the Bangladesh Interest-Free Loan, 206

Q

Qatar–Gulf crisis of 2017, 64
Qingdao Port, 209
Quadrilateral Security Dialogue (Quad), 23, 159–161
  partners, 250
  security dialogue mechanism, 217

R

Radcliffe, Cyril, 187
Rahman, Mujibur, 19, 49, 115, 203
Rahman, Mustafizur, 196
Rahman, Shafiqur, 80
Rahman, Ziaur, 52, 204, 205, 223
Rapid Action Battalion (RAB), 158
Rashtriya Swayamsevak Sangh (RSS), 142
Refugee movement, 3
Regional Comprehensive Economic Partnership (RCEP), 124, 128, 145
Rizvi, Gowher, 157
Robinson, Gwen, 113
Rohingya
  crisis, 40, 210, 213
  refugees, 13, 41, 63, 174, 176, 245
  repatriation, 125
Rushdie, Salman, 85

S

Safeguard Supply of Water, 229
Satanic Verses in 1988, 85
Schuchert, Brigitta, 11
Security and Growth for All in the Region (SAGAR), 256
Sen, Amartya, 78
Shah, Amit, 254
Shanghai Cooperation Organisation, 216
Shanghai Stock Exchange Consortium, 214
Shanti Bahini, 193
Shenzhen Stock Exchange, 214
Shimla Accord, 222
Silk Road Fund, 214, 216
Singh, Manmohan, 188
Sinha, Surendra Kumar, 6
Sino-Bangladesh relations, 205
Sino-Bangladesh strategic partnership, 206
Sino-Indian relations, 193
Sino-USA relations, 32
'Six Point Programme', 221
Sobhan, Rehman, 191
South Asian Association for Regional Cooperation (SAARC), 9, 38, 101, 119, 126, 161, 271
  summit, 229
South Asian Free Trade Area (SAFTA), 123
South Asian neighbours, 1
South–South Network for Public Service Innovation, 100
Soviet Union, 24, 53, 204
Straits Times, 54
Sunday Times, 19
Supreme Court, 198
Sustainable Development Goal (SDG), 100

T

Tablighi Jamaat, 85
Teesta River, 189, 197
Tejgaon airport, 223
The Daily Star, 157
The Economist, 60
The Last Days of United Pakistan, 221
The Wire, 142
Track II dialogues, 190
Transit and Trade Agreement, 161
'Treaty of Peace and Friendship', 224
Tripartite Agreement, 222
Troop contributing countries (TCCs), 122
Two-nation theory, 49

U

Ukraine crisis, 2
UN General Assembly, 117
United Liberation Front of Assam (ULFA), 194
United Nations Convention on the Law of the Sea (UNCLOS), 188

United Nations Development Programme, 98
United Nations General Assembly (UNGA), 175
United Nations Population Fund (UNFPA), 177
United Nations Security Council (UNSC), 23
United States Agency for International Development (USAID), 102, 238
UN Mission, 120
UN peacekeeping cooperation, 209
UN Security Council, 176
UN's Framework Convention on Climate Change (UNFCCC), 93
Untranquil Recollections, 191
US-Bangladesh Partnership Dialogue, 237
US Chamber of Commerce, 239
US Cooperation Afloat Readiness and Training, 240
US Development Finance Corporation, 239
US immigration programs, 80
US-led Indo-Pacific strategy, 217

V
Vishva Hindu Parishad (VHP), 142
Voluntary process, 86

W
War of Liberation of Bangladesh, 116
Warsaw Pact, 23, 53
Water Development Board, 91
Western nations, 1
Western Pacific Naval Symposium (WPNS), 209
West Pakistan's genocidal campaign, 1
World Bank, 117, 140, 143
World Trade Organization (WTO), 121, 141

X
Xiaoping, Deng, 205

Y
Yarlung Zangbo River, 207
Yemen war, 64
Young Muslim Organisation (YMO), 85

Z
Zia, Khaleda, 58, 193, 205, 226, 244